PENGUIN BOOKS

# FIGHTING FAITHS

Richard Polenberg is the Goldwin Smith Professor of American History at Cornell University. He is the author of *One Nation Divisible* (Penguin Books).

# FIGHTING FAITHS

## The Abrams Case, the Supreme Court, and Free Speech

RICHARD POLENBERG

PENGUIN BOOKS

PENGUIN BOOKS
Published by the Penguin Group
Viking Penguin Inc., 40 West 23rd Street,
New York, New York 10010, U.S.A.
Penguin Books Ltd, 27 Wrights Lane,
London W8 5TZ, England
Penguin Books Australia Ltd, Ringwood,
Victoria, Australia
Penguin Books Canada Ltd, 2801 John Street,
Markham, Ontario, Canada L3R 1B4
Penguin Books (N.Z.) Ltd, 182–190 Wairau Road,
Auckland 10, New Zealand

Penguin Books Ltd, Registered Offices:
Harmondsworth, Middlesex, England

First published in the United States of America by
Viking Penguin Inc. 1987
Published in Penguin Books 1989

1 3 5 7 9 10 8 6 4 2



LIBRARY OF CONGRESS CATALOGING IN PUBLICATION DATA
Polenberg, Richard.
Fighting faiths: the Abrams case, the Supreme Court, and free speech/ Richard Polenberg.
p. cm.
Bibliography: p.
Includes index.
ISBN 0 14 01.1736 9 (pbk.)
1. Abrams, Jacob—Trials, litigation, etc. 2. Trials (Anarchy)—New York (N.Y.). 3. Freedom of speech—United States. I. Title.
[KF224.A34P65 1989]
342.73′0853—dc19
[347.302853] 88–21844

Printed in the United States of America by
R. R. Donnelley & Sons, Harrisonburg, Virginia
Set in Bodoni Book

*To the memory*
*of my mother,*
*Leah Polenberg*

". . . when men have realized that time has upset many fighting faiths, they may come to believe even more than they believe the very foundations of their own conduct that the ultimate good desired is better reached by free trade in ideas—that the best test of truth is the power of the thought to get itself accepted in the competition of the market, and that truth is the only ground upon which their wishes safely can be carried out. . . ."

OLIVER WENDELL HOLMES, JR.<br>
Dissenting Opinion,<br>
*Abrams et al.* v. *United States*

# PREFACE AND ACKNOWLEDGMENTS

IN THE SUMMER of 1980, while examining various manuscript collections at the State Historical Society in Madison, Wisconsin, I came across a letter which led me, eventually, to write this book. The letter was written by Mollie Steimer in 1920 when she was serving a sentence in the Missouri State Penitentiary. It was a joyful letter, addressed to her mother, sisters, and brother. It described her happiness on reading newspaper reports about workers who had refused to transport munitions to supply the Allied armies of intervention in Soviet Russia. Here, she thought, was proof of international working class solidarity, a sure sign that a new day was dawning. The letter, much of which is quoted on pages 321–22, concluded: "I just feel like embracing the whole world and crying out: 'Come—do not stop—keep marching on—and we shall be victorious.' "

What most affected me was Steimer's buoyant spirit. I knew little about her at the time other than that she was one of the defendants in the landmark free speech case, *Abrams* v. *United States,* which I had always thought significant chiefly because of Justice Oliver Wendell Holmes's famous dissenting opinion. But I knew that she had begun serving a fifteen-year prison sentence for violating the World War I Sedition Act, and I was impressed that under the circumstances she remained so hopeful, indeed so cheerful.

I began to consider writing a book about the Abrams case, which, I soon realized, offers a way of approaching broader issues of radicalism, reform, ethnicity, bureaucracy, and civil liberties which have always been of interest to me. I also discovered that the sources for studying the case are wonderfully rich. Steimer's papers are deposited at the International Institute for Social History in Amsterdam, as are the papers of her friends, Emma Goldman and Alexander Berkman. The papers of Harry Weinberger, the defendants' lawyer, are available, and so are those of the trial judge, Henry DeLamar Clayton, Jr., and the two dissenting Supreme Court Justices, Oliver Wendell Holmes, Jr., and Louis D. Brandeis. The National Archives houses the Records of the Bureau of Investigation, the Military Intelligence Division, the Department of Justice, the Supreme Court, and the federal district court for the Southern District of New York. The Freedom of Information Act made it possible to obtain more than 600 pages of formerly classified documents, mostly from the files of the Bureau of Prisons, but also from the files of the State Department, the Bureau of Immigration, and the Office of Naval Intelligence. In all, I located important material in nearly 100 manuscript collections.

In addition, several scholars generously gave me access to material they had collected in the course of their own research. Paul Avrich, the author of numerous books on anarchism in the United States and Russia, made available his correspondence with Steimer and other material pertaining to the case, including original documents, notes of interviews he had conducted, and photographs. Margaret Marsh, the author of *Anarchist Women,* gave me copies of her correspondence with Steimer, including newspaper clippings which Steimer had sent her. When I found that the 800-page transcript of the Abrams trial was missing from the National Archives branch at the Military Ocean Terminal in Bayonne, New Jersey, I called on Fred D. Ragan, who had once made a photocopy of the transcript which he graciously loaned to me.

I received help from many other people as well. For a correct translation of the central document in the case, a leaflet written in Yiddish, I relied on Chana Kronfeld. To translate an important letter written in Russian, I turned to Carol Sheade. Neil Basen kindly forwarded references to pertinent newspaper articles which he had come across in his research. Dr. Willard Cates, Jr., sent me a copy of his Yale honors thesis on Harry Weinberger. Dr. Michael Goodfriend, a cardiologist, explained the significance of the medical terms used on the death certificate of one of the anarchists.

Many librarians proved helpful in a multitude of ways. I especially wish to acknowledge my indebtedness to Erika Chadbourn of the Harvard Law School Library; Thea Duijker of the International Institute for Social History in Amsterdam; Edward C. Weber of the Labadie Collection at the University of Michigan; Richard Strassberg of the Labor-Management Document Center at Cornell University; and Marcia Zubrow of the Charles B. Sears Law Library at SUNY–Buffalo.

Over the years a number of Cornell students have served as my research assistants. I am happy to express my appreciation to Lesa Gelb, Deborah Moss, E. Catherine Loula, Laurie Strauch, Joyce Hausner, Margaret McNamara, Carol Jennings, Debra Eisenstadt, Jessica Wang, and Margaret Autry. In addition, Mindy Roseman, Naomi Cohn, and Beth Lobel helped locate library materials for me. Garth Kliger's Cornell honors thesis on the Schenck case proved extraordinarily useful.

Although I alone am responsible for this book, I am deeply indebted to my friends who read the entire manuscript and offered many valuable suggestions. For their assistance, I wish to thank Paul Avrich, Deborah Gesensway, Don Herzog, Walter LaFeber, Margaret Marsh, Larry Moore, and Lorri Staal. My father, Morris Polenberg, made numerous suggestions; almost every page of the manuscript has benefited from his sound judgment. Gerald Howard, my editor at Viking Penguin, offered encouragement at each stage of this project, and gave astute advice regarding the style and substance of the book. My thanks also go to Shirley Brownrigg, an excellent copy editor.

My research was supported, in part, by the Colonel Return Jonathan Meigs First (1740–1823) Fund. A Humanities Research Grant from Cornell University helped defray the expense of doing research at the International Institute for Social History in Amsterdam. I had hoped to interview Mollie Steimer in Cuernavaca, Mexico, but she had died in the summer of 1980.

RICHARD POLENBERG
*Ithaca, New York*

# CONTENTS

# LIST OF ILLUSTRATIONS

*(following page 196)*

# FIGHTING FAITHS

PROLOGUE

# A Farewell Dinner

ON THE EVENING of November 21, 1921, one hundred and seventy-five people attended a ceremonial dinner at Allaire's Restaurant, on Third Avenue and 17th Street in New York City. The purpose of the gathering was twofold: to say farewell to four radicals—Mollie Steimer, Jacob Abrams, Hyman Lachowsky, and Samuel Lipman—who were about to be deported to Soviet Russia, and, since they were being deported at their own expense, to raise money to pay for their passage. The deportees, however, were not present. Their lawyer, Harry Weinberger, had begged the Commissioner General of Immigration to allow them to leave Ellis Island for the occasion and had even told that official he was more than welcome to attend, but the request was rejected. Four empty chairs in the center of the dining room symbolized the deportees' absence.

The toastmaster, Albert Rhys Williams, a Congregationalist minister turned journalist, was an outspoken partisan of the Russian Revolution. The other speakers, well-known anarchists, socialists, communists, and civil libertarians, all said the appropriate and expected things. They denounced the arrest of Steimer, Abrams, Lachowsky, and Lipman in August 1918 for distributing leaflets opposing American intervention in Soviet Russia, and their conviction in October under the wartime Sedition Act. The speakers attributed the death of a fifth comrade, Jacob Schwartz, to police brutality. They condemned the trial judge, Henry DeLamar Clayton, for his biased conduct, and termed the fifteen-to twenty-year sentences he imposed a "legal monstrosity." They asserted that the Supreme Court's decision upholding the convictions in November 1919 was misguided, mitigated only by the powerful dissent of Justice Oliver Wendell Holmes, Jr. They called the imprisonment of the four radicals and their deportation "mean and despicable."

The most emotional moment may have come when Weinberger read a message from Mollie Steimer. Twenty-four years old, Steimer had spent much of the last three years in one prison or another, but these experiences had only strengthened her belief in anarchism and her faith in its eventual triumph. She asked her comrades not to lose heart but to "unite all your forces and work among the exploited to . . . inflame in them the desire for freedom." Government officials, even though they persecuted radicals, were not "naturally mean." Rather, it was the capitalist system, based on exploitation and force, that cultivates "the most vile instincts"; it was the state that "deliberately corrupts its citizens." Prisons, she continued, "vile and ruinous institutions," "schools where the most disgusting deeds are practiced," would vanish when workers created a free society based on "the principles of non-rulership and non-exploitation," a society "where Love and Joy will prevail instead of hatred and pain."

The evening had its share of the unexpected, the dramatic, and the contentious. A surprise speaker, a former Assistant United States Attorney who had helped prosecute the case, now said he was sorry. The government, he declared, "should have paid no attention to the act for which these four persons were sent to prison." Charles Recht, an attorney who represented Russia's legal interests in the United States, electrified many of those present by flamboyantly exhibiting the Soviet passports he had obtained for the four, documents starting with the salutation "Comrades" and urging that the deportees be shown every consideration "in the name of the revolution." But not all the guests were impressed by this gesture. Alluding to Soviet Russia's persecution of political dissenters, a socialist editor predicted that the deportees would receive "a rather chilly reception" and would discover that "nowhere in Russia would their treatment be any better than it was in this country." A chorus of hisses, mixed with applause, greeted his remarks.

Among the many diners at Allaire's that evening, at least one was neither a comrade nor a friend but rather an undercover agent of the U. S. Army's Military Intelligence Division. The theme of most of the speeches, his report duly noted, was "condemnation of America, its government and those in authority." Perhaps weary after listening to hours of such impassioned rhetoric, the agent seemed relieved to relate that "the dinner broke up after midnight in a verbal combat between the various factions, everybody yelling at once and wanting to speak for their particular brand of radicalism." The Department of Justice, which had been spying on the deportees and their friends for three years, apparently did not send anyone to the dinner, but faithfully clipped newspaper accounts for the Bureau of Investigation's weekly report on "Radical Activities in the Greater New York District."[1]

Two days later, when the deportees left on the S. S. *Esthonia,* the American chapter of their lives ended. But as the speeches at Allaire's Restaurant and the reports filed about them suggest, a study of that chapter can help explain the appeal of anarchism to working-class Jewish immigrants; the special brand of justice radical aliens could expect at the hands of the law; the fashioning of techniques for the systematic surveillance of political dissidents by federal, state, and local officials; the moral dilemmas confronting liberal bureaucrats in an illiberal era; the Supreme Court's application of the "clear and present danger" standard to define the permissible limits of free speech; the ways in which political criminals survived behind prison walls; the impact of the Russian Revolution on the American left; and the use of deportation as a preferred means of dealing with anarchists.

By following the four deportees across the ocean, moreover, we can draw a comparison between methods of suppressing dissent in Soviet Russia and in the United States, two nations that had little in common besides a profound distaste for anarchists. That common distaste ensured that the story of Jacob Abrams, Mollie Steimer, Hyman Lachowsky, and Samuel Lipman would in many respects be a tragic one, as is necessarily the case when idealists are made to suffer for their ideals. Yet their story is not merely one of victims and defeat. It is also a story of courage and dedication, of people who refused to perceive themselves as victims or admit defeat, and as such is especially worth telling.

# 1

# Anarchism and War

## The Immigrant Experience

JACOB ABRAMS, Mollie Steimer, Hyman Lachowsky, Samuel Lipman, and Jacob Schwartz emigrated to the United States from Russia between 1908 and 1913. Abrams arrived in 1908 when he was twenty-two years old, and Schwartz in 1910 when he was twenty-three; the others made the journey when they were fifteen or sixteen years old: Lachowsky in 1908, Steimer and Lipman in 1913. In all, 425,000 Jews left Russia for the United States in that five-year period. A total of 1.6 million emigrated between 1881, when the Czar's government began enforcing harsh anti-Semitic policies, and 1914, when the outbreak of World War I made it virtually impossible for immigrants to cross the Atlantic. Most Jews who fled Czarist rule would have given much the same reason Mollie Steimer's parents gave: so their "children would be brought up in a free country."[1]

Nothing better symbolized the absence of such freedom in Russia than the existence of a Pale of Settlement. Since the late eighteenth century the great majority of Jews had been forced to reside in the fifteen western provinces in Russia and ten in Poland that comprised the Pale. Later, Czars Alexander III (1881–1894) and Nicholas II (1894–1917) sharply restricted mobility within this already restricted region, stripping Jews of the right to move from one village to another, forcing them to leave small villages for larger towns, and redefining the boundaries of the Pale so as to exclude Jews from the cities they had once called home. About 5 percent of the Jewish population—university students and graduates, merchants, certain artisans, and older army veterans—could obtain permission to live outside the Pale. But these groups, too, found themselves in an increasingly untenable position. They were often expelled on the flimsiest of pretexts, and even if they were not, their children, on reaching maturity, were banished to the Pale. The right of free domicile was not a right at all but a privilege arbitrarily given or taken away by local officials.

Residential restrictions were reinforced by an intricate web of political, economic, and legal disabilities. Jews were barred from voting in municipal elections and denied the right to buy or lease land. They were excluded from state service and prevented from entering many professions. Conscripted out of proportion to their numbers, they were yet deprived of any chance for military advancement. Jewish lawyers could not be called to the bar without the permission of the Minister of Justice, permission seldom if ever granted. After 1886, Jewish students faced a quota on their admission to secondary schools and universities: 10 percent within the Pale, 5 percent outside the Pale, but only 3 percent in Moscow and Saint Petersburg. Schools of engineering, veterinary medicine, and agriculture usually excluded all Jews. Such discriminatory edicts were the least of the Jews' troubles. Brutal pogroms, carried out with the connivance of the police, claimed thousands of victims. The very name of the town of Kishinev, the site of a 1903 massacre of Jews, came to stand for officially licensed slaughter.

In describing Czarist policies, contemporary Jewish observers used metaphors that would later acquire a literal meaning. Lucien Wolf's *The Legal Sufferings of the Jews in Russia,* published in 1912, branded the expulsion of Jews from villages in the Pale and their resettlement in larger towns "the campaign of extermination."[2] Another author, writing in 1914, referred to the pogroms that erupted in Odessa and other cities after the revolution of 1905 as "a veritable holocaust."[3] Commentators had little hope that Russia's anti-Semitic policies could be reversed and thought that Jews would have to make new lives for themselves elsewhere. As one writer said, "The Russian Jews who cling to their native land are on the road to ruin."[4]

Russian subjects did not have the legal right to emigrate, but the

Czar's government did little to prevent Jews from leaving. Few sailed from Russian ports, however, for that required a passport, an expensive document, difficult (when not impossible) to obtain. Instead, Jewish immigrants usually crossed into Germany by train, passing through a border control station, and continued on to one of the northern ports, the most important of which were Bremen, Hamburg, Liverpool, Antwerp, and Amsterdam. Whatever their destination, they encountered immigrants of many different national, religious, and ethnic backgrounds. The steamship lines maintained compounds, often housing thousands of people, where steerage passengers awaited departure. Separate facilities were provided for men traveling alone, women traveling alone, and families. Within each category Jews were usually segregated. At the North German Lloyd line's facility in Bremen, "Russian Jews were not allowed at the new building, but were housed at one of the older buildings."[5]

Most immigrants underwent medical examinations at every stage of their journey—sometimes when purchasing their tickets, and always when entering Germany, arriving at the port of embarkation, and boarding ship. The steamship lines had instituted these examinations in 1891 when the United States provided for the exclusion of aliens who had a "loathsome or dangerous contagious disease" and required the lines to furnish such individuals return passage. Twelve years later Congress stiffened the penalty: a line which knowingly transported an alien who had such a disease would not only have to provide a return ticket but also would be fined one hundred dollars. For the steamship companies, careful medical inspections were a simple matter of profit and loss.

When at last immigrants boarded ship, they were herded into steerage compartments. These varied greatly from one line to another, even from one vessel to another. In the years before World War I, the steamship lines had begun to modernize their facilities, but the process was hardly complete. The differences between old-style and new-style steerage were vividly described by Anna Herkner, an investigator for the United States Immigration Commission. Disguised as a Bohemian immigrant, Herkner made three transatlantic crossings in 1908, each lasting about two weeks. She carefully observed everything that went on around her, and she submitted detailed accounts of her experiences.

On July 30, 1908 Herkner sailed on a ship providing old-style steerage. She landed at Ellis Island twelve days later, twelve days during which she and the other passengers were treated "as so much freight." The compartment for single women was divided into three areas—for Germans, for Jews, and for everyone else. Berths were two feet wide, six feet long, two and one-half feet high, and were used not only for sleeping but also for storing possessions. There were no hooks on which to hang garments. There were no garbage cans. Floors were swept but never washed, so "the vomitings of the seasick are often permitted to remain a long time before being removed." Food, although sufficient, was "wretchedly prepared," the meat "old, tough, and bad smelling," the vegetables "a queer, unanalyzable mixture, and therefore avoided." Passengers had to scramble to get a place on the food line, and scramble again to find a place to eat. It was next to impossible to keep utensils (or anything else) clean because the washrooms were inadequate and the tap water was mostly cold and salty.

To escape "a congestion so intense, so injurious to health and morals that there is nothing on land to equal it," steerage passengers tried to spend as much time as they could on deck. But outdoor space was also pitifully inadequate. The two decks, each forty by fifty feet, were cluttered with machinery, ventilators, and other equipment. There were no chairs or benches, no protection from the sun, rain, or showers of hot cinders that poured from the smokestacks. Crew members mingled with the passengers, treating the women contemptuously. "Their language and the topics of their conversation were vile. Their comments about the women, and made in their presence, were coarse. What was far worse and of continuous occurrence was their handling the women and girls. Some of the crew were always on deck, and took all manner of liberties with the women in broad daylight as well as after dark." Harassed by a crew member, Herkner finally punched him in the face. "The atmosphere was one of general lawlessness and total disrespect for women," she concluded.[6]

By contrast, new-style steerage accommodations seemed almost luxurious. Well-lighted and well-ventilated, the staterooms, each with two to eight berths, provided storage space, seats, mirrors, and even washstands. There was plenty of hot water, soap, and clean towels. Stewards kept the floor spotlessly clean. The dining room, which served as a recreation room between meals, was equipped with a piano. As for the meals, "absolutely everything was such as might be eaten without hesitation by anyone." Jewish passengers, assigned to their own rooms, were looked after by a Jewish cook, who prepared kosher food. Crew members respected the passengers' privacy. The decks, spacious and partially covered, lent themselves to friendly socializing. In the evenings "there was considerable singing, dancing, walking, and merrymaking generally." After experiencing the comforts of such a voyage, Anna Herkner was appalled at the continued use of the old-style steerage, with its oppressively claustrophobic environment.[7]

Once in New York harbor, steerage passengers took ferries to Ellis Island for a final medical screening. The Public Health Service prided itself on having developed a system which permitted a handful of physicians to inspect several thousand immigrants daily. Entering a large room in four lines, immigrants filed slowly past a medical officer stationed at the head of each line, who, it would seem, glared at them with an eagle eye, for one examiner boasted, "Experience enables him in that one glance to take in six details, namely, the scalp, face, neck, hands, gait and general condition, both mental and physical."[8] Acquainted with every stratagem a frightened person might employ to hide a real or imaginary defect, doctors might ask one immigrant to unbutton a collar in order to check for goiter, another to put aside a blanket in order to check for "a deformed forearm, mutilated or paralyzed hand, loss of fingers or favus nails," a third to remove a hat in order to check for ringworm. The slightest deviation from the norm warranted further attention. "Pompadours are always a suspicious sign," one doctor explained. "Beneath such long growths of hair are frequently seen areas of favus."[9]

The four lines eventually funneled into two, with a doctor posted at the end of each. Standing in front of windows, so that sunlight shone in the immigrants' eyes, the doctors examined each person for visual defects, particularly for symptoms of trachoma. The Public Health Service had decided to add trachoma to the list of dangerous contagious diseases in 1897. A disease of the eyelid that always causes pain and, if untreated, can result in a loss of vision or blindness, trachoma can be communicated only by direct contact with the secretion from the eye of an infected person, usually by common use of a towel or washbasin.

As one specialist explained, "Trachoma infection, then, must be planted in the eye in order that it may grow, exactly as corn and potatoes are planted to have them grow."[10] The contagion doctors feared, however, was social as well as medical, for the disease, even if not transmitted to anyone else, would surely make a person less productive. Reduced earning power, in turn, would lead a man "to satisfy himself with a progressively lower standard of existence" and reduce his family to "increasing poverty, filth, and unhygienic surroundings which are known especially to foster the disease."[11]

Inspectors made chalked notations—"B" for back, "E" for eye, "L" for lameness—on the outer garment of anyone who appeared to have a disability, and these people would then have to undergo more thorough examinations, perhaps over a period of days. A coat marked with an "X" inside a circle meant that the doctor suspected that the immigrant was "stupid and inattentive to such an extent that mental defect is suspected." These individuals would then take a battery of tests (either in English or in their native language) to determine whether their "common knowledge, retentiveness of memory, reasoning power, learning capacity and general reaction were severally and distinctly below normal." They were asked to count backwards from twenty to one, to name the months of the year, to repeat a story in as much detail as possible, to arrange a series of objects in the same order as the examiner. "What is the difference between a house and a stable?" an inspector might ask. The answer, "The family lives upstairs, stable is underneath," was considered correct, but "Stable is dirtier, no other difference" was not, however, considered accurate, ironical as the response may have been.[12]

No more than 15 to 20 percent of the immigrants ordinarily took the complete physical or mental examinations, and very few of them were finally barred. The average rate of exclusion was less than 2 percent. In 1912 and 1913 more than two million immigrants entered the country; only 36,000 were turned away, and this number included not only those deemed physically or mentally unfit but also paupers and contract laborers (workers who had already made contractual arrangements with employers, who imported them). Some immigration inspectors undoubtedly regretted that the grounds for rejection were so limited, or so it would seem from the reaction of one doctor. After watching

5,600 immigrants pass through Ellis Island on Easter Sunday in 1912, he complained that the "changing and deteriorating character" of immigrants from southern and eastern Europe offered a breeding ground for the "morally delinquent."[13] Another official noted, "It is a no more difficult task to detect poorly built, defective or broken down human beings than to recognize a cheap or defective automobile."[14]

An immigrant who passed all these examinations would then be questioned briefly to "see that he is not an anarchist, bigamist, pauper, criminal, or otherwise unfit." Anarchists, of course, could not be detected by inspecting eyelids. (In 1912 and 1913 only four immigrants were turned away as anarchists.) Officials had more latitude in their definition of pauperism. In 1909 the newly appointed New York Commissioner of Immigration, William Williams, decided that immigrants would need to have twenty-five dollars rather than only ten dollars to enter the country. This ruling had a limited effect: in one year, the number barred as "likely to become a public charge" rose from 4,402 to 15,918. Protests from the Hebrew Immigrant Aid Society, which took Williams to court, soon led to a relaxation of the order. Williams held office until 1913, and tried always to construe the law in a manner that, in his own words, would bar "a great deal of the riffraff and the scum which is constantly seeking to enter."[15]

Jews left Czarist Russia early in the century for many reasons besides religious persecution. Young men ran away to avoid serving in the military; young women, to liberate themselves from lives of domestic drudgery mapped out for them by their parents. There were some, men and women alike, wanted by the police for their revolutionary activities, and others, seeking fortune and fame, for whom revolution was the last thing on their minds. Nor did all immigrants encounter the same problems in making their way to the United States. Although most traveled in steerage, a lucky few could afford a second-class or even a first-class cabin. They crossed the ocean in comfort, and they never even left the boat for inspection at Ellis Island. Disembarking directly at a pier, they could be welcomed by relatives and whisked away to their new homes.

Whether Jacob Abrams, Mollie Steimer, Samuel Lipman, Hyman Lachowsky, Jacob Schwartz, and the family members who accompanied them felt Czarist oppression more or less keenly than other Jews, whether they experienced the horrors of the old steerage system or had a more comfortable journey, whether they passed the various inspections easily or underwent more elaborate tests, whether they were exposed to the barbed insults of immigration officials or escaped such hostility—much of this is not known. But whatever their individual experiences, whatever hardships they had known in their lives, they surely shared the common conviction that things would be different, and better, in America.

## The World of Work

Russian Jews brought with them a kaleidoscopic array of trades and skills. They were carpenters and cabinetmakers, glaziers and shoemakers, butchers and bakers, locksmiths and blacksmiths, weavers and spinners, barbers and clockmakers, furriers and bookbinders, actors and architects, doctors and rabbis, electricians and engineers, teachers and musicians, artists and editors. Of the immigrants who were skilled workers, however, nearly half were tailors, dressmakers, seamstresses, or in some other way connected with the needle trades. About two-thirds of the immigrants settled in New York City, where some managed to find jobs in familiar lines and others took whatever jobs were available. Abrams, Lachowsky, and Schwartz worked as bookbinders, Lipman as a furrier, and Steimer as a ladies' shirtwaist maker. Enough is known about conditions in those industries to catch at least a glimpse of what their lives as workers must have been like.

New York City was the heart of the bookbinding trade, responsible for more than one-third of the industry's output. There were 280 binderies in Manhattan in 1913, nearly half of them located within a mile radius of City Hall. Bookbinders did indeed bind books, but they also worked on pamphlets, theater programs, calendars, telephone directories, trade catalogues, business ledgers, albums, and advertising brochures. The work was highly seasonal, with the busy months concentrated in the winter and spring, when workers toiled ten or eleven hours a day, sometimes working through the night in order to earn enough to tide them over slack times. As machine binding replaced hand binding in the years before the war, the proportion of women in the industry increased. By 1917 Manhattan binderies employed about 5,000 women and 4,000 men. Depending on their skill and experience, men earned, on the average, sixteen to twenty dollars a week, and women a little more than half that amount.

Mechanization made the work less arduous but no less fatiguing. A worker's daily activities typically included "operating complicated machines, repeating one process hour after hour, standing at work all day, carrying loads of heavy paper from one part of the shop to another, stooping frequently to lift the folded sections of books, pressing a foot pedal rapidly and incessantly."[16] Doing such work was hard enough, but doing it in dark and dingy shops magnified both the difficulty and discomfort. Entering a Fulton Street shop, one investigator was nauseated. "One is attacked by an offensive odor of burning glue and decayed paste," he reported. "The men also complain of the putrefactive odor of rats which are found among the bundles of paper and board." Floors were swept only once a day, and "this produces an agitation of dust particles and the men invariably complain of dryness in the nose and throat after sweeping." Windows could have let in light and air, but often they were shut "for fear that the papers may fly apart from the breeze or the glue dry up while it is being handled."[17]

The special occupational hazard facing the bookbinder was the loss of fingers or a hand. Feeding paper into cutting machines, workers "have to put their hands under the knife and draw them back before the knife comes down."[18] The dimmer the lighting, the longer the working day, the more exhausted or distracted the worker, the greater was the danger. To read letters written to the union journal, *The International Bookbinder,* is to realize how swiftly and unpredictably tragedy could occur. "Brother Oscar Plushhell," a letter from Omaha, Nebraska, begins, "met with a serious accident while operating a cutting machine. The brother was trimming calendar pads which bulged out as the clamp descended, and to avoid this, Oscar was pressing against them, but the last cut he made, instead of bulging out, they went in and the knife caught his left hand severing the thumb and two fingers, mashing the third finger so bad it is feared amputation will be necessary."[19]

In the event of accident or illness, workers who were union members could turn for help to the International Brotherhood of Bookbinders. Founded in 1892, the union was well entrenched in many cities, including Chicago and Philadelphia. The New York City bookbinders, plagued for years by factional disputes, finally resolved their differences in 1917. Rival unions agreed to amalgamate, and this helped boost national membership from 10,600 in 1916 to 15,700 in 1918. Members were entitled to strike benefits, and their families to a modest death benefit. The union built up a fund to assist those who fell ill, with the goal of granting benefits as a matter of right rather than charity so as not to rob recipients of their self-respect. The older custom of "passing the hat in case a brother is ill," one official explained, "has in the past been a nuisance not only to the members of the local, but also has always carried a sting with it to the brother."[20]

The Brotherhood exemplified a traditional style of bread-and-butter unionism. Even while battling for better conditions, the union took pride in workers who managed to become capitalists, and regarded "the advancement of one of our loyal members to the ranks of the employing class" as an occasion for general rejoicing.[21] After the United States entered the war, the union printed patriotic poems in its journal, sang chauvinistic songs at its convention, and informed members that savings certificates "will be the credentials of patriotism without which an individual will have no right to claim to be an American."[22] Bookbinders who enlisted in the army wrote enthusiastic letters from boot camp: "And believe me if we ever get over the pond the Huns will know that they were in a fight when they tangle with us."[23] In much the same spirit, articles in *The International Bookbinder* condemned American socialists and their "weird, dreamy Bolshevist theories."[24]

For Abrams, Lachowsky, and Schwartz the union may have served many useful purposes but would not have offered a congenial ideological home. The Brotherhood was too conservative, its predominantly Irish leadership too ethnically remote, for the Yiddish-speaking antiwar anarchists to have found it a suitable vehicle for political expression. That his shopmates elected Jacob Abrams president of their local probably had less to do with his politics than with his personal qualities. But Abrams' friend, Samuel Lipman, a socialist rather than an anarchist, would have felt quite comfortable in the International Furriers' Union, a radical organization whose membership was largely Jewish. Abrams would have read *The International Bookbinder,* which backed the war, berated socialists, and routinely printed Yiddish-dialect jokes which were offensive even by the forbearing standards of the day.[25] But Lipman would have received *The Fur Worker,* which was published in Yiddish as well as in English, endorsed the socialists as "the only party that believes in the emancipation of the workers from wage slavery," and held that "no war for whatever purpose waged, ever in any way benefited the worker."[26]

The fur industry prospered during World War I and so did many of the 16,000 fur workers in New York City. In March 1917, rather than risk a strike when profits were rising, the Manufacturers' Association had accepted most of the union's demands. The agreement provided for a 48-hour week: 8 to 12 and 1 to 6 on Monday through Thursday, 8 to 12 and 1 to 5 on Friday, and 8 to 12 on Saturday. The union won improved wage scales for the different grades of finishers, operators, cutters, and nailers, ranging from fifteen to twenty dollars a week for second-class finishers to twenty-five to thirty-five dollars for first-class cutters. Women always received the lower rate in each category, and wages below even the minimum were allowed for learners, "the feeble and the old." The owners agreed to hire only workers with union cards, to limit overtime (paid at time and a half), to grant ten legal holidays, and to permit periodic inspection to ensure compliance, terms the union regarded as a decided victory.[27]

The agreement reflected in many respects the predominantly Jewish character of the fur industry. The terms had been hammered out by Jewish owners and Jewish laborers at a meeting held at the Jewish Community Building, presided over by Dr. Judah L. Magnes, a prominent labor reformer and an ordained rabbi. The conferees made special provisions for orthodox or observant Jews: firms could substitute the nearest Jewish holiday for a legal holiday, closing, for example, on Yom Kippur instead of Columbus Day; and firms which shut down on Saturdays could instead operate on Sundays. Implementation was supervised by the Bureau of Industry of the New York "Kehilla," a federation of Jewish religious, charitable, and social organizations. Although immigrants from Italy, Greece, and many other countries became furriers, nearly three-fourths of the workers and virtually all the employers were Eastern European Jews.

The typical shop in the fur industry was modest in size, employed perhaps eight to twelve workers, and was owned by a man, himself recently a worker, who had managed to accumulate enough capital to open his own establishment. The shops remained small enough, the ethnic ties close enough, and the relationship between worker and employer intimate enough, so that illness or incapacity could elicit a shared sense of responsibility. So, in July 1918, when a worker in Berkowitz Bros. shop took ill, his friends took up a collection. Each man gave what he could, some twenty-five cents, others fifty cents or a dollar; another man donated five dollars to mark the birth of a grandson; and the Berkowitzes contributed five dollars too.[28] Poor people found ways to help those less fortunate than themselves. For example: "The employees of B. Geller & Sons worked an extra hour for the benefit of a sick brother, a cutter. This realized $65. The firm contributed $25, and the sum of $90 was handed to the sick brother."[29] Like the bookbinders, the furriers attempted to put medical benefits on something other than a charitable basis. As one worker explained, "Sick benefit is a good thing for anyone who needs it. And God forbid, how often the fur worker needs it."[30]

Any furrier would have instantly recognized the truth of those words. Every day, workers were exposed to hazardous conditions that impaired or ruined their health. This was a result partly of the absence of safety measures, and partly of the nature of the manufacturing process. The raw fur was first scraped, or "fleshed," with razorlike blades to remove fat and connective tissue. Then, placed in huge revolving drums, which had been prepared with sawdust, salt, sand, and water to soften the skins and remove the grease, the fur went through a process known as "dressing." When the drums were opened, "clouds of dust arise, for the collection of which no devices exist at present." The furs were next brushed with vegetable or chemical dyes. "Pools of dyestuff and water accumulate on the floors," a visitor observed; "the men stand in them." Finally, the furs were cut, stretched, and nailed to designs on tables, and the pieces were sewn together. Workers who treated the furs with hydrogen peroxide, chrome salts, and nitrate of mercury solution, very seldom wore gloves.[31]

In 1915 the New York City Department of Health reported the results obtained from physical examinations of 585 furriers, results which may well have understated the gravity of the situation because workers feared they might lose their jobs if certain infirmities were discovered. Even so, the study found that furriers exhibited a "lowered state of physical vigor, and hence a greater predisposition towards disease." Mercury poisoning, the most common occupational illness, usually revealed itself in tremors of the hands and face, arms and tongue, and in gingivitis, which, in severe cases, produced "a blueish metallic appearance of the gums." The report recommended installing proper ventilating systems, requiring workers to wear protective garments and rubber gloves, and sweeping dust and loose hair with a vacuum cleaner when the working day was done—sensible enough proposals which were generally ignored.[32]

As an "operator on ladies' waists," which is how she described herself, Mollie Steimer's working environment would have differed conspicuously from that of a furrier or bookbinder. The manufacture of dresses and shirtwaists was a branch of the ladies' garment industry which also produced cloaks and suits, sheets and spreads, house dresses, and infant's and children's wear. There were 100,000 ladies' garment workers in New York City, of whom 30,000 made dresses and shirtwaists. They worked in about 600 shops, located mainly in midtown Manhattan lofts. In 1916 the International Ladies' Garment Workers' Union, which claimed two-thirds of the dress and waist makers as members, won a reduction in the work week from 50 to 49 hours, and in 1917 negotiated a further reduction to 48 hours. But seasonal fluctuations in the garment industry were even more pronounced than in other trades. For two months in the fall and four in the spring there was too much work to do, and for the rest of the year too little. In the slack season, especially in July, one-third of the workers were laid off, and wages fell by one-half, since many employees worked only three or four days a week.

To say that 84 percent of shirtwaist workers were women would only begin to convey the actual ambience of the shops. Men most often worked as cutters or pressers, so virtually all the sewing machine operators were women. Generally speaking, they were young women; 50 percent were under twenty years of age, and another 25 percent under twenty-five years. Most were the children of immigrants from southern and eastern Europe; more than half were Jews, more than a third Italians. Most still lived at home with their parents, and their earnings—averaging about $400 a year—meager as they were, supplemented their families' incomes. Fully 85 percent of these young women were single, and many of them regarded work as a transitional stage. Observing that 5,000 young women married and left the trade each year, a male ILGWU official said, "It should be remembered that men, even when they marry, come to work the very next day, as if nothing happened. Very rarely a working man can afford to go on a honeymoon trip unless he marries in the slack season. For girls, however, particularly Jewish girls, the marriage license is an automatic withdrawal from the union. In plain words, when a girl marries she replaces shop work by housework. . . ."[33]

A few gifted women found an outlet for their talents in the shirtwaist shops, particularly in the field of design, which called for creativity and imagination. A woman who was "quick to see the trend of fashions, clever in adapting new ideas, and skilled in combining materials and colors" could aspire to such a position.[34] By and large, though, working on waists was not rewarding. Specialization of labor meant that each worker repeated the same process, experiencing the "stupefying and wearying effect of machine work."[35] How stupefying and wearying may be suggested by listing the operators' usual designations: sleeve makers, body makers, closers, sleeve setters, skirt makers, belt makers, joiners, hemstitchers, tuckers, hemmers, binders, pipers, lace runners, trimmers, buttonhole makers, markers, and button setters. But this was not all, for in the larger shops "even these subdivisions are further subdivided. At times four or five workers can be found working on one sleeve."[36] Speed, dexterity, and concentration were indispensable, especially for pieceworkers. To earn a penny, a woman had to sew six buttons, or four hooks and eyes, or two belts.

However wearisome the work, it was not hazardous. "There were no vocational diseases peculiar to the garment trades," a 1914 study concluded, and added that many of the most common ailments associated with the industry—backaches and eyestrain—could be remedied if employers provided chairs that had backs and could be adjusted to the worker's height, and installed lights that were shaded to reduce glare.[37] Fire remained the gravest danger. In 1913, owing partly to the tragic blaze at the Triangle Shirtwaist Company, which had killed 146 women two years earlier, the dress and waist industry agreed to cooperate with the Joint Board of Sanitary Control, a body representing labor, management, and the public, which endeavored to make the plants cleaner and safer. The Joint Board inspected and, if necessary, reinspected every shop to ascertain that flammable materials were removed, exits and aisles were kept clear, and doors were unlocked. Fire drill instruction was to be given, fire escapes made accessible, and fire extinguishers or buckets placed where they would be available in an emergency. Yet the risk was never entirely removed, if only because many shops were in the same buildings as non-garment industry tenants, who were not held to the same standards. More than half the women worked in shops located on or above the sixth floor, from which escape was necessarily difficult. Memories of the Triangle inferno must have haunted many workers.

Mollie Steimer went to work in a shirtwaist factory at the age of sixteen, two days after arriving at Ellis Island. By 1918 she had spent five years in front of a sewing machine. When she could get a full week's work she earned about fifteen dollars. She made less than her friends in the bookbinding and fur industries, but her job was less dangerous than theirs and her surroundings were somewhat better. By contemporary standards, workers in these three trades were not badly off. Militant unions looked after their interests, and working conditions had gradually been improving. Looking back on her experience, however, Mollie Steimer explained why she became disenchanted with a working world marked by long hours, low wages, and periodic layoffs. "Life was hard," she recalled. "Came home late, got up early. Things began to protest in me against a system of life where people who are hard workers have to struggle bitterly just to be able to exist."[38]

## Anarchism and East Harlem

"I began to read," Steimer continued, "to search for a way out." Coming across Peter Kropotkin's *The Conquest of Bread* in a Lower East Side library, she found what she was looking for.[39] Kropotkin, the Russian anarchist who had been living in exile in England since 1886, had published *The Conquest of Bread* in France in 1892; the first English edition appeared in 1906. The book contended, simply yet eloquently, that the formation of a society based on anarchist principles was natural, inevitable, and right. In the better world to come, Kropotkin maintained, government would be dissolved, property held in common, and law replaced by mutual agreement. Social distinctions would vanish. All would contribute what they could and take what they needed. In a system capable of producing more than enough for all, none would know want. Promising an extraordinary amount of individual freedom, Kropotkin did not appeal to his readers' selfish impulses but to their sense of community. He approvingly quoted the moral philosopher Jean Marie Guyau: "We are not enough for ourselves: we have more tears than our own sufferings claim, more capacity for joy than our own existence can justify."[40]

It must have seemed to some of Kropotkin's readers that a sixth sense had enabled him to fathom the desperation of their everyday existence. "To do manual work now," Kropotkin wrote, "means in reality to shut yourself up for ten or twelve hours a day in an unhealthy workshop, and to remain riveted to the same task for twenty or thirty years, and maybe for your whole life. It means to be doomed to a paltry wage, to the uncertainty of the morrow, to want of work, often to destitution . . ."[41] So long as the worker "comes home in the evening crushed by excessive toil with its brutalizing atmosphere," there could be no opportunity for personal growth, no chance for a creative use of leisure.[42] If Kropotkin's description of work under capitalism seemed uncannily accurate, why doubt his prediction concerning work in an anarchist society? According to *The Conquest of Bread,* men and women would be expected to perform some kind of socially useful work for no more than four or five hours a day until they reached the age of forty-five or fifty, devoting the rest of their time to scientific or artistic pursuits, cultural or intellectual interests, hobbies, recreation, and rest. With the factory "made as healthy and pleasant as a scientific laboratory," even routine jobs would become attractive.[43]

In this, as in his other writings, Kropotkin considered the practical objections commonly raised to anarchism. In "a society that recognizes the absolute liberty of the individual, that does not admit of any authority, and makes use of no compulsion to drive men to work," he conceded, some might try to exploit others, seek special privileges, or refuse to do any work at all.[44] Yet the satisfaction derived from purposeful labor would be so great, Kropotkin believed, the desire for social approval and the fear of ostracism so strong, that nearly everyone would recognize the advantages of the new order and willingly work for the common good. Those refusing to do their fair share would be expected to leave. If no place would have them, they would be permitted to take what they needed—provided that there was enough to go around—but would be regarded as outcasts or misfits. It was inconceivable to Kropotkin that any number of people would choose such a barren, isolated existence. Anarchist society, then, would not in any sense be chaotic. Order would prevail, not because individuals were forced to obey externally imposed laws but because "social habits and the necessity . . . of finding cooperation, support and sympathy" would lead people voluntarily to accept internal restraints.[45]

Like an anxious gardener, Kropotkin thought he could detect the buds of the new society all around him: museums, libraries, schools, parks, gardens—all were already free, all were available on the basis of need, as were such urban amenities as "water supplied to every house without measure or stint."[46] The desire to cooperate for the common good was instinctive, he observed. Even in a system of private enterprise, which put a premium on selfishness, people found ways to help each other, organizing the English Lifeboat Association, for example, to save shipwrecked sailors, or the Red Cross to care for victims of war and disaster. During the Franco-Prussian War of 1870–1871, Kropotkin said, volunteers "were only too glad to occupy the most dangerous posts" and "continued their work under fire," assisting the wounded without regard to nationality as need dictated.[47] If kindness and mutual aid could sprout even under the arid conditions of capitalism, Kropotkin thought, they would surely flower in the fertile soil of anarchism.

Enraged by social injustice and exasperated by the passivity of the masses, Kropotkin's followers, often the gentlest of souls, frequently justified or excused cold-blooded acts of violence. As revolutionaries they readily accepted the need for collective violence. But they also defended the use of assassination threats and, sometimes, the premeditated murder of the rich and powerful. Even Kropotkin, who knew that terrorism was often self-defeating and that some fanatics might be attracted to violence for its own sake, could not find it in his heart to condemn such deeds, not when they were motivated purely by a hatred of oppression, directed at despots, and aimed at sparking a popular insurrection. Kropotkin attempted to reconcile such behavior with anarchist morality by adding three crucial words to the Golden Rule: "Treat others as you would like them to treat you under similar circumstances." He then concluded that "we ourselves should ask to be killed like venomous beasts," were circumstances such that we were in danger of becoming tyrants.[48]

Most anarchists were confirmed atheists. Their standard text was Michael Bakunin's *God and the State,* first published in 1882 and reprinted as an inexpensive pamphlet in the United States in 1916. Following Bakunin, who believed that "the idea of God implies the abdication of human reason and justice," anarchists attacked organized religion for imposing a repressive code of morality, for preaching a doctrine of passive submission to evil, and for siding with wealth and privilege.[49] Yet anarchism's appeal was spiritual as well as secular, for it offered adherents an opportunity to dedicate their lives to a higher cause.[50] Devoted to ideals which, in Mollie Steimer's revealing phrase, "would really make life worth while," they could entertain millenarian hopes for the not-so-distant future. Jacob Abrams once explained, only half facetiously, how to convince Steimer to do something: "She must be approached like a good Christian, with a bible, of Kropotkin or Bakunin, otherwise you will not succeed."[51]

Kropotkin's adherents shared some of the same beliefs as the socialists: that human nature was perfectible, that a collectivist system would provide enough for all, and that revolutionary impulses could be guided into constructive channels. But unlike socialists, whose goal was to seize state power, anarchists wanted to destroy the state. To many Marxists, a dictatorship of the proletariat was a necessary step in building a new classless society; then, and only then, would the state gradually "wither away." In Kropotkin's view, an authoritarian regime, even if directed by the proletariat, would still be authoritarian. "It could not last," he insisted, "general discontent would soon force it to break up, or to reorganize itself on principles of liberty."[52] In the short run, socialists worked for useful reforms and took pride in their practical accomplishments. They ran candidates for office and solicited all the support they could. Anarchists rejected this incremental approach. Arguing that participation only legitimized existing institutions, they usually turned their backs on electoral politics.

The differences between anarchists and socialists in this era involved tone and style as well as ideology and tactics. Anarchists were quicker to anger and more intemperate than socialists. Their hatred of capitalist exploitation was more visceral, and their disappointment with workers unable or unwilling to see the revolutionary light less easily concealed. Anarchist rhetoric was, if anything, more extravagant; listening to it, one might well imagine the apocalypse was imminent. "I believe with all my heart in resistance and warlike action," Alexander Berkman told an anarchist rally in Union Square in July 1914. "We are on the verge of a social revolution," he cried; "when the time comes we will not stop short of bloodshed to gain our ends."[53] Socialist periodicals had such titles as *Advance*, *The Call*, *Appeal to Reason*, and *Revolutionary Age;* anarchists preferred less circumspect, more combative names: *The Agitator*, *Revolt*, *The Social War*, and *The Blast.*

In 1917 a new Yiddish-language anarchist publication appeared whose name, *Der Shturm*, "The Storm," exemplified this intransigent spirit as, undoubtedly, did its editorial policy. Although no copies seem to have survived, we know that it was put out by a "Group" (in the locution anarchists favored) consisting of Abrams, Steimer, Lachowsky, Schwartz, and Lipman. There were some twenty participants in all, including Mary Abrams, Jacob's wife; Ethel Bernstein and her sister, Rose; Sonya and Zalman Deanin; Hilda Kovner; Sam Adel; and other comrades who drifted in and out on an informal basis. *Der Shturm* was succeeded in January 1918 by *Frayhayt*, "Freedom," whose masthead proclaimed, "The only just war is the social revolution." More than fifty years later, Hilda Kovner (who married Sam Adel), reminisced, "That was holy work, you know, to distribute our literature, to spread the word."

The Group endeavored, in anarchist fashion, to arrive at decisions collectively, but if anyone can be said to have been the leader by virtue of age, experience, and temperament, it was Jacob Abrams. "Abrams was a wonderful boy," a friend recalled. "He claimed to be an anarchist but wanted to be the chief." Jacob Abramovsky, for that was the family name, was born in Uman, a town in the Ukraine, located about 150 miles north of Odessa, in 1886. His mother died when he was four, and his stepmother treated him harshly. He attended a Hebrew school, studying the Talmud, until he was twelve. Later he took part in the 1905 revolution. His older sister, Manya, emigrated to the United States in 1906 and by 1908 had saved enough money to send for her brother. He arrived, a revolutionary but not yet an anarchist, began to work as a bookbinder, and met his future wife, Mary Damsky, at a May Day rally in 1911. A short, slender man with dark brown eyes and chestnut hair, Abrams, according to Sonya Deanin, "was an extreme militant. He and Schwartz were tough and fanatical. Whoever disagreed with them was an enemy, to be beaten up. It didn't matter whether they were capitalist enemies or anarchist enemies." Abrams also had a gentler, more amiable side, and it is hard to say which contributed more to his influence on those around him.[54]

In June 1918 Abrams, using the alias "Abram Dean," rented a six-room apartment on East 104th Street, off Fifth Avenue. The woman who rented it to him remembered that he looked at the apartment with Mollie Steimer who "started to cry, that she didn't like the flat; so he said to her 'Don't be disgusted, the flat will be cleaned.' She said 'I don't like it.' . . . He said 'You keep quiet, you don't like the flat,' he said 'You don't know what you like.' "[55] The apartment became home for some members of the Group and also served, for the next two months, as their meeting place. In July Abrams rented a basement store a few blocks away, on Madison Avenue near East 107th Street. He purchased a press and several cases of type, which were delivered in August and enabled his friends to do their own printing. The Group was now situated in the very center of East Harlem, an area that provided a highly congenial environment for Jewish anarchists.

At the time, nearly 120,000 people were crowded into the East Harlem area bounded by 100th Street and 112th Street, by Fifth Avenue and the East River. Half the residents were immigrants, and most of the others their children. The census listed 4,800 people, a mere 4 percent of the total, as "native white of native parentage," and 2,650, a little more than 2 percent, as "Negroes or mulattoes." Of the 60,000 immigrants, 33,300 were Russian, Polish, or Rumanian Jews, and 16,300 were Italians. To a great extent, different national groups kept to their own neighborhoods. In one district, running from 99th Street to 104th Street, and from Fifth Avenue to Park Avenue, there were 10,000 foreign-born residents; 7,800 were Eastern European Jews and 110 were Italians. A few blocks to the east and north was a very dissimilar district, bounded by 104th Street and 109th Street, by Third Avenue and First Avenue, in which there were 11,000 foreign-born residents; 900 were Eastern European Jews and 9,400 were Italians. Even without formal boundaries, the lines between ethnic enclaves were reasonably clear.

Eastern European Jews had begun moving into Harlem in 1900, and before long they greatly outnumbered the smaller, more affluent and assimilated community of German Jews. Many of the new arrivals had moved from the Lower East Side, where overcrowding had become a more acute problem when a new building code mandated the demolition of some older dwellings, and when work on the Williamsburg Bridge (completed in 1903) and the Manhattan Bridge (completed in 1909) led to the tearing down of other buildings. Just when Jewish immigration was reaching record proportions, housing became scarcer in the older ghetto and more available in East Harlem. There, contractors demolished private homes and replaced them with six-story apartment houses. Real estate boomed. Jobs, especially in the building trades, followed people uptown, and even those who worked downtown could commute quickly and conveniently. The first subway line, running from City Hall along Broadway, opened in 1904, and a Lenox Avenue spur was added in 1908. Three years later construction began on a Lexington Avenue line which would run through East Harlem.

In 1918 East Harlem housed a multitude of religious, cultural, and social institutions embracing all aspects of Jewish life. There were dozens of congregations, some housed in imposing synagogues, others in movie theaters, homes, or stores; many had only fifteen or twenty members, but one boasted 1,000 members. Along two blocks on East 104th Street there were four synagogues. The largest Jewish school in the United States, the Uptown Talmud Torah, was located on East 111th Street; 1,475 boys attended classes on weekdays from four to eight-thirty and on Sundays from nine to two. Jewish fraternal orders, social clubs, and literary societies met in Harlem, a Hebrew Home for the Aged and a Hebrew Sheltering Society were located there, and

Jewish settlement houses offered classes in music, dance, art, and what was called "physical culture." A community center on East 101st Street, founded "to take care of the social needs of the neighborhood," not only sponsored lectures but also provided hot showers, offered legal aid, and ran an employment bureau. Mount Sinai Hospital, the largest Jewish Institution of its kind, was located at East 100th Street between Fifth Avenue and Madison Avenue. It "minister[ed] to the needs of all classes, the poor sick being treated free of charge, while those who are able pay from $7.00 per week and upwards."[56]

A radical Jewish subculture, woven of socialist, socialist-Zionist, and anarchist strands, flourished in this environment. Within a ten-minute walk of the Group's apartment on East 104th Street was a meeting hall for more than a dozen branches of the Arbeiter Ring, the Workmen's Circle. The goal of this socialist-affiliated benevolent society was "to help the working class as a whole, to improve the conditions of the worker, to increase his wages and to strengthen his social and political influence." Pictures of Marx and Bakunin decorated the walls of its reading room, and copies of such radical Yiddish newspapers as the socialist daily *Forverts*, "The Forward," and the anarchist weekly *Freie Arbeiter Stimme*, "Free Voice of Labor," were always available. The headquarters of Poale Zion, the Zionist socialist organization, were also located on East 104th Street. Members worked for "the restoration of the Jewish people in Palestine; the establishment of a socialistic commonwealth."[57] Rallies, meetings, impromptu gatherings or "commune festivals and balls" could be held at the Labor Lyceum, Harlem Terrace Hall, Clairmont Hall, or New Star Casino, all of which were located between East 103rd and East 107th streets. Sectarian as the organizations sponsoring these affairs might be, the network of radical Jewish organizations, taken as a whole, was as inclusive as it was extensive.

The nerve center of anarchism in East Harlem, however, was not a specifically Jewish institution at all but the Ferrer Modern School, located at 63 East 107th Street. Named for the Spanish educator Francisco Ferrer, who had been executed in Barcelona in 1909 for his alleged participation in a bloody insurrection, the school stressed spontaneity and freedom, not order and discipline. The Modern School tried to implement Ferrer's beliefs, which historian Paul Avrich has described as "learning by doing in a natural environment, cultivation of manual as well as intellectual skills, recognition of the rights and dignity of the child, give and take between pupil and teacher, participation of children and parents in the administration. . . ."[58] In 1915 the school moved to Stelton, New Jersey, but the Ferrer Center remained on East 107th Street for three more years, offering art lessons, English-language classes, plays, and concerts. At its weekly revolutionary forum, speakers engaged in arguments over anarchism and socialism, birth control and free love, Freudianism and feminism, modern art and drama, syndicalism and the general strike.

In 1917 the two topics uppermost in the minds of anarchists everywhere, certainly at the Ferrer Center and the Group's meetings, were the United States' entry into the World War and the Bolshevik Revolution. The war divided anarchists, although to a lesser extent than it did socialists. Peter Kropotkin disappointed many of his own disciples when, asserting that working-class advancement required the defeat of German militarism, he supported the Allies. A few American anarchists followed him, but most denounced the war. Emma Goldman and Alexander Berkman, for example, argued that intervention was designed to protect "the vilest plutocracy on the face of the globe."[59] They organized a No-Conscription League in May 1917, held meetings which Jacob Abrams and his friends attended, and predicted that war would destroy the last vestiges of freedom in the country. In June they were arrested and charged with advocating violence and conspiring to prevent draft registration. Convicted in July, they were sentenced to two years' imprisonment.

Although in later years anarchists would bitterly condemn the Russian Revolution, in November 1917, dazzled by its success, they convinced themselves that it represented a fulfillment of their dreams. Goldman praised the "glorious work" of the Bolsheviks and insisted that they had "libertarian plans." Berkman agreed, adding that Lenin was not "the narrow-minded Socialist type whose ideal is a strongly centralized Socialist government."[60] Describing their emotions when they heard the news of the revolution, anarchists resorted to the language of ecstasy, rapture, or exaltation. "I am wild with joy," Berkman wrote in his prison diary; "this is the happiest moment of my life."[61] Nearly thirty years later, Milly Rocker, a Jewish anarchist, recalled her reaction. She wrote to her friend, Mollie Steimer: "My heart was heaving with happiness. There was so much light, sunshine, though it was a rainy and chill day."[62]

People were attracted to anarchism for a variety of reasons. Harsh economic circumstances could prompt a person to join the movement, as could one's intellectual inclination, psychological disposition, cultural environment, or a supportive institutional network. For those who became converts, the year 1918 was a crucible that tested their belief. As Abrams, Steimer, Lipman, Lachowsky, and Schwartz were preparing to engage in a new round of anarchist activity in East Harlem, the United States government was taking two ominous steps that would soon reshape their lives: in May Congress approved a wartime Sedition Act, and in July President Woodrow Wilson decided to send American troops to Soviet Russia.

## The Justice Department and the Sedition Act

The origins of the Sedition Act can be traced to the village of Ashland in Rosebud County, Montana. Only sixty people resided there, about as many as in a single tenement house on East 104th Street. One of them was a man named Ves Hall. A rancher who did not disguise his dislike for the war, Hall allegedly declared in January 1918 "that he would flee to avoid going to the war; that Germany would whip the United States, and he hoped so; . . . and that the United States was only fighting for Wall Street millionaires." Hall apparently reserved some of his choicest invective for Woodrow Wilson, labeling him "a Wall Street tool" and "the crookedest——ever President." Whatever expletive the stenographer deleted, it landed Hall in some "hot and furious saloon arguments" and, before long, helped get him arrested.[63] He was indicted under the Espionage Act of June 15, 1917, which made it a crime for anyone to "willfully make or convey false reports or false statements with intent to interfere with the operation or success" of the armed forces, to "willfully cause or attempt to cause insubordination, disloyalty, mutiny, or refusal of duty" in the armed forces, or to "willfully obstruct the recruiting or enlistment service of the United States, to the injury of the service of the United States."[64]

Hall's trial began on January 13, 1918, before George M. Bourquin, a resident of Montana for thirty-five years, a state judge since 1904, and United States District Judge since 1912. After a two-week trial Bourquin directed a verdict of acquittal. Even if the jury were to find that Hall had made the statements attributed to him, Bourquin ruled, he would not be guilty. The judge asserted that a person's "beliefs, opinions, and hopes," however wicked, could not be considered false statements within the meaning of the law. Bourquin conceded that actual "slanders of the President and Nation" did, indeed, violate the law, but only insofar as they threatened to interfere with the conduct of the war. The Espionage Act required a "specific intent to commit specific crimes," the judge said, and intent depended on "magnitude and proximity." Hall's statements did not satisfy either criterion, for they were made in a kitchen, at a picnic, and in a saloon where they were less likely to cause interference with the war than a fistfight and, perhaps, "a broken head for the slanderer." Bourquin tried to link the concepts of magnitude and proximity to intent with a simple analogy: "if A shot with a .22 pistol with intent to kill B two or three miles away," the judge observed, "A could not be convicted of attempted murder."

Bourquin added two further qualifications to his stringent interpretation of the Espionage Act. Its reference to "military and naval forces," he said, meant "those organized and in service, not those merely registered and subject to future organization and service." Since there were no soldiers or sailors to be found within hundreds of miles of Rosebud County, Hall's statements did not violate the law. To obtain a conviction for obstructing recruitment, Bourquin added, the government had to demonstrate that some actual obstruction had taken place. "The espionage act does not create the crime of attempting to obstruct, only the crime of actual obstruction, and when causing injury to the service." In Bourquin's view, the Espionage Act was truly intended to punish espionage, not seditious speech. "Congress," he noted, "has not denounced as crimes any mere disloyal utterances, nor any slander or libel of the President or any other officer of the United States."[65]

The decision brought on a tornado of criticism which swept away free speech safeguards. On January 28, the day after Bourquin's ruling, the Governor of Montana declared that its citizens were so outraged they might resort to violence. He summoned the state legislature into special session, and when it met on February 14 he provided the verbal thunder and lightning, reiterating that unless steps were taken to curb sedition the people "may be provoked into becoming a law unto themselves."[66] It took only nine days to pass a criminal syndicalism act that made it a crime "to utter, print, write, or publish any disloyal, profane, scurrilous, contemptuous, or abusive language" about the form of government of the United States, the Constitution, soldiers or sailors, the flag, or the uniform of the Army and Navy; to use language calculated "to incite or inflame resistance" to any duly constituted authority; or to "urge, incite or advocate any curtailment of production" of any vital materiel with intent to hinder the war.[67] Before the storm had subsided, the legislature had impeached a judge who had testified as a character witness for Ves Hall.

Within three months the provisions of the Montana statute would be incorporated, nearly verbatim, into a federal Sedition Act. The Senators from Montana, Henry L. Myers and Thomas J. Walsh, were kept fully informed of events at home, and they soon began to badger the Department of Justice, inquiring first whether Judge Bourquin's ruling could be appealed, and then, when informed it could not be, asking support for additional legislation. The Attorney General, Thomas W. Gregory, had been informed by aides that Bourquin's "occupancy of the bench at this time is a most unfortunate thing for the people of Montana."[68] Late in March, therefore, when Walsh told Gregory that Hall's acquittal made it advisable to amend the Espionage Act "so as to make the escape of those similarly traitorously inclined impossible," the Attorney General replied in a cautious but sympathetic manner. He advised Walsh to have a talk with the responsible officials in the Department's War Emergency Division.[69]

The head of that Division was John Lord O'Brian, and his chief assistant was Alfred Bettman. The two men had much in common. Both were in their mid-forties, graduates of Harvard (O'Brian '96, Bettman '94), and lawyers. Both had practiced law in the cities in which they had grown up, O'Brian in Buffalo and Bettman in Cincinnati, and had then plunged into reform politics. O'Brian had served in the New York State Assembly, held an appointment as United States Attorney for the Western District of New York, and, when war was declared, helped administer the draft as chairman of the appeals board. Bettman, "a person with delicate and refined sensibilities," who was "somewhat retiring and shy in his nature," did not run for office but rather devoted himself to city planning.[70] Calling for a scientific approach to urban problems, he supported a measure enabling cities in Ohio to create planning boards.[71] In 1917, Bettman would recall, "I had such an urge to get into a war job, preferably in the law line, that I could hardly stand it."[72] His friend, O'Brian, provided the opportunity he craved. O'Brian went to the War Emergency Division on October 1, 1917, and Bettman joined him within a month.

Regarding themselves as enlightened liberals, cosmopolitan in outlook, and sensitive to questions of individual liberty, O'Brian and Bettman believed that "freedom of discussion is of the very essence of democracy."[73] Prosecutions under the 1917 Espionage Act, in their view, were constitutionally justifiable as long as they were "not directed at sedition or disloyalty" but at protecting "the orderly execution of the laws relating to the raising of armies."[74] Themselves members of the legal profession, they considered the Department of Justice the most dependable of all government agencies because it "consists of lawyers habituated to weighing facts carefully in their relation to law and having, so to speak, a judicial point of view."[75] Well acquainted with left-wing literature, they were scornful of less knowledgeable officials, especially those in military or naval intelligence, who seemed unable to tell the difference between socialists, communists, and anarchists.[76] American institutions were so sturdy, Bettman thought, that revolutionary doctrines "if permitted to bloom in the open . . . will soon wilt."[77]

At the same time, the two officials, as political realists, were dismayed by the ruling in the Ves Hall case. As O'Brian wrote, Judge Bourquin's unnecessarily strict construction would result in "practically nullifying prosecutions."[78] More dismaying still was the prospect of mob violence against radicals, several incidents of which had recently been reported. A federal law would calm public hysteria, they believed, and also leave the crucial decisions concerning prosecution in the hands of moderate, responsible officials. Bettman and O'Brian probably knew that such a law would claim innocent victims, but, in view of the public's ugly mood, so would the absence of a law. An associate of theirs in the Department of Justice later conceded that the Sedition Act "was hard on the defendants," but saw no viable alternative. "Would it not have been harder on them," he asked rhetorically, "if they had been lynched or tarred and feathered?"[79]

If, as Bettman admitted, "the only excuse" for the Sedition Act was "to allay the public sentiment," this seemed reason enough for the Department of Justice to cooperate with Senator Walsh in drafting the measure.[80] The task of enacting appropriate legislation was greatly simplified because the House of Representatives, on March 4, had passed an amendment, although quite a limited one, to the 1917 Espionage Act. A Liberty Loan drive had been scheduled for April, and so the House, with little discussion, had added a new crime to the existing list: willfully making false statements "with intent to obstruct the sale" of war bonds.[81] This measure then went to the Senate Judiciary Committee, of which Walsh was a member. The Committee rewrote the bill, greatly expanding its scope by incorporating the provisions of the Montana criminal syndicalism act. On April 4 Walsh introduced the Sedition Act—technically, the Senate version of an amendment to the Espionage Act—and, in doing so, asserted that Judge Bourquin's "strained construction" of the earlier statute made enactment necessary.[82]

Someone listening to the statements made on the Senate floor in behalf of the bill might well have concluded that the best of all possible ways to protect freedom of speech was to abridge it. Senators argued, as had officials in the Department of Justice, that the alternative to passing the legislation would be mob violence. Occasionally it was alleged that the reign of terror had already begun, more often that the lawlessness was imminent. Senator Walsh heard from one irate constituent who, on a visit to the West Coast, detected a widespread feeling that "traitors and spies should be shot," and reported "the demand is that some positive action be taken or vigilante committees will be organized and the citizens take it into their own hands."[83] There were, in fact, several instances of vicious beatings and even one ghastly lynching, but there was no evidence to suggest that this brutality was motivated by the government's inability to indict people for seditious speech, or that any such number of indictments would end it.

The opposition came chiefly from Republicans, many of them quite conservative, who feared that the bill could be construed broadly so as to curb their own criticisms of the Wilson administration. Theirs was not a plea for freedom, tolerance, or diversity, much less for respecting the rights of radical dissenters, but rather an argument for exempting their own attacks on the President's policies, however harshly worded, from the strictures of the act. The same Senators who feared that the measure could be used "to suppress free and legitimate discussion by the great mass of the loyal people of this country" did not hesitate to brand a speech by a Socialist candidate for Congress "so disloyal as to border on treason" or to denounce the Wilson administration for coddling spies and saboteurs.[84] The bill's Republican critics were as anxious as its advocates to punish speech that interfered with the war so long as the ground rules were understood: Republican rhetoric was to be considered fair, while radical rhetoric would be declared out of bounds.

But how could one guarantee that these rules would be observed? Joseph I. France, a Maryland Republican, hit upon a possible solution. Employing the language of the state criminal libel laws, he introduced the following amendment: "Nothing in this act shall be construed as limiting the liberty or impairing the right of an individual to publish or speak what is true, with good motives and for justifiable ends."[85] Such a proviso, Republicans believed, would protect loyal but not disloyal speech, for to their way of thinking the former was inherently truthful while the latter manifestly was not. No one expressed this view more clearly than former President Theodore Roosevelt. A bitter critic of the administration, he favored "any legislation, no matter how extreme, that will reach the men who vilify and defame America . . . or who preach sedition directly or indirectly," yet he also defended the people's right "to speak the truth freely of all their public servants, including the President, and to criticize them in the severest terms of truth whenever they come short in their public duty."[86] The Senate narrowly rejected the France amendment on April 9, but the next day the bill's sponsors, eager to win final approval, withdrew their opposition. The Senate quickly adopted the amendment, and then the Sedition Act, by voice votes.

While a conference committee tried to reconcile the Senate and House versions, the Department of Justice threw its considerable influence behind an effort to have the France amendment deleted. To introduce the element of motive, Bettman informed O'Brian on April 15, would render the act practically useless. Under existing law, "intent" to interfere with the war merely implied that individuals knew, or could be assumed to know, that certain acts were likely to produce certain effects, not that their "motive" or purpose was to produce those results. The act's effectiveness, Bettman observed, depended on "the principle that the motive prompting the propaganda is irrelevant." Otherwise, it would be impossible to move against groups whose propaganda impeded the war effort but which claimed to be acting out of high motives—indeed, in the case of religious pacifists, "out of the highest possible motive." The nightmarish prospects were endless; even socialists said they wanted to promote human happiness, and certainly, Bettman added, "the promotion of human happiness is a good motive."[87] O'Brian summarized these arguments for the House and Senate conferees. "In the field of propaganda," he noted, "especially that dangerous form of propaganda known as pacifism, it would in many cases be very difficult for the prosecution to actually disprove assertions of loyalty and justifiable purpose."[88]

The conference committee did what it was urged to do. On April 22 it reported a version of the Sedition Act which omitted the controversial amendment, a version, France commented bitterly, "altered at the behest and under the direction, as it seems to me, of Mr. John Lord O'Brian of the Department of Justice."[89] On May 4 the Senate voted 48 to 26 to accept the committee's recommendation. The vote divided largely along party lines: 38 Democrats and 10 Republicans favored the measure; 2 Democrats and 24 Republicans opposed it. On May 7 the House approved the measure after an impressive display of magniloquent jabber about "pernicious vermin," "spawn of the lower regions," "poison dark spreaders of revolution," and "white livered rabbits who try to tear down the Army and the Nation under the guise of free speech." The final vote was 293 to 1, with Meyer London, a Socialist from New York, the lone dissenter.[90]

The Sedition Act amended the Espionage Act in a number of significant ways. It was now a crime not only to obstruct, but also to attempt to obstruct, recruitment for the draft, or to "say or do anything" with intent to block the sale of war bonds (although bankers still could offer "bona fide and not disloyal advice" regarding their clients' investment portfolios). Modifying slightly the language used by the Montana legislature, the Sedition Act made it a crime to "willfully utter, print, write, or publish any disloyal, profane, scurrilous, or abusive language" about the United States' form of government, Constitution, military or naval forces, or flag, or about the uniform of the Army and Navy, or to use any language designed to bring any of these various things "into contempt, scorn, contumely, or disrepute." The act also forbade anyone to "willfully urge, incite, or advocate any curtailment of production in this country of any thing or things . . . necessary or essential to the prosecution of the war . . . with intent by such curtailment to cripple or hinder the United States in the prosecution of the war." Violations were punishable by a fine not to exceed $10,000, by a prison term of up to twenty years, or both. Finally, the Act augmented the Postmaster General's power. He was already authorized to deny second-class mailing privileges to publications he deemed disloyal; now, "upon evidence satisfactory to him" that individuals were using the mail in violation of the Act, he could stop all their mail deliveries.[91]

The provisions appalled but did not surprise a small, active group of civil libertarians who had monitored the progress of the Act closely. Roger Baldwin, head of the National Civil Liberties Bureau, appeared almost resigned to the inevitable, writing in April that "hysteria and intolerance will get its victims, regardless of the legislation. If the authorities don't do it, a mob will, and the authorities will act with or without law."[92] Almost resigned, but not quite, for Baldwin did urge Colonel Edward M. House, the President's closest political advisor, to alert Wilson to the bill's dangers. Baldwin even intimated that if dissent was tolerated, liberals and radicals might endorse the administration's war policies. "The general terrorization of public opinion by overzealous officials," Baldwin asserted, "makes it exceedingly difficult for these forces to speak."[93] House did not offer any encouragement, however, and Baldwin did not expect Wilson to veto the bill. He predicted, correctly as it turned out, that the President would defer to the appropriate members of his Cabinet, especially to Attorney General Thomas Gregory.[94]

On May 10 Wilson asked Gregory's advice, and he, in turn, asked Bettman's. "The most valuable feature of the new act," Bettman replied, was that it permitted prosecutions for attempting to obstruct, as well as for actually obstructing, the draft. The provisions curbing seditious speech, he added, resulted from the public outcry and "will have the advantage of calming this clamor. If administered with some discretion, these features of the act ought have no consequences detrimental to the best interests of the country." There was, however, "no possible justification" for granting the Postmaster General discretionary authority to halt mail deliveries. "This very serious and dangerous extension of purely executive action," Bettman warned, could "make everybody so cautious as to practically destroy all freedom of discussion of the war."[95] Yet Bettman did not recommend a veto, and neither did Gregory, whose reply to Wilson contained a similar listing of virtues and defects. Except for the clause permitting the Postmaster General "to practically determine . . . guilt or innocence, and inflict punishment without regard to whether the . . . man could be legally tried and convicted"—an exception, one might imagine, important enough to give an Attorney General pause—Gregory declared, "I know of no proper objection to this bill."[96] On May 16, 1918 Woodrow Wilson signed the Sedition Act.

From the administration's perspective, the Act seemed to steer a safe middle course between the Scylla of repression and the Charybdis of indulgence, the former represented by those, as Gregory later described them, who believed "that even slight criticisms of the Government should be drastically dealt with by criminal prosecutions, if not by firing squads," and the latter by those who thought "that the most unbridled license should be permitted in criticizing . . . the conduct of the war."[97] Even this middle course, however, would prove difficult to navigate, because the standards governing what could and could not be said under the new Act were admittedly "vague and broad." Those standards, Gregory concluded, "are necessarily made thus broad because they deal with the one subject most difficult to define, namely the legitimate limits of free speech."[98]

The definition of those limits would await a test case. It was to be provided by the arrest of the Group of anarchists in East Harlem, four men and a woman who had most likely never heard of Judge Bourquin's decision in the Ves Hall case and were certainly unaware of the concerns expressed within the Department of Justice by John Lord O'Brian and Alfred Bettman. What Jacob Abrams and his friends knew, and knew all too well, was that Congress had passed a restrictive "gag bill," that President Wilson had signed it, and that their Group's membership had consequently dwindled because the new law meant that "work was possible strictly underground and few were ready for that."[99] On the night she was taken into custody by the police, Mollie Steimer said that the Sedition Act was aimed at "anyone who attacked the United States, or who speaks against the uniform of the United States Army or Navy or insults the President, and a lot of other things." She also knew what would happen to anyone who violated the law. "It said if you did any of these things you would get twenty years in prison."[100]

## Woodrow Wilson and Russian Intervention

The day after Woodrow Wilson signed the Sedition Act, an incident occurred in Chelyabinsk, a remote city in central Siberia, that would have as profound an effect on Abrams, Steimer, Lipman, Lachowsky, and Schwartz as the Act itself. On May 17, 1918 the first armed clash took place between Soviet authorities and a Legion of Czechoslovakian soldiers who were attempting to proceed westward along the trans-Siberian railway from Vladivostok. The incident triggered a military conflict which, escalating rapidly over the course of the next few weeks, would provide a plausible excuse for Wilson to send American troops to Russia. Attracted to such a course of action as early as April, Wilson, like a moth darting around a flame, moved steadily closer to intervention. In July he finally made the decision, and in August the first American troops landed in Siberia.

The White House had undoubtedly faced formidable pressure to intervene, especially after March 15, 1918, when the Soviet government ratified the Treaty of Brest-Litovsk. That pact not only took

Russia out of the war, thereby freeing German troops to return to confront the Allies on the western front, but also granted the Germans extraordinary territorial concessions. Many American officials concluded that the Bolsheviks were merely German pawns, and that military intervention would be a reasonable way of blocking German domination of Russia. At the same time, England, France, and Japan were pressuring the United States to join in a concerted action against a Bolshevik regime they hated and feared. Some of Wilson's advisors, however, pointed out that a military response would contradict the principles of self-determination and nonintervention that the President himself had so eloquently pronounced. Wilson's initial response, in March, was to raise practical questions about intervention, which, he said, had not yet been answered. "Namely, what is it to effect and how will it be efficacious in effecting it?"[101]

The hostilities that erupted in May between the Czechoslovaks and the Bolsheviks answered both questions to the President's satisfaction. Indeed, for Wilson the conflict was providential. A Czech Legion numbering 70,000 soldiers, which had been engaging German and Austro-Hungarian forces in the Ukraine, was left stranded by the Treaty of Brest-Litovsk, unable to continue fighting on Russian soil. Seeking to return to the western front, the Czechs decided that the shortest route would in fact be the most dangerous, for it required traveling in a northwesterly direction to Archangel, and then attempting to sail to France in waters that were controlled by German submarines. Instead, the Czechs opted for the longest way out of Russia: eastward, along the trans-Siberian railway to Vladivostok, and then a lengthier, but presumably safer, ocean voyage to France. The Czechs and Bolsheviks reached an agreement, so they thought, on safe passage: the Legion would demonstrate it had no counterrevolutionary designs by turning over its arms to the Soviet authorities, and the Bolsheviks, for their part, would help provide supplies and transportation for the arduous journey.

The agreement was no sooner concluded than it broke down. A convoy of 70,000 foreign soldiers, occupying eighty trains, was attempting to travel 6,000 miles across a country devastated by war, wracked by revolution, and besieged by hostile forces. The situation was inherently unstable. When the Czechs were reluctant, or unwilling, to surrender their arms, the Bolsheviks refused to assist them. As the Czechs moved east, they encountered and inevitably clashed with German, Austrian, and Hungarian soldiers, former prisoners of war who had been released (and, so the Czechs believed, rearmed) by the Bolsheviks, and who were moving in the opposite direction with the same ultimate destination: a return to the war zone. Then, too, an advance guard of Czech soldiers, having reached Vladivostok by the end of May, turned around and marched west in order to reinforce the remainder of the Legion out along the trans-Siberian railway. As the Czechs gained control of Russian towns and villages, anti-Soviet groups rallied to them, confirming the Bolsheviks' worst fears. By June a full-scale war raged between the two sides, with each accusing the other of being the first to violate the original agreement.

Whoever was to blame, it did not take American officials long to realize that the conflict provided a perfect rationale for dispatching troops. Sending aid to the beleaguered Czechs, who were attempting to return to the western front and who had already fought sporadic battles with former German prisoners in Siberia, was much easier to justify than sending an army to eradicate Bolshevik rule, although, to be sure, the one might very well accomplish the other. The Czech Legion's exploits were reason for jubilation in normally staid quarters in the State Department. "This is a 'God-send!' " one official exclaimed. "It is just the news we want."[102] Others, more subdued, were no less alert to the implications. On June 13 an American diplomat noted some of the possibilities raised by the presence of the Czech troops and suggested that "with only slight countenance and support they could control all of Siberia against the Germans." On June 17, after he had read this letter, the President told Secretary of State Robert Lansing that he found in the suggestion "the shadow of a plan that might be worked out with Japanese and other assistance."[103]

The shadow soon acquired considerably more substance. On June 19 Wilson met with Thomas Masaryk, the leading Czech nationalist. Masaryk had been with the Czech Legion in Siberia until early March, when he left for the United States and went to Washington, where he waited patiently for an appointment at the White House. The two men hit it off at once, possibly, as Masaryk thought, because "we had both been professors," but more likely because both had left academic life and entered politics in order to advance certain principles and because those principles were remarkably similar.[104] American intervention, the former Professor of Classics at Prague now told the former Professor of Political Science at Princeton, would enable the Czechs to leave Siberia, return to the war, and so win their independence from the Austro-Hungarian Empire that much more rapidly. Masaryk never advocated intervening to crush the Soviet government. He insisted, in fact, that the conflict in Siberia was "not an anti-Bolshevist undertaking" but was "forced upon us by the obligation of self-defense."[105] Urging the President to send military aid to the Legion, Masaryk appealed to their shared faith in liberalism, nationalism, and democracy. In all his dealings with Wilson, then and later, Masaryk viewed intervention as "a guarantee that these American principles will be realized."[106]

The prospect of intervention, tempting in late May, became irresistible by late June, for Wilson now believed he had a principled basis on which to act. So, on June 22, when the U. S. Ambassador to Russia, David Francis, cabled that workers and peasants had turned against the Soviet government and would welcome Allied intervention, the President was undoubtedly in a receptive frame of mind. When, on June 23, Lansing spoke of an obligation to the Czech troops who had proven "most loyal to our cause," Wilson was almost certainly in a favorable humor.[107] And when, that same day, the British warned that failure to intervene would mean "we shall suffer a blow to our prestige in Russia from which it will take us years to recover," Wilson was surely disposed to agree.[108] There were risks to going in, but, it seemed, even more serious risks to staying out: Japan was prepared to intervene unilaterally in order to enhance its influence in Siberia, and the democratic anti-Soviet elements in Russia might, in despair, turn to Germany for redress. By early July the Czech Legion had taken Vladivostok, and so when Lansing prepared a memorandum that emphasized America's responsibility to send arms and men to help the Czechs in "disarming and dispersing" enemy forces, the President must have been all ears.[109]

On July 6 Wilson met with three Cabinet members—the Secretaries of State, War, and the Navy—and with his two highest-ranking military advisors, the Army Chief of Staff and the Chief of Naval Operations. By now Wilson was less interested in receiving advice than in gaining consent for intervention, and he easily won approval for the sending of 7,000 soldiers to Siberia. He expected that Japan would send an equal number. "The present situation of the Czecho-Slovaks" warranted this policy, Wilson said; it was incumbent on the United States and its Allies "to make an effort to aid those at Vladivostok in forming a junction with their compatriots in western Siberia." Wilson reasoned that "this Government on sentimental grounds and because of the effect upon the friendly Slavs everywhere" would be criticized if it failed to act, and would be held responsible if the Czechs were defeated. Sounding more like Thomas Masaryk every minute, Wilson maintained that the purpose of intervention was not to interfere in internal Soviet affairs but to "cooperate with the Czecho-Slovaks" by helping them hold Vladivostok, by supporting their efforts against the former German and Austrian prisoners, and by guarding their lines of communication.[110]

These purposes, so narrowly defined, were amplified on July 17 when Wilson formally presented the Allies with an *aide-mémoire* outlining his plan. The document, which Wilson composed and even typed himself, began innocently enough. The President actually condemned military intervention, declaring that it "would add to the present sad confusion in Russia rather than cure it, injure her rather than help her, and . . . would be of no advantage in the prosecution of our main design, to win the war against Germany." The United States, he said disarmingly, could not "take part in such intervention or sanction it in principle." It did not take long, however, for the other shoe to drop, and it did so with a hollow thud. Military intervention, the paper continued, was "admissible . . . only to help the Czecho-Slovaks consolidate their forces and get into successful cooperation with their Slavic kinsmen and to steady any efforts at self-government or self-defense in which the Russians themselves may be willing to accept assistance." Wilson had thereby linked the goal of assisting the Czechs with that of promoting self-government in Russia, a phrase open to whatever interpretation one chose to give it.[111]

The public learned of the decision on August 3 when Wilson issued an edited version of the *aide-mémoire.* On August 4 Secretary of War Newton Baker met General William S. Graves at a hotel in Kansas City and told him he was to head the mission. Baker handed Graves a copy of the unedited *aide-mémoire,* warned he would "be walking on eggs loaded with dynamite," and wished him good luck.[112] American soldiers arrived in Vladivostok on August 16, Graves himself on September 1. British troops were already on the scene, as were the 72,000 soldiers—not 7,000—that Japan had decided it was necessary to send. Graves immediately found that the objectives Wilson had listed in July were useless in planning military strategy. The Czech forces were already reunited and were, indeed, firmly in control of Vladivostok. With Japanese help, they were busily mopping up Bolshevik resistance throughout much of eastern Siberia. As for central Siberia, the historian George F. Kennan has written that "in alliance with the White Russian forces, these Czechs had thrown themselves with vigor and with initial enthusiasm into the struggle against the Bolsheviki." In all, 7,500 American soldiers were sent to Siberia, where they remained until April 1920.[113]

On the whole the public reacted favorably to the August 3 announcement. The move appeared to serve a proper military purpose, and it could not be foreseen, of course, that the armistice ending the war would be signed in November 1918 or that American troops would remain in Siberia long after any justification had disappeared. The President's promise to respect Russia's territorial integrity convinced many people that his intent was honorable, but not everyone was persuaded. Former President William Howard Taft, a resolute conservative who applauded the decision to send troops, thought Wilson's rhetoric was "gush" intended to "camouflage . . . our motives." Taft would have dispensed with the hypocrisy, for "no matter how the administration tries to masquerade it, it is action against the Bolsheviki."[114]

That was precisely the reason why American radicals were so horrified. For months they had been hoping that Wilson would not succumb to interventionist pressure, even as they feared that he would. The President's August 3 announcement, although not entirely unexpected, had a shattering effect on them. A week later Socialist Party officials gathered in Chicago to plan a response. They adopted a statement praising Soviet Russia as "a government of the workers, by the workers and for the workers" and denouncing both Germany and the "imperialists in the countries at war with Germany" who supported "the crushing of the Soviet Republic by Allied armies." The same conference heard John Reed declare, "If the American Socialist movement is going down, if we are all going to jail and the movement is going to be disrupted, we will have it disrupted on the Russian situation."[115]

The response of the socialists in Chicago was mild compared to that of the anarchists in East Harlem. To the small but militant Group that met in Jacob Abrams' apartment on East 104th Street, the thought of American forces invading a nation which had attained a new social order was unbearable. And of course it was not just any nation that the United States was invading. These Jewish immigrants had themselves left Russia years before to escape oppression, only to find that conditions in the United States were not as they had imagined them. Living in a land which, to their way of thinking, thwarted aspirations for individual freedom and then enacted repressive laws that would have done credit to Czar Nicholas II, they realized that this same country was preparing to attack their homeland, Russia, which had, miraculously, "achieved the freedom of her toiling class." In the summer of 1918 Mollie Steimer remembered, she and her comrades still believed that the Russian Revolution "would lead to the Int[ernational] Social Revolution and the freeing of mankind." That being so, the question the Group asked in a leaflet written just before the formal announcement of intervention—"Will we allow the extinguishing of the first spark of the Social Revolution?"—surely allowed only one answer.[116]

On July 17 Jacob Abrams signed an agreement to purchase a printing press and the suitable cases of English and Yiddish type from the Bursch Brothers, a firm located on Bleecker Street. By coincidence, that was the day on which Woodrow Wilson wrote the *aide-mémoire* justifying intervention in Siberia. On August 14, as the first boatload of American troops neared Vladivostok, the press was delivered to the basement store on Madison Avenue, a five-minute walk from the Group's apartment in East Harlem.

# 2

# The Arrests

## August 23, 1918

EVEN A CASUAL READER of New York City newspapers on Friday, August 23, 1918 would have come across the following headlines: "Seditious Circulars Scattered in Streets"; "Wilson Attacked in Circulars from Roofs of East Side." On Thursday evening, the stories related, leaflets condemning the policy of intervention in Russia had been thrown from the roofs of buildings on Second Avenue near Eighth Street. Some of the leaflets were printed in English, others in Yiddish. A storeowner who picked up a copy of the English leaflet, entitled "The Hypocrisy of the United States and Her Allies," was so infuriated that he raced up the stairs to find the culprits, but arrived only "in time to see several men running across the neighboring roofs in a northerly direction." He then brought the leaflets to the police, who "scoured the neighborhood in search of the perpetrators." A house-by-house search, however, failed to locate those responsible. The newspapers quoted a few sentences from the leaflet and reported that "excitable persons" believed the circulars had been dropped from airplanes.[1]

So the police had undoubtedly been alerted when, on Friday morning, four men showed up with additional copies of the leaflet. At about 7:45 A.M., three of the men explained, they were standing at the intersection of Crosby and Houston streets, waiting to enter the building around the corner, at 610 Broadway, where they worked. Happening to look up, they saw the leaflets floating down from an open window. The fourth man was already at work when someone told him about the leaflets and brought him copies. None of the four could read Yiddish, but they were sufficiently incensed by the English circulars to bring them to police headquarters, located a few blocks away at 240 Centre Street. There Captain Fuller Potter of the U. S. Army's Military Intelligence Division read the English leaflet and concluded it was "of a decidedly seditious character." He assigned two detectives, Henry Barth and Thomas Jenkins, to "what seemed to be a rather hopeless task of finding the person who had distributed the literature."[2]

The task proved not so hopeless after all. Arriving at 610 Broadway, Barth and Jenkins began a methodical search. The first and second floors were occupied by a firm which employed two hundred workers; the officers checked every name but found nothing suspicious. They then moved to the third floor, which was occupied by the American Hat Company. Barth and Jenkins quickly examined the time cards of all three hundred employees to see if anyone had punched in early. They discovered that a man named Hyman Rosansky "had arrived at the shop that morning earlier than was customary for him, and this time of arrival tallied with the time the circulars were thrown from the window." Other employees reported that Rosansky "was an anarchist and was constantly trying to stir up trouble among his fellow workmen." So Barth and Jenkins approached Rosansky and asked to see his draft registration card. He said he had left it in his coat pocket, went to get it, and when he produced the card "he also had other papers in his pocket, and they were looked over, and we found two of those pamphlets, one in English and one was in Yiddish, such as the boys had said were thrown out of the window . . ." Rosansky claimed he had found the leaflets on the building's fire escape that morning, but men working near the window denied having seen him. "Being convinced that Rosansky was not telling the truth," the officers reported, "we made him take us to his home."[3]

Rosansky lived with his wife and children in East Harlem, at 97 East 107th Street, a few doors from the Ferrer Center. When Barth and Jenkins entered his apartment, their suspicions were immediately confirmed. "A careful survey of the premises disclosed two more of the pamphlets above mentioned and a large quantity of other anarchistic literature. There were pictures of anarchistic 'martyrs' on the walls, and the atmosphere in general was of an anarchistic nature."[4] Moreover, poking through a bureau drawer, the policemen found a loaded .32 caliber revolver and two boxes of cartridges. Barth later testified, "Well, I says to Rosansky, 'Now,' I says, 'you better stop lying, because the more you lie the worse you are off, and the worse you will get it. You better tell us the truth.' "[5] Rosansky replied that he did not want to say anything more in the presence of his wife, who was understandably distraught, but promised to make a statement at headquarters. For purposes of verification, the officers told Rosansky to make his mark on the two leaflets (since he evidently could not write his name, at least in English) and told his wife to sign them. Then they took Rosansky to 240 Centre Street.

There, at two-thirty in the afternoon, Rosansky was grilled by Sergeant Barth, Lieutenant Colonel Nicholas Biddle, and Inspector Thomas Tunney. Speaking at times in Yiddish, with Patrolman Abraham Brody as interpreter, Rosansky told the following story: Born in Brest-Litovsk, he had emigrated to the United States in 1910 but had not become a citizen. He was twenty-five years old, married, and the father of three children. He did not belong to the Ferrer Center or any other anarchist group. As for the revolver, "a fellow gave that to me two weeks ago, when he went to Chicago," but he did not know the person's name. Rosansky said that some men he had known for a few weeks had, on the evening of August 22, given him the leaflets to distribute. "I know the fellows but don't know exactly the names. Lachowsky I know by name." Rosansky remembered this exchange: "I says, 'What kind of leaflets.' 'It is all right, you don't have to know what kind of leaflets.' 'What I got to do with this?' He says, 'You have got to throw them from the window.' " Rosansky said that he had arrived at work early so he could distribute the leaflets without being observed.[6]

When asked, "Why did they take you into their confidence to distribute these?" Rosansky answered, "I don't know, they wanted to give me more things."[7] The "they" to whom he referred were, as we know, Abrams, Steimer, Lipman, Schwartz, and Lachowsky. Although none of them knew Rosansky well, Lachowsky had vouched for his reliability. As Mollie Steimer later explained, Rosansky "was not in the Group, but said he was a sympathizer." He "knew that we were doing some work and expressed a wish to participate. . . . We therefore gave him copies of the leaflets . . . and told him that if he agrees, he can help spread same, which he did." But when Rosansky was "caught and questioned, he gave us all out."[8] Obviously frightened, and anxious to protect his family, Rosansky volunteered a crucial piece of information: he had arranged a rendezvous with the Group on East 104th Street, at seven-thirty that evening, when he was to receive additional copies of the leaflets.

Even as the police were questioning Rosansky, incoming reports quickened their sense of urgency. According to Lieutenant Colonel Biddle, the Washington office of the Military Intelligence Division had sent a message "to the effect that an important anarchistic or I.W.W. meeting was to be held at the Central [Opera] Palace on 67th Street that night at which . . . well known radicals were to speak. A similar notice had reached us from our secret agents in the city." The conjunction of the two events—the distribution of the leaflets and the calling of a public meeting—convinced Biddle that "the matter was one of real importance and was being handled by somebody high up in anarchistic circles." He arranged to have the meeting covered by plainclothes agents and by "a sufficient number of stenographers to take down any utterances made by the speakers." With men assigned to the Central Opera House on 67th Street, and with others accompanying Rosansky to East 104th Street, "all the addresses which we then had in our possession were covered and there was nothing further to do but await results."[9]

The meeting at the Central Opera House, however, was on the verge of being canceled. It had been called not by anarchists but by the Socialist Party as a forum for John Reed, Scott Nearing, and others who opposed United States intervention in Soviet Russia. On Friday a Socialist Party functionary, Julius Gerber, met with the police and the manager of the Central Opera House to make sure that the rally proceeded smoothly. The police produced the leaflets and insinuated that the Socialists had distributed them. The terrified manager of the hall withdrew permission for the meeting. Gerber, disclaiming all responsibility for the leaflets, sputtered "that we were not irresponsible nor responsible for what irresponsible outside people do," but he might just as well have been speaking to the wind. The manager, Gerber said, "was frightened by the circular he read, and he would not let us have the hall."[10]

Calling off a widely publicized rally hours before it was scheduled to begin was not easy. On Friday evening an expectant crowd gathered on 67th Street only to be informed of the cancelation. Some of the people proceeded downtown to a Socialist meeting hall on 29th Street, where Reed, Nearing, and the others appeared and spoke. By far the larger number, perhaps five hundred marchers, headed uptown to East Harlem, hoping to hold a rally at the New Star Casino on East 107th Street. When they arrived, they found the doors locked; several youths climbed in through a fire escape but were told by the proprietor they could not use the hall. So the crowd resorted to marching through the streets of East Harlem, singing Russian songs and chanting revolutionary slogans. Copies of the two leaflets were handed around. On East 106th Street the police tried to arrest some of the more vocal demonstrators, while the crowd struggled to prevent the arrests. "Then police clubs began to swing freely," and one of the marchers hurled a brick, hitting a policeman in the head and knocking him down. As the marchers dispersed, the police arrested three young men and three young women on charges of disorderly conduct.[11]

Two blocks from all this commotion, Sergeants Barth, Jenkins, and six other detectives had staked out East 104th Street. Standing shadowed in doorways, they waited for the other members of the Group to make contact with Hyman Rosansky. At about seven-thirty Mollie Steimer appeared, talked briefly to Rosansky, then entered the apartment at 5 East 104th Street. A few minutes later Hyman Lachowsky appeared, carrying two bundles of leaflets, one of which he gave to Rosansky. At eight o'clock Jacob Abrams and Samuel Lipman approached Rosansky, and Steimer, now carrying some of the leaflets, soon joined them. They walked a short way together, then Abrams went into a restaurant and a little later Lipman went off in another direction. Lachowsky and Steimer were then arrested and taken, with Rosansky, to the 39th Precinct station house on East 104th Street near Second Avenue, where they were searched and found to be carrying the leaflets. Two other detectives trailed Lipman, stopped him, and asked his name. He replied, "Louis Levine." He was also taken to the station house. By nine o'clock Steimer, Lipman, and Lachowsky were in a paddy wagon.

As it left for police headquarters on Centre Street, a crowd gathered and Mollie Steimer "got up on the seat of the patrol wagon and addressed the people to revolutionize and to come to her assistance."[12]

Meanwhile, the police waited patiently for Abrams to emerge from the restaurant on East 104th Street. When he did, Jacob Schwartz was with him. Four detectives trailed them for two blocks, then collared them and demanded to see Abrams' draft card. He produced a card which, it was later found, had been forged. The police asked where they lived, and, according to Barth's account, "We asked them to direct us to the place." The two men took the detectives to their apartment. Abrams did not have a key, but obtained one from a neighbor. The apartment was so sparsely furnished, the police reported, that "it looked more like a place, a place of assemblage, than a residence."[13] One of the bedrooms had only a cot, another only a mattress on the floor. Wooden packing boxes served as desks. The police ransacked the apartment, finding hundreds of copies of the English and Yiddish leaflets, as well as other anarchist literature, a book inscribed, "Alexander Berkman, his friend, to comrade Abrams," and, in the bottom drawer of a dresser, a loaded revolver.

While the police were rummaging through the apartment, the doorbell rang. "It is all right, it is me. Let me in," said a bruised, disheveled man, who, it turned out, was Gabriel Prober, a friend of Abrams'. Prober was a bookbinder who lived in Brooklyn. He explained that he had gone to the Central Opera House that evening, then marched uptown to East Harlem, and was caught in the ensuing free-for-all. "He was crying and his face was all swollen and he had no hat, and he was breathing heavily," the policemen reported. "His face was all puffed up and bleeding as though he had been through a pretty rough deal."[14] Prober said he had come to Abrams' apartment to wash up and tend to his injuries. Risking nothing, the detectives took Abrams, Schwartz, and Prober into custody, put them in taxicabs, and set out for 240 Centre Street.

The next day newspapers carried accounts of the arrests which, if not entirely accurate, were nonetheless revealing. The *World* reported that "the attitude of all the persons arrested was that of martyrs for a holy cause. The Crowd is known as the Blast Group and all are long-haired Anarchists who came here from Russia." The *Journal* described the men as "long-haired, heavily-bearded and sullen. The girl is defiant and of a quick and alert manner."[15] "Some of them boasted of their anarchistic allegiance," another account said, "and expressed themselves as willing to die for the cause."[16] *The New York Times* informed its readers that "all of the prisoners are said to be of Russian origin and followers of Leon Trotsky and Nicholas Lenine, the Bolshevist leaders."[17] The stories played up the forged draft card and the loaded revolvers. The newspapers reported that the young anarchists had been arraigned before United States Commissioner Samuel M. Hitchcock and charged with violating the Sedition Act. They were being held in the city prison, with bail for each set at $10,000.

## Two Leaflets

The document which had so disturbed everyone—the Second Avenue storeowner, the workers at the corner of Houston and Crosby streets, the officers of the Police Department and the Military Intelligence Division, the manager of the Central Opera House, the Socialist Party official, the newspaper reporters and, presumably, their many readers—was the English-language leaflet. Printed on a thin sheet of paper, measuring four and one-half by twelve inches, it contained fewer than four hundred words. Samuel Lipman was its author, and the errors in spelling, grammar, and punctuation, as well as its mannered, stilted tone, can be accounted for by the fact that English was not his or any of his comrades' native language. The leaflet, as it appeared in its original form, stated:

THE
HYPOCRISY
OF THE
UNITED STATES
AND HER ALLIES

"Our" President Wilson, with his beautiful phraseology, has hypnotized the people of America to such an extent that they do not see his hypocrisy.

Know, you people of America, that a frank enemy is always preferable to a conceald friend. When we say the people of America, we do not mean the few Kaisers of America, we mean the "People of America." you people of America were deceived by the wonderful speeches of the masked President Wilson. His shameful, cowardly silence about the intervention in Russia reveals the hypocrisy of the plutocratic gang in Washington and vicinity.

The President was afraid to announce to the American people the intervention in Russia. He is too much of a coward to come out openly and say: "We capitalistic nations cannot afford to have a proletarian republic in Russia." Instead, he uttered beautiful phrases about Russia, which, as you see, he did not mean, and secretly, cowardly, sent troops to crush the Russian Revolution. Do you see now how German militarism combined with allied capitalism to crush the russian revolution?

This is not new. The tyrants of the world fight each other until they see a common enemy—WORKING CLASS—ENLIGHTENMENT—as soon as they find a common enemy, they combine to crush it.

In 1815 monarchic nations combined under the name of the "Holy Alliance" to crush the French Revolution. Now militarism and capitalism combined, though not openly, to crush the russian revolution.

What have you to say about it?

Will you allow the Russian Revolution to be crushed? YOU: yes, we mean, YOU the people of America!

THE RUSSIAN REVOLUTION CALLS TO THE WORKERS OF THE WORLD FOR HELP.

The Russian Revolution cries: "WORKERS OF THE WORLD! AWAKE! RISE! PUT DOWN YOUR ENEMY AND MINE!"

Yes friends, there is only one enemy of the workers of the world and that is CAPITALISM.

It is a crime, that workers of America, workers of Germany, workers of Japan, etc., to fight THE WORKERS' REPUBLIC OF RUSSIA.

AWAKE! AWAKE, YOU WORKERS OF THE WORLD!

REVOLUTIONISTS

P. S. It is absurd to call us pro-German. We hate and despise German militarism more than do your hypocritical tyrants. We have more reasons for denouncing German militarism than has the coward of the White House.

Despite its strong and occasionally provocative language, the leaflet is on the whole cautious and even circumspect, written, most likely, so as to avoid violating the Sedition Act. There is a strident denunciation of President Wilson's insincerity, but no attack on the form of government of the United States. Workers are exhorted to "awake" and "rise," but not to take concrete action of any kind. The leaflet blames the Allied intervention in Russia on capitalist intrigue, but the postscript explicitly disavows any sympathy for German militarism. What emerges most clearly, perhaps, is the sense of betrayal at Wilson's double-dealing. "We really thought he would not consent to intervention," the Group wrote in an unpublished leaflet, seized by the police.[18] It was the President's cant, his sanctimonious refusal to own up to his real reasons for sending troops to Russia that infuriated Lipman.

Jacob Schwartz wrote the Yiddish leaflet which was, by contrast, far more militant. Ironically, it seems not to have been translated into English until after the arrests. The police assumed that the two leaflets said the same thing. When Lachowsky was taken into custody, he was handed both leaflets and asked, "Are these the same in English and Yiddish?" "There are some words a little different, but it is the same," he replied.[19] Within a matter of days, however, the Yiddish leaflet was translated into English—the records do not reveal by whom—and this official translation would provide the strongest basis for the indictments, would be quoted extensively at every stage of the legal process, and would, eventually, form the basis for the Supreme Court's ruling. This translated version reads as follows:

WORKERS—WAKE UP!!

The preparatory work for Russia's emancipation is brought to an end by his Majesty, Mr. Wilson, and the rest of the gang; dogs of all colors!

America, together with the Allies, will march to Russia, not, "God Forbid", to interfere with the Russian affairs, but to help the Czecho-Slovaks in their struggle against the Bolsheviki.

Oh, ugly hypocrites; this time they shall not succeed in fooling the

Russian emigrants and the friends of Russia in America. Too visible is their audacious move.

Workers, Russian emigrants, you who had the least belief in the honesty of our government, must now throw away all confidence, must spit in the face the false, hypocritic, military propaganda which has fooled you so relentlessly, calling forth your sympathy, your help, to the prosecution of the war. With the money which you have loaned, or are going to loan them, they will make bullets not only for the Germans but also for the Workers Soviets of Russia. Workers in the ammunition factories, you are producing bullets, bayonets, cannon, to murder not only the Germans, but also your dearest, best, who are in Russia and are fighting for freedom.

You who emigrated from Russia, you who are friends of Russia, will you carry on your conscience in cold blood the shame spot as a helper to choke the Workers Soviets? Will you give your consent to the inquisitionary expedition to Russia? Will you be calm spectators to the fleecing blood from the hearts of the best sons of Russia?

America and her Allies have betrayed (the workers). Their robberish aims are clear to all men. The destruction of the Russian Revolution, that is the politics of the march to Russia.

Workers, our reply to the barbaric intervention has to be a general strike! An open challenge only will let the government know that not only the Russian worker fights for freedom, but also here in America lives the spirit of revolution.

Do not let the government scare you with their wild punishment in prisons, hanging and shooting. We must not and will not betray the splendid fighters of Russia. Workers, up to fight.

Three hundred years had the Romanoff dynasty taught us how to fight. Let all rulers remember this, from the smallest to the biggest despot, that the hand of the revolution will not shiver in a fight.

Woe unto those who will be in the way of progress. Let solidarity live!

THE REBELS

This translation, however, is at best inadequate and at worst misleading. Where Schwartz's use of Yiddish is lyrical, witty, and incisive, the translation makes it appear turgid, humorless, and dull. A few examples, in transliterated Yiddish, will illustrate how the document's tone and meaning were transformed. The sentence "too visible is their audacious move" reads, in the original, *"tsu ofen is zeyr chutzpahdike shtelung,"* which might better be translated as "too open is their audacious attitude," although the Yiddish word *chutzpah* denotes a quality of nerviness that has no precise English equivalent. The sentence "Woe unto those who will be in the way of progress" actually reads *"vey iz tsu di vus shtehn in veyg fun prahgres,"* a play on the oft-invoked exclamation *"vey is* [*tsu*] *mir"* or "woe is me," which conveys in common usage a feeling of mock sympathy rather than any kind of threat. Statements which appear to be ungrammatical ("must spit in the face the false, hypocritic, military propaganda") are just poorly translated ("must spit in the face of the lying, hypocritical, military propaganda"). The translator rendered *"shverdn"* as "bayonets" rather than as "swords." Where the word "emigrant" appears, Schwartz actually wrote *"oisgevanderte"* (or *"ahngevanderte"*), a term suggesting that Russian Jews who had moved to America had not left Russia permanently but were only "out-wanderers" who would, one day, return to Soviet Russia, in the author's view the modern equivalent of the Promised Land.

The official translation not only disregarded these nuances, but in three instances distorted the leaflet's meaning. Two phrases were made to seem more incendiary than they actually are, and one less so. Schwartz did not write "Mr. Wilson and the rest of the gang." He wrote, satirically, "Mr. Wilson and his comrades," using a Hebrew, not a Yiddish, word. The government's version rendered *"dem klensten gloiben in der erenstkeyt fun der regirung"* as "the least belief in the honesty of our government," thereby making the leaflet appear to attack the United States government. A better translation is "the least faith in the earnestness of the government," for Schwartz meant to say that Russian Jews knew from bitter experience that they could never place their faith in any government. Later, at the trial, Jacob Abrams pointed out both of these errors. He did not, however, mention a third in which the translator inadvertently softened the language. In the next to last paragraph Schwartz warned that the hand of the "revolutionary"—*"revolutsyoner"*—would not tremble in a fight—not simply "revolution."

I am indebted to Dr. Chana Kronfeld for a new translation of the leaflet, which reads as follows:

## WORKERS WAKE UP!!

The preparatory work for Russia's "deliverance" is finished, and has been made clear by his Majesty, Mr. Wilson, and his comrades: dogs of all colors.

America together with the Allies will march after Russia, not, God forbid, to intervene in its internal affairs but only to help the Czecho-Slovaks in their fight against the Bolsheviks.

Oh, the ugly hypocrites! This time may it not work out for them to lie to the Russian emigrants and the friends of Russia in America. Too open is their audacious attitude.

Workers, wanderers from Russia, you who had the least faith in the earnestness of the government, must now throw away every trust, must spit in the face of the lying, hypocritical, military propaganda, which has lied to you in an ugly way in order to elicit your sympathy and your help in conducting the war. With your poor monies which you have loaned or will loan, they will make bullets not only for the Germans but also for the Workers' Soviets in Russia. While working in the ammunition factories you are creating bullets, swords, cannons to murder not only Germans but also your most beloved, your best ones, who are in Russia and who are fighting for freedom.

Wanderers and friends of Russia, will you carry on your consciences cold-bloodedly the stain of shame as accomplices in the strangulation of the Workers' Soviets? Will you add your vote to the inquisition-like expedition after Russia? Silent bywatchers of the blood flowing from the hearts of the best sons of Russia.

America and the Allies have lied. Their larcenous goals are clear to every person—the elimination of the Russian Revolution—this is the politics of the march after Russia.

Workers, our answer to the barbaric intervention has to be a general strike! A public resistance alone can let the government know that not only the Russian worker fights for freedom but that also here in America lives the spirit of revolution. Let the government not frighten you with its wild penalties of imprisonment, hanging and shooting.

We must not and shall not betray the brave fighters of Russia.

Workers, up to the battle!

Three hundred years the Romanovs have taught us how to fight.
Let all rulers remember this, from the smallest to the biggest despot, that the hand of the revolutionary will not tremble in the fight.
Woe to those who stand in the way of progress!
Solidarity lives.

REBELS.

The leaflet postulates a few key themes. Confronted by blatant governmental hypocrisy, the people will arise as if from a troubled sleep; silence and acquiescence will give way to outspoken resistance; punishments inflicted by the ruling class will count for nothing; betrayal will be transformed into faithfulness to a noble cause, and guilt, thereby, into redemption. Schwartz's leaflet differs not only from the awkwardly rendered official translation but also from Lipman's more cautiously worded English leaflet. One cannot but wonder why those differences existed. Was it because Schwartz was an anarchist and Lipman a socialist? Because Schwartz, writing in Yiddish, felt an ease and freedom from constraint that Lipman, writing in English, did not? Unfortunately, these questions were of no concern to the police officials at 240 Centre Street, who, on the night of August 23, 1918, had other purposes in mind: to make sure that all the radicals they had just arrested incriminated themselves and went to jail.

## The Bomb Squad

The telephone call from police headquarters came late, after eleven o'clock at night, but not too late for Inspector Thomas Tunney. An officer informed Tunney that several "important anarchists" had been arrested, and asked him to come to headquarters to continue the interrogation. He did not need to be asked twice. Arriving shortly before midnight, after Lachowsky and Lipman had been questioned, Tunney questioned them further and then interrogated Abrams, Schwartz, Prober, and Steimer. "By five in the morning," Lieutenant Nicholas Biddle related, Tunney "had succeeded in getting a sufficient confession from each of them to warrant their being held for the District Attorney."[20]

For Tunney, those few hours capped a four-year career as head of the Police Department's Bomb Squad, years Tunney recalled in a memoir not too modestly entitled *Throttled! The Detection of the German and Anarchist Bomb Plotters in the United States.*

Thomas J. Tunney had joined the police force in 1897, at the age of twenty-four. A few years later "a number of mysterious explosions in New York which caused considerable property damage" awakened his interest in explosives. "I found myself before long forced to become something of a student of chemistry," Tunney remarked.[21] His newly developed interest caught the attention of higher-ups in the department, and in August 1914, when Police Commissioner Arthur Woods organized the Bomb Squad, he placed Tunney in charge of it. This special squad was created in the aftermath of an accidental, although lethal, dynamite explosion which occurred in a Lexington Avenue apartment in East Harlem. The blast killed several young anarchists, habitués of the Ferrer Center, who were at the time manufacturing a bomb earmarked for John D. Rockefeller's estate in Tarrytown, New York.

Tunney greatly admired Arthur Woods, paying him the ultimate compliment (or so he may have imagined) by dedicating *Throttled!* to him. Woods, a graduate of Harvard and a former teacher at Groton, had been appointed Commissioner in April 1914 because of his friendship with John P. Mitchel, the recently elected Mayor of New York City. Influenced by the tenets of Progressive reform, Woods embarked on a crusade against crime, vice, and corruption. He also streamlined the Police Department. He encouraged the use of the merit system in appointments and promotions, upgraded the police training schools, and installed modern signal boxes for summoning patrolmen. One winter, when unemployment caused widespread distress, the police raised several thousand dollars for the jobless, much of it from their own pockets. Woods urged the men in blue to cultivate the goodwill of youngsters by paying informal visits to classrooms and by setting aside special "play streets." Woods's door was always open to any policeman who had a gripe, and, by most accounts, he was widely respected.

Woods took office firmly committed to protecting First Amendment freedoms. "People in this country have a constitutional right of free assemblage and of free speech," he remarked, adding, "It is the duty of the police, not merely to permit this, but to protect people in the enjoyment of free speech and assemblage." Woods recognized that some limits had to be established: demonstrators could not be permitted to interfere with the rights of others, to obstruct traffic, or to provoke "immediate violence." But that phrase, he cautioned, had to be construed narrowly. "It cannot properly be construed as provocative of immediate disorder if speakers criticize, no matter how vehemently, the existing order of things, or if they recommend, no matter how enthusiastically, a change which they believe would improve things."[22] Woods took justifiable pride in how the police had handled anarchist demonstrations in 1914. When a bystander at one such rally complained about a speaker who was denouncing the government, Woods noted, a policeman responded in just the right way: "If you want to hold a meeting, go over to the other side of the street there and I'll protect you too."[23]

The war forced Woods to modify these views, as evidenced by his reply, in August 1917, to a letter from his friend, Theodore Roosevelt. Speakers on street corners who proclaimed support for Germany or who attacked the United States were traitors, Roosevelt wrote, who should be summarily arrested. Woods replied that speech which was "not interfering with the rights of others . . . and not inciting to violence" should be protected, but he then made a crucial concession. In wartime, he admitted, "some of these matters have to be looked over again to see what, under the changed conditions, constitutes incitement to violence, and interference with the rights of others." Words that were patently harmless in peacetime "may have the effect of sowing seeds of disloyalty in the minds of some of those that listen." The problem for the authorities, Woods thought, was that seditious speech was not illegal, at least not yet. To rectify this, "a Federal statute should be enacted making criminal any sort of propaganda, printed or spoken, in favor of the enemy, or tending to weaken our country." But until that time, Woods assured Roosevelt, "we shall not let free speech be used to cloak sedition."[24]

Tunney and the detectives on the Bomb Squad had little interest in the abstract question of free speech. In their view, anarchism and bomb-throwing were cut from the same red cloth. Not only was there the evidence of the Lexington Avenue explosion, but in October 1914 two more bombs went off in New York City, one in the nave of St. Patrick's Cathedral and the other in front of the rectory adjoining the Church of St. Alphonsus. Tunney then assigned an undercover agent, Amedeo Polignani, to infiltrate the "Bresci Circle," an anarchist group which met in the Italian section of East Harlem. Using whatever subterfuge and deception were required, Polignani succeeded in winning the anarchists' confidence. According to Tunney's account, the agent was approached by two young men, Carmine Carbone and Frank Abarno, who had grown impatient with their comrades' cautious tactics. The disgruntled pair allegedly invited Polignani to help them build some bombs. In March 1915 Abarno was arrested in St. Patrick's Cathedral, seconds after he had placed a bomb near a pillar, and Carbone was also soon taken into custody. To the anarchists, this was a clear case of police entrapment. They claimed that Polignani had hatched the plot, inveigled the others into participating in it, and built the bombs himself. A jury found Carbone and Abarno guilty, and they were sentenced to six to twelve years in Sing Sing.

In the next few years more arrests and convictions followed. Those apprehended, however, were not anarchists but rather German agents who were attempting to sabotage merchant ships sailing from the United States with supplies for the Allies. The Bomb Squad's quarry had changed but not the tactics of the hunt, which resembled those it had employed against the anarchists. Agents were again selected with a careful regard for their ethnic background. In this case, Tunney said, he chose detectives who were "fine Americans of German descent, with an excellent command of the German language." Assuming false identities, even posing as German agents, Tunney's men frequented waterfront dives with instructions to "fish about for whatever might take their bait." The bait must have been tempting because the detectives managed to uncover the laboratories where explosive devices were being made, and the agents who were manufacturing them. When the Bomb Squad was sure it had located the right man, Tunney admitted, "we pounced on him without the formality of an examination, and searched his room" for incriminating evidence and further leads.[25]

Assessing the wartime work of the Bomb Squad, Commissioner Woods commented that it was engaged "not in trying to bottle up the preachers of any particular doctrine, but simply in finding out who were the plotters of violent deeds and bringing them to justice."[26] For the members of the Bomb Squad, the distinction was blurred. The same detectives, impelled by a similar sense of urgency, went on missions that may well have seemed analogous, some directed at anarchists, others at enemy agents. Detectives Henry Barth and Thomas Jenkins, who, on August 23, 1918, were sent to find the man who had tossed the leaflets from the building near Crosby and Houston streets, had worked together on other assignments. Earlier, the same team had searched a German-American clubhouse in Brooklyn, where, in the toe of an old boot stored in a locker, they had found one of the "infernal machines" they were looking for. So it is not surprising that they pursued the man who had thrown the leaflets as doggedly as if he had been hurling bombs.

Nor is it surprising that their chief, Thomas Tunney, passed himself off as an expert on anarchist affairs. Alexander Berkman and Emma Goldman had no more faithful reader than the good Inspector. In *Throttled!* and in testimony he gave before Congressional committees, Tunney expressed a grudging admiration for the anarchists' literary skill and oratorical ability. He termed Berkman's *Prison Memoirs of an Anarchist* "a very interesting book indeed," and acknowledged that Berkman's other writing "at times shows a certain cheerful tenderness underneath its bombast."[27] Goldman, he granted, was "a very able and intelligent woman and a very fine speaker."[28] Yet Tunney believed that anarchists had "disorderly minds," favored "unrestrained guerilla warfare on law and class," and were addicted to violence. He had no difficulty in justifying the arrests of Abrams, Steimer, Lipman, and Lachowsky on the grounds that they were "the ringleaders of a group who circulated leaflets denouncing armed intervention in Russia and advocating a general strike."[29]

For more than three years Tunney ran the Bomb Squad as he pleased, choosing its personnel, setting its priorities, prescribing its tactics. Tunney had Woods's complete confidence, and Woods had Mayor Mitchel's. This cozy arrangement came to a sudden end, however, in November 1917, when Mitchel was defeated in his bid for reelection. The Mayor-elect, John F. Hylan, was a little-known judge with strong ties to Tammany Hall. The votes had hardly been counted when Hylan announced that he expected Woods, whose appointment, technically, did not expire until April 1919, to resign before he, Hylan, assumed office on January 1, 1918. Woods, a proud man, immediately announced his intention to resign, pointedly stating that a Police Commissioner's success depended on "the whole-souled understanding and cooperation of the Mayor."[30] Tunney and the Bomb Squad now faced the bleak prospect that a Tammany flunky would be appointed Commissioner—a threat they regarded as ominous as any posed by secret agents, however devious, or by anarchists, however hot-blooded.

The threat was narrowly, although only temporarily, averted. On December 13, 1917, Woods, in one of his last official acts, announced that Secretary of War Newton D. Baker had asked him to transfer the entire Bomb Squad to the Army's Military Intelligence Division. Woods wasted no time in complying with the request. The arrangement was a simple one: high-ranking Bomb Squad officials received commissions, while detectives were made noncommissioned officers. Their day-to-day duties were no different, and their autonomy remained unimpaired. Some fifty members of the Bomb Squad and several Deputy Police Commissioners appointed by Woods were, for the duration of the war, removed from the Police Department's jurisdiction and were placed under the Army's. It was an open secret that the move was inspired by "the fear that when the Tammany regime takes over the affairs of the city Tammany's favorites would be placed in charge of the bomb squad" and Woods's appointees, including Tunney, dismissed.[31]

Mayor Hylan's actions early in 1918 followed the predicted course. Dipping down into the uniformed ranks, he named Richard E. Enright, a man known for his Tammany Hall ties, as the new Police Commissioner. One of Arthur Woods's first moves, shortly after his appointment in 1914, had been to remove Enright from his position at police headquarters—where, to the delight of favored contractors, he headed the Bureau of Repairs and Supplies—and to assign him to a remote station house in Flatbush. An observer said of Woods's motives, "It may be that he does not care to have a man with Enright's connections in the department in a position to grant special favors."[32] In 1918 these connections brought Enright back from exile in Brooklyn, and the special favors followed close behind. Hylan's chauffeur was eventually hired by the Department as an investigator, and his brother-in-law appeared on the payroll of the Bomb Squad.[33] Enright buttered up the

Mayor by offering to provide him, at every public function, with a police escort of six men on motorcycles, thirty-four men on horseback, and a band playing "flourishes and ruffles, these being the same as the honors paid to a Major General of the Army."[34] When the war ended and the Bomb Squad was returned to the Commissioner's less-than-tender mercies, Tunney would be forced out and his elite corps made over in Enright's image.

On the night of August 23, 1918, however, when Tunney received the telephone call summoning him to headquarters to question Jacob Abrams and his comrades, the Bomb Squad was still riding high. Tunney was on loan to the United States government, courtesy of the Police Department, and so were the other officials who awaited his arrival at 240 Centre Street. Two were conservative, civic-minded businessmen whom Woods had appointed Special Deputy Police Commissioners. Under the new dispensation, they held officers' rank in the Military Intelligence Division: Nicholas Biddle, a bank director and a trustee of the Astor estate, as a Lieutenant Colonel; and Fuller Potter, of the brokerage firm of Potter, Prentice, and Choate, as a Captain. Also present were Henry Barth, Thomas Jenkins, and six other men—Edward Meagher, Vincent Hastings, Michael Santaniello, James Murphy, Edward Caddell, and John Dillon—all Bomb Squad detectives who were now Sergeants in Military Intelligence. These men wore the uniform of the United States Army, but their attitude toward anarchists had been shaped by their experiences over a period of several years as members of the Bomb Squad.

## The Confessions

Lieutenant Colonel Biddle and Captain Potter first interrogated Hyman Lachowsky, at about nine-thirty. Lachowsky admitted that he had given leaflets to Rosansky and that he was also planning to distribute them himself, but refused to answer questions that would implicate anyone else. When Biddle asked whether he had given the leaflets to others, or belonged to the same Group as Mollie Steimer, Lachowsky replied, "I refuse to answer." "Will you tell me why you refuse to answer?"

"I object to answer." "Why?" "It is too much that I answer this." Moments later Biddle lost his temper. "Does it make any difference to you whether you tell the truth or not . . . now don't lie." "I don't lie." "Yes, you do, and you know it damned well." Captain Potter told Lachowsky he was "making a big mistake" by not answering Biddle's questions. "He is a Colonel in the Army," Potter said, and added misleadingly, "By telling the truth you certainly can do yourself no harm." Lachowsky said he would explain, in Yiddish, why the leaflets were in his possession, but a translator was not provided and was, perhaps, not available at that hour.[35]

Shortly after midnight Inspector Tunney questioned Lachowsky but was no more successful in making him divulge names. "Are you a Revolutionist?" "Yes." . . . "Do you think you were doing right by distributing these, according to the dictates of your conscience?" "Yes." . . . "Do you know who printed these articles and dictated the manuscripts on them?" "I won't answer." "Do you know them?" "I refuse to answer."[36] Lachowsky described, on the witness stand, what happened next. "Somebody turned out the light. . . . I felt the first punch in my eye. Then they took me in the other room, and there was four men with blackjacks. . . . He [Sergeant Edward Meagher] walked in there and said, 'Never mind, he will tell the truth.' He took a gun out of his pocket and put it to my chest and said, 'Tell the truth or I will shoot you.' I said, 'If I have anything to tell, I will tell it before the Judge.' He said, 'Judge, my eye, you must tell me, not the Judge.' They tore out my hair."[37] Lipman, Abrams, and Steimer later testified that they had seen Lachowsky, "lying with his head on the desk," his eyes black and blue, "all beaten up, with some of his hair on the floor."[38]

Samuel Lipman was interrogated next. Inspector Tunney, Lipman claimed afterwards, "said he will do to me as he did to Lachowsky, and Lachowsky was sitting in the back room, half dead. . . . Of course, I answered all the questions I was asked."[39] Lipman admitted that he had known the other members of the Group "for several months"; they "are my friends and I know that they are Anarchists and I exchange views with them." Tunney seemed less interested in forcing Lipman to identify others than to incriminate himself, which is exactly what he did. Lipman was asked whether he approved of the views expressed in the leaflet "in which the President of the United States is abused?" "Yes, I do approve of it." "Are you opposed to the draft?" "Yes." . . . "Did you distribute any of these pamphlets?" "No, but I know they were going to be distributed." "Who told you that?" "My friends, whom I met on the street."[40] Lipman also confessed that he had told the policeman his name was Louis Levine and had produced a fraudulent draft registration card in order to avoid arrest.

When Lipman had been arrested, the police had searched him and found a piece of yellow paper on which there was a hand-written draft of a leaflet entitled "Revolutionists! Unite for Action." During the interrogation Lipman admitted he had written it and then read it aloud for the stenographer. The paper urged radicals to put aside their differences in order to support the Russian Revolution. Further, Lipman asked, "Why don't we protest against the action of 'Our Kaiser' who without asking the Congress has sent troops to crush the Russian Revolution?" The radical press, Lipman went on, failed to point out "the hypocrisy of the United States and her Allies," and "the printed prostitute, i.e. the Yellow press, keeps the masses in darkness by telling them that troops are sent to Russia to fight Germans." Lipman closed with an injunction, "Know you lovers of freedom that in order to save [the] Russian Revolution, we must keep the Armies of the Allied countries busy at home." The police asked what he meant by that, and he answered, "I meant that we should start protest meetings all over the country and keep the soldiers busy preventing them and stopping them after they had started." To the query, "When you speak of the 'action of Our Kaiser' whom do you refer to?" Lipman obligingly replied, "President Wilson."[41]

Unlike Lachowsky, Lipman had told the police what they wanted to know, but according to his testimony and that of his friends, he was nevertheless mistreated. Five or six policemen took him into a room, Lipman recalled, "and they put me in the middle and they tried to throw me one to another, and one that I told you about—Eddie [Meagher], pulled me [by] the hair and dragged me all over the floor, and then when I asked for a little water, they threw some water and poured over me. I was all wet. It lasted about forty-five minutes." Five feet five inches tall, somewhat overweight, dependent on thick eyeglasses, Lipman was easy prey for his brawny captors. He remembered being punched and kicked—"They took all kinds of ways with their feet and with their fists."—and being humiliated and taunted—"They tried to ridicule and beat, and they pulled from me the hair and jerked me over the floor." Mollie Steimer testified that a policeman "took the glasses off Lipman and said, 'I will fit these glasses into your head." He knocked him with his fist in his heart several times." Later, at the trial, Lipman recalled the hallucination produced by the terror he had felt that night. "I found myself as I supposed, lying in a grave—all around me and they had all kinds of drugs . . ."[42]

Jacob Abrams later testified that he was threatened at police headquarters but not harmed. He claimed, however, that while still at his apartment, a policeman had hit him in the face "and I knew what to expect"; at headquarters an officer warned him not to talk to Lachowsky "because you are going to get it next." Abrams also remembered that a mahogany cabinet with a glass door occupied a conspicuous place in the room; it contained "cotton bandages, iodine, peroxide—everything that is needed when somebody gets hit." So, during the interrogation, he said, "I really—I was physically afraid to deny things that I don't remember today that I said . . ." Abrams explained that when Inspector Tunney began the examination, "I was not touched . . . but once he jumped at me and I felt that it was a question of his going to kill me and I said 'Go right to it,' and he didn't touch me but they took me out."[43] Abrams had the presence of mind to ask one of the officers "if there is chance to call up for counsel, and he said not at that late hour of the night, but he will do that in the morning."[44] Another officer, disturbed by the mistreatment of the anarchists, had tried to stop it. "He interfered because Lachowsky had been beaten in that room," Abrams said, "and he didn't want to see any more beating done there."[45]

During the interrogation, which began shortly before midnight, Abrams answered some preliminary questions about his background and beliefs. He said that he knew Emma Goldman and Alexander Berkman and had testified at their trial. He was asked about the revolver found in his room, and explained, "Well, a certain fellow, I don't remember his name came into my place and bought some stuff and left this revolver as security." Shown the galley proofs of a circular, printed in Yiddish, which had been taken from his apartment, Abrams said he had written it; asked what it said, he acknowledged that it described the horrors of war. Abrams admitted that he had forged a draft classification card by erasing the original name and substituting his own. The inquiry closed with three questions which elicited purposely vague and evasive answers: "How much money was collected altogether for printing and distribution of these disloyal and revolutionary pamphlets?" "I really don't know how much, there was some money collected but I don't know how much." "How many of you were together when you were discussing this revolutionary pamphlet?" "About five or six." "Won't you please tell me where the press is that prints these circulars?" "I really don't know where it is. Some of the other fellows can tell you if they want to."[46]

If Abrams is to be believed, Jacob Schwartz was brutally beaten at police headquarters. Abrams said that he saw Schwartz lying "on the floor, all sweating and wet with sweat, and his handkerchief was full of blood . . . and he said to me 'I am all beaten up.' "[47] It is not clear from Abrams' testimony whether Schwartz was beaten before, during, or after his interrogation. He was questioned at 1:45 in the morning, in a session lasting only a few minutes. Schwartz admitted that he had been an anarchist for about two years. He claimed that he first saw the leaflets "last night . . . Lachowsky showed them to me, and he said we are going to distribute them," but insisted he had not distributed any. According to the transcript of the interrogation—which was never introduced at the trial since Schwartz died before it began—the final exchange was, "Do you believe that the President of the United States should be called the Kaiser of America?" "No, I don't believe that he should be called the Kaiser of the United States."[48]

Gabriel Prober, whose misfortune it was to show up at Abrams' apartment to minister to his injuries just when the police were conducting their search, was also questioned briefly. He stated that he knew Abrams, Schwartz, and Lachowsky from the Bookbinders' Union, and that he had first visited the East 104th Street apartment five weeks earlier. Tunney asked Prober whether he was an anarchist; he replied, "I am an Internationalist." He denied having had any part in printing or distributing the leaflets, but admitted being present when "the other fellows" discussed the project. "What other fellows do you mean?" "Lachowsky, Steimer, and Abrams." Prober did not allege that the police had mistreated him or that he had seen anyone else who showed physical signs of having been manhandled.[49]

The last of the interrogations, Mollie Steimer's, began at two-fifteen in the morning, nearly five hours after she had arrived at headquarters. Like Lachowsky, Lipman, and Abrams, she talked about her own actions but only about her own. She admitted distributing the leaflets at various locations on the Lower East Side—on Rivington Street, Clinton Street, and East Broadway—and said she knew this violated the Sedition Act. "Did you have anything to do with the dictating of the manuscript?" "I am in sympathy with every word in that circular." "Did you dictate it?" "No." "Do you know who did dictate it?" "No." "Did you contribute to the expense of printing it?" "Yes." "Well, how much did you contribute?" "I am a working girl and therefore I couldn't contribute very much." Asked when she had become an anarchist, Mollie Steimer answered defiantly, "I have always been an Anarchist."[50] She later testified that she had seen Lachowsky, Lipman, and Schwartz after they had been beaten. "I started to holler, but . . . one of those beasts put his hand on my mouth and shoved me into a different room."[51]

At the trial, members of the Bomb Squad denied that they had even laid a finger on any of the anarchists. The detectives who allegedly had been the worst offenders—Edward Meagher and Thomas Jenkins—took the witness stand, and, with an air of injured innocence, denied any and all wrongdoing. Sergeant Henry Barth, who, according to Abrams, had interceded to stop the brutality, denied that he had done so. The defendants' tales, he said, were fabrications; in his professional judgment, "it would take but one blow of a blackjack to kill a man. It would be impossible to beat a man for two hours." Besides, Barth added, "There was no cause for beating them. Why should we?" Inspector Tunney also testified that "no cruelty occurred there."[52]

Lieutenant Colonel Biddle emphatically rejected the anarchists' allegations. He told the Director of Military Intelligence that the claim of brutality "is an invariable defense at all Anarchist trials where there is no other defense," but then tried to strike a note of impartiality: "Laying aside, as far as possible, all prejudices on my part in the matter, and considering only the evidence pro and con, there would appear to be no justification in the charges accusing these men of brutality." The anarchists' testimony, he believed, was more than outweighed by evidence on the other side. Gabriel Prober did not allege he was abused, and every one of the detectives swore no one else was. Moreover, at the arraignment on Saturday morning the prisoners "not only showed no evidence of having been badly treated . . . but did not enter any complaint on this score," and, during three pretrial appearances, "no mention was made of any brutal treatment." It was in the defendants' own interest to try to show that their statements had been given involuntarily, Biddle pointed out, but he and Captain Potter had been present and "at no time did we see any brutality, nor was any complaint made of such measures having been used." Although the police arrested other radicals at the demonstration in East Harlem on the night of August 23 and took them to headquarters, none, Biddle said, "were produced as witnesses to substantiate these charges."[53]

One of those radicals, who was not asked to testify at the trial, did in fact later substantiate the charges. Boris Aurin, like Prober, had gone to the 67th Street rally and then marched to East Harlem. He claimed that he met a young woman who had been injured in the melee, and assisted her to Abrams' apartment, arriving, again like Prober, while the police were there. He too was taken to police headquarters, where he saw a beaten, injured Jacob Schwartz, and Hyman Lachowsky, who was "a terrible sight. Lachowsky's clothes were dirty, torn, and in blood; his face was in blood and all blue, his hair missing from his head in a number of places." Then the police ushered him through the room where Samuel Lipman was being assaulted. "Four secret service men, in shirt sleeves, were standing each in one corner of the room, with blackjacks in their hands and revolvers protruding visibly from their pockets, and were playing ball, with Lipman as the flying ball. They were throwing him from one corner of the room to the other with the remark 'Let him die there, the dog.' " Aurin claimed that he, too, was punched, threatened, and given a "verbal third degree" before being released for lack of evidence against him.[54]

There is no way of proving conclusively which side was telling the truth. Although it was obviously self-serving for the anarchists to claim brutality, it was equally self-serving for the police to deny it. On balance, the anarchists' version seems more convincing. The accounts given by Lachowsky, Lipman, Abrams, and Steimer, and by Boris

Aurin too, are internally consistent. They are also understated. Abrams and Steimer did not assert that they had been mistreated. They made a distinction between what they saw and what they heard. No one alleged that Biddle or Potter was present when any of the beatings occurred. Abrams claimed that two detectives, upset by the brutality, attempted to stop it, hardly the claim of a man fabricating a story to suit his own purposes. Most important, the anarchists' accounts are rich in details which have an authentic ring—Lachowsky remembering a policeman saying, "Judge, my eye, you must tell me . . .," Lipman recalling a terrifying vision of a grave and drugs; Steimer and Abrams remembering Schwartz bathed in a pool of sweat.

The third degree was generally accepted as a necessary and useful procedure in the New York City Police Department. Verbal threats, menacingly rolled-up sleeves, blackjacks and rubber hoses, groans from behind closed doors—all were part of a night's work at 240 Centre Street. Two detectives later wrote books which described these practices in the World War I era. Both justified the use of head-bashing as a way to obtain information which otherwise would be withheld, in instances where the police were sure of a person's guilt and the crime was especially flagrant. In such a situation, one of the detectives remembered, "I . . . got myself a sawed-off baseball bat and walked in on those dogs."[55] The other recalled, "I've forced confessions—with fist, blackjack and hose—from men who would have continued to rob and to kill if I hadn't made them talk."[56] Three former United States Attorneys for the Southern District of New York signed a bar association report in 1928 deploring the long-standing use of the third degree to extract confessions.[57]

By prevailing standards, Lachowsky, Lipman, and even Schwartz had gotten off lightly. They had been abused primarily because the police wanted to know where the leaflets had been printed. At some point during the night, however, continued abuse became unnecessary. Looking through papers they had removed from Abrams' apartment, the police found the bill of sale for the printing press. On Monday morning, August 26, Sergeants Barth and Jenkins went to the printing shop run by the Bursch Brothers on Bleecker Street. Alexander Bursch told them that he had sold Abrams the press, and that his brother had set it up in a basement shop at 1582 Madison Avenue, near East 107th

Street. By that afternoon the two officers had obtained a warrant to search the shop, where they found everything they were looking for and more: the press, the type, the paper, copies of discarded leaflets, and a pail containing the charred fragments of leaflets that someone had set on fire and then doused with water. Back at headquarters, Lieutenant Colonel Biddle was elated, for it seemed that his men had uncovered sufficient evidence on which to build an airtight case against people "who have been a dangerous element in the community for many months past."[58]

## The Indictments: Francis G. Caffey

Military Intelligence officials were not the only ones who were pleased with the work of the Bomb Squad. So was the United States Attorney for the Southern District of New York, Francis Gordon Caffey. Writing to Captain Fuller Potter on September 4, Caffey expressed his appreciation to Sergeants Barth and Jenkins for "the splendid way in which the evidence was obtained and presented."[59] Caffey had been appointed United States Attorney in May 1917, and held the position for four years. It was his presentation of the case to the grand jury that led to the indictments of Abrams and the others. That much accomplished, Caffey found it necessary to convince Department of Justice officials, whose outlook he considered pusillanimous, that his decision to prosecute under the Sedition Act had been correct.

Caffey was born in Gordonsville, Alabama, in 1868. His father, Hugh William Caffey, was a well-known surgeon, and his mother, Alabama Gordon, came from a prominent Southern family. Caffey went north in 1887 to attend Harvard, graduating in 1891 and then entering the Law School. He returned to Alabama in 1894 to practice law in Montgomery. In 1898, when the Spanish–American War began, Caffey signed up and served as Lieutenant Colonel in the Third Alabama Infantry. He left his native state in 1902 to accept a partnership in a prestigious New York law firm with strong Democratic Party affiliations. Caffey also took on the thankless task of defending Southern political mores to skeptical Northerners. He published an article justifying the stringent educational and property qualifications for voting which Alabama had written into its 1901 Constitution. The pressing need, Caffey said, was to ensure "a clean and intelligent electorate" by eliminating "the venal and ignorant among white men as voters" since "it is a mistaken assumption of fact to say . . . that in their present temper the negroes as a body are anxious to vote."[60] He remained actively involved in Harvard Law School alumni affairs, and in the reform-minded National Child Labor Committee. In 1913 Caffey was appointed Solicitor for the Department of Agriculture in the new Wilson administration.

Caffey took pride in his family's heritage of military service. An ancestor had fought in the American Revolution, his father had been a surgeon in the Confederate Army, and he had served in the Spanish–American War. In October 1917 he informed the French Ambassador that the Caffey clan was almost single-handedly repaying America's debt to Lafayette. "In our family we are proud of the fact that these six representatives are to be a part of the military force which will return the visit of General Lafayette during the Revolution." He was prouder still when he discovered that not six but ten of his relatives were in the armed services.[61] Approaching age fifty, Francis Caffey had to do his fighting closer to home. Assuming his duties as United States Attorney just as the country entered the war, Caffey told reporters, "Alien enemies, slackers, anti-draft agitators, conspirators of all sorts who seek to prevent the successful prosecution of the war must be ferreted out and put where they can do no harm." In case anyone had missed the message, he added, "The process of extermination must be swift."[62]

Caffey's view of dissent in wartime, and the deference shown him by Department of Justice officials, were illustrated by the decision to hold the second *Masses* trial. The editors of *The Masses*—among them Max Eastman, John Reed, Art Young, and Floyd Dell—were charged with having violated the Espionage Act by publishing articles, editorials, and cartoons attacking the war and the draft. The first trial, which took place in April 1918, ended with a hung jury. Civil libertarians implored the Wilson administration not to retry the case, and they found a well-placed ally within the Department of Justice in the person of Alfred Bettman. He told John Lord O'Brian that a new trial would serve no useful purpose. Eastman and the other editors of *The Liberator,* the successor to *The Masses,* had "grown more enthusiastic about the President and the war aims of the President," Bettman declared. To prosecute them for articles published a year earlier, when they were now singing "a very different tune," would do more harm than good.[63]

In this case, however, O'Brian did not accept Bettman's advice, largely because of Francis Caffey's determination to proceed. O'Brian informed Attorney General Thomas Gregory that, Bettman's doubts notwithstanding, the Department should support a new trial "in view of the attitude taken by the United States Attorney." Caffey had spoken with the judge about the jury's behavior in the first trial, and was convinced that two jurors held radical views which they had concealed during the pretrial examination and which should have disqualified them. O'Brian reminded the Attorney General that Caffey, "who is a competent official occupying an important executive position, insists that the case should be retried."[64]

Caffey was not at all swayed by the argument that the case should be dropped because the editors' view of the President's policies had mellowed. He cited antiwar articles appearing in *The Masses* in the summer of 1917 which were intended, in his view, to obstruct military recruitment. If the editors had recently taken a more moderate tack, Caffey said, it was not because they had suddenly gained respect for the nation's laws but, rather, because they believed that the revolutionary cause would be furthered by a German defeat. Nor was Caffey moved by the argument that the editors were "sincere humanitarians." Laws must be enforced, he commented, "whether they are violated by persons actuated by sordid motives or by humanitarian motives. I feel further that to drop the prosecution of this case at this time would afford encouragement to persons to engage in similar obstructive activities for the purpose of assisting German propaganda in this country." To Caffey, it was scandalous that the editors posed as martyrs to the cause of free speech. "It was and is the Government's contention that no right of free speech as such is involved in their case," Caffey concluded, "but merely the question whether under cloak of that right persons may willfully obstruct the raising of an army to wage a war which has been declared by the Congress."[65]

The second *Masses* trial got under way in September 1918, two weeks before the Abrams trial, in the same courtroom, and nearly before the same judge. It was scheduled to begin on September 23 before Judge Henry DeLamar Clayton, but the defense gained a one-week postponement to enable a new team of lawyers to familiarize themselves with the case. As a result, the trial judge was Martin F. Manton rather than Clayton. One of the defense attorneys, Charles Recht, recognized that the defendants made an excellent impression. "Max Eastman, soft and willowy and dignified looked every inch the matinee idol, Jack Reed the type of a Western cowboy hero, Art Young resembled a Yankee cherub, while Floyd Dell was something of a Peter Pan of Greenwich Village." The trial ended on October 5; the next day the jury returned with a divided verdict. Seven jurors had voted to convict, five to acquit, and one of the holdouts told Recht, "You fellows were just lucky in not having a Jew or a foreigner among the defendants."[66]

Four days later jury selection began in the trial of the anarchists, a case in which all the defendants were Jews and all of them foreigners. The most important difference between the two trials, however, was not the defendants' religious or ethnic backgrounds but what law they were accused of having broken. *The Masses'* editors had been indicted under the June 1917 Espionage Act which required proof of an intent to interfere with the conduct of the war. At their first trial, in April, Judge Augustus N. Hand instructed the jury that "every citizen has the right, without intent to obstruct the recruiting or enlistment service, to think, feel, and express" any opinion.[67] The anarchists, though, were indicted under the more restrictive provisions of the May 1918 amendment to the Espionage Act, the Sedition Act, under which thinking, feeling, and expressing were not necessarily protected.

The grand jury had handed up an indictment under that Act on September 12. The first three counts charged that Abrams, Steimer, Lipman, Lachowsky, Schwartz, Prober, and Rosansky had engaged in a conspiracy "to utter, print, write and publish" two leaflets containing "disloyal, scurrilous and abusive language about the form of Government of the United States," "language intended to bring the form of Government of the United States into contempt, scorn, contumely and disrepute," and "language intended to incite, provoke and encourage resistance to the United States" in the war with Germany. An additional count charged that the defendants had conspired "to by word and act oppose the cause of the United States in said war."[68] After the judge rejected demurrers filed by the defense, Caffey decided that this final count should be spelled out more explicitly.[69] In a revised indictment which the grand jury returned on September 27, the defendants were charged with conspiring "to urge, incite and advocate curtailment of production of things and products, to wit, ordnance and ammunition, necessary and essential to the prosecution of the war, . . . with intent by such curtailment to cripple and hinder the United States in the prosecution of said war."[70]

Each of the four counts (in both versions) cited the same six overt acts: Abrams purchased the press and type with which the two leaflets were printed; Abrams arranged for the press and type to be delivered to the basement shop on Madison Avenue; Abrams and Lachowsky printed the leaflets; Rosansky distributed the leaflets from a building at Crosby and Houston streets; Steimer distributed the leaflets on Rivington Street, Clinton Street, and East Broadway; Lachowsky delivered a package containing the leaflets to Rosansky. Schwartz, Lipman, and Prober were indicted as co-conspirators but not themselves charged with any overt acts. The acts attributed to Abrams, Lachowsky, Steimer, and Rosansky were either ones they acknowledged during their questioning at police headquarters or those that could very easily be proven on the basis of the bill of sale for the printing press.

It was not until October 21, after the trial was under way, that Caffey notified the Department of Justice that he had obtained the indictments. Caffey wrote, belatedly, because he was concerned that newspaper accounts of the proceedings might include "propaganda antagonistic to the interest of the Government." He assured the Attorney General that the record offered "a definite and concrete illustration of the position of the pro-German supporters in this country of the Bolsheviki course of action in Russia in its relations with Germany."[71] This was Caffey's convoluted way of saying that those who opposed intervention in Russia supported the Bolsheviks, that those who supported the Bolsheviks were pro-German, and that those who were pro-German belonged in jail. John Lord O'Brian and Alfred Bettman quickly recognized the dangers lurking in that false syllogism. On October 25 they told Caffey that the United States had not "officially recognized the friendly affiliations between the Bolsheviki leaders and the German Government." They even added a stern warning: "As we have pointed out to you, praise of the Bolsheviki *per se* and an attack upon the Allied intervention *per se,* that is, without proof of the intents or purposes against which the Espionage Act is directed, do not constitute violations of law."[72]

Although he received this letter after the trial ended, Caffey was anxious to gain the Department's approval, if only retroactively, and its support for his attempt to deny bail. He wrote to the Attorney General on November 1, and after a telephone conversation with Bettman on the second, wrote again. Attempting to justify the decision to prosecute, Caffey embellished the facts. He wrote that on the night of the anarchists' arrest, "10,000 of their adherents congregated at the New Star Casino . . . and afterward several thousand marched through the street," thereby exaggerating the size of the demonstration and misrepresenting the political affinities of the demonstrators. Caffey said that the draft of a leaflet in Lipman's possession "contained the boast that an up-rising of the workers would keep the soldiers so busy at home that it would be impossible for any to be sent abroad." Yet Lipman had referred not to an uprising but to the holding of protest meetings. Treating unfounded reports as plain truth, Caffey reported that he had grounds to believe that Abrams "is a lieutenant of Berkman and Goldman, and has been carrying on their propaganda here in New York," that Lipman "is the representative of Trotzky here in New York," and that the "defendants arrested in this case are ring-leaders in an international Bolsheviki movement."[73]

Caffey also alluded indirectly to the language in the Yiddish leaflet which called on munitions workers to strike. The leaflets, he noted, were distributed on the Lower East Side and "as you know the homes of a great number of workers in factories are located in this part of New York."[74] This was what ultimately convinced Bettman. On November 6, when a copy of the translated Yiddish leaflet finally reached his desk, he told an associate that he found "the Yiddish circular . . . to be different from and much more objectionable than the English circular."[75] Bettman was later asked about his role in the case. He remembered that the English leaflet contained "a bitter and violent criticism of the use of our soldiers in Russia," but that he had insisted such criticism did not constitute a violation of the Sedition Act "without clear proof that the attack on the Russian policy was a disguised method of trying to assist a German victory." The defendants, however, had "circulated a second leaflet, which was a distinct appeal to munition-workers to quit work; and as these munition-workers were presumably turning out munitions to be used against our enemy, the Central Empires, that second dodger, in connection with the surreptitious method of distribution and some other circumstances" warranted prosecution. Although the trial was held "before we heard of the case . . . we did not feel called upon to interfere."[76]

Ever since Congress had passed the Sedition Act in May, Bettman and O'Brian had hoped to "keep some sort of supervisory control" over its application.[77] Francis Caffey's prosecution of Jacob Abrams, Mollie Steimer, and the others illustrates how illusory that hope was. Faced with a tenacious, influential, xenophobic United States Attorney, and dependent, to a considerable degree, on that Attorney's version of the facts, however garbled or misleading, there was little choice other than to go along. This was all the more true because O'Brian's and Bettman's position on freedom of speech, while less restrictive than Caffey's, was sufficiently restrictive—or ambivalent—to permit their acquiescence in such prosecutions.

## The Lawyer: Harry Weinberger

Radicals who were arrested during World War I often had a difficult time finding a lawyer. Few attorneys were willing to handle their cases, and those so inclined were overworked and underpaid. Charles Recht, who had assisted in *The Masses* defense, recalled that "very seldom in political cases . . . did an individual pay me a fee."[78] His associate, Rose Weiss, feared she might have to "abandon the 'honorable' profession altogether as the only phase that appeals to me is the labor work and it is impossible to earn a living at that."[79] The firm of Isaac Shorr, Walter Nelles, and Swinburne Hale defended radicals, some of whom could not afford to cover the lawyers' expenses, much less pay a fee. "We are in a hot bed of repression here," Hale once wrote, "with only a very few lawyers who are willing and able to handle the situation, and who are hopelessly overworked."[80]

One such hopelessly overworked lawyer was Harry Weinberger, who devoted much of his time to defending anarchists and aliens, including, most prominently, Emma Goldman and Alexander Berkman. In 1918 he was thirty-two years old, and had been in practice for ten years. His parents, Moritz and Rose Weinberger, were Hungarian Jews who had emigrated to the United States from Budapest. Weinberger was born in New York City and raised, as he recalled, "in an Irish neighborhood on the East River." Self-conscious about his height—he remarked that he had never "been picked on as an easy mark or a pushover, though I am only 5 feet 4½ inches tall"—Weinberger compensated, or over-compensated, by becoming a battler, a scrapper, a mixer-upper. He described himself as "a pugnacious little East-sider who fought for the love of fighting." He boasted that he became a good street fighter, and he certainly became an outstanding runner, excelling in the 100- and 400-yard dashes and in the mile relay. "It must have appeared to people who knew me through the years," he said, "that I would rather fight than eat."[81]

At the age of twelve Weinberger tried to enlist in the Spanish–American War, if not as a soldier then as a drummer boy, but could not convince the recruiting agent to accept him. So he went to high school, and then he went to work. He got a job as a stenographer, and in the evenings attended New York University Law School. At the time it was not uncommon for a young man, particularly if he was an immigrant or the child of immigrants, to skip college, work full time, and enroll in a night law school in preparation for the bar examination. Deans and professors at established, prestigious—and expensive—law schools often disparaged evening students and the quality of instruction the students presumably received. "A host of shrewd young men, imperfectly educated," was how one such biased observer described these neophyte lawyers, many of them Jewish, "all deeply impressed with the philosophy of getting on, but viewing the code of Ethics with uncomprehending eyes."[82] But night schools were indispensable for immigrants, and poor people generally, who sought careers in the law. In 1908, when Harry Weinberger received his degree, one in three law students was attending a night school, and fewer than one in ten lawyers admitted to the bar was a college graduate.

Weinberger's early political views were quite conventional. A registered Republican, he served as an election district captain, debated Democrats and Socialists, and even held a post as a special assistant to the New York Attorney General. Weinberger apparently had political aspirations of his own, but they came to an abrupt end in 1916 when he bolted his party and backed the Democrats on the strength of Woodrow Wilson's promise to keep the country out of war. "I had wrecked my political career," Weinberger recalled, and any hope of rebuilding it as a Democrat ended in April 1917 when Wilson, despite his promise, took the nation into war.[83] Weinberger was left in political limbo, but he had already formulated a creed—incorporating elements of Single-Taxism, individualism, and pacifism—which brought him closer to anarchists and socialists than to either Republicans or Democrats.

The Single Tax was a radical cure for social ills originally proposed by Henry George in *Progress and Poverty* (1879), a book which had a transforming effect on many of its readers, and certainly on Weinberger. The chapter entitled "The Central Truth," he said reverently, was "the greatest chapter in any book ever written."[84] George reasoned that the unequal distribution of wealth, "the curse and menace of modern civilization," existed only because land was privately owned. The remedy, therefore, was obvious: a "Single Tax" on land, which would make it "common property." When this solution was adopted, and George believed it surely would be one day, liberty and justice would triumph. Men and women would live in a world "with want destroyed; with greed changed to noble passions; with the fraternity that is born of equality taking the place of . . . jealousy and fear . . .; with mental power loosed by conditions that give to the humblest comfort and leisure." This would be "the culmination of Christianity—the City of God on earth, with its walls of jasper and its gates of pearl."[85]

Henry George once quoted Voltaire's acerbic definition of lawyers as "conservators of ancient barbarism."[86] George's disciple, Weinberger, believed rather that "the purpose of law was to assure justice." In his view, justice was synonymous with liberty, liberty with individualism, and individualism, in turn, with limitations on the power of the state. Weinberger asserted that "there always comes a time when the rights of the individual ought to rise above even that of the state."[87] What is perhaps more remarkable is that, in a legal career spanning thirty-five years, he rarely, if ever, thought a time had come when the rights of the state should rise above even those of the individual. To believe in personal liberty, Weinberger said, is to recognize that "absolute compulsion is repugnant to the sense of a free people."[88]

He made that comment in a speech opposing a New York State law which required children attending public school to be vaccinated against smallpox. As early as 1912 Weinberger aligned himself with opponents of compulsory vaccination, writing articles for the movement's journals, testifying on the subject before committees of the State legislature, and representing—unsuccessfully—a man who was penalized for refusing to permit his child to be vaccinated. "Under the guise of vaccination doctors are allowed to cut into the perfectly healthy human body and inject disease by indirect compulsion—free education—against the actual wish of the child or its parents," Weinberger asserted.[89] Vaccination did not necessarily offer protection against smallpox, he went on, but rather exposed the individual to disease, or even death, since the vaccine virus could not be guaranteed to be "free from bacterial taint." Weinberger condemned a 1905 United States Supreme Court ruling which upheld compulsory vaccination. "It stands with the Dred Scott decision," he remarked, "which would not stay settled because it was not settled right."[90]

The Court had justified its decision by noting that the Constitution "does not import an absolute right in each person to be, at all times and in all circumstances, wholly freed from restraint," and by citing, as an example, the government's power to draft an individual into the armed forces.[91] Yet this, too, was a power that Weinberger rejected, not only because he believed that conscription subverted individual liberty but also because he was a pacifist. He said that he had become a "confirmed pacifist" by the age of eighteen, and added, "I had read and studied Mark Twain's 'The Mysterious Stranger' and knew by rote its unanswerable argument against all war."[92] Since Twain's novel was not published until 1916, reading it could only have strengthened

Weinberger's pacifist convictions. Among the passages he probably memorized was one in which Twain described how, in the face of rising war hysteria, "you will see . . . the speakers stoned from the platform, and free speech strangled by hordes of furious men. . . . And now the whole nation—pulpit and all—will take up the war-cry, and shout itself hoarse, and mob any honest man who ventures to open his mouth; and presently such mouths will cease to open."[93]

When the United States entered the war, Weinberger joined Emma Goldman's and Alexander Berkman's No-Conscription League. He had met Goldman in 1915, and had represented her in 1916 when she was indicted for disseminating birth control information.[94] Now, in 1917, Weinberger spoke at a rally she organized, though he confined himself to arguing that the Selective Draft Act, passed in May, was unconstitutional. In June Goldman and Berkman were indicted under that law (not under the Espionage Act) for forming a "conspiracy to induce persons not to register." With no hope of gaining an acquittal, but with every hope of using the trial as a showcase for revolutionary, antiwar propaganda, the two anarchists handled their own defense. Weinberger was a "wonderful fighting spirit," Goldman said, "but we decided it was more consistent for us to conduct the case."[95] After their conviction Weinberger arranged for their release on bail, filed the necessary papers for an appeal, and, in December, argued the case before the Supreme Court.

Weinberger contended, as did attorneys appearing on behalf of other opponents of conscription, that the Act violated the Thirteenth Amendment, which prohibited involuntary servitude. Weinberger's more intriguing argument, however, focused on the statute's provisions which granted an exemption from combatant duty to men who belonged to religious organizations opposed to war. Weinberger contended that this provision, amounting to a "new combination of church and state," discriminated against those who did not belong to certain preferred religious groups but who nevertheless conscientiously objected to the war.[96] According to *The New York Times*, Weinberger "confined his attack principally to the assertion that the law deprives citizens of religious liberty."[97] In January 1918 the Supreme Court, speaking through Chief Justice Edward White, rejected all challenges to the constitutionality of the draft. The Chief Justice refused even to reply to Weinberger's argument about religious freedom "because we think its unsoundness is too apparent."[98]

Commenting on the Supreme Court ruling, Weinberger could not help but recall Mark Twain's warning. "The conscientious objectors are being sent to jail," he said, "and the mind and heart of the people are voiceless, and the press is choked."[99] Ironically, it was Emma Goldman, sentenced to the penitentiary, who tried to lift Weinberger's spirits. "I am better off than you," she wrote, "since I expected nothing else."[100] Goldman also urged Weinberger to take consolation in the success of the Bolsheviks in Russia, which he was only too eager to do. In January 1918 Weinberger, along with other radicals, believed that the Bolsheviks "are still the hope of the world, and are doing more at the present moment to educate the world and give it a new hope and a new vision than anything that has happened since the American and French revolutions."[101]

By virtue of his convictions, commitments, and connections, it followed logically that Harry Weinberger would defend Jacob Abrams and the other anarchists arrested in August 1918. A committed civil libertarian who believed that "the great crime is repression of honest thought," Weinberger also took seriously an obligation that most lawyers conveniently ignored.[102] As he put it, the "highest and most sacred duty of a lawyer" was to ensure that "the weakest and most despised" received the same protection in the courtroom as the richest and most powerful.[103] Weinberger must have been in a receptive mood when he received a letter from Emma Goldman, written from prison on September 1, with the comment, "I see some more of our N. Y. boys in trouble, Abrams & others." Worried that the young anarchists would unwittingly blurt out information that would be used against them, Goldman asked the lawyer to find out what he could about their situation.[104]

Whether at Goldman's prompting or someone else's, Weinberger agreed to take the case. On September 10 he wrote to the defendants—the letter was addressed to "Mr. Jacob Abrahams"—to inform them that he would be present, on the eleventh, "to take care of their interests" when they made their pleas.[105] When the date of their appearance was rescheduled, Weinberger wrote that "there is nothing that we can talk over until we actually see the indictments and know what the charge is."[106] In the weeks that followed, Weinberger handled various legal and personal matters: he tried to gain permission for the prisoners to meet with their relatives; he arranged for Abrams to be seen by a doctor; he began to raise bail; and he entered a demurrer to the original indictment, which led the United States Attorney to secure a new indictment from the grand jury. At the end of the month Weinberger told his clients he would see them on September 30 "to begin to prepare for trial."[107]

A case involving anarchists who were defending the Russian Revolution held a particular appeal for Weinberger, both temperamentally and intellectually. More clearly than compulsory vaccination, more clearly even than conscription, the prosecution of people merely for distributing leaflets posed the question of where the line should be drawn between freedom of expression and restraint. An idealist, an individualist, a pacifist, Weinberger viewed freedom of speech from a perspective that placed him at odds not only with the bully boys of Inspector Thomas J. Tunney's Bomb Squad, and with Francis G. Caffey, the saber-rattling United States Attorney, but also, most significantly, with self-styled liberals in the Department of Justice, such as Alfred Bettman and John Lord O'Brian, who were attempting, without much success, to stake out a moderate, middle-of-the-road position.

This became evident when Weinberger filed a demurrer which indicated the lines along which he wanted to conduct the defense. After asserting that the revised indictment "does not set forth facts sufficient to constitute a crime," he quickly moved to the fundamental issue: "The law the defendants are alleged to have violated . . . is unconstitutional on the following ground: It violates Article I of the Amendments to the Constitution, which reads: 'Congress shall make no law abridging the freedom of speech; or the press . . .' The law being unconstitutional," Weinberger concluded, "defendants cannot be guilty of a violation of same."[108]

# 3

# The Trial

## War Fever

ON FRIDAY, October 11, 1918, as jury selection for the anarchists' trial was being completed, President Woodrow Wilson visited New York City, intending to march in the Liberty Loan parade on Saturday. On Friday evening he and his wife attended a Broadway play, *The Girl Behind the Gun,* which one reviewer had described as "a military musical comedy up to the minute." During an intermission following the second act, the cast stepped forward to urge everyone to buy Liberty Bonds. When the leading man asked who would take the first subscription, the President said, "I will take a two-thousand-dollar bond." Then "an epidemic of bond buying and cheering and general patriotism swept through the theatre." Bonds were bought almost faster than the ushers could sell them, and when a lull occurred, "a fifteen-year-old lad who had gotten into the Marines by hiding his age and who had returned wounded from France," offered to buy a fifty-dollar bond. "Look at that lad," the actor shouted, "he was ready to sacrifice his life, and now he is ready to give his money." Someone offered to buy as many fifty-dollar bonds as there were men in uniform in the audience, and, to deafening applause, eighty-seven men jumped to their feet. "Does anyone want the show to go on?" "No—get the money! Let everybody come across!" people cried. An hour later the audience had come across to the tune of $750,000.[1]

During the next two weeks the nationwide Liberty Loan drive, the fourth of the war and the largest, reached its peak in New York City. Signs and posters everywhere called on people to give as much as they could and even more. Condemning "LIBERTY BOND SLACKERS, Fair Weather Patriots and Duty Shirkers," the publicity campaign contrasted the minuscule demands made of civilians with the sacrifices expected of soldiers.[2] In one cartoon Uncle Sam, his hand on the shoulder of a doughboy who had lost a leg, was saying to "Mr. Stay-at-Home": "This boy has given his limit—have you?"[3] Newspaper advertisements vilified Germans in harsh and offensive language: "We have the Hun on the run, but it takes a good deal longer than you think to beat defeat into the thick skulls of the baby-killing beasts from the Rhine."[4] Those who bought bonds were advised to display the buttons they received, for otherwise the public might conclude that their patriotism "consists of talk and not purchase."[5]

In the fall of 1918 it was virtually impossible to spend a day anywhere in New York City without encountering a Liberty Loan rally, hearing a band playing martial music, or finding oneself in the middle of a patriotic parade. In East Harlem, where Jacob Abrams and his friends were arrested, "gatherings of the people at war meetings are almost a daily and nightly occurrence," one journal reported. "The Liberty Loan rallies have brought out immense audiences in halls at streetcorners and other places."[6] The newspapers carried daily dispatches about the final Allied military drive, the Meuse-Argonne offensive, and daily lists of American soldiers killed and wounded in the fighting. To the journalist Lincoln Steffens, the city seemed keyed to a fever pitch, its mood at once volatile and ominous. "It is sick, the public mind is," he told a friend on October 15, "the streets feel excited, nervous and the sight of them reminds one of the circus."[7]

As crowds are drawn to a circus by daredevil displays, so movie-goers were attracted to war films by the chance to experience, even if only vicariously, the danger and thrill of combat. *Private Peat,* which opened during the first week of the Abrams trial, told the story of a man, rejected by the Army, who somehow managed to enlist and make his way to the trenches in France. It was part of a double-feature with *Yellow Dog,* a film with a simple message: "The yellow dogs of the nation are the Americans with German souls who seek to sow dissatisfaction and distrust. The picture shows how the evil may be stamped out . . ."[8] *Lafayette We Come,* a film about a young woman falsely suspected of being a German spy, included actual footage of American troops in France. This technique had been used earlier by D. W. Griffith in *Hearts of the World,* which had opened in April and was still playing to large, appreciative audiences in New York City. Ghoulish scenes supposedly showed German officers "forcing their unwelcome attentions upon French girls, who are condemned to virtual slavery." Lillian Gish portrayed a woman who was "subjected to the 'German lash' because she was not strong enough to lift a basket of potatoes." Artfully splicing battle scenes filmed at the front with others staged in the studio, Griffith blurred the line between reality and illusion, so that, as a reviewer noted, "sometimes one does not know whether what he is seeing is a real war or screen make-believe."[9]

The inflated nationalism, the pervasive tension, the highly charged atmosphere—all were illustrated by the "slacker" raids in September. Agents of the Department of Justice, assisted by military personnel and members of the American Protective League, a superpatriotic organization, stopped every man they saw who appeared to be of draft age and demanded to see his registration card. Those who could not produce their cards were held, sometimes overnight, until they could prove they had a legitimate exemption. Having tried out this procedure in Chicago and other cities, and having found it effective, federal agents moved on to New York City. For three days, beginning on September 3, they blanketed the city, stationing themselves at subway entrances, patrolling parks and squares, and guarding the ferries and bridges. More than 20,000 hapless men, accosted on the streets, were hauled off to armories or to jail, often at bayonet-point. Most gained their release quickly, but others, especially visitors from out of town, experienced considerable hardship. Defending the dragnet, Attorney General Thomas Gregory said that most citizens "will cheerfully submit to the minor inconveniences which the execution of any such plan of necessity entails." The raids, he noted, led to the apprehension of a number of deserters and of 1,500 draft dodgers.[10]

Slacker raids had their counterpart in raids on radical organizations, or those which defended the rights of radicals, such as the National Civil Liberties Bureau. The Bureau's director, Roger Baldwin, had for some time had his telephone tapped by federal agents. His conversations, the agents believed, "constantly deride and ridicule the military arm of the Government, military preparations, etc., and in fact if these conversations could only be introduced and established, each constitutes a clear-cut violation of the Espionage Act."[11] On August 31, agents of the Bureau of Investigation showed up at Baldwin's office on Fifth Avenue near Union Square. After flashing a search warrant, they proceeded to pick through the relevant files and cart away whatever looked interesting. Baldwin improvised a strategy that he hoped would satisfy Department of Justice officials. He assured them that his group had "not the slightest intention of violating the law," offered to "modify our methods wherever it could be shown to us that they are prejudicial to the country's interest," and even agreed to submit publications for advance clearance. He also retained the services of a conservative lawyer with strong Democratic Party connections. Although the Bureau was not prosecuted, Baldwin was, in October, for refusing to appear for a draft-board physical examination on the grounds that he was conscientiously opposed to conscription. So while Jacob Abrams and his comrades were being held in the Tombs, as the city prison was known, Roger Baldwin, who had refused bail, was there, too. He was tried on October 30, convicted, and sentenced to a year in prison.[12]

Many radicals wound up behind bars in the fall of 1918, and many more assumed they would. What else could they expect, when eighty-three members of the Industrial Workers of the World had just been sentenced to long prison terms in Chicago for supporting strikes that, the government claimed, interfered with war production, or when Eugene Debs had just been given a ten-year jail term in a Cleveland courtroom for speaking against the war? On September 14, the day after Debs's conviction, the authorities in New York City arrested John Reed and Socialist Assemblyman Abraham Shiplacoff. They were indicted for speeches they had made at Hunt's Point Palace in the Bronx, denouncing American intervention in Russia. The speeches had been phrased cautiously, but not cautiously enough to suit the federal agents present. Meanwhile, Rose Pastor Stokes, another New York Socialist who was appealing a ten-year sentence under the Espionage Act, was resigned to serving time. "The class struggle is on—on as never before," she wrote, "and in the struggle some who are in the front trenches must expect to suffer the brunt of it."[13] Radicals faced imprisonment everywhere, and as one sympathetic attorney wrote, "Things will be worse before they are better and we may as well prepare for it."[14]

Undercover agents of the Army's Military Intelligence Division and the Department of Justice's Bureau of Investigation tended to exaggerate the influence of the radicals on whom they spied, but by October even these informants were commenting on the weakness, fear, and disarray in left-wing circles. One such report concerned a group of anarchists who were friends of Jacob Abrams. Meeting in a tearoom in Greenwich Village, they grumbled about his treatment, denouncing it as "an outrage of the 20th century" and adding that "even the czar of Russia would blush to do a thing like this." Yet, according to the undercover informant, "the conviction of the I.W.W. leaders and their Members, the arrest and conviction of Debs and the indictments of Reed . . . and Rose Pastor Stokes, and several others, put a fright in more of the radicals, as to the course of their future actions." Unable to attract new members, hard put to raise more money, "the Bolsheviki are contenting themself with nothing else but talk, being afraid for their safety of their life and limbs."[15]

A city already stirred up by forays against radicals, by anti-German harangues, and by overblown patriotic rhetoric was subjected to still another source of tension: an influenza epidemic. The 1.5 million American soldiers who were sent overseas in 1918 arrived at a time when Spanish influenza was ravaging Europe. Many of them caught the disease and, inevitably, brought it back to the United States. The flu first appeared among sailors in Boston late in August, and then made its lethal way across the country, hitting large, densely populated cities the hardest. Over the next sixteen months 25 million Americans came down with the illness. Approximately 675,000 of them died, either of the flu itself or pneumonia, its most frequent fatal complication. Since under normal circumstances an estimated 125,000 people would have succumbed to either flu or pneumonia, the epidemic claimed the lives of 550,000 Americans.[16]

It was not only the awesome toll but also the nature of the disease that made people so jittery. The most susceptible were not small children or the elderly, but those in their twenties; the highest mortality rates occurred among men and women aged twenty-five to thirty. The illness struck without warning. "The onset is very sudden," doctors reported, "the patient sometimes passing from an apparently well condition almost to prostration within one or two hours."[17] There was no cure, indeed no treatment other than providing the patient with "fresh air, nutritious food, plenty of water, cheerful surroundings, and good nursing."[18] Dramatic symptoms usually accompanied the illness. Patients became delirious, running fevers as high as 104 or 105 degrees, and then coughing and spitting blood. "Epistaxis occurs in a considerable number of patients," it was reported, "in one person as much as a pint of bright red blood gushing from the nostrils." Death, when it came, often resulted from choking, with "large quantities of frothy blood-tinged fluid exuding from the mouth and nostrils."[19]

The epidemic reached its height in New York City in October, just when Jacob Abrams and his comrades were standing trial. During that two-week period about 5,000 New Yorkers came down with the flu every day and a total of 9,450 people died of the illness. Soon there were barely enough doctors and nurses to care for the sick, or morticians and gravediggers to bury the dead. To relieve overcrowding on the transit lines, and thereby reduce the danger of infection, the Board of Health introduced a staggered schedule of working hours. To reduce still further the risk associated with riding in stuffy subways, the city turned off the heat in the cars, left the windows open, and urged riders to wear warm clothing. But these measures were unavailing, and no one seriously considered canceling the patriotic parades and bond rallies which effectively exposed many who had not yet caught the flu or pneumonia to many who already had.[20]

It was simpler and more satisfying to blame the epidemic on German espionage agents. "It would be quite easy for one of these German agents to turn loose Spanish influenza germs in a theatre or some other place where large numbers of persons are assembled," said an army officer responsible for health and sanitation. "The Germans have started epidemics in Europe, and there is no reason why they should be particularly gentle with America."[21] Whether or not such rumors were widely believed, they were widely circulated in New York, a city gripped by fear. And as New Yorkers went about their daily business that October—going to the theater or the movies, buying bonds and marching in parades, discussing the slacker round-ups and reading about the legal predicaments of socialists and anarchists—a great many experienced the telltale symptoms of the Spanish flu: headaches, fever, weakness, pain in the muscles and joints. "As frequently described," one physician wrote, "the patient feels as though he had been beaten all over with a club."[22]

## John Reed and the Death of Jacob Schwartz

The anarchists' trial opened on Monday morning, October 14, but Jacob Schwartz, one of the defendants, was not in the courtroom. He had died, the night before, in the prison ward at Bellevue Hospital. On Thursday a funeral service was held at the chapel of the city morgue. Three fellow members of the Bookbinders' Union gave eulogies. The mourners, wearing red sashes, placed floral wreaths adorned with revolutionary slogans on the coffin. "You can kill men. You can't kill ideals," read one inscription. "To a Comrade of wage slaves," read another. The long funeral procession then made its way from the chapel, located at First Avenue and 29th Street in Manhattan, to Mount Carmel Cemetery in Queens. There, in a plain pine coffin, with his widow, Florence, standing by the graveside, the body of Jacob Schwartz was laid to rest. The tears that were shed were not only tears of sorrow but tears of rage. Although an official autopsy had attributed the death to pneumonia, none of Schwartz's friends accepted that finding. Convinced that he was a victim of police brutality, they placed another wreath on his coffin with the angry inscription: "Jacob Schwartz, as the result of the Third Degree, on the night of his arrest, Aug. 23, died Oct. 14."[23]

Among anarchists and other radicals, too, Schwartz's martyrdom achieved legendary status. Word spread quickly that he was a victim of police brutality, "so beaten by the officers that he died last night."[24] The news reached Emma Goldman, in prison, who grieved: "Dear Schwartz, he paid with his life for his ideas. . . . He was such a devoted and ardent boy. One more victim to brutality."[25] Many years later, when she was writing her autobiography, Goldman received a letter from Mollie Steimer reminding her that "The Boys were put to the 3rd degree as a result of which Schwartz died."[26] In *Living My Life* Goldman wrote that Schwartz's death resulted "from injuries inflicted upon him by police blackjacks."[27] Similarly, in 1928, when Upton Sinclair published a novel about the Sacco-Vanzetti case, he used Schwartz's death to illustrate the excesses resulting from anti-radical hysteria. "In New York four Russian boys and a girl . . . attempting to distribute a circular protesting against the invasion of Russia, were seized by the police and tortured until one of them died."[28] "The government pronounced his sentence without trial on the night of August 23," Mollie Steimer always believed. "It was death."[29]

Two letters Schwartz had written while imprisoned in the city jail, the Tombs, were frequently quoted to support this view. In the first, dated September 5, he graphically described his treatment, and that of his friends, at police headquarters on the night of their arrest. Comparing the behavior of their captors to "the Spanish Inquisition and the blackest pages of man's brutality to man," Schwartz claimed the police stopped at nothing, "from tearing the hair to pulling the tongue; from black-jacks to the leg of a chair was used on us because we would not speak." Yet these "horrible tortures," he said, had not broken his spirit or that of his comrades. "The morning found us weakened bodily but strong spiritually—stronger than the iron of our bars and more powerful than the stone walls." The authorities, he added, might as well have tried to imprison the very idea of anarchism itself. "What are the red spots of blood on our clothings in comparison with the greatness of our Ideal!" Schwartz exulted. "Our Ideal is the Future. They are the Past." The second letter, written in Yiddish, was found, only half-begun, in Schwartz's cell after he was taken to Bellevue. It said, in its entirety, "Farewell, comrades. When you appear before the court I will be with you no longer. Struggle without fear, fight bravely. I am sorry I have to leave you. But this is life itself. After your long martyr . . ."[30]

While Schwartz may have overdramatized the readiness of the authorities to resort to Torquemada-like tactics, he had, in fact, been beaten up and the punishment had a harmful effect on a man who already suffered from what was described as a "weak" or "leaking" heart. These were references to an unsound heart valve, which could have resulted either from rheumatic fever in childhood or a congenital defect. Schwartz suffered from chronic endocarditis, an infection of the inner lining of the heart valves, and from mitral stenosis, a thickening and consequent obstruction of the mitral valve on the left side of the heart. He also developed, toward the end, an acute verrucous infection, which occurs when bacteria enter the bloodstream of a person with endocarditis and attack the already damaged heart valve. It is possible that the punches which landed on Schwartz at police headquarters on the night of August 23, especially any which bloodied his mouth, might have caused just such a bacterial infection, which could then have worsened over a period of weeks and eventually proven fatal.

When the police were threatening him, Schwartz, according to the eyewitness account of Boris Aurin, a fellow radical, protested "that he is sick and got a weak heart, and that they should not use force, they answered that who cares for his heart. . . . He made the impression on me of a dead man. He was pale as snow and continually coughing and spitting."[31] Mollie Steimer remembered that Schwartz, when he emerged from the interrogation room, was "deathly pale, breathes heavily, coughs and spits blood,"[32] all symptoms of a person with a severe heart ailment. In delicate health to begin with, Schwartz's strength must surely have been sapped by the sadistic treatment.

Yet it appears that Schwartz's death seven weeks later resulted not only from heart disease but also from pneumonia, which often accompanied the flu. Indeed, his cardiac condition would have made Schwartz particularly susceptible—and vulnerable—to any respiratory infection. Moreover, autopsies performed on the victims of pneumonia revealed such a distinctive pathology that it is hard to imagine (short of actual misrepresentation) that the medical examiner's report could have been mistaken. That report attributed the death to "Acute Broncho-Pneumonia" but also listed "Chronic Endocarditis/Mitral Stenosis—Acute Verrucous" as contributing causes.[33] Even Harry Weinberger, the anarchists' attorney, who charged the police with brutality, later conceded that Schwartz had finally succumbed to pneumonia. As Weinberger put it, "His heart bled from the third degree, thus weakening him and he developed pneumonia which was the secondary and apparent cause of death."[34]

Conditions in the Tombs—the overcrowding, the stuffiness, the lack of exercise, the unwholesome diet—made the prison a veritable incubator of respiratory disease. Confined in these unhealthful surroundings, it would have been miraculous if a man in Schwartz's weakened condition had escaped. The Tombs had eight floors, and each of them had thirty-eight cells arranged in a double row, back to back, with the doors opening into the corridors. None of the cells had windows. Each cell, seven feet in width, eight in length, was designed for two inmates. Prisoners were allowed in the yard for an hour a day. The unfortunate inmates who became ill were treated with neglect. "I never suffered so much in my life," recalled a man who came down with the flu that terrible fall. "I could get no water, because the spring faucet was too strong for me to press, and I had to stay there all night, locked in my cell, burning up with fever."[35]

By October 2, Schwartz may have been too sick to get out of bed. His wife, Florence, visiting the prison that day, gave five dollars in pocket money, probably intended for her husband, to Mollie Steimer.[36] On October 10, Schwartz, running a fever of 103 degrees, was moved to the prison ward at Bellevue, a hospital whose resources were already strained beyond the breaking point by the flu epidemic. The medical staff was depleted by illness. There were twice as many patients as beds to accommodate them, and the hospital's morgue had run out of room for the corpses. Conditions in the prison ward were frightful. Its fifty beds were filled with "coughing and moaning patients who crowd the ward, all suffering from influenza." In these "horrible surroundings," one patient later wrote, the cries of the delirious mingled with the screams of a "derelict suffering from alcoholism" and the "curses, ravings and vile language" of a dying drug addict. "How any man could get cured in a bedlam like this," he commented, "I could not understand."[37] Jacob Schwartz was one of the many who were not cured.

On October 25 a memorial rally to honor Schwartz was held at the Parkview Palace, on Fifth Avenue and 110th Street, a few blocks from where the anarchists had been arrested. More than 1,200 anarchists, socialists, and members of the Bookbinders' Union packed the hall. Harry Weinberger and John Reed gave the first two speeches, transcripts of which were made for the rally's organizers. Talks in Yiddish and Russian followed, transcripts of which are not available. Sitting unobtrusively in the audience, however, was an undercover agent of the

Army's Military Intelligence Division who understood both languages and filed a report summarizing what was said. The meeting got under way at nine o'clock in the evening in what was obviously an electric atmosphere. The chairman, Max Cernak, whom the agent described as "a Hebrew but with a German accent," said nervously, "We are looking for as little trouble as possible, and maybe there are some people here in the hall that are really looking for trouble, so we are not to give them any chance." He set the tone for the evening by telling his listeners they had assembled not merely to commemorate Schwartz's death but to celebrate it, "for every martyr upon the cause for the social revolution is a new step to victory . . . as more people are sacrificed on the altar of revolt, the quicker the victory will be—the better the victory will be."[38] Then, to loud cheers, he introduced Harry Weinberger.

For about ten minutes Weinberger played unblushingly on his audience's emotions. Schwartz, he said, was one of those rare individuals who "leave behind them a memory of idealism—a memory of having fought and worked for the betterment of their fellowmen everywhere." A hush surely fell over the hall when the lawyer read the unfinished letter found in Schwartz's cell, the letter ending "after your long martyr . . ." "Can you picture anything more heroic than that?" Weinberger asked. "Dying slowly in a dark prison cell, all alone, without friends, without medical attention, without nurses, in a cold, clammy, dark cell—and yet, his heart goes out to his fellow comrades . . . and he sends that small, pitiful letter, which like words of living fire, will be remembered . . . as long as anyone who has heard of this case will live." Walking through Central Park on his way to the rally, Weinberger continued, he looked up and saw the stars and the first glimmer of moonlight, and then he noticed the dead leaves scattered by the wind as they fell from the trees. If only things were reversed, he said, and the harmony in the heavens could replace the decay on earth. Then peace and goodwill would prevail, poverty and bitterness vanish. "We would not be like the cold, dead leaves that now cumber the ground in the parks, but we would be like the stars above, each doing his work as he sees it, each living his life to the fullest—real men, real women, with real intellects, with real hopes, with real aspirations and real ideals."[39]

When he had finished, Weinberger introduced John Reed, whose presence undoubtedly had much to do with the large turnout. War correspondent, bohemian rebel, formerly an editor of *The Masses,* Reed was even better known as an eyewitness to the Bolshevik Revolution, which he later described so effectively in *Ten Days That Shook the World.* Since his return to the United States late in April 1918, Reed had himself been a target of government repression. One of the defendants in the second *Masses* trial, which ended in acquittal on October 5, Reed, when he appeared at the Schwartz memorial rally, still faced two outstanding indictments. In Philadelphia, on May 31, he had spoken on a street corner after being denied access to a rented hall. Charged with inciting to riot and making seditious remarks, he was released on $5,000 bail. His New York Sedition Act indictment—for the speech in September attacking intervention in Soviet Russia—had required him to put up another $5,000 in bail. Reed was trailed by detectives who sometimes grilled him after his appearances, and who once confiscated his belongings. They awaited the day they would put him behind bars. In September a federal agent said he "is a most dangerous man to be walking around the streets at liberty. His bail should have been $50,000 instead of $5,000. Put John Reed in jail beyond the reach of bail, and much of the prevalent agitation would cease. He is worshipped by his followers as a hero today, and they constitute fertile soil for his poisonous heresies."[40]

Now, facing the expectant crowd at the Parkview Palace, Reed began with the salutation: "Comrades and friends." Unlike Weinberger, who had been careful to say that even those in the audience who did not share Schwartz's belief "that the Bolsheviks are right" would mourn his death, Reed tied the martyred man's fate directly to the Russian Revolution. Quoting a line from Schwartz's prison letter, "this is life itself," Reed said that the only worthwhile life was "to be in some way helping the cause of the people—that there is no other life, and that all opposition to us is death. (Applause) The only life is in the warm blood of the Proletariat, which will mount and wash the world clean! (Great applause)—and soon!" He had brought a message, he went on, for everyone to take home, and think about, and dream about: "The Russian Soviet Republic is winning! The Russian Soviet Republic has won! Socialism is safe! (Hurrah! Tremendous and prolonged applause.)"

Then Reed described what he had seen and heard during the November days in Petrograd, when workers rose to defend the revolution against "Kerensky's cossack forces." Men and women appeared, "some with guns, some with spades, some with axes, and the little children carrying sacks to fill with earth to make barricades against the cossacks. (Applause)" The proletariat, "the unled, the leaderless, the unorganized Proletariat," checked the assault and rolled it back. But the victory was not without cost, for many were wounded and many died. At the Smolny Institute, Reed reported, he had found a bulletin issued by the Bolsheviks. On the back a man had jotted down the names of his friends who had died in the battle, and had written a poem in their honor, "and the poem was blotted with his tears." Reed said he would read the poem, and "I want you to apply it to Jacob Schwartz, who fell in the fight as well as any of them." In a voice that almost certainly was trembling with emotion, he recited: "Sleep, warrior eagles;/ Sleep with peaceful soul!/ You have deserved, our own ones,/ happiness and eternal peace./ Under the earth of the grave,/ You have strongly closed your ranks./ Sleep, citizens!"[41]

Finally the applause died down. The meeting lasted for almost two more hours. An appeal for funds to help defray the legal costs of the Abrams trial netted $378, some in cash and some in the form of jewelry which was auctioned on the spot. Max Cernak then made a speech in Yiddish. According to the agent's report, he "attacked the Police for causing the death of Schwartz" and urged everyone to work for the liberation of the working class, the cause for which Schwartz had given his life. A member of the Union of Russian Workers, Peter Bianky, spoke next. Addressing the crowd in Russian, he "spoke of the good work which Schwartz did, and called his hearers to further organization." When Bianky asked everyone to stand in Schwartz's honor, "some one proposed to sing the Russian funeral march, and the crowd picked it right up." The meeting ended after eleven, with people singing revolutionary songs as they streamed into the streets.[42]

In the next few days radicals throughout the city paid homage to Jacob Schwartz, and on the first anniversary of his death his friends again met in honor of his memory. As the years passed, however, Schwartz was forgotten by all but a few anarchists. The circumstances of his death were too ambiguous to sustain the allegation that the police had murdered him. Ironically, in 1931, when the government formally got around to filing a *nolle prosequi* in his case, the entry stated inaccurately: "While the defendant was awaiting trial, he died in the Tombs Prison. This information is given to me by the Assistant who handled the case for the Government at the time . . ."[43] In October 1918, however, the radicals' belief in Schwartz's martyrdom confirmed a larger set of convictions: that democratic America was no better than Czarist Russia, that the policeman's nightstick was as deadly as the cossack's knout, that those who fought for a better world could expect to die for their trouble, and that, dying, they would find redemption. Not long after addressing the memorial meeting in Jacob Schwartz's honor, John Reed scribbled a note to himself. The carrying out of wartime prosecutions under the Espionage Act, he commented, "was simply a capitalist weapon in the class struggle."[44]

## The Judge: Henry DeLamar Clayton, Jr.

In 1918, in the Southern District of New York, there were three federal judges in whose courtrooms the Abrams case might have been heard: Julius M. Mayer, Augustus Noble Hand, and Learned Hand. The youngest of the three, Learned Hand, was senior by appointment, having been elevated to the federal bench in 1909, where he was joined by Mayer in 1912 and by his cousin, Augustus Hand, in 1914. To help relieve the three judges' crowded dockets, it was customary to designate federal judges in less populous districts to hold court in the Southern District usually for a period of four to six weeks. So, in the summer of 1918, several district judges were invited to come to New York City. Informing United States Attorney Francis G. Caffey of these arrangements, Learned Hand asked his cooperation in scheduling cases in a way that would make efficient use of the visiting jurists' time. "I do not think that they expect to run on a three-shift basis twenty-four hours a day, but you will understand that I may have difficulty in getting them here again if they get the impression that there is not much to do." The first of these judges, Hand explained, would arrive in July, a second in August, and the third, Henry DeLamar Clayton, Jr., of Alabama, in

September.[45] Assigned to try the Abrams case, Judge Clayton brought to the task a set of values shaped over a lifetime in politics, farming, and the law.

Henry DeLamar Clayton, Jr., was born in Barbour County, Alabama, in 1857. The year before, his father, a staunch defender of slavery, had led an armed expedition to Kansas where pro- and anti-slavery forces were contending for control. Clayton Senior was serving in the Alabama legislature when the Civil War began. He enlisted in the Confederate Army and eventually rose to the rank of Major General. He fought at the battles of Chickamauga, Rocky Face Mountain, and New Hope Church. He was wounded at Murfreesboro, had three horses shot from under him at Jonesboro, and later survived an attack of typhoid fever. Returning to his plantation after the war, the elder Clayton was elected a circuit court judge. The newly emancipated black, he said, was "helpless by his want of self-reliance, or experience, of ability to understand and appreciate his condition." In 1868 Clayton lost his judgeship when a Reconstruction measure barred certain categories of Confederate sympathizers from holding office. In 1868 another son was born to the Claytons: they named him Jeff Davis. With the end of Reconstruction in Alabama in 1874, Clayton was again elected a judge. He believed he treated blacks paternally, with "all the leniency the law would permit."[46] In 1886 he became president of the University of Alabama, an office he held until his death in 1888.

While Clayton Senior had been fighting for the Confederacy, his wife, Victoria Hunter Clayton, was raising their son, Henry, Jr., and their other children on the family plantation. Years later Mrs. Clayton published *White and Black Under the Old Regime,* a memoir which painted slavery in a most attractive light: slaves were "always happy in their innocent childhood"; they were "exempt from care"; their wants were provided for, so they "took no thought for the morrow"; the master who was "too exacting" was the exception; as a rule, "love and trust . . . existed between the master and his slave in our Southern land." From 1861 to 1865 Victoria Clayton and her children were the only whites on a plantation whose continued operation depended entirely on the labor of black slaves. More than a defense of slavery in the antebellum South, her memoir is a testimonial to those "good and honest" slaves who remained loyal. But during Reconstruction, Mrs.

Clayton observed sadly, blacks who were "unfitted for anything except to obey and to do their duty each day as directed by a superior" were given "all the privileges of citizenship." The last chapter of her book describes how, years after emancipation, a former slave asked her to care for a seven-year-old black boy who was then "bound by law" to her until he reached the age of twenty-one. She wistfully entitled the chapter, "Becoming a Slaveowner Again."[47]

The Civil War and Reconstruction—or, more properly speaking, his recollection of those boyhood events filtered through his parents' perceptions—apparently left a lasting imprint on Henry DeLamar Clayton, Jr. Even in his sixties, he rarely missed a chance to reminisce about slavery, the South, and the Civil War. He accepted his mother's view that masters loved their slaves, and slaves their masters. He regretted the widespread misreading of Harriet Beecher Stowe's *Uncle Tom's Cabin,* a novel, he believed, that "pays a high compliment to the way in which Southern folks treated their slaves. It was slavery which made Uncle Tom into a fine, honest, Christian man." Simon Legree, on the other hand, was "a New England Yankee."[48] "The Negroes are a docile race—the most docile race in the world," Clayton said in 1918. "They will do almost anything a white person tells them to do."[49] For Clayton, after more than half a century, Robert E. Lee remained the "great Confederate general and incomparable Southern gentleman."[50]

If his views of the old South approximated his mother's, his paternalism toward blacks, at least toward those who were properly deferential, resembled his father's. Clayton conceded that he was inclined, as a judge, to be lenient toward black defendants and to give them "a little bit the lighter punishment." Just such a situation arose in October 1918, a day or two before the Abrams trial began. A black woman, Helen Johnson, was convicted in Judge Clayton's court of selling whiskey to a United States soldier. In passing sentence, Clayton told the woman he would call her "Helen," not "Mrs. Johnson." "Down where I come from we do not call Negroes 'Mister' or 'Mistress'—we call them by their first names," he explained, "not to belittle them" but because Southerners understood blacks better than Northerners. He told Mrs. Johnson that when his father was in the Confederate Army, "there were five of us children on the old plantation with mother and the Negroes. There were Uncle Joshua and Aunt Rachel, and there was the slave woman who took care of me. And when we ran short of food she divided a little corn meal she had hoarded up between her own boy and me. . . . And Helen, that woman loved me to her dying day—and I loved her." One can only guess at the thoughts racing through Helen Johnson's mind as the judge continued his maudlin autobiographical excursion. When Clayton asked her to promise never to break the law again, she quickly complied and was fined only ten dollars.[51]

Before he became a judge, Clayton had been a congressman. His political style, like his father's, was that of the patriarch: the gentleman farmer and lawyer of impeccable ancestry, who parlayed his family's name and connections into a public career, who cut a fine figure and made a fine speech, who represented a stable agrarian constituency, who remained aloof from patronage battles, and who regarded regular reelection more or less as a matter of right.[52] The town of Eufala provided an ideal base for such a politician. Clayton moved there in 1880, after receiving a law degree from the University of Alabama. The town then had about 4,000 inhabitants, and thirty years later its population was 4,250. There was a buggy factory and a brick "manufactory," but the local economy rested primarily on cotton, grown on surrounding plantations and ginned and milled in the town.[53] Entering Democratic Party politics, Clayton was elected to the Alabama legislature in 1890, was appointed United States Attorney for the Middle District of Alabama in 1893, and was elected to Congress in 1896. From that year until 1914 he never faced a serious challenge for renomination or a real threat to reelection. His campaign expenses, he recalled, were "very nominal," amounting to "only a few hundred dollars each election."[54]

Woodrow Wilson's victory in 1912 undermined this comfortable political arrangement. This was doubly ironic: not only did Clayton admire Wilson ("History will write him down as one of the very few of the very great Presidents of our country," he wrote in 1915. "He is so thoughtful, considerate, wise and courageous") but he warmly supported the New Freedom.[55] By 1913 he was chairman of the House Judiciary Committee, and therefore well positioned to expedite the enactment of antitrust legislation, one of Wilson's chief objectives. Clayton cooperated with the administration in drafting, then introducing, the antitrust bill for which he is best remembered. Designed to exempt labor unions from antitrust prosecution, although worded too ambiguously to accomplish this, the bill catapulted Clayton to national attention and won him the praise of such labor leaders as Samuel Gompers, who thanked him for "the sterling service you rendered the people of our country."[56] The measure went to the Judiciary Committee in April 1914, and was passed by the House in June. But Clayton was not there to vote for it. He had resigned from Congress on May 25 to accept an appointment as a Federal District Judge.

Clayton left the House partly because a judgeship was inherently appealing, but also because the political style that had served him so well for so long was becoming anachronistic. During the Republican administrations of William McKinley, Theodore Roosevelt, and William Howard Taft, Clayton, a Democrat, had little federal patronage to dispense. Relatively few demands for jobs were made on him, and those were rather easily satisfied. But with Wilson's election, Alabama Democrats, starved for federal patronage, began to behave in a fashion best described as piranha-like. To throw a tasty morsel to one group, Clayton found, was to cause furious teeth-gnashing by all too many others. Clayton was caught in a bitter fight over a postmastership in Dothan, Alabama, a fight that involved just the kind of intrigue and internecine conflict for which his temperament and style were particularly ill-suited. In the spring of 1914, for the first time in his career, he faced a serious challenge from a Democratic opponent who, one historian notes, "never missed an opportunity to pick at the raw wounds of disappointed office seekers." Judicial robes were, for Clayton, the last refuge of a patriarch.[57]

After a year or two, however, Clayton, grew somewhat dissatisfied with his district judgeship. Early in 1916 he discreetly let it be known that he wanted to be considered for a Supreme Court vacancy.[58] When Wilson instead nominated Louis D. Brandeis, Clayton, lowering his sights, took aim on the Chief Justiceship of the Court of Appeals for the District of Columbia.[59] Unsuccessful once again, Clayton complained that the rewards of a federal district judgeship were inadequate. He earned only $6,000 a year, less than the $7,500 he had received as a member of Congress, and he told the sympathetic Learned Hand, and whoever else would listen, that the salary scale for district judges should be raised to $9,000 to $10,000. It was galling to Clayton that "no lawyer of any considerable practice in the federal courts fails to make two or three times as much as the judge's salary." Although enjoying lifetime tenure, he grumbled that "a judge is prohibited from doing almost everything under the sun, except to draw his meager salary and to breathe. Out of his salary he must pay his living expenses and those of his family, carry a little life insurance and dress like a modest gentleman."[60]

As a Federal District Judge for the Middle and Northern Districts of Alabama, Clayton spent much of his time in Montgomery. Yet he maintained his two-hundred-acre farm at Eufala, on the west bank of the Chattahoochee River, and regularly sent the manager detailed instructions for sowing wheat, purchasing alfalfa seed, selling oats, and picking cotton. He told a relative in 1917 that, had he a choice, he would reside year round in Eufala "in my own house, under my own scuppernong vine, under my own fig trees . . ." Writing, only half-humorously perhaps, about his farm animals, the judge offered a clue to some of his most deeply held values: "And my cow would be my friend and my horse would delight in serving me. My dog would greet me with friendly salutes and grateful wags every day and every hour if I wanted him to. I'd rather hear the neigh of a good horse, the moo of the faithful cow, the cackle of the business-like speckled hen, the crowing of the vigilant rooster, and the bark of an honest dog than to hear the screams of the whistles of a hundred industrial establishments." In the fall of 1918, holding court in New York City where the urban cacophony was considerably louder than the moos of faithful cows or the crowing of vigilant roosters, Clayton continued to regard himself as a man of the soil and clung to a belief in the supremacy of the agrarian way of life.[61]

On most issues Clayton agreed with Woodrow Wilson. But there were two on which he, like many Southern Democrats, broke with the President. The first was woman suffrage, which Wilson eventually acknowledged to be a necessary war measure. To Clayton, woman suffrage threatened the principle of states' rights. Moreover, Clayton reported, his wife, Bettie, had assured him "that she does not want to be burdened with the duty of voting" and that suffrage would "do great harm in the Southern States."[62] Clayton also disagreed with Wilson over literacy tests for immigrants. The President opposed these tests, but

Clayton favored them as a way to protect American workers against competition from the "cheap pauper labor of Europe," and, perhaps, to exclude those whom he thought incapable of becoming good citizens.[63] In 1916 Clayton declared that even naturalized citizens who "unfairly" criticized the government "should get off the face of the earth, or at least go back to the country they left. . . . I have no sympathy with any naturalized citizen who is given to carping criticism of this Government or who cannot say that he loves America first, last, and forever."[64]

A tragic incident converted Clayton's distrust of immigrants into a passionate hatred of Germany and everyone whom he suspected of aiding the German cause in World War I. On May 30, 1918, his younger brother, Bertram Tracy Clayton, was killed by a German bomb in France. A graduate of West Point, a civil engineer, and a career officer, Bertram Clayton had told his brother, when war was declared in 1917, that "the only thing worth while is to be in with the troops."[65] In 1918 he arranged for an overseas assignment and was promoted to the rank of Colonel. He was the highest-ranking American officer to be killed in World War I, and when the terrible news arrived, Henry DeLamar Clayton described himself as "heart-broken."[66] Later, when the armistice was signed, he told his wife, "I fear that I have too much bitterness in my heart to be as thankful as I should be on account of the German surrender. I wanted our army to trod German soil. I wanted the German army annihilated."[67] Five months after his brother's death, presiding at the Abrams trial, Clayton was still wearing "a black band on his arm, and a gold star."[68]

So it is little wonder that the judge was favorably impressed by the patriotic fever then raging in New York City. He noted with satisfaction that "everybody is giving to the Red Cross and the like and buying War Savings Stamps and Liberty Bonds."[69] The September roundup of men without draft cards led him to comment that "the people of New York are certainly out of patience with slackers."[70] Deeply moved by the sight of soldiers in the streets, Clayton commented, "Some of them show the effects of war—more or less wounded and some of them partially maimed."[71] He was proud of his wife, who had hosted a tea for women who were knitting sweaters and mittens for soldiers. They went to the movies together, saw *Pershing's Crusaders,* and, Clayton noted, looked forward to seeing "*Hearts of the World,* which is said to be a marvelous movie production, rivaling, if not surpassing, *The 'Birth of the Nation.'* "[72] The Claytons spent several weekends at a friend's thirty-two-acre estate at Islip, Long Island, where, on Sundays, everyone went to the golf course in horse-drawn wagons rather than automobiles. In all, the Southern judge found his stay in the North a pleasant one. "Barring the relatively few extreme socialists and anarchists," he commented, "I must say that the citizens of New York are splendid in their loyalty and devotion to our country in these sad and trying hours which demand so many sacrifices."[73]

On October 10, 1918, Clayton told a friend that he would have to spend the rest of the month in New York City. "I am engaged in the trial of a very important case," he explained.[74] It was, of course, the Abrams case. Henry DeLamar Clayton brought to the trial attitudes that had been instilled by his parents, molded by his childhood memories, confirmed by his political experiences, strengthened by the personal loss he had suffered, and hardened by the wartime atmosphere of superheated patriotism. As he peered down at the defendants and their lawyer, the judge could not help but feel that his most cherished values—pastoralism, paternalism, and 100 percent Americanism—were under attack.

## The Prosecution's Case

The United States Attorney for the Southern District of New York, Francis G. Caffey, a graduate of Harvard Law School, enjoyed the company of other Harvard men. No fewer than eight of twenty-two Assistant Attorneys in his office were fellow Harvard graduates, one of whom, John M. Ryan, class of '96, was assigned to the Abrams case.[75] Born in Galena, Illinois, Ryan had attended Georgetown, then Harvard, and had worked for the New York law firm in which Caffey was a partner before being appointed a prosecutor in 1918. Harry Weinberger later recalled that Ryan was "a little taller than I, built somewhat on my style, smooth shaven, shell rim glasses, iron grey hair, with a habit of putting his glasses on and taking them off." Ryan was assisted by a younger attorney, Sanford Lawrence Miller, whom Weinberger described as "tall, raw boned, almost 6 feet high, built in proportion, smooth shaven, brown hair."[76]

The jurors' names were not reported in the newspapers and do not appear in the surviving court records. According to Weinberger, they "were men about 45 years of age and over. Many of them retired. Most of them in business for themselves." The lawyer thought that the jurors, as businessmen, had an ingrained bias against radicals.[77] Judge Clayton saw it differently. Insisting that the selection process had been scrupulously fair, he pointed to the exclusion of all potential jurors "who might be so enthusiastic and ardent in their patriotism as perhaps they might not accord the defendants a fair trial." The twelve men who were finally seated, the judge added, came "from the different walks of life. They appeared also to me to be, for the most part, poor men, or men in very moderate circumstances. They did not appear to me, any one of them, to belong to what is sometimes called the capitalistic class. They seemed to be plain, ordinary American citizens from the humble walks of life."[78]

Even so, it is more than likely that the jury was inclined to be sympathetic to the government's case. Leaving as little as possible to chance, United States Attorney Caffey habitually provided the Bureau of Investigation with a list of all potential jurors in Espionage Act and Sedition Act cases. In this way, well before the actual selection, discreet inquiries could be made and undependable or untrustworthy individuals identified. Prosecuting attorneys could then be told whom to challenge.[79] Whether this screening procedure was employed in the Abrams case is uncertain, but Ryan and Miller may well have been trying to convince jurors who needed little convincing. Defense attorney Weinberger was right when he said that, in the Southern District of New York, "juries are convicting juries. . . . There are no laboring men, or even socialists and liberals, on United States juries."[80]

The four counts in the indictment charged each of the defendants—Abrams, Steimer, Lipman, Lachowsky, Rosansky, and Prober—with conspiring to publish two leaflets that contained disloyal, scurrilous, and abusive language about the government, that were designed to bring the government into contempt, scorn, or disrepute, that were intended to incite resistance to the United States' war effort, and that advocated the curtailment of essential production with the intent of crippling the prosecution of the war. But beyond introducing "The Hypocrisy of the United States and Her Allies" and "Workers—Wake Up" as exhibits, reading them to the jury, and terming them "seditious," Ryan and Miller did not attempt to show that the leaflets were intended to do any of these things, much less that they had succeeded in doing any of them. The prosecution set out to prove only that the defendants had written, printed, and distributed the two leaflets.

The parade of government witnesses began on Monday, October 14, and lasted four days. Several police officers described how the leaflets, brought to headquarters on August 23, had been traced to Rosansky, who had broken down and incriminated the others. The officers also explained how they had arrested Abrams and his friends that night, searched their apartment, and taken down their statements. A police stenographer read those statements into the trial record. The policemen recounted how they had followed the trail, which started with the bill of sale for the printing press, and led to the basement shop on Madison Avenue, where they discovered the press, trays of type, and paper. The prosecution called the three workers who had found the leaflets at the corner of Crosby and Houston streets and brought them to the police, the two janitresses who had rented the East 104th Street apartment and the Madison Avenue basement shop to Abrams, the photographer who had taken pictures of the shop, the man who had sold Abrams the printing press and trays of type, and a printer who could identify the type as that used in the leaflets. In all, the prosecution called twenty-two witnesses and introduced thirty exhibits. As Lieutenant Colonel Nicholas Biddle said, "There was not a missing link in the testimony."[81]

In presenting their case, Ryan and Miller emphasized that the anarchists had acted surreptitiously, and had thereby demonstrated a consciousness of guilt. Nellie Ryan, who had rented the East 104th Street apartment to Abrams, reported that he had lied about his name, using an alias, Abram Dean. Eva Kraus, who had rented the Madison Avenue shop, said that Abrams had lied again, introducing Lachowsky as his brother, and that the two of them had preferred to work after nightfall. The police officers who went to the shop testified that they had found some copies of the leaflets in a pail, only scorched in a botched attempt to destroy the evidence. Even the anarchists' refusal to answer questions about their confederates during the interrogations at police headquarters conveyed an impression that they knew they had something to hide. Mollie Steimer's answer to a loaded question was read into the record: "Didn't you know at the time you distributed these pamphlets that it was a violation of the law?" "Yes, sir."[82] All this testimony, Caffey believed, offered "proof of the criminal intent with which the defendants committed the acts."[83]

Harry Weinberger cross-examined most of the government's witnesses, but, other than insisting that Gabriel Prober had nothing to do with printing or distributing the leaflets, he did not challenge the accuracy of their accounts. "There will be no attempt to escape the fact that we did what we did," Weinberger said in court; "the acts which we did will be acknowledged by each of these defendants."[84] The acts, he quickly added, were simply not criminal. As one government witness followed another to the stand, Weinberger even offered to speed up the proceedings by "stipulat[ing] on the record that I am not going to question that part of the testimony."[85] Nevertheless, the opportunity to cross-examine police officers permitted Weinberger to raise the issue of the third degree, which, he hoped, would expose that vicious practice and perhaps even cast doubt on the admissibility of the confessions.

Questioning the policemen as aggressively as the court would allow, Weinberger tried to show that several officers had mistreated the defendants while several others had stood by and watched. Edward J. Meagher, a member of the force for three years, was singled out as the chief culprit. "Are you not known in your department as the 'Tiger'?" Weinberger snapped, but Ryan objected and the judge upheld the objection. To the lawyer's barbed questions, Meagher gave dead-pan answers: "Did you pull Lachowsky at any time by the hair around the examination room?" "I did not." "Did you beat Lipman over the heart at any time in that examination room?" "No." . . . "Did you tell Lipman that you would take his eye glasses and put them into his eyes if he didn't tell you all about where these pamphlets were made?" "I did not." . . . "Did you strike Schwartz at any time over the heart?" "No, I did not." Eventually, as Weinberger's tone became even more accusatory, the judge interceded. "I am trying to get information from the witness," Weinberger protested. "I know what you are trying to do," Clayton replied, "you are trying to do more than you ought to do as an attorney."[86]

Although he did not permit Weinberger to press this line of inquiry too hard, Clayton was anxious to set the record straight on the matter of the third degree. Perhaps anticipating appeals to a higher court, the judge asked the policemen whether they had seen or heard of "cruelty or oppression of any sort, kind or description exercised on or towards any of these defendants," or whether, on the night of the arrests, one of the defendants had "made all of those answers freely and voluntarily, with no threat or promise made to him, to induce him to answer?" When Inspector Thomas J. Tunney, Chief of the Bomb Squad, was testifying, Clayton interrupted Weinberger's cross-examination in order to rephrase Tunney's argument to the effect that all the defendants' statements were made "freely and voluntarily, without any coercion or force or the practice of any cruelty, or anything of a similar condition."[87] Faced with police officers who blandly denied any improper conduct, and a judge who never doubted the denials, Weinberger could not substantiate his allegations of police brutality.

Judge Clayton also prevented Weinberger from turning to the defendants' advantage the prosecution's decision to place an undercover informant on the stand. At first the testimony of one Harry Rein hardly seemed momentous: on August 23 he had "instructions to cover" a meeting at the Central Opera House, he had seen Gabriel Prober waiting to enter, and, when the meeting was canceled, he, Rein, had gone with the crowd to East 107th Street where a policeman had shown him a copy of the leaflet. Weinberger, hearing the witness say he had been asked to "cover" the meeting, assumed he was a reporter. The lawyer asked which paper he worked for, only to be told "I have volunteered my services to the Department of Justice . . . and the Military Intelligence. . . . I have covered most of these Bolsheviki meetings, and I have made my reports." He understood Yiddish, Rein added, and "I was requested, since August first, to cover these Russian meetings." Weinberger then asked about the nature of the meeting at which Rein had seen Prober, but Clayton instructed the witness not to answer, and became angry when Weinberger persisted. "Take your seat!" Clayton shouted. "May I respectfully say—," the lawyer began, only to be told, "You may not do anything else right now but take your seat. I have ruled on it." Weinberger then asked Rein why he planned to contact a special agent of the Bureau of Investigation at the meeting, but even before the prosecution had time to object, the judge disallowed the question. Unable to conceal his annoyance with Weinberger, Clayton made what he surely imagined was a humorous remark: "I have tried to out-talk an Irishman, and I never can do it, and the Lord knows I can not out-talk a Jew."[88]

The judge's habit of joking, often inappropriately, about matters that troubled him would reassert itself as the trial progressed. Now, on Thursday, October 17, as the government prepared to conclude its case, Clayton mentioned a sensitive subject that was undoubtedly of concern to everyone in the courtroom. Addressing the members of the jury, he said that the prosecutors had kept them "sitting in this stuffy court room" where "the air is very foul." "Outside there is some good air," he continued, ". . . and I suggested that we open these doors, and then it was suggested that it would cause a draught and might give us this grippe that is going around, so I don't want to do that." Again resorting to humor, Clayton announced an adjournment. "While there are plenty of attorneys, there are not so many good jurors, and I know that good judges are scarce, and I shall take care of the jury and the judge in this case, as far as I know how, as the District Attorney does not seem to be any too solicitous about our health, and we will disregard him."[89]

## Raymond Robins and the Sisson Documents

One of the spectators in Judge Clayton's stuffy courtroom was Raymond Robins, who had been subpoenaed to appear as the first defense witness. "Long wait & nothing doing," he wrote in his diary on Thursday night. On Friday, however, he would take the witness stand, as would Albert Rhys Williams. Both men had recently returned from Russia where they had observed the Bolshevik revolution, and both, for very different reasons, were bitterly opposed to Woodrow Wilson's policy of military intervention. Harry Weinberger had decided to base his defense on the claim that the Bolsheviks, before ratifying the Treaty of Brest-Litovsk with Germany in March 1918, had proposed a policy of military and economic cooperation with the United States, but that Wilson had spurned the offer and left the Bolsheviks no alternative to ratification. If this claim was true, as Robins and Williams were prepared to testify, then the defendants, Weinberger argued, "were absolutely correct when they objected to the intervention in Russia by a military armed force."[91] To show that Lenin's government had been ready to make a deal with the United States, however, Weinberger first had to disprove the authenticity of a set of documents, brought back from Russia by Edgar Sisson, and recently released, which alleged that the Bolsheviks were, in reality, German agents.

A well-known journalist and a former editor of *Collier's,* Edgar Sisson had taken a position with George Creel's wartime propaganda agency, the Committee on Public Information. In October 1917 Wilson had sent him to Russia to help boost the Kerensky government's morale, but the timing was terrible. By late November, when Sisson arrived in Petrograd, his instructions were obsolete, for the Bolsheviks had seized power. Sisson nevertheless remained in Russia until March, a period he later described in a memoir entitled *One Hundred Red Days.* Every day was, for Sisson, a harrowing one. The actions of the Bolsheviks, the "new tyrannical rulers" of Russia, horrified him, and the sight of Lenin was enough to make his flesh crawl. Writing to his wife, Sisson characterized the Russian leader as "the Wildest of the Wild men of Russia." Unlike other Americans who were impressed by the mingling of idealism and fanaticism in Lenin's makeup, Sisson saw only his sinister side. Observing Lenin as he spoke to the All-Russian Congress of Soviets, Sisson thought he saw "a leering, animated gargoyle. Frequently his face set in lines of animal ferocity."[92]

In this mordant mood Sisson was prepared to believe the worst about the Bolsheviks, and what could be worse than that they were German agents? Early in February 1918, he came into possession of documents, supposedly filched from Bolshevik files, which, if authentic, revealed that Lenin, Trotsky, and others "had been the accredited and financed agents of Germany."[93] For about a month Sisson devoted himself to obtaining additional documents, and soon acquired copies of letters and memoranda presumably written by German generals and bankers which made it appear that Soviet officials were taking orders from Germany. Sisson left Russia on March 4, arriving in the United States, after an arduous journey, on May 6. Seventy-two hours later his report was on the President's desk. Convinced that "the present leaders of the Russian Bolsheviki government were installed by Germany for German use against the nations at war with Germany," Sisson drew the obvious conclusion: America should intervene in Russia "to take a stand against the present Bolsheviki leaders, charging them with the betrayal of the liberty of all free peoples, and calling upon Russians themselves to rise and stand with us against their German masters and against such Bolsheviki leaders as are servants of those German masters."[94]

Presenting his sixty-eight documents to George Creel, Sisson asserted that Germany had masterminded the Russian Revolution and, through "mazes of deception," had continued to dictate the Bolsheviks' policies. Creel was dazzled by the find, but others in official circles remained skeptical.[95] The State Department suspected that the documents were forgeries as did Wilson's advisor, Colonel Edward M. House, partly because the British government, after examining the same documents, had concluded they were counterfeit. So the months passed, Sisson's frustration mounted, but the papers were not made public. When the President decided to intervene in Russia, however, the documents' potential propaganda value outweighed any doubts as to their authenticity. Wilson, without bothering to consult the State Department, authorized publication. On September 15 the Committee on Public Information began releasing the documents, which then appeared in major newspapers over a period of several days. Widely accepted at first, they soon were challenged so sharply that Creel asked a committee of historians to render an opinion as to whether the documents were genuine.[96] He made the request on October 18, the same day that Raymond Robins was scheduled to testify in the Abrams case.

Raymond Robins had traveled a roundabout route to Russia. As a young man, he had spent three years prospecting for gold in Alaska, and, apparently, had found what he was looking for. As a relative explained discreetly, he "had come out of the Klondike with enough gold for financial independence."[97] Moving to Chicago in 1900, Robins became active in the fields of social welfare, political reform, and

Christian evangelicalism. He supported Jane Addams' Hull House, backed reform candidates for municipal office, and lectured for the "Men and Religion Forward" movement. A good friend of Theodore Roosevelt, he campaigned for the Progressive Party in 1912, and even ran for the Senate on the party's ticket in 1914, but lost. In 1916 Robins chaired the Progressive National Convention. His wife, Margaret Dreier Robins, an equally prominent figure in the world of reform, was a leader of the Women's Trade Union League (as was her sister, Mary E. Dreier) and a militant supporter of woman suffrage. Raymond and Margaret Robins spent many of their happiest hours at "Chinsegut," their hilltop estate on Florida's Gulf Coast.

In the summer of 1917 Raymond Robins was sent to Russia as a member of the American Red Cross Commission. He arrived in September, his assignment to help arrange for the more efficient distribution of food and medicine in the war-torn nation, and to help attract economic and financial support for Kerensky's government. Yet while he backed Kerensky, the ardent Robins could not resist being caught up in the emotional fervor of the Bolshevik revolution. The Soviet experiment, he thought, enjoyed enormous popular support, and was "as spontaneous, as Russian, as a folk-song on the Volga."[98] For a time Robins worked closely with Edgar Sisson, but the two men, miles apart in their views, were light years apart temperamentally, and soon came to detest each other. The cold, suspicious, cynical Sisson had nothing in common with the emotional, trusting, idealistic Robins. When the two Americans met Lenin, their reactions, as recorded by Sisson, provided a classic illustration of psychological projection. "Where Robins saw a sensitive person I saw a calculating one."[99]

Ironically, it was Robins who had given Sisson the first batch of controversial documents, but Robins, of course, considered them utterly worthless. Far from regarding the Bolsheviks as German agents, he thought that they were revolutionaries doing their best to instigate revolution in Germany itself. Moreover, Robins believed that during the Brest-Litovsk negotiations in March 1918 Lenin and Trotsky had asked him to convey an offer to the Wilson administration, an offer carefully couched as a series of questions. In the event that the Soviet government refused to ratify the peace treaty with Germany, "What kind of support could be furnished in the nearest future, and on what conditions—military equipment, transportation supplies, living necessities?" And if Japan should attempt to seize Vladivostok, what action would the United States take "to prevent a Japanese landing on our Far East?"[100] If the right answers were forthcoming, the Russian leaders indicated, they would be ready to do business, ready, in fact, to give the United States control over much of Russia's railroad system, thereby preventing Germany from capturing essential war materiel. Here, Robins believed, was an opportunity to inaugurate an era of good feeling between Soviet Russia and the United States, an opportunity, he further believed, that was lost, perhaps forever, when the Wilson administration ignored the feeler.

Setting sail on the high seas, Robins, thinking over what had happened, was more than ever astounded by the shortsightedness of American policy. Soviet Russia had wanted western capitalist investment, Robins believed, and such investment would have made possible "Allied economic organization and control and would have stabilized the Soviet power, softening and modifying its hard formulas to meet the necessities of actual life. The policy would have given for Allied enterprise the last greatest remaining market for secondary production left in the earth, and would have opened to Allied exploitation the greatest unappropriated primary resources and products of field, forest and mine left in the world." Noting ruefully what had been lost—"the vast natural resources of the most fruitful portion of the earth," "the vast Russian market for the benefit of Allied capital and products not only for the period of the war but for generations thereafter," the "vast untouched deposits of minerals, platinum, copper, gold and virgin forests"—Robins concluded that those who claimed communism was a menace failed to realize that "a year of trade will do more to harmonize Bolshevism with the rest of the world, and with the safety of the rest of the world, than a generation of invective and invasion."[101]

Robins finally reached Seattle on June 20. For the next four months he offered a vivid account of Russian events to all who would listen. His audience included Secretary of State Robert Lansing, Secretary of War Newton D. Baker, Supreme Court Justice Louis D. Brandeis, AFL President Samuel Gompers, *New Republic* editor Herbert Croly, Republican Senator Hiram Johnson of California, and his old friend, Theodore Roosevelt. But it was only in private that Robins could express himself freely. On the advice of the Military Intelligence Division, which learned that Robins had been speaking to influential individuals, "setting before them at length and with great ardor the purity of Lenine and Trotsky," and urging them to support recognition of the Soviet government, the State Department requested him not to discuss any diplomatic matters relating to Russia in public.[102] "If I do not get into action again somewhere I will burst," Robins complained to his wife, but in the meantime, however unhappily, he remained silent.[103]

Writing to his wife, Robins called Lenin "that Great Heart of the Russian revolution—the foremost economic adventurer among the sons of men," and she, in turn, called him "the one great courageous builder and statesman of the new world—and his strength is as the strength of ten because his faith is great."[104] Understandably, then, Robins regarded Wilson's July decision to intervene militarily in Russia as only the sorry culmination of a policy best described as "a tragedy of stupid errors."[105] His old nemesis, Edgar Sisson, was still at work, he knew, engaging in his "ferret and snake-like activities," even though it was obvious that "his great story was as stale as a last year's bird's nest."[106] On September 15, when the documents were released, Robins told Margaret Dreier Robins, "I have just read the Sisson poisonous forgeries. Their publication now shows how much they need support for their policy in Russia. . . . It will carry with it the seeds of its own discredit."[107]

On the same day that Robins wrote this letter to his wife, John Reed sent her a hastily scrawled note. Explaining that he had just been arrested in New York City for a speech denouncing intervention, and adding that "whether I am to go to prison or not is a minor matter," he told her that "Raymond Robins' testimony on the stand, I believe, can do great service for the Russian Revolution." He asked Margaret Robins to put this request before her husband as soon as possible.[108] So a month before the Abrams trial began, Reed recognized that Robins could be an important witness in such cases, and it is even possible that he suggested as much to Weinberger. In any event, the strategy had obvious advantages. The government had persuaded Robins not to speak out in public, but in a courtroom he would be sworn to tell the whole truth. His testimony could discredit the Sisson Documents, strike a blow against Russian intervention, and, in the process, provide justification for the anarchists' leaflets. For the defense lawyer's purposes, Raymond Robins was an ideal witness.

For Robins, however, the witness box was hardly an ideal place. He apparently feared that if he talked about Russia, even under oath, he would risk prosecution, and if he did not, he would risk a contempt citation. However unfounded the fear, the excitable, overwrought Robins regarded himself as a marked man. He thought that his mail was being opened and his phone tapped. "If you hear that I have been committed to prison for refusing to violate confidential relations with Russia do not be disturbed," he told Theodore Roosevelt. "Going to prison is a small thing for the privilege of the Russian experience."[109] The former President then reported to a mutual friend, Gifford Pinchot, that, as Pinchot wrote to Robins, "the Administration had gone after you on some ridiculous charge of disloyalty." Pinchot added reassuringly, "I have no doubt the charges will break down."[110]

On Monday, October 14, following a long talk with Theodore Roosevelt at Sagamore Hill, Robins went to his sister-in-law Mary E. Dreier's apartment on lower Fifth Avenue. Before long a marshal arrived to serve him with a subpoena. Robins, locking himself in the apartment, refused to let the marshal enter. Once, he ventured out on the fourth-floor fire escape, but spying the subpoena-server on the sidewalk, prudently retreated. Later that afternoon Weinberger asked the court to authorize a marshal to break into the apartment, apprehend Robins, and serve a writ charging him with contempt of court. The order was granted. But five minutes before the marshal arrived to arrest Robins, he emerged from the apartment to accept the subpoena, accompanied by his lawyer, George W. Wickersham, whose credentials included service as Attorney General in the Taft administration, and a term as president of the Association of the Bar of the City of New York. "I am Mr. Wickersham," he announced. "I will be responsible for Mr. Robins's appearance in court tomorrow morning."[111]

It was one thing to get Robins onto the witness stand, quite another to get Judge Clayton to admit his testimony. When Robins testified on October 18, he was permitted to answer questions about his background, but when Weinberger asked about his responsibilities in Russia, the prosecution objected, and the judge warned that the relevance of such testimony would have to be demonstrated. Weinberger then laid out the lines along which he planned to proceed. Since the indictment charged the defendants with putting out leaflets attacking United States intervention, he was going to try to show, first, that President Wilson had acted illegally in sending troops to Russia without a declaration of war, and, second, that the Bolshevik government was not pro-German but had actually offered "the United States control of the railroads of Russia, so that America could control all goods and keep them within the border of Russia, so that Germany could never get them." Consequently Jacob Abrams, Mollie Steimer, and the others were entirely within their rights when they criticized the decision to send American troops into action against a Soviet government which had been willing, all along, to cooperate with the United States in the war.[112]

This line of defense, Clayton responded, was inappropriate: persons accused of violating a statute which forbade making certain statements condemning the government's policy could not claim, as justification, that their statements were true and the policy was misguided. To allow such a defense, the judge added, would permit defendants in Sedition Act cases to assert "a superior wisdom to the organized government of the United States and the authorities who have spoken and acted for it." Having made a reasonable point, and one Weinberger probably expected him to make, Judge Clayton then interjected an inappropriate characterization of the defendants' behavior. The charge, he claimed, is "that these defendants, by what they have done, conspired to go and incite a revolt; in fact, one of the very papers is signed 'Revolutionists,' and it was for the purpose of avoiding . . . the purposes of the government and raising a state of public opinion in this country of hostility to the government of the United States, so as to prevent the government from carrying on its operations . . . Now they can not do that. No man can do that, and that is the theory that I have of this case, and we might as well have it out in the beginning." When Weinberger, recognizing that Clayton had gone too far, asked him to instruct the jury "to disregard your Honor's opinion as to the legality," Clayton, perhaps sensing he had indeed gone too far, did so. But it is unlikely that his statement, or his admonition to Weinberger—"your theory and mine are at war, they can not be reconciled"—could be erased from the jurors' minds.[113]

The judge decided that in order to define the issue fairly for a later appeal, Weinberger would be allowed to ask Robins the questions he wanted, thereby placing them on the record, but the witness would not be allowed to answer them. The lawyer began firing a series of questions designed to draw from Robins the views he was not supposed to state publicly. Hadn't Robins investigated the Sisson Documents and concluded that they were forgeries? Hadn't the Soviet government, before ratifying the Treaty of Brest-Litovsk, asked him "to bring about an understanding with the Allies, with a view of continuing the war, on the part of the Soviets against Germany, on condition of material aid, and that was to consist of transportation, instructors for the army, materials and food?" Hadn't the United States failed to reply to this offer, but indeed kept it secret? Hadn't the Soviets agreed to put key railroad lines under American control, in order to prevent Germany from acquiring vital material?[114] Robins was satisfied by the arrangement which required him to remain silent, or so it appears from his diary entry: "Court & Clayton are the call of the day's work. . . . The power is great & majestic & kindly withal." His testimony finished, it was with a sense of relief that Robins boarded an evening train to Chinsegut, his Florida retreat.[115]

Robins was followed to the witness stand by Albert Rhys Williams, an ordained minister who had left his Congregationalist pulpit in East Boston and now described himself as a "journalist and lecturer." The thirty-four-year-old Williams, a socialist, had gone to Russia in June 1917, and, after the Bolsheviks came to power, had worked in the Commissariat of Foreign Affairs, preparing propaganda to be used among German soldiers. Like Robins he believed that the United States had rejected friendly overtures from Lenin's government and had embarked instead on a disastrous policy of military intervention, but Williams also had a commitment to the Soviet system which Robins never shared. "We are fighting for a new, free, just order," he said in Russia in June 1918, "a society without warring classes, where the beaten, despised and oppressed of the earth shall come into their own."[116] His radical beliefs made Williams, on his return to the United States in September 1918, an obvious candidate for government surveillance. His papers were seized by the authorities, and on October 16, two days before he testified at the Abrams trial, a State Department report branded him "extremely dangerous" and suggested that "his activities should be very closely watched. It may well be that if his suspicions are not aroused he will shortly say or do something which will make it possible for the Department of Justice to prosecute him."[117]

The questions Weinberger asked Williams, like those he had asked Robins, were designed to show that the Soviet government had been willing to continue the war against Germany. Once again, Judge Clayton permitted the questions to be entered on the record, but upheld the prosecution's objections and instructed the witness not to respond. "Isn't it a fact," Weinberger asked Williams, that the Bolsheviks had issued propaganda calling for a working-class revolution in Germany, and had dismantled factories in Petrograd "when it was feared that the Germans would capture the city?" "Did Lenine tell you that any Soviet leader who allowed any material to fall in the hands of the Germans ought to be shot? . . . Were Bolsheviki officers court-martialed when they ordered a retreat before German troops . . .?" As Weinberger continued to read, Clayton informed the jury that the questions "are not in any sense a part of the evidence here."[118]

Williams may have been frustrated by not being able to use the courtroom as a forum, but not as frustrated as Harry Weinberger, who had repeatedly seen his strategy thwarted. When he put Robins and Williams on the stand, Weinberger had intended to call Edgar Sisson himself in order to prove that the controversial documents were fraudulent. But when it became clear that Clayton would not allow Sisson, any more than he had the other two witnesses, to answer questions about his Russian experience, Weinberger decided it would be futile to persist. He merely asked that the record note that the defense had wanted to hear Sisson's testimony. Clayton obliged, stating that Weinberger had proposed to "put Mr. Sisson on the stand, and propose[d] to ask him those questions, and, upon objection by the Government, the Court declined to let you do so, and you except." By granting the exception, the judge allowed Weinberger to raise the exclusion of this testimony when he filed an appeal.[119]

So the Abrams trial provided only a muted sounding board for critics of the Wilson administration's Russian policy, and did not help resolve the controversy over the Sisson Documents. Scholars have since concluded that Raymond Robins, Albert Rhys Williams, and Harry Weinberger were right to doubt the papers' authenticity. "With the possible exception of a few relatively unimportant items," George Kennan has concluded, "these documents were unquestionably forgeries from beginning to end." At the same time, Robins, Williams, and Weinberger undoubtedly exaggerated the willingness of the Soviet government to remain in the war on the side of the Allies. The message Trotsky and Lenin handed to Raymond Robins before the Treaty of Brest-Litovsk was ratified, setting forth certain hypothetical questions to which the Soviets wanted answers, was no forgery. But Edgar Sisson and George Creel had good reason to question its significance. As Kennan also points out, the paper "committed the Soviet government to nothing. It constituted merely a query as to what aid would be forthcoming in certain contingencies."[120]

By Friday afternoon, October 18, the Abrams trial had lasted for a week, and both sides seemed eager to bring it to a conclusion. When the judge asked how much longer the case would take, Weinberger said the defense would need only two more days, and the prosecution said it planned to offer no rebuttal. Thanking the lawyers on both sides for conducting themselves appropriately, and warning the jury "not to talk about this case amongst yourselves nor to anybody else," Henry DeLamar Clayton was quite satisfied to adjourn court for the weekend. Yet the judge could not resist the opportunity to proclaim his patriotism, noting that "we are all interested in this [liberty] loan, and everybody is trying to do their bit."[121] It had been, after all, exactly a week since President Wilson had done his bit for the bond drive at the Broadway theater.

# 4

# The Conviction

## The Judge as Prosecutor

The courtroom flare-up occurred on Monday afternoon, October 21, 1918. Jacob Abrams had spent a grueling day on the witness stand, and the hour was growing late. Judge Clayton was himself questioning the witness, and Abrams, speaking in a soft voice with a distinct Yiddish accent, was earnestly attempting to defend his anarchist beliefs. "This government was built on a revolution," Abrams said. ". . . When our forefathers of the American Revolution—" That was as far as he got. "Your what?" Judge Clayton interrupted. "My forefathers," Abrams replied. "Do you mean to refer to the fathers of this nation as your forefathers?" Clayton asked. Abrams said, "We are all a big human family," and "Those that stand for the people, I call them father." But the judge had made his point, and the jury had no doubt gotten it.[1]

It was not uncommon, in 1918, for a judge in either a civil or criminal case to question a witness directly. A judge, in fact, was assumed to have a duty to do so "when it appears that the witness is evasive, diffident, or ignorant." To get at the whole truth, a judge was even permitted to call witnesses on his own volition. The legal community disagreed over how much latitude to allow the Court, but there was no disagreement that the judge "must so frame his questions that he gives no impression of partiality to the jury."[2] The distinctive feature of the Abrams trial is not that Judge Clayton actively interrogated the defendants, but rather that his questions were framed in such a hostile, argumentative manner, and were so clearly designed to put the anarchists' behavior in a sinister light. The judge, by making damaging remarks about the defendants, and what he called their "puny, sickly, distorted views," helped make the case for the prosecution.[3]

More than once Judge Clayton implied, in the jury's presence, that Abrams, Steimer, Lipman, and Lachowsky had violated the Sedition Act. For example, when Weinberger asserted that their intent in printing and distributing the leaflets had been lawful, Clayton, noting the secrecy with which the anarchists had acted, interjected that when we "do things that we are not ashamed of, and we are not violating the law . . . we come out in the open, but when we do things questionable, that is the time when other methods are resorted to, and I am going to leave it to the jury to determine whether the intention is honest or not."[4] Again, when Abrams was explaining his view of United States intervention in Russia, the prosecutor objected, and the judge said that he had permitted the witness to continue "just to show that my idea was right . . . that he was trying to justify the violation of this law by repeating, in another form, what we have been hearing from the soap boxes—or we used to hear here from the soap box orators on the street corners—but that is what the law does not permit now."[5] And yet again, when Abrams, discussing his concept of revolution, commented that the rulers of the United States "have succeeded through trickery ways to get all of the wealth in their power," Clayton commented that "he would be properly arrested if he should get out on the street and make a talk similar to what he is making now."[6] The judge never let the jury forget what was at stake in the trial. "If we have got to meet anarchy," he said, "let us meet it right now."[7]

When Abrams was sworn in, and Weinberger began to ask about his early life in Russia, the prosecutor jumped to his feet to object. The defense attorney tried to explain that it was necessary to delve into Abrams' background in order to establish his intent in publishing the leaflets. For if "he was doing it as a proper form of criticism of a government, and not as an aid to Germany," Weinberger claimed, then he had not violated the Sedition Act.[8] Judge Clayton, however, upheld the prosecutor's objection. Furthermore, he charged that Weinberger was maintaining, improperly, that his clients' unlawful behavior was justifiable. According to Clayton, the defense was trying to show that "because these men were Anarchists, and actually thought and believed that they had a right to revolutionize and destroy the government, therefore they could not have been guilty of a wilful intent to violate the laws."[9] Weinberger protested that nothing was further from his mind: he was not claiming that a belief in anarchism justified breaking the law, but rather that a commitment to the Russian Revolution, not any desire to hinder the war effort, had motivated publication of the leaflets.

Although the judge misconstrued the defense attorney's argument, the question of intent was not nearly as obvious as Weinberger made out. The legal definition of "intent" refers not to what a particular individual wants to happen as the result of certain behavior, but to what a reasonable and prudent individual knows, or should know, will happen as the result of that behavior. Thus, a man or woman who sets fire to a building may "intend" only to burn it to the ground, not kill its inhabitants; yet the person who sets the fire can nevertheless be charged with murder, or attempted murder, for the deaths could have been foreseen. At the Abrams trial Assistant U.S. Attorneys John M. Ryan and S. L. Miller pointed out that "motive" and "intent" were two quite different things. So even if Weinberger could show that the defendants' "motive" had been a desire to support the Russian Revolution, the government could still maintain that their "intent" had been to interfere with the prosecution of the war, in the sense that they should have known that their leaflets could have had that effect.

Judge Clayton, having ruled that Weinberger could not inquire into Abrams' anarchist background, then announced that he would permit the witness to answer such questions—but that he, the judge, would ask them. He proceeded to do so, in an unfriendly, if not accusatory, manner. Had Abrams been taught anarchy in the school he had attended in Russia? Abrams answered that he had been taught Hebrew; "I was taught anarchy here in America." The judge continued, "You are not a citizen of the United States? . . . Never been so far as to have taken out your first papers? . . . You know you can not become a citizen because you are an Anarchist, don't you? . . . And you are an Anarchist?"[10] Clayton asked Abrams if he "was against the government of the United States and all other governments?" When the witness said that he opposed governments that rested on violence, the judge, impatient with such fine distinctions, snapped, "You are against the government? Yes or no."[11] Not once but twice Clayton actually asked, "Why don't you go back to Russia?" Harry Weinberger replied that Abrams and his friends would have been delighted to return to Russia to fight for the ideals of the Revolution. Still fuming, Clayton remarked, "Well, I wish these people were over there now, if I may be allowed to have a wish!"[12]

In responding to the judge's questions about his anarchist convictions, Abrams said, "Christ was against government. I can prove by the Bible that Jesus Christ himself was against government. He said no man shall be a judge of his neighbor." Judge Clayton could not allow such a remark to go unchallenged. Jesus, he intoned, had said "render unto Caesar that which is Caesar's," and that proved that He "was very much in favor of government. . . . Christ taught that you should obey your rulers, and Christ was not an anarchist." When Weinberger pointed out that Jesus had also said "blessed are the peacemakers," and had driven the money lenders out of the temple, the judge was virtually beside himself. "I think that is in the nature of a profanation," he bellowed. "I don't think you are authorized to say what Christ did." To Weinberger's further assertion that he had studied Christian belief, the judge replied curtly, "But you have studied it, I am afraid, without profit."[13]

Facing someone who was not only an alien and a Jew, but a man who earned his living as a bookbinder, Judge Clayton felt called on to preach the virtues of the agrarian life. He asked Abrams why, if he thought so much of the producing class, he remained in New York City, "instead of going out on the land of this country, the fertile land which you can get . . . The Government is giving away so much land and you can get the land—fertile soil—why don't you go out and really produce something yourself?" "I haven't got the knowledge how to produce. I can bind books," Abrams replied. But this did not satisfy the judge. "Do you think it is very difficult to learn how to plow? Couldn't you see a man hook a couple of horses to a plow, and couldn't you imagine in half an hour or an hour's demonstration that you could plow? . . . But you don't want to work, isn't that it?" "No, I want to work," Abrams answered. Clayton then added, "You don't want to really produce?" and even as the witness tried to explain that he worked eight hours a day, the judge defended his query. "I just asked him for my own satisfaction . . . to see what his philosophy is."[14]

When Abrams criticized capitalism and the inequality it fostered, the judge was moved to rebut his assertions. Accordingly, the trial began to resemble a verbal sparring bout with each side looking to score points, if not a knockdown. Abrams said he wanted to bring about a change from the present system "where it is impossible to live," to one "where everyone should work and get the full production of his labor" and "where every man is treated alike and nobody has a right to interfere with his private life." Judge Clayton had heard enough. He asked Abrams if he thought a man who owned land and property was necessarily a criminal. "Where did he get it?" Abrams asked the judge, who answered, "It doesn't make any difference, his possession . . . makes that individual a criminal?" Abrams said that John D. Rockefeller could not have earned all his money honestly. Rockefeller, the judge responded, "is not so bad as you think he is." By donating money for medical research, he went on, the millionaire had done a great deal of good. "Yes," Abrams shot back, "done a great deal in 1914 in Colorado, by burning up the tents of the workers." Seeking to end the exchange, Clayton said, "We are not going to try Rockefeller." For once, Abrams had the last word. "It is about time he should be on trial."[15]

When Harry Weinberger resumed the questioning of his own witness, Abrams testified that Lipman had written the English leaflet, and Schwartz the Yiddish leaflet, that he had himself set the type and printed 5,000 copies of each, and that Steimer and Lachowsky had distributed them. Abrams explained why he believed that Wilson, in sending troops to Soviet Russia after pledging not to, and in acting without Congressional authorization, had taken "a cowardly action, saying one thing and doing the other." The witness also recorded his view of German militarism. "I say it is absurd I should be called a pro-German, because in my heart I feel it is about the time the black spot of Europe should be wiped out." Weinberger asked if he would be willing to go to Russia to fight against Germany. "Any time," Abrams answered. "First chance. I wish I would be aviator—flyer."[16]

Weinberger then led Abrams through a line-by-line reading of both leaflets. The judge permitted this, after reminding Weinberger not to omit "the scurrilous words that are used, the epithets, taking it all together."[17] As Abrams was explaining the Yiddish leaflet, Clayton twice coaxed him into accepting the more incriminating translations. When Weinberger, relying on the official translation, read, "Mr. Wilson, and the rest of the gang; dogs of all colors!" Abrams said, "I object to the word 'gang' because in the original I did not have a gang. It is comrades in Hebrew. It is wrong translated." Clayton, ignoring the correction, demanded to know whether Abrams meant to refer to President Wilson "as a dog, one of the dogs, one of the gang."[18] Later Weinberger came to the crucial phrase "the least belief in the honesty of our government," crucial because the Sedition Act barred making contemptuous statements about the United States government. As we have seen, the accurate translation was "the least faith in the earnestness of the government." Clayton asked whether the leaflet specifically referred to the United States government. Abrams said he was referring "to every government . . . I mean the government in general, because I speak to workers in general." "You mean the government of the United States, do you?" the judge persisted. "All government." "Don't you mean the government of the United States?" "I included it also." ". . . did you mean by 'our government' to say the government of the United States, yes or no?" Wearily, Abrams said, "Yes, I did."[19]

Shortly after the judge extracted this admission, the flurry over Abrams' use of the phrase "our forefathers of the American Revolution" erupted, and soon after that the court adjourned for the day. The trial resumed, on Tuesday, October 22, with cross-examination. Assistant U. S. Attorneys Ryan and Miller, after trying to bait Abrams into admitting he believed in some "human" laws—and failing, since Abrams defined a "human" law not as one that was man-made, but as one that benefited humanity—sought to make him out a liar. Miller asked Abrams whether he was a truthful person and then confronted him with the fact of his having rented the East Harlem apartment under an assumed name. Then Miller brought up Abrams' possession of a forged draft card and asked under what name he had registered. Since Abrams was facing a separate indictment for possessing the card, Weinberger advised him not to answer the question but to claim the constitutional privilege against self-incrimination. Judge Clayton ruled that Abrams had to answer the question. When Weinberger again advised his client not to answer, Clayton shouted, "Sit down. . . . Not another word. Sit right down now and shut up your mouth. Shut up your mouth right now."[20] Weinberger continued to argue, and Clayton to admonish him angrily. Then Weinberger protested that the judge's remarks "are prejudicing me before the jury." Furious, Clayton told him that his remark constituted contempt of court and fined him ten dollars. Weinberger paid the clerk and assured Judge Clayton he had meant no offense. Accepting the apology, the judge said, "Give him back his money."[21]

Samuel Lipman followed Abrams to the stand on Tuesday afternoon. He had written "The Hypocrisy of the United States and Her Allies," he said, because President Wilson, after making statements that were sympathetic to Soviet Russia, had proceeded to send, "without announcing to the people, a military expedition to crush the Russian Revolution." Lipman explained, "My only intent to write this leaflet was to raise a protest against intervention in Russia by capitalistic nations."[22] Judge Clayton asked Lipman, as he had Abrams, if he thought he was justified in trying to "break up the Government of the United States?" Lipman replied that the leaflet "speaks about capitalism and not government. . . . I am a Socialist and believe in government." Lipman added, "I called for a protest, which, as I understand it, from my knowledge of the Constitution, the people of America had a right to protest."[23] Judge Clayton repeatedly tried to refute Lipman's argument that he had criticized only the President's acts rather than the government's. "Who was acting for the Government, if the President was not?" the judge asked. Lipman replied, "I thought it was the Congress and Senate that was supposed to represent the people of America." Clayton tried again. "The President is the Executive Head." Lipman shot back, "He is not the Kaiser."[24]

Hyman Lachowsky also testified on Tuesday afternoon. He admitted that he had printed the leaflets, but claimed their purpose was to call attention to military intervention in Soviet Russia. Judge Clayton, questioning the witness, reminded the jury whom they were judging. "Have you ever been naturalized in this country?" "No." "Never taken out any first papers, have you?" "Never." "Are you an anarchist?" "Yes, sir." "You could not be naturalized. Go on."[25] Gabriel Prober was then called as a witness. He explained the circumstances of his arrest on the night of August 23 at Abrams' apartment, where he had gone to wash the cuts and bruises he had received in the scuffle at the outdoor rally. Prober, a bookbinder who had known Abrams for two years, denied having had anything to do with the leaflets, and the prosecuting attorneys made only a halfhearted effort to prove any such connection. Hyman Rosansky did not testify in his own behalf. Although he was one of the defendants in the case and was represented by Weinberger, the others regarded him as a stool pigeon and cold-shouldered him throughout the trial.

At one point during the defense's presentation, Harry Weinberger asked the judge if he was claiming that the Sedition Act made it a crime for his clients to have voiced any criticism at all of the government. Clayton replied, "I stated that they could not criticize the government of the United States and obstruct its operation, as they were doing, and Congress, to meet that thing, passed this law."[26] The remark passed unnoticed, perhaps because in light of Clayton's conduct of the trial one more prejudicial assertion seemed unexceptional. The judge had assumed the role of prosecutor by sniping at the witnesses, by misstating their attorney's position, by insinuating that their failure to acquire citizenship could be held against them, by prodding them into accepting an unfavorable translation of the Yiddish leaflet, and by rebuking their lawyer when he advised them to exercise their constitutional privilege. Henry DeLamar Clayton's bilious reaction when Jacob Abrams mentioned "our forefathers" expressed not only the animosity of the native-born American for the immigrant, but the hostility of the countryside for the city, of the patriot for the "slacker," of the reformer for the radical, and of the patriarch for the rebel. In that sense, the courtroom proceedings revealed a clash of cultures, of rival visions of what the nation had been and was becoming. Nothing better illustrated this than the judge's response when Mollie Steimer strode briskly to the witness stand.

## "The Feminist Radical"

She was not quite twenty-one years old and looked even younger. Four feet nine inches tall, weighing about ninety pounds, Mollie Steimer was often taken for a teenager, and her round face, her short, curly black hair, and her habit of clenching her fists when she was angry strengthened the childlike impression. Harry Weinberger, who referred to her as "this little girl," may have thought she was younger than she actually was, but he surely recognized as well that emphasizing her youthfulness was likely to arouse sympathy for her. Friends described Steimer as a "little kiddie," or a child, "diminutive and quaint-looking, altogether Japanese in features and stature."[27] During the trial, the New York *Call* reported, Steimer wore a Russian silk tunic of "dark, modest red," and, like her comrades, a black band in memory of Jacob Schwartz.[28] Unlike them, however, she spoke English with only a trace of an accent. Those who met Mollie Steimer at the time remarked that she was "the incarnate spirit of youth," or, as Emma Goldman said, that she "looked stern in her youthful fervor."[29] On the day she took the witness stand, she surely had that same stern look in her eyes.

Mollie Steimer was the eldest of six children. Her parents lived in Elizabethport, New Jersey, where her father worked at a low-paying job for the Standard Oil Company. She never forgot his "thin and weary-looking appearance" and, especially, his exhaustion every evening. "How tired he usually comes home from work, and how much so when the day's work lasted fourteen hours! He would just have supper, glance at the newspaper and go to bed. Early in the morning, when all were yet asleep, father rose, took his little bundle and again went to the plant. In this manner of miserable existence the years rolled by. What did this hard laboring man get out of life? Nothing! Absolutely nothing (except suffering)."[30] When she testified at the trial, Steimer could have had no inkling of the twin tragedies that would, the following month, overtake her family. In little more than a week her father died suddenly, and her fourteen-year-old brother, Jack, succumbed to Spanish influenza. Remembering Jack, she had to fight back the tears "which came into my eyes as I thought of that lovable boy, so handsome, so eager to read and to learn, so kind to everybody."[31]

Joining the anarchist movement in January 1917, Steimer later attributed her radical convictions to a number of things: dissatisfaction with her family's poverty-stricken way of life, the bleak prospects that stretched before her in the shirtwaist shops, her reading of such books as Peter Kropotkin's *The Conquest of Bread,* August Bebel's *Women and Socialism,* and Sergei Stepniak's *Underground Russia,* her anger at United States intervention in the Mexican Revolution in 1914, and her opposition to World War I. Yet once, in writing to Emma Goldman, she emphasized another reason, more closely related to an awakening feminist consciousness, for attending anarchist gatherings. From about the age of seventeen, she related, she had attended Goldman's meetings: "I was terribly interested in Birth Control. Not for myself, but for my mother who had 6 children which I considered the greatest misfortune that could befall our family and sought help from such as you and Marguerite [Sanger] to save our house from more babies."[32] As an anarchist, Steimer was distinguished by her uncompromising spirit. Even among men and women who were known, as a group, for their implacable, unyielding ways, she gained a reputation for obstinacy and inflexibility. Whatever others may have thought, Steimer never regarded herself as contumacious. "Since I first joined the Fr[eedom] Group, I refused to be a follower," she stated matter-of-factly. "I tried to be myself."[33]

Steimer's courtroom demeanor served notice that, even when standing trial, she would continue to be herself. When the judge entered the chamber, for example, and the bailiff ordered everyone to rise, Steimer kept her seat. One newsman reported, half-wonderingly, half-admiringly, "The marshals in charge of the prisoners are totally at a loss what to do about Mollie when the judge comes in. She resolutely refuses to rise. They could lift her up with one of their little fingers, but content themselves with looking in bewilderment at her silk back and her curly hair and holding their breath till everybody sits down again."[34] Taking the witness stand, she brushed aside the usual formalities. She "refused to take the oath and it was ruled that her testimony should go into the record for what it was worth."[35] Harry Weinberger made the mistake, in asking his first question, of calling her by her first name, a liberty he had not taken in addressing the male defendants. "Mollie, where were you born?" When there was no reply, he rephrased the question. "Miss Steimer, where were you born?" Then he got an answer: "In Russia."[36]

Steimer was considerably less willing than her codefendants to allow Weinberger to lead her through his direct examination. While they answered all his questions about the printing and distribution of the leaflets, she would talk only about her own role, and then only circumspectly. When she admitted distributing the leaflets, Weinberger asked, "Where did you give them out?" "In various places," she replied. When he repeated the question, she admonished him, saying, "I don't think it necessary to mention the places." He insisted. "Now, mention just one or two of those places. That is what I want," and her answer, again, "I don't see the necessity of it." "You leave the necessity to me," Weinberger said, understandably exasperated. "I don't think it necessary to do that," she replied firmly. Henry DeLamar Clayton, finally thinking he had found a common ground with Harry Weinberger, made a rare, fraternal comment: "Well, it is the old adage, maybe, Brother Weinberger, 'Convince a woman against her will, she is of the same opinion still.' " Ignoring the gibe, Steimer calmly volunteered the information that she had distributed the leaflets "in places where the most workers were working. I have been trying to reach masses of people, and it does not matter where or in what places I did that."[37]

Steimer, of course, cooperated fully with Weinberger when it came to eliciting her "intent," that is to say, her reason for distributing the leaflets. Her purpose, she said, was "to call the attention of the workers to the fact that international capitalism seeks to crush the Russian Revolution, that the Allies were acting just as tyrannic, just as cruel as the Germans, by invading a neutral country and assailing those workers who were defending the revolutionary freedom." Disclaiming any sympathy for Germany, for militarism anywhere was always an evil, she insisted that she had only wanted to point out the hypocrisy of the United States government which said it supported the right of national self-determination and yet "sought to crush the Russian Revolution and abolish the present government that the Russian workers established." Since the Bolsheviks represented the producing classes, she argued, "I do uphold the Bolshevik movement."[38] With that Weinberger ended his direct examination.

Miller began his cross-examination by asking Steimer if she was an anarchist. Unwilling to provide the simple "yes" or "no" the prosecutor was looking for, she insisted on explaining what she meant by anarchism. Judge Clayton ruled that she was entitled to offer such an explanation. So Steimer stated, "By anarchism, I understand a new social order, where no group of people shall be in power, or no group of people shall be governed by another group of people. Individual freedom shall prevail in the full sense of the word. Private ownership shall be abolished. Every person shall have an equal opportunity to develop himself well, both mentally and physically. We shall not have to struggle for our daily existence, as we do now. No one shall live on the product of others. Every person shall produce as much as he can, and enjoy as much as he needs—receive according to his needs. Instead of striving to get money, we shall strive towards education, towards knowledge." She added that "the workers of Russia are trying to establish such a system." "They are only trying to?" Miller asked. "Yes," the witness said, "if you should not crush them they would succeed."[39]

Steimer similarly stood her ground when Miller badgered her about her concept of law. The prosecutor asked if she believed in laws, only to have her reply, "Explain to me first what you mean by law." Judge Clayton then decided to take a hand in the proceedings. Did she believe in the law under which she had been indicted? "No, I don't believe in such laws." "And you are trying to defeat that law?" "I am." Miller tried again, with the same result: "Do you believe in any laws?" "Please [tell] me what do you mean by law." "Will you answer the question?" "I will not, unless I know exactly what you mean by your question." When, answering another of the judge's queries, Steimer granted "that the people ought not to kill each other," Clayton asked whether that did not justify passing a law against murder. Steimer, following Kropotkin, insisted that in a just society, where everyone "should be well developed mentally" and "able to enjoy life," crime would vanish. "We would not need any laws to punish, and we would not need any courts." Miller asked, "But at the present time we need some laws?" "Because the system is rotten," she answered.[40]

After listening to Steimer's testimony for a few minutes, Judge Clayton began to argue with her, not about the leaflets whose distribution had led to her arrest, nor even about intervention in Soviet Russia, but about marriage and free love. He asked whether she believed in any of the laws designed to protect public morality. "I do not think the laws which are in existence today do protect morality," she replied. What of the laws regarding marriage, the judge asked. Steimer said that women usually got married for economic reasons, "not because of love," and stayed married for the wrong reasons. "What is the use of a law combining them, when their hearts are not combined any more?" she asked. The judge said, "And when the love grows cold, you think they ought to end the marriage relation; that is your idea?" The witness responded icily, "Well, I do not think that this has anything to do with this trial." The judge agreed, but a few minutes later was again asking Steimer whether she believed in polygamy, or in polyandry, or in free love. Thereupon, Steimer turned the tables on Clayton, and began asking the questions. Noting that laws against infidelity were notorious failures, she continued, "May I ask you . . . do not thousands and thousands of such cases prevail anyhow? You have the law." "People may violate vows," the judge conceded. "They do sometimes, and society is trying to protect itself." "It does not succeed," Steimer commented.[41]

Judge Clayton told Steimer that her answers to these questions would "not affect your guilt or innocence in this case," but defended his asking them on the irrelevant grounds that a belief in polygamy was one of the bases for denying citizenship to an alien. Since Steimer had already admitted to being an anarchist, she was legally subject to deportation, and was surely not going to be applying for citizenship. More likely, Clayton's questions were intended to put the witness, or at least her views, in a ludicrous light. Steimer, however, never wavered. "I believe that two people should combine, only when they love each other, honestly and truly, and not because of any other circumstances."[42] Her unwillingness to exhibit the least deference—indeed, her continued defiance—obviously offended the Alabama patriarch. Later in the trial, when she tried to address the courtroom spectators directly, Clayton barked, "You turn around and address the Court. This is one time, Mollie, when you are brought in touch with a knowledge that there is some authority, even over an anarchistic woman."[43]

His curiosity as to Steimer's view of conjugal bliss and the nuptial bond satisfied, the judge permitted the prosecution and defense to resume their sparring over the issue of intent. When Steimer said she favored a general strike to block intervention in Russia, Miller asked, "Did you include the workers in the ammunition factories in your general word 'workers' here?" "Yes," she replied.[44] Weinberger immediately tried to repair the damage. He again asked Steimer whether the purpose of the general strike "was to prevent intervention in Russia" rather than "to interfere in the war against Germany." "The war between Germany and the United States does not concern me," she answered, "because I wish to see militarism throughout the entire world crushed by the workers."[45] Miller returned to the attack, centering on the legal distinction between intent and motive. "If all of these munition workers stopped making munitions, do you think that would hinder the United States in the war with Germany?" All Steimer could say, lamely but truthfully, was, "It did not matter to me."[46]

Once, when Steimer refused to give as specific an answer as District Attorney Miller thought she should, he asked the judge to find her in contempt. Clayton responded, "If I ordered her to jail, that would stop the trial. What good would that do? You will just have to do the best you can, Brother Miller."[47] During the entire trial it was only when a woman was testifying—and being uncooperative!—that Judge Clayton addressed the prosecuting and defense attorneys as "Brother," leading one to suspect that he used the term not merely in its familiar courtroom sense but androcentrically, as if to suggest that menfolk shared a common outlook, which, in the very nature of things, was beyond any woman's comprehension. Although Steimer was arrested, indicted, and tried for expressing views deriving from her anarchism, not her feminism, the fact that she was a woman had a great deal to do with the kind of anarchist she became, with her behavior in the courtroom, and with the response she elicited from the judge.

There was, therefore, a good reason for the New York *Tribune* to term her "the young feminist radical," and an even better reason for Emma Goldman, learning, in prison, of the courtroom proceedings, to write, "Mollie's stand is the most inspiring event in my public career. Young boys have made such a stand before . . . But not one girl. . . . So it was left to a child of 18, a Russian Jewess, to redeem our sex & a great principle at that. My work has not been in vain. . . . I am supremely happy to know that the ideals which have meant life itself to me, have now found a new champion, one so brave and clear & consistent."[48]

## The Verdict

In her testimony on Tuesday afternoon, Mollie Steimer echoed her comrades' assertion that the police had beaten Lipman, Lachowsky, and Schwartz on the night of the arrests. In rebuttal, the prosecution recalled two members of the Bomb Squad, Henry L. Barth and Edward J. Meagher. Each detective again denied that he had seen or heard anything improper, and a frustrated Weinberger decided it would be pointless to prolong the cross-examination. He then formally moved for dismissal of the indictments on the grounds that the Sedition Act was unconstitutional, that it was "too indefinite, and, therefore, does not advise the people as to exactly what is permitted," and that "there is absolutely no evidence of a conspiracy or violation" of the law.[49] The judge quickly denied the motions. The attorney also made a special plea on behalf of Gabriel Prober, asking that the jury be directed to acquit him, a plea that was similarly unsuccessful and may only have reflected Weinberger's awareness that the other defendants' fate had already been settled.

Such a realization could explain the kind of summation Weinberger delivered to the jury on Wednesday morning. The speech was not included in the trial record, but was later printed in a pamphlet issued in the defendants' behalf. Lasting more than two hours, the summation was devoted to a defense of free speech and a celebration of nonconformity. Persecution for the expression of opinion, of anyone, anywhere, at any time, had always proven harmful, Weinberger claimed. He proceeded to draw analogies between his clients and famous figures who had been punished for their beliefs but vindicated by history: Moses (who "objected to the third degree being applied to some of his people"), Socrates, Galileo, Spinoza, and the abolitionists John Brown and William Lloyd Garrison. Above all, there was the example of Jesus, who "preached against those in control of the government and pointed out their evils. Then we see him arrested, tried, tried because his ideals and ideas were different from those in power, and we find the self-same kind of a Court as this, and the self-same kind of a District Attorney, working for a conviction and getting it." Judge Clayton, as devout a Southerner as he was a Christian, may have found the comparisons to John Brown and to Jesus equally offensive.

Eventually Weinberger came to what he considered the central issue in the trial. Contrary to what the Sisson Documents purported to show, he stated, the Bolsheviks were not German agents but had been prepared to cooperate with the Allies. Therefore, "these defendants, in giving out these leaflets, were standing with the Bolsheviki for liberty, and not for militarism." Although Raymond Robins and Albert Rhys Williams had not been permitted to testify, he continued, the jury knew that the United States, without having declared war on Russia, had sent troops to Vladivostok. The defendants, Weinberger insisted, "have the right to question and protest against an army being sent to Russia, to fight the Bolsheviki. They had the right, not because they are American citizens, because they are not, but because they are here and free speech is guaranteed to all citizens and noncitizens." The attorney, quoting Woodrow Wilson's comment that "a man that is afraid of the truth is afraid of life," asked why people should be so pitilessly pursued merely for questioning the administration's policy.

Weinberger suggested an answer, however unedifying, to his own question. He speculated that the President was probably not even aware of the indictments. The problem was that "there are always these underlings, these intelligence bureaus, these men with a little power who always abuse that power; these little doggies sent out on the scent of what they think may be a crime, and feel that they must deliver the goods." So the Bomb Squad had arrested the anarchists, and when they refused to tell where the leaflets had been printed, brutal officials had put the men "and this little girl" through the third degree. The detectives' denials could not be taken seriously, for "you know, I know, the Court knows, the District Attorneys know, and the Intelligence Bureau knows that they lied." On the other hand, the defendants, no ordinary criminals, had told the truth, not only about their radical beliefs, but also about their treatment at headquarters and about their activities. "These defendants tell you they did do what they are charged with. That is, they did do the act but they deny that the act was a violation of law. They say under the right of free speech they had a right to say these things."

Weinberger then launched into a defense of anarchism. As envisioned by its leading theorists, he said, it would create a cooperative, noncoercive society. "You and I may not think that this is possible," Weinberger conceded, but the defendants were entitled to their dream, a dream, after all, which had inspired some of the world's greatest thinkers. Abrams and the others, convinced that the dream was on the verge of coming true in Soviet Russia, had naturally protested against Allied military intervention and had called on the workers to support their protest. Weinberger reminded the jury that the postscript to the English leaflet proclaimed that "we hate and despise German militarism." Far from being pro-German, the defendants were "liberty-loving Russians." Their argument could not be answered by throwing them in jail. "You may close their mouths but for every . . . idealist that goes to jail, ten thousand more step forward." Whatever else one thought of them, the defendants only wished to help Russia by bringing to the American people their views of "what they thought was a wrongful act by the President of the United States, without authority of Congress, sending an army to invade a nation we were at peace with, calling to the American public to protest."[50]

Weinberger's speech passed over the narrow, technical issue of intent under the Sedition Act. Hoping against hope that he could strike a small spark of sympathy for the young, idealistic radicals, he emphasized instead the broad themes of free speech and toleration. By contrast, S. Lawrence Miller's summation for the prosecution, delivered on Wednesday afternoon, was briefer, terser, and more legalistic than Weinberger's. According to one report, Miller's speech, which is not included in the trial transcript either, "laid special stress on the phase of the Espionage law which forbids any act which would tend to interfere with the production of things necessary for the prosecution of the war, and claimed that the defendants in urging a general strike as a protest against Russian intervention were attempting to block production of war materiel."[51] Dousing whatever sympathetic sentiments Weinberger may have kindled, Miller adroitly fanned the flames of indignation against the defendants. Stressing that they were anarchists, the District Attorney "declared they had defied the laws of the United States and had advised others to do likewise."[52]

Following Miller's summation, Judge Clayton gave his charge to the jury. He began, fairly enough, by reading the relevant sections of the Sedition Act of May 1918 and by summarizing the four counts of the indictment. He explained that his refusal to dismiss the indictments, his overruling of defense motions, and his unwillingness to admit certain evidence should not be held against the defendants. Moreover, any "reference or comment or expression of opinion which the Court may have made or hereafter may make in respect to the evidence . . . or the contentions of the respective parties, is not evidence nor to be understood as expressing my own opinion or personal belief in either the guilt or innocence of the defendants." The defendants, added the judge, were to be presumed innocent until proven guilty beyond a reasonable, that is to say, a substantial, doubt. "It is not a mere vague conjecture, or a flimsy, fanciful, fictitious doubt which you could raise perhaps about anything or everything." It was up to the jury to decide how much weight to give to the testimony, based on "the appearance of the witnesses on the stand, their candor or lack of candor, their feelings or bias, if any; their interest in the result of the trial, if they have any interest; their means of information, and the reasonableness of what they have said."[53]

The judge then proceeded to define the terms "willful," "conspiracy," and "intent" for the jury's benefit. To do something willfully meant, in legal parlance, to do it purposely or intentionally, he said, rather than accidentally or inadvertently. In passing the Sedition Act, Congress had not intended to hold an individual criminally liable for thoughtless, unpremeditated words "that, upon second thought, he perhaps would agree he should not have said."[54] A conspiracy was an agreement by two or more persons to do something unlawful, Clayton added. Once a conspiracy existed, each participant could be held responsible for the acts of all. Moreover, since conspiracies were by nature secret, it was "not necessary to prove by direct evidence that the defendants came together and agreed, combined or confederated to commit the crime." All that the law required was evidence from which one could "reasonably infer that the defendants had a common object."

Conceding that it was perhaps "improper" of him to say, the judge nonetheless said that "it may be" that some defendants wrote the leaflets, others printed them, and others distributed them. Yet if they had acted "in pursuance of the common purpose of the conspiracy to violate this law, the act of one of the conspirators is the act of all."[55]

The issue of intent was, of course, pivotal. The judge stated, "The rule is that the person charged with any crime or offense is presumed to intend the natural and probable consequences of what he knowingly does." So if the defendants had willfully conspired to write, print, or distribute certain leaflets which urged the curtailment of production of ordnance and munitions, "with intent by such curtailment to cripple and hinder the United States . . . this would constitute criminal intention, notwithstanding you may also find that the motives of the defendants were to serve a certain faction in Russia in so doing, and the defendants were not conscious of doing anything [un]lawful, because they did not know the law." Drawing a distinction between motive and intent, the judge said, "A motive is that which leads a person to do a certain act. The intention is a design or plan or purpose to use a particular means to effect a certain definite result." If he were himself starving, and stole a loaf of bread from a bakery, his motive would be to appease his hunger but "my intention is to steal, to violate the law, within the meaning of the law."[56]

Instructing the jury further on the meaning of intent, Judge Clayton let his thumb rest rather heavily on the scales of justice. He invited the jurors to disregard the defendants' own version of their intent, first, by saying that "you will bear in mind that they are defendants in this case and, necessarily, vitally interested in the result of your verdict"; then by encouraging the jurors to use their "good, common, out-of-doors sense," the kind of sense "that men had before Law books were written," in assessing intent; and finally by returning to the consciousness-of-guilt argument he had made while the trial was in progress. "It is perhaps not amiss for me to say," he remarked, that those who are "actuated by pure and lawful motives as a rule act in the open daylight. People who have circulars to distribute, and they intend no wrong, go up and down the streets circulating them. So it is proper for you to consider how these leaflets were printed and how they were circulated, as bearing upon the question of the intent that animated these defendants."[57] Even before hearing these instructions, the jury might well have found the defendants' intent criminal within the meaning of the law. After hearing the judge out, no other verdict was possible.

When he had finished, the judge announced that Harry Weinberger had submitted a list of thirty-five charges on which he wanted the jury to be instructed. Clayton read each one, accepting some, rejecting others, and, when necessary, explaining his rationale. Even when granting one of Weinberger's points, the judge somehow found an opportunity to state a view that could only be construed as hostile to the defense. For example, Weinberger asked the judge to tell the jury that an indictment was not itself evidence of guilt. Clayton agreed, since he had already given a similar instruction, but then noted that "the defendants are not justified in violating the Act of Congress because of any peculiar belief that they have of government or the wrongfulness of any law." Congress, he added, "was within its constitutional authority in passing this Espionage Law, and although the defendants may think that law wrong, they can not violate that law with impunity and set up their opinions in justification of their violation of the law."[58]

The judge rejected many of the points Weinberger wanted him to make. Two were especially crucial, the first of which, predictably enough, related to the issue of intent. Weinberger asked the judge to inform the jury that the government had offered no proof that the defendants "had any desire to help Germany in this war," or that they "intended to hinder the United States in any way whatsoever in its war against Germany," but that, to the contrary, they had all said "that their intention was only to protest against intervention in Russia." Refusing this request, the judge stated that Weinberger's version of events "does not embrace a full, fair and correct statement of what the evidence in the case is." He told the jury, "It is true that the defendants testified that they had no desire to help Germany in this war, but you are not bound to believe what they said." Were he to give such a charge, he remarked, "it would be tantamount, in my opinion, to taking this case away from the jury."[59]

Judge Clayton's rejection of a second, seemingly unobjectionable point raised by the defense attorney is even more revealing. Weinberger asked the judge to tell the jury that if it had obtained any impression of the judge's opinion as to the defendants' guilt or innocence, "that Your Honor, as a matter of fact, has no such opinion and that the jury should not speculate as to what it might be, but should decide for itself on the evidence and the law." A reasonable enough request, it would seem, but one that Judge Clayton found unacceptable. He explained, "The vice of that charge is contained in these words: 'that Your Honor, as a matter of fact, has no such opinion.' Now, that is going a little too far . . . I have not formed or intended to express any opinion on the guilt or innocence of these people in this case which should in any wise bias your verdict. It would perhaps be unfair to the defendants were I to express an opinion, either as to their guilt or innocence." Having gratuitously announced that if he were to give his honest opinion of the defendants he would be prejudicing their case, the judge blandly instructed the jury to reach a verdict solely on the basis of the evidence, and, in deliberating, "do not imagine that I have an opinion at all on that subject, one way or the other."[60] This, more or less, is all that Weinberger had wanted.

The judge completed his reading of Weinberger's proposals at five o'clock on Wednesday afternoon. The jury retired at 5:12. While it was out, the courtroom was cleared of spectators, many of whom were supporters of the defendants, or, as *The New York Times* described them, "Bolshevist agitators, anarchists, and other radicals."[61] When the jury returned at 6:18, many spectators were denied readmission, but not those, according to the New York *Call,* who were the "friends of the district attorney."[62] When Weinberger protested, Judge Clayton ordered the marshal to admit "such people as you think are proper." But many of the anarchists' friends were still barred and, according to Weinberger, were handled "with rudeness and brutality." The officers, he later wrote, "man-handled the women and young girls and punched many of the men."[63]

Weinberger continued to protest, arguing that the exclusion in effect deprived his clients of the right to a public trial. Furious at the allegation, the judge threatened him with a reprimand or worse. "Behave yourself like a lawyer. You know that you have offended against propriety, and it is an insult to this Court for you to undertake to make the impression that anything has been done here improperly, sir."[64] When the hubbub died down, the foreman of the jury announced the verdict: Gabriel Prober had been found not guilty on any count, and the others had been found guilty on all four counts of the indictment. After polling the jury, Clayton thanked its members. "I feel that the defendants have had a fair trial at your hands," he commented. "I approve of your verdict."[65] The judge discharged the jury and scheduled sentencing for ten-thirty on Friday morning.

"The defendants received the news of their convictions in a mood almost enthusiastically gay," one reporter observed. ". . . They smiled and laughed and exchanged 'congratulatory' handshakes before being taken back to the Tombs."[66] Another account, using virtually identical language, said that the defendants heard the verdict "in a mood almost fantastically gay."[67] The smiles, the laughter, the handshakes were, almost certainly, an attempt by the anarchists to buoy their own spirits and their friends', and to demonstrate their contempt for legal proceedings that they thought farcical. Perhaps, too, their bravado was a way of denying what they feared the future held, for in thirty-six hours they would face sentencing at the hands of a judge from whom they had little reason to expect mercy. Their mood, in truth, was anything but gay. A telegram to Jacob Abrams from his sister, Manya, and her husband, Joseph Spivak, struck a more somber and, under the circumstances, a more convincing note: "Have our sympathy and admiration at the courageous stand you and your codefendants took at the trial of freedom."[68]

## The Sentencing

Henry DeLamar Clayton, Jr., did not regard himself as a vindictive man. In the month before the Abrams trial, he often complained that it fell to his "unpleasant lot" to have to imprison guilty individuals. "It does not give me much pleasure to send the poor devils who are convicted to the penitentiary," he sighed, "but it is the law I pronounce in such cases."[69] On Friday, October 25, however, when Jacob Abrams and the others stood before him for sentencing, entirely unrepentant, and when Assistant U. S. Attorney Ryan urged the maximum penalty to protect the law-abiding citizens of the Southern District of New York from further exposure to seditious matter, the judge was not inclined to be forgiving. On the contrary, he finally felt free to vent his anger and hostility, emotions which, in his own mind at least, he had successfully kept concealed from the jury while the trial was in progress.

Three of the defendants, Abrams, Lipman, and Steimer, attempted to make statements before sentence was handed down, not to ask for mercy, but rather to explain why they believed the court lacked the moral authority to pass sentence. Clayton cut them off impatiently. Then, to Abrams' assertion that "if it is really a crime to stand up for the people you love, if it is a crime to believe in ideals . . . I am proud to be a criminal," Clayton responded, "I am glad you got that out of your system, very glad." The judge added that it was permissible to criticize the government, but not to call for strikes by munitions workers and thereby "render our soldiers, now fighting in France, helpless for the lack of powder and bullets." The right of free speech, he continued, did not give people a right "to slander and libel their government—to slander and libel those in authority" in order to "cripple the government in its operations," to bring public officials into disrepute, and to "create a condition where the government's activities will be wholly thwarted."[70]

Samuel Lipman was the next to step forward. "I do not care for the punishment that you impose upon us," he said. "That makes my labor a little bit easier," the judge replied. Lipman added that Jacob Schwartz had given his life for the truth, and so he would gladly sacrifice a portion of his own life, but he wanted the record to show that the trial was one of "Capitalism against Labor." Responding that there wasn't "a word of truth in that," that it was "a piece of slander," Clayton snapped, "Now, go ahead and tell another lie." Lipman said he did not care how severe his sentence was. Clayton said, "And that renders my duty in that regard less painful." Lipman remarked angrily that "a Judge of a free country that fights for wide world democracy, is going to impose a sentence upon us for telling the truth as we see it." No less angrily, Clayton told the prisoner, "You understand thoroughly the maliciousness of anarchy, but you do not understand democracy." Lipman vainly protested that he was a socialist, not an anarchist, but his words made no impression on the judge. "You talk like an anarchist, or worse, if possible." Undeterred, Lipman concluded by saying that the more laws the government passed to suppress speech, and the more critics it jailed, "the nearer will be the end of poverty, misery and starvation, autocracy, despotism and tyranny." Judge Clayton said, "You want to be martyrs. You are not going to be, but you are going to be punished, and justly punished. Now, Mollie, what have you to say."[71]

"I do not believe in any authorities," she began, and, after Judge Clayton ordered her to face him, not the audience, Steimer continued, "Though you have sent military troops to Russia to crush the Russian Revolution, though you may succeed in slaughtering hundreds of thousands of revolutionists, you will by no means succeed in subduing the revolutionary spirit. On the contrary, the thought of truth and life [in] every heart and mind of the workers is always present, and the sooner the social—the international social revolution [is] bound to come." With respect to the charges in the indictment, she added, "I am responsible for my deeds, and ready to stand the consequences, no matter what they be." In what was surely intended as a mocking comment, Clayton told Steimer that he wished to commend her for "having the merit of brevity, and Shakespeare said that brevity is the soul of wit."[72]

Then Harry Weinberger made some remarks on his clients' behalf that might better have been left unsaid. They did not wish to request any special consideration, he said, but only to affirm that their views, whether they were right or wrong, "whether they violated the Espionage Act or not," reflected their honest convictions. Publishing the two leaflets, he went on, certainly served no selfish purpose. Weinberger conceded that the defendants "may have violated the Espionage Law, as the jury found, and the Court so directed, but at least they stood up for what they believed on behalf of Russia . . ." Unlike others, who were out to make a financial killing from the war by defrauding the government, the convicted radicals had "stood for their ideals as they saw them, even though they may have violated the law by doing it." While this did not constitute an actual confession of guilt, it went a lot further than was necessary. It is difficult to imagine what Weinberger hoped to gain. If he was hoping to curry favor with the judge, his hopes were misplaced.[73]

Before imposing sentence, Judge Clayton subjected Weinberger and the anarchists to a tirade lasting nearly two hours. No longer bound by the canons of judicial propriety, since the jury had already rendered its verdict, he could say exactly what he thought. He reiterated what he had been saying throughout the trial, but where he had formerly made his points by intimation, insinuation, and innuendo, he now made them a good deal more directly. Recapitulating the testimony that stood out most sharply in his mind, the judge talked about a wide range of subjects—Germany and Russia, free speech and sedition, anarchism and morality, capitalism and Christianity, Americanism and citizenship—all with a view toward proving, once and for all, that "you never can get the American idea into the head of an anarchist . . ."[74]

It was a surrealistic world into which Judge Clayton led his listeners, a world inhabited by diabolical enemies. Germany's "repeated hostile, unjustifiable and cruel acts" had thrust war on the United States, the judge said, and all loyal Americans realized that "the insidious and despicable work" carried on by German propagandists actually extended to "planning to get up a Bolshevik Revolution in this country." Proceeding with "devilish ingenuity," German agents had fomented strikes in munition plants, planned the destruction of railroad bridges, and plotted to obstruct the government. They had even acquired control of a few newspapers, the better to cause trouble, agitate the populace, and spread "their covert German propaganda stuff." But Americans had finally awakened to the danger, and Congress had passed the Espionage Act, and later the Sedition Act, the authority for which derived simply from the "inherent right of self-defense." Such laws were vital, Clayton said, to thwart the "devilish and artful German Kaiser and his military satraps."[75]

Like the Kaiser's minions, Clayton continued, Abrams and the others had done their best to cover their tracks. They did not make their plans openly, in broad daylight, but rather made them "in a little hid out secret meeting in the night time. The wicked seek the cover of the darkness. The righteous stand in God's sunlight, or in the blazing glare of electricity." The secrecy with which the anarchists had acted betrayed their sinister purposes. "Do law abiding citizens print their utterances in that way?" the judge asked rhetorically. "Do they seek to hide them?" The "surreptitious manner" in which the leaflets were distributed—from rooftops, early in morning, when they could not be observed—further demonstrated their evil intent. "The criminal hides out and is secretive in his methods. The law abiding citizen . . . is open and has nothing to conceal."[76]

The judge proceeded to defend the trial, which, he said, was as fair as any he had witnessed in forty years. He had taken great pains to ensure the selection of an impartial jury, and to give the defense the broadest discretion in presenting its case. Clayton noted that he had allowed Weinberger to proceed, even when "he likened the nefarious work of this set of criminals" to the achievements of great Americans, and "then, to cap the climax, likened their conduct to the conduct of Jesus Christ himself." The claim that Jesus was an anarchist still rankled. "Now, did you ever hear of such rot, and yet I sat here patiently and heard it ad nauseam, because I did not want to say anything that would influence the jury." Again quoting Jesus' admonition to "render unto Caesar," the judge commented, "What does that mean? Obedience to the laws, respect of the property rights, respect of the individual rights, respect of orderly government and decency in your conduct." For Weinberger to have said what he did was a "profanation." "Oh, that these people with their half-baked ideas would submit to some good instruction," he mused.[77]

Such instruction, the judge ventured, was no less needed in economics than in theology. The witnesses, he said, constantly talked about capitalism, "and as I can get it from their definition, any man who is out of jail and has got on a decent suit of clothes, and got one dollar and twenty-five cents in his pocket above his indebtedness, he is a capitalist, provided he has got a good character. Capitalism, Capitalism, Capitalism, a crime! Great goodness!" It was capitalism that gave people "a full and fair chance in the race of life," Clayton observed, and who should know that better than Jews? "Talk about your old Jerusalem! I don't blame our good, free American Jewish citizens for not wanting to go back to Jerusalem. They have got a better thing in old New York." It used to be said that "the Irish had all of the offices and the Jews had the money," but now, Clayton observed, Jews "actually have taken some of the offices away from the Irish." Living in a land of opportunity, the defendants had never thought of doing productive work themselves. "Not one of them ever has produced one potato. They never produced anything, but to the extent of their full ability they raised all the hell they could." He recalled asking why Abrams did not "go out and produce something and get some good honest work instead of raising the devil around here in New York?" only to discover "they don't want to work."[78]

The judge also recalled another incident distinctly. Although the anarchists were aliens, he said, they had acted as if the United States were their country, theirs, indeed, to run as they saw fit. "One of them on the stand said our forefathers did so and so. I said, 'What? You were born in Russia and came here four or five years [ago] and not a citizen, and an anarchist, and never can become a citizen.' Our forefathers, the signers of the Declaration of Independence and the Constitution! Why, just look at it." The defendants, in the judge's view, had no grasp of American government or understanding of the nation's institutions. Although well-read and articulate, they had a tendency to quote snippets from respected authors, taking the words out of context to justify their fallacious positions. In their desire to abolish all forms of authority, including the courts and the police, they would force people "to live in a world of outlaws."[79]

Then the judge turned, at last, to the crime of which the anarchists had been found guilty. "Here are people who deliberately set to bring about, for instance, among other things, a strike in our munitions plants," he said, and he began to read excerpts from the two leaflets, with frequent caustic comments. Just the title, "The Hypocrisy of the United States and Her Allies," was enough to make him seethe. "When everybody is trying to do his part for the success of the cause for which our boys are fighting and dying on Flanders field," he commented, the leaflet "was an effort to throw a monkey-wrench into the machinery of the United States." As he continued to read the leaflets' condemnation of Woodrow Wilson's Russian policy, Clayton offered arguments to refute those made by Abrams and "that bunch of choice criminals." Freedom of speech, the judge concluded, meant the right to express "a just and fair criticism, not to break up the operations of the government." Freedom implied restraint, liberty a respect for the rights of others. Continuing to search, even as he spoke, for the crucial sentence—"Workers, our reply to the barbaric intervention has to be a general strike"—the judge finally located it and said triumphantly,

"That is what they were indicted for, and the Court and jury heard all the evidence and found them guilty."[80]

The time had come for Judge Clayton to ask for the U.S. Attorney's recommendation with respect to sentencing. Two considerations to bear in mind, the judge said, were the deterrent effect of "the public example to be made by punishment" and "the reformation, if possible, of the defendants, the ones punished." John M. Ryan requested prison sentences of twenty years, the maximum the law allowed, for Abrams, Lipman, Lachowsky, and Steimer. They had planned to distribute their leaflets at monster rallies, he reminded the judge, and he conjured up the fearful image of "ten thousand such people as these spreading this literature in the Southern District of New York. I ask your Honor to protect the Southern District of New York by imposing the maximum sentence, that that shall not occur again."[81]

Ryan asked for leniency, however, in the case of Hyman Rosansky, whose confession had led the authorities to the others. Without his help, Ryan explained, the police could not have apprehended the anarchists so quickly, "and before the effect of the circulars reached the workers in the munition factories." Ostracized by his former friends, Rosansky now lived "in fear of bodily harm." His wife, impoverished, and responsible for three small children, was "in a pitiable condition." She had admitted that Rosansky "is ignorant and easily led," an opinion the District Attorney evidently shared. Taking into account the mitigating circumstances, Judge Clayton fined Rosansky $1,000 and sentenced him to a term of three years in the penitentiary.[82]

The judge then sentenced Jacob Abrams, Samuel Lipman, and Hyman Lachowsky to twenty years in the federal penitentiary on each of the four counts of the indictment, the sentences to run concurrently, and to fines of $1,000. Abrams, making an exaggerated bow in the judge's direction, said, "Thank you." Lipman commented, "I did not expect anything better," to which the judge replied, "I do not think you deserve anything less." Lachowsky said, "I expected it," and the judge responded, "I am glad you expected it—glad to know that, at least, because you are not disappointed." In a final gesture of condescending chivalry, Clayton sentenced Mollie Steimer, who appeared in court with a garland of roses, to serve fifteen years in the Missouri State Penitentiary and fined her only $500. The transcript does not record that she made any comment at all.[83]

And so, after two weeks, the trial came to a close. Harry Weinberger announced that he had prepared an appeal to the United States Supreme Court. John M. Ryan asked the judge to have the trial record sent to the immigration authorities in Washington with a view, eventually, toward deporting the convicted anarchists. Henry DeLamar Clayton declared he would rule on the question of bail on Saturday morning. As the spectators were filing out of the courtroom, the police arrested Henry Golobow, a friend of Abrams and a fellow member of the Bookbinders' Union. Golobow was asked for his draft registration card, but when he offered to produce it, was nevertheless charged with disorderly conduct. He was taken to police headquarters, questioned, and released only after a call to his draft board showed he was properly registered.[84]

Those who considered the anarchists a menace applauded Judge Clayton's handling of the trial. *The New York Times* editorialized that the judge "deserves the thanks of the city and of the country for the way in which he conducted the trial" and especially for "the half-humorous way in which he repressed [the defendants'] eager inclination to deliver impassioned speeches about imaginary wrongs."[85] A lawyer in New York City was even more effusive. After reading about the harsh sentences, he told Clayton, "It made my blood tingle—with pride, with approbation. The dignity, allow me to say the majestic dignity, force and decision with which you conducted the matter was bound to impress people of their ilk with the power of our law and to understand that liberty of thought is not license."[86] The judge also received an anonymous letter vilifying Weinberger. "He thinks he is a knowall and after being able to send his client back to Russia you send him and his family there too."[87]

Radicals and their sympathizers naturally saw things differently. They termed Clayton's behavior "a combination of stupidity, vituperation and falsehood, seasoned with cheap wit and flat jokes at the expense of his victims."[88] To Emma Goldman, Clayton was a hanging judge and the sentences were "really gruesome."[89] According to an undercover agent of the Military Intelligence Division, who attended a fund-raising meeting for the convicted four, a speaker called Clayton "an ignorant western farmer who knows little or nothing at all of the great teaching that our comrades believe."[90] *The Nation,* while critical of the anarchists and their views, carried an editorial, "Our Ferocious Sentences," which condemned Clayton's "total lack of dignity and judicial poise."[91]

There is surely good reason to question the judge's conduct of the trial and his mean-spirited display in passing sentence. But although Judge Clayton had failed to conceal his prejudices, it is doubtful that they caused the jury to reach a guilty verdict. Given who the defendants were and what they had done, and given, too, the prevailing public sentiment, the jury probably would have returned a guilty verdict even if the Court's behavior had met the highest standards of disinterestedness. The problem was not so much the judge as the law. The Sedition Act of May 1918 could all too easily be construed to make what the anarchists had said a crime.

## Bonds for Bail

On Saturday morning, October 26, Harry Weinberger appeared in Judge Clayton's chambers to request that his clients be admitted to bail, a request, he probably thought, that would be routinely granted. After all, the proposed appeal to the Supreme Court might take many months, even a year, to be decided. Since their arraignment the anarchists had each been held on $5,000 bail. So far they had not been able to raise that sum, but the defense attorney thought that the publicity accompanying the trial would make it possible to raise the needed amount from their supporters. The lawyer's sanguine outlook, however, failed to take account of U.S. Attorney Francis G. Caffey's dogged determination not to allow the anarchists to set foot on the streets of New York City, or of Judge Clayton's ready acceptance of Caffey's arguments.

The judge at first appeared amenable to fixing bail, Weinberger reported, but, in view of Caffey's opposition, asked the two sides to return that afternoon "when he would further decide whether to raise the amount of bail or lower it." When the lawyer and the members of the District Attorney's staff returned, however, Judge Clayton "stated he understood he did not have the power to admit to bail, and as he was immediately leaving for Alabama, he could not hear further legal argument."[92] Furthermore, the judge said, "I have doubt as to whether they are entitled to bail at all," since the Sedition Act was constitutional, the trial had been fair, and the convictions were proper. Clayton, however, granted the convicted radicals a twenty-day stay, so that their lawyer could appeal to the Supreme Court, to the Circuit Court of Appeals for the Second Circuit, or to any Justice of either of those courts "to pass upon the question of whether they are entitled to bail or not, and, if they are so entitled, to fix the amount and conditions." If a judge did not accept the anarchists' petition within twenty days, they would go to the pentitentiary.[93]

The judge left for Alabama that afternoon, and on Wednesday, October 30, Weinberger filed the necessary petition with the Supreme Court along with the "Assignments of Error," which stated briefly the grounds on which he would ask the Court to overturn the convictions. He was appealing directly to the Supreme Court, he said, because the Sedition Act violated the free speech provisions of the First Amendment and because reversible errors had been committed at the trial.[94] On October 30 the lawyer also wrote to W. J. Hughes, the Assistant Solicitor General in the Department of Justice, alerting him to the petition for bail. The next day Hughes told Alfred Bettman of the Department's War Emergency Division that Weinberger was formally going to present his motion for bail to the Supreme Court on November 4. Hughes asked Bettman, "What is the attitude of your office towards the matter? Personally I do not think that we ought to make any opposition."[95]

Bettman, however, came to view the matter differently, especially after Francis Caffey asserted a strong interest in the case. He wrote to Bettman on November 1 and spoke to him on the telephone on the second, reminding him, in no uncertain terms, that the anarchists, ever since their convictions, were being hailed as martyrs. Caffey continued, "I would urge as was urged before Judge Clayton when he denied bail to these defendants, that it would be a calamity and a menace to the City of New York, and also to our army abroad, if these defendants were let loose to spread similar seditious utterances and literature. There are so many places in the City of New York where they could hide, that it would be extremely difficult, if not impossible, to find them."[96] Bettman was convinced, to the point where he prepared a draft of the memorandum that the Assistant to the Attorney General, G. Carroll Todd, submitted to the Supreme Court opposing the petition to admit Abrams and the others to bail.

The evidence at the Abrams trial, Todd began, showed that the anarchists were "engaged in an agitation against the Government of the United States and the war." Operating an underground press, "proceeding with elaborate precautions against discovery of their identity," and acting in "a most secret, intriguing and surreptitious manner," they had concocted an elaborate plan to print and distribute their leaflets. Such propagandists could not be permitted to remain at large during a wartime emergency, the memorandum continued. Once convicted, such people were, if anything, more dangerous. Having little more to risk, they would be even more likely to continue their work. So the Department of Justice had instructed United States Attorneys to oppose the granting of bail for "prominent and influential propagandists." Abrams and his friends had not engaged in "frank and open political agitation" in order to change public opinion, as they were entitled to do, but had deliberately attempted to weaken the United States "by an attack upon the purity of its motives and an attack upon our political and social system." To release such people on bail, Todd concluded, would be to defeat the purpose of the Sedition Act and infuriate the public.[97]

This memorandum was submitted on November 5, and within twenty-four hours Weinberger had fired off a reply. Incensed and incredulous in turn, he reiterated that his clients had not opposed the war with Germany. He conceded that they had used bitter, even harsh language in criticizing intervention in Soviet Russia but insisted that "mostly it is proper criticism." He contrasted the Draconian sentences imposed on Abrams, Lachowsky, Lipman, and Steimer, "a nineteen-year-old girl," with the much lighter sentences European governments had given for similar, and indeed more serious, political crimes. Weinberger explained what he thought should have been obvious: the anarchists had acted covertly because agents of the Department of Justice had been swooping down on public meetings, and arresting people who had tried to distribute leaflets. "Even appeals for defense funds for men on trial have been stopped, and legal defense committees broken up," he added, "while the postmaster has stopped all mail of certain individuals and newspapers without giving them their day in court."[98]

To make his argument more persuasive still, Weinberger then made a promise on behalf of his clients that, in all likelihood, he was not authorized to make. He began, soundly enough, by pointing out that in the event any of them "should violate the law while on bail, they could be arrested on a new charge, and then bail would perhaps be properly refused." The Court, on short notice, could even revoke any existing bail. But then Weinberger crawled out on a dangerously slender limb. Abrams, Steimer, Lipman, and Lachowsky, he said, "give their words through me that they will not continue propaganda of any kind while the case is pending before this Court." Over a period of two months, Weinberger explained, he had come to know them intimately, "their views, their ideals, their ambitions, their hopes, and can vouch for the honesty of their promise in reference to not continuing propaganda of any kind while on bail." Appealing also to precedent, Weinberger cited a Supreme Court decision which held that no one should be compelled to go to jail until "finally adjudged guilty in the court of last resort."[99]

As things turned out, one sentence in Weinberger's November 7 memorandum—"We are probably on the threshold of peace."—proved prescient. Only four days later the Allies and the Central Powers crossed that threshold by signing the armistice ending World War I. The justification for denying bail to the Abrams' group—the need to safeguard war production—however specious before November 11, vanished altogether afterward. By coincidence, it was on the same day that the Supreme Court decided to grant Weinberger's request to admit the anarchists to bail. The amount was set at $10,000 for each defendant. Weinberger attempted to convince Caffey to accept $5,000 for each individual, but on November 16 agreed to furnish $10,000 for each of the defendants. From Weinberger's perspective, the vital principle had been upheld. He told Judge Learned Hand that the Supreme Court order "should settle the practice once for all that defendants after conviction are entitled to bail pending appeal."[100]

It took Weinberger less than three weeks to obtain the necessary funds. On November 14 Judge Augustus Hand granted a further extension of the twenty-day stay to permit time to raise bail. On November 16 Weinberger deposited $10,000 in Liberty Bonds to set Abrams free. Two days later he deposited an additional $10,000 in Liberty Bonds to obtain Mollie Steimer's release. Judge Hand granted a second extension on November 24, so Lipman and Lachowsky would not have to go to the penitentiary while efforts to raise their bail continued. By the next day Weinberger had put together $10,000 more, partly in Liberty Bonds and partly in real estate, to gain Samuel Lipman's release. On November 27 Abrams returned to the Tombs so that his bail could be used to free Hyman Lachowsky, who, according to a deposition of Weinberger's, was "in a very bad physical condition" but who, perhaps recalling Jacob Schwartz's fate, refused to be taken to Bellevue for treatment. Abrams' stay in prison was brief. On November 30 Weinberger deposited the final installment of $10,000, again in Liberty Bonds.[101]

Weinberger raised the money for bail from a number of sources. Small sums, of $50 and $100, poured in from friends and family members who lived in the South Bronx, in East Harlem, or on the Lower East Side. Substantially larger amounts came from wealthy sympathizers at fashionable Riverside Drive and lower Fifth Avenue addresses. Mary Dreier, Raymond Robins' sister-in-law, in whose apartment Robins had hidden while trying to avoid a subpoena, sent Weinberger $1,000 in Liberty Bonds. Frederick A. Blossom, a socialist and well-known birth control advocate, borrowed $6,000, paying interest on the loan, to assist the cause. (He later asked Weinberger for help in paying the interest, complaining "you know how these Wall St. sharks get around the usury laws.")[102] The lawyer sometimes had to reassure nervous contributors that they would remain anonymous, explaining that the money would be deposited in his, Weinberger's, name "and in that way there will be no publicity for those giving bail."[103] A separate bond, of $500, had to be given as surety for the appeal to the Supreme Court. It was provided by a prominent anarchist, Dr. Michael Cohn, who, Weinberger proudly informed Judge Clayton, was "worth more than $25,000."[104] The irony of using Liberty Bonds to release a group of people imprisoned for conspiring to interfere with the war appears to have escaped notice. The more profound irony, of course, is that the authorities, patriotic to the last degree, presumably accepted the Liberty Bonds at face value.

So three months after their arrests, and a month after their convictions, all the anarchists were out of jail. All, that is, except Hyman Rosansky. Bail had been set at $10,000 for him, as for the others, but neither Weinberger nor any radical sympathizers were interested in raising so much as a penny to help him. As Weinberger explained, the other defendants resented Rosansky "because of his practical squealing [and] not desiring to have anything to do with them."[105] His fate was now tied to theirs, but since Rosansky, in Weinberger's words, had "turned States evidence, we have nothing to do with, and are making no request for him."[106] Toward the end of November Rosansky was transferred from the Tombs to the federal penitentiary in Baltimore, Maryland.

Weinberger eventually relented, when, in February 1919, the United Hebrew Charities told him that Mrs. Rosansky was in pitiable condition and "under our continuous care for relief."[107] Weinberger then applied both for a reduction in Rosansky's bail and for a pardon, pointing out that Rosansky's family was destitute and that he had helped the prosecution's case. In his appeal, Weinberger even managed to enlist the support of the prosecuting attorney, John M. Ryan. Late in April 1919, his bail lowered to a nominal $250, Rosansky was released from the penitentiary. He visited Weinberger, who promptly reported to Emma Goldman that "he has really improved a thousand percent physically, aye, even mentally by his stay in Baltimore. That is, the fat, flabby mushiness has been knocked out of him and his body hardened. . . . Rosansky was scared that something would be done to him, but I merely said that he should just keep away from everybody and that he would be all right."[108] Goldman, still cooped up in the penitentiary, replied disapprovingly that confinement could perhaps improve a man's body "but never a man's mind. . . . His character will probably never be anything else but putty."[109]

To secure Rosansky's release, Weinberger had obtained the backing of the U.S. Attorney's office, but only after Francis G. Caffey had cleared the arrangement with Judge Clayton. In February 1919 Clayton informed Caffey that he had no objection to granting executive clemency to Rosansky, a weak man, who had been "led by his codefendants, each one of whom appeared to be of strong intellect, and of positive vicious disposition." The judge noted that Mrs. Rosansky was in poor health and unable to support her three children, the youngest of whom was less than a year old. Rosansky had already served a reasonable sentence, the judge added, and besides, as an alien anarchist, he would probably be deported as soon as he was released. Yet Clayton took the occasion to reaffirm his view that the other four defendants deserved all the punishment the law would allow. "They are very vicious, bold and active anarchists and have great command of 'soap box' oratory and seem to use their power of speech on every occasion for spreading among the weak and ignorant misinformation and doctrines subversive of government."[110]

From the anarchists' perspective, and from their lawyer's, it was the judge who was "vicious" and the government which was "subversive" of First Amendment freedoms. The judge's conduct of their trial, the severity of their sentences, the vindictiveness of the United States Attorney's office and the Department of Justice in attempting to deny them bail—not to mention their three long months in the Tombs—all served to confirm their perception of themselves as embattled revolutionary martyrs. This was evident when, on the first night of freedom, Mollie Steimer went with Jacob Abrams to a Greenwich Village tearoom frequented by anarchists, and so, inevitably, by an undercover federal agent. "There was Abrahams and Molie Steiner just released from jail," he reported. An excited crowd surrounded her, asking all sorts of questions. The agent recorded one of her replies. "She said that the several weeks of jail did her a great deal of good . . . and hereafter she will know how to act when necessary."[111] Her words convey an impression of wariness, of suspiciousness, that cannot be fully explained by the ever-present, and in this instance fully justified, fear of spies. Yet it is unlikely that Steimer or her comrades, entering their final months of freedom in America, understood exactly how wary and suspicious they, and radicals everywhere, were going to have to be in the year 1919.

# 5

# The Surveillance State

## Aliens, Anarchists, and the Law

MR. LUBIN and Mr. Greenfield owned a small fur-manufacturing shop on East 21st Street. In October 1919 they received a surprise visit from Mr. J. G. Tucker, an agent of the Bureau of Investigation. Introducing himself and producing his credentials, he asked whether they remembered an employee named Samuel Lipman, who had worked for them in the summer of 1918, and whether he "had ever made any statements to his fellow workmen tending to show that he was an anarchist." The two men said "that they had no personal knowledge of Lipman having ever made any statements to any of his fellow workmen." But they promised to talk to "the only man now in their employ who was employed by them at the same time with Lipman," and to tell Tucker what they found out. Two days later the investigator returned, only to learn that while Lipman had, indeed, worked there, the man who had worked with him "had stated that Lipman had never discussed socialism or anarchism with him."[1]

This was no idle mission the agent had undertaken, for if he could prove that Lipman was an anarchist, rather than the socialist he claimed to be, the government could much more easily deport him. Abrams, Steimer, and Lachowsky had all admitted that they were anarchists, in statements to the police and in testimony at the trial, and they were, consequently, marked for eventual deportation. If not for their appeal, still pending, before the Supreme Court, the authorities could already have sent them back to Russia. Harry Weinberger was well aware that three of his four clients, as aliens and anarchists, lacked a legal basis for remaining in the United States.

Over the years Congress and the courts had devised a formidable system of laws to bar aliens who were anarchists from entering the country, and, further, to deport aliens who became anarchists at any time after their arrival, no matter how peaceful their inclinations or law-abiding their behavior. It was even possible to strip naturalized persons of their citizenship and then deport them if it could be shown that they had believed in anarchism prior to their naturalization. The last brick in this anti-anarchist wall was mortared firmly into place on October 16, 1918—during the first week, coincidentally, of the Abrams trial—when President Woodrow Wilson signed a newly passed immigration bill.

The scaffolding had been erected twenty-five years earlier when, in 1893, the Supreme Court decided that Congress had the right to deport, as well as to bar, "all aliens, or any class of aliens, absolutely or upon certain conditions, in war or in peace." This right, said Justice Horace Gray, speaking for the majority in *Fong Yue Ting* v. *U.S.*, was essential to the safety and welfare of any sovereign nation. The Court therefore upheld the constitutionality of an act which provided for the deportation of Chinese aliens who had failed to obtain a certificate of residence. Three justices dissented; one, David J. Brewer, while conceding that Congress might exclude whomever it wished, held that aliens, once lawfully admitted, were entitled to a reasonable measure of protection. Although they admittedly were not citizens, they were nevertheless "denizens" who intended to live their lives in the United States. Brewer quoted an injunction from King Canute's codification of English law in the eleventh century: "Verily he who dooms a worse doom to the friendless and the comer from afar than to his fellow injures himself." The majority, however, rejected Brewer's benevolent approach as well as the ancient wisdom of the King.[2]

Congress also had the authority, in the opinion of the Supreme Court, to treat the deportation of aliens as an administrative rather than a judicial matter. In 1903, in *Yamataya* v. *Fisher*, the Justices (with Brewer again dissenting) held that Congress could delegate the enforcement of laws concerning deportation "exclusively to executive officers, without judicial intervention." In this instance a warrant had been issued to the immigration inspector at Seattle, Washington, ordering the deportation of a Japanese woman on the grounds that she was a pauper, and therefore should have been barred from entering the country. Speaking for the Court, Justice John Marshall Harlan maintained that the designated official was the "sole and exclusive judge" of the facts in such cases, and courts had no power to reexamine such a ruling. Harlan insisted only that officials observe "the fundamental principles that inhere in 'due process of law.' " That is, aliens had to be notified of any deportation proceedings brought against them and given an opportunity to make statements in their own behalf. But they did not have the same rights as defendants in a court of law. At deportation hearings the usual rules governing admissibility of evidence, cross-examination of witnesses, or the right against self-incrimination did not apply.[3]

Armed with this broad-gauged authority to deport aliens, and to do so through administrative action, Congress, over the years, gradually tightened the noose around foreign-born anarchists. The earliest immigration laws, enacted in the 1880s and 1890s, had barred people who were considered undesirables, such as convicted criminals, the insane, polygamists, paupers, contract laborers, and those with contagious diseases. Following the assassination of President William McKinley in 1901 by an alleged anarchist, Congress barred the entry of anarchists, or persons who believed in or advocated the violent overthrow of the United States government, all government, or all forms of law, or who favored the assassination of public officials. Under the new law, passed in 1903, the holding of these beliefs became grounds for deportation as well as exclusion. Aliens who held such radical views but had concealed them when entering the country, and aliens who later came to hold these views, could be deported at any time within three years. In 1910 Congress began to tinker with this "probation" period during which aliens could be deported. An act aimed ostensibly at aliens who engaged in immoral behavior (prostitutes, for example, or procurers) also established a more general precedent: such persons could now be deported at any time after entering the United States.[4]

In February 1917 Congress passed a comprehensive immigration bill which selectively incorporated the restrictive aspects of the earlier measures. The most controversial feature was the requirement that all immigrants over the age of sixteen be able to demonstrate literacy in some language. This prompted a presidential veto, but Congress passed the bill over the veto, and it is unlikely that Woodrow Wilson had any objection to the provisions regarding the exclusion and deportation of radicals. Building on the act of 1903, the new law provided for the exclusion of aliens who were "anarchists, or persons who believe in or advocate the overthrow by force or violence of the Government of the United States or of all forms of law, or who disbelieve in or are opposed to organized government, or who advocate the assassination of public officials, or who advocate or teach the unlawful destruction of property." Taking a cue from the act of 1910, the law provided for the deportation of "any alien who at any time after entry shall be found advocating or teaching" anarchism, forcible overthrow, or assassination. The law provided that aliens who were anarchists at the time they entered the country (illegally, of course), but who did not thereafter advocate the doctrine, could be deported only within five years of their arrival.[5]

A powerful weapon in the arsenal of the immigration authorities, the 1917 act made it possible to deport a quiet, law-abiding man, an anarchist who was opposed in principle to the use of force, and who had resided in the United States for fifteen years. In June 1918 Frank R. Lopez, a Boston resident, was taken into custody. After a deportation hearing the immigration inspector ordered his deportation because he "is an anarchist, and, in my opinion, a dangerous one" and because he admitted having taught the "idea of social revolution and anarchy." A warrant was issued for his deportation in November. A writ of habeas corpus was obtained, but in December a circuit court of appeals dismissed it, holding that although Lopez believed in peaceful change, he was, in the eyes of Congress, "none the less a dangerous presence." Congress had not made any distinction between anarchists who were "honest and law-abiding visionaries" and anarchists who hatched bomb plots in cellars. "The constitutional power to exclude or to deport," the court added, "does not depend upon whether the alien is or is not a criminal, or the advocate of lawless ideas."[6]

The 1917 act also allowed the government to bring denaturalization proceedings against anarchists. Michael Stuppiello had emigrated to the United States in 1900 at the age of fourteen. Moving to Rochester, where he worked as a cobbler, he married a woman who was a United States citizen, and they had two children. In 1909, when he took out his first papers, and in 1915, when he was naturalized, he stated that he was not an anarchist and believed in the principles of the Constitution. But in May 1918 the Bureau of Immigration arrested Stuppiello. An inspector asked him if he believed in anarchy, and he replied that he did; asked for how long, he answered for "six or seven years." Like Lopez, Stuppiello believed in the theory of anarchism but not in the use of violence. A district court, however, decided that he would not have been admitted to citizenship in 1915 if he had owned up to his convictions. Asserting that all anarchists sought to discredit constituted authority, the judge added, "Such philosophical anarchism as he professes is fully as dangerous as the anarchism of one who advocates violence to bring about a state of society without a government." Stuppiello's certificate of citizenship was therefore canceled.[7]

So the government was far from defenseless in its war against alien anarchists. Yet by mid-1918 the administration and Congress had become increasingly alarmed about four glaring loopholes in the existing law. The purpose of the Immigration Act passed in October 1918 was to close them securely. The first required only a minor grammatical change. The 1917 act, using the same language as in 1903, excluded or expelled "anarchists, or persons who believe in or advocate" the violent overthrow of the government, the assassination of officials, or the unlawful destruction of property. But some argued that the language following the comma after "anarchists" could be construed merely as descriptive, as a definition, that is, of anarchism. If this construction was accepted, aliens who were anarchists but who did not believe in violent overthrow would be exempt from the law, and so would aliens who did believe in violent overthrow but were not anarchists. To correct this potentially disastrous defect, the bill was simply amended to say: "anarchists; aliens who believe in or advocate . . ." In effect, the government held that changing a comma to a semicolon would go far toward assuring the safety of the republic.

The Immigration Act of 1918 amended the older statute in three other significant ways. It eliminated the five-year rule, thereby enabling the government to deport alien anarchists regardless of when they had entered the country. It also amplified the existing guilt-by-association clause. Under the 1917 statute officials had only been able to move against aliens who, before their arrival, had belonged to organizations advocating anarchy, assassination, or destruction of property; now aliens who joined such groups in the United States could be deported. The new targets were "aliens who are members of or affiliated with any organization that entertains a belief in, teaches, or advocates the overthrow by force or violence of the Government . . . or opposition to all organized government." Finally, a provision was added to punish aliens who, after being deported, reentered the United States, or attempted to return. Such individuals would be guilty of a felony, subject to a prison term of up to five years, and deported again after they had served their time.[8]

The measure sailed smoothly through a xenophobic Congress eager to vote for "An Act to exclude and expel from the United States aliens who are members of the anarchistic and similar classes." The House of Representatives approved the bill on June 21 after a perfunctory debate in which no one rose to speak in opposition. The sponsors explained that the bill's purpose was to give the government "a summary means of getting rid of these people without the long delays of the court." One Congressman said, "It seems to me the quicker you can get rid of cattle of this kind the better"; another wanted to exterminate "the rats gnawing at the very foundations of our Government"; and a third added, "There is no punishment which can be meted out to them which would be too great for the infamy and doubledealing."[9] The Senate took up the measure in July. One Senator asked if the intent was "to send a man out of the country simply because he holds a belief?" and was assured, "A certain description of belief; yes sir."[10] With virtually no discussion, the Senate passed the bill by a voice vote on October 3. When he signed the act on October 16, 1918, President Wilson gave legal sanction to the view, expressed by one Congressman, that "this country has no place for the anarchist."[11]

However carefully the new measure had been drafted, a number of questions remained open. How was the government to prove that an alien was a member of, or affiliated with, a proscribed organization? How, indeed, was the word "affiliated" to be defined? Radical groups were not known for keeping reliable records, and were not, in any case, about to turn their membership lists, accurate or otherwise, over to government agents. What kinds of information would be used in deciding which organizations should go on the proscribed list? Would public statements and official manifestos be considered, or, as Anthony Caminetti, the Commissioner General of Immigration, suggested, would the "private conversations" of the group's "officers or agents" also be taken into account?[12] Although these questions were as yet unanswered, there was no denying that the government now possessed a rapier-sharp weapon to use against alien anarchists, one that made the older implements seem, by comparison, blunt and unwieldy.

In June 1918, during the brief discussion preceding House passsage, one Congressman posed a hypothetical situation: suppose an alien was arrested for violating the Espionage Act, and while still under a federal court's jurisdiction, "it should appear that he came within the purview of this bill also." How would such a jurisdictional conflict between the judicial branch, which enforced the Espionage Act, and the executive branch, which handled deportation, be resolved? The bill's sponsor replied, "I hardly think an executive officer could take away a defendant who was already in the hands of a court." While a court could compel the Secretary of Labor to hand over an alien to stand trial, the Secretary of Labor could not proceed against an individual who had been indicted, unless the court agreed to dismiss the charge. The usual procedure, in the hypothetical case, would be for an alien anarchist first to stand trial, go to jail if convicted, and then be deported.[13]

As things turned out, this was not so hypothetical a case after all. It described exactly the position in which Jacob Abrams, Mollie Steimer, and Hyman Lachowsky found themselves. And if J. G. Tucker, the Bureau of Investigation agent who was making discreet inquiries of Messrs. Lubin and Greenfield, had any luck, it would also describe the status of Samuel Lipman. For a year the anarchists remained in legal limbo: if their appeal to the Supreme Court failed, they faced long penitentiary sentences, followed by deportation; if, by chance, their appeal succeeded, they faced immediate deportation.

## The Machinery of Surveillance

In December 1918, shortly after his release from the Tombs, Hyman Lachowsky appeared at a socialist rally at the Brownsville Labor Lyceum in Brooklyn, where he was overheard to denounce Hyman Rosansky as a "damned squealer."[14] In January 1919 Jacob Abrams and Mollie Steimer were seen at a meeting, held at the Forward Hall on the Lower East Side. The meeting had been called to devise ways to aid political prisoners, but pandemonium broke out when Abrams proposed a resolution pledging to work for the release not only of socialists but also of anarchists. "Mollie Steimer shrieked and tried to get hold of the Chairman of the Resolution Committee," an observer reported; "the hall was in an uproar for about ten minutes."[15] In March 1919 Samuel Lipman wrote to Alexander Berkman, then serving a two-year sentence in the Atlanta penitentiary. Trying to raise Berkman's spirits, Lipman joked that while he had once doubted that there was any point in writing to a stranger, he now knew, having himself been a guest "in Hotel De Tombs," that "any letter to a prisoner is good & interesting."[16]

In May 1919 Abrams participated in a debate in East Harlem. He spoke in favor of replacing the existing system of trade unions organized along craft lines with "workmen's councils," which, if "established in all industries . . . will be available when action is necessary."[17] Abrams spent that summer at the Ferrer Colony in Stelton, New Jersey, living in a tent in the woods. Mollie Steimer spent a less bucolic summer in the city. In August, however, she went to a picnic to raise funds for the benefit of political prisoners, and was seen "selling stamps for 'Freedom's Cause' in ten and fifteen cent denominations."[18] On October 14, the first anniversary of Jacob Schwartz's death, Abrams spoke at a memorial meeting at the Forward Hall. Recounting the story of the third degree, Abrams asked the audience to rise and "take a vow to revenge the death of Schwartz, by propaganda."[19]

These and other reports on Lachowsky, Abrams, Steimer, and Lipman were filed by federal, state, and local officials who had been assigned to cover radical activities. Some of those officials worked openly, making no effort to disguise their identity. Others operated covertly, frequenting radical hangouts, browsing in left-wing bookshops, and quietly sipping cup after steaming cup of tea in Russian tearooms. Government agents took copious notes at meetings, opened suspects' mail, listened in on telephone conversations, and, to the extent possible, planted such primitive recording devices as were then available. Surveillance had been carried on during the war, but not on the same extensive scale. In 1919, gripped by a fear of revolution, the government stepped up its coverage of radicals throughout the United States. Surveillance became more systematized than ever.

The new system developed largely in response to a terrifying series of bomb plots. On April 28 a package containing a homemade bomb was delivered to the Mayor of Seattle. The next day a similar package, delivered to the home of a former United States Senator from Georgia, exploded when it was opened. On April 30 a New York City post office employee, reading newspaper accounts of these two incidents, remembered that sixteen packages, matching the description of those he was reading about, had been put aside for lack of sufficient postage. The police were summoned, and all sixteen parcels were found to contain lethal mechanisms, timed to explode on May Day. They were addressed to John D. Rockefeller, J. P. Morgan, and prominent political leaders, including several Cabinet members. Even before worried law enforcement officials could react, the would-be assassins struck again. On June 2, bombs exploded in eight cities at almost the same time. One of them went off outside the rectory of a Catholic church in Philadelphia, and another outside Attorney General A. Mitchell Palmer's home in Washington. The other targets were the private residences of a silk manufacturer in Paterson, New Jersey; a state legislator in Newtonville, Massachusetts; the Mayor of Cleveland; and municipal judges in Boston, Pittsburgh, and New York City, all of whom had presided, in recent years, at anarchists' trials. Miraculously, there were only two fatalities: a watchman standing near the New York City judge's apartment, and the man who had planted the bomb near Palmer's home. There the police found a circular entitled "Plain Words." It was signed "The Anarchist Fighters" and read, in part, "There will have to be bloodshed; we will not dodge; there will have to be murder; we will kill." Copies of the same leaflet were found at the sites of all the explosions. Two Italian anarchists, Robert Elia and

Andrea Salsedo, were implicated in the June 2 bombings. They were arrested in New York City after a manhunt lasting nine months.[20]

The investigation sparked a nationwide program of radical surveillance. In New York City it was carried out by four agencies, one of which, not unexpectedly, was the Police Department's Bomb Squad. As previously noted, the Bomb Squad had been transferred to the United States Army's Military Intelligence Division in December 1917 by the outgoing Police Commissioner, Arthur Woods. But this was only a makeshift arrangement, devised to keep the squad safely removed from the clutches of the then newly elected Tammany Hall Mayor, John F. Hylan, and his Police Commissioner, Richard Enright. When the armistice was signed in November 1918, control of the Bomb Squad reverted to the Police Department. After nearly a year's wait Hylan and his crony Enright took command. Inspector Thomas J. Tunney, the head of the Bomb Squad but no lackey of the new regime, was detailed to the pickpocket bureau, and then, to complete his humiliation, to the traffic squad. In August 1919 Tunney retired from the force.[21] By then the Bomb Squad had been turned over to Sergeant James J. Gegan.

Enright and Gegan formed quite a team. The Police Commissioner persuaded the Mayor—who, in fact, needed very little persuading—to issue an edict banning the display of the red flag at any public gathering. Enright told Hylan that the red flag was "emblematic of unbridled license and anarchy; it, like the black flag, represents everything that is repulsive to the ideals of our civilization and the principles upon which our Government is founded. . . . I consider that the preservation of public order and the peace and welfare of the community at large, demand the absolute prohibition of its employment."[22] Gegan, the new head of the Bomb Squad, used the term "Bolsheviks" to encompass all that was evil. "Bloody revolution is their aim. Massacre, robbery, rape, riot and arson are their program."[23] Once, when he was sued by a man who claimed he had been brutally beaten by the Bomb Squad, Gegan snapped, "Naturally radicals hate me, for I have warred on them a long time. I am going to keep right on warring on them."[24]

Under such leadership the Bomb Squad created a city-wide spying apparatus. No radical group was exempt, no tip too unlikely to pursue. In February 1919, when socialists were discussing the prospects for a general strike, Enright assured Hylan, "A close watch is being kept upon their meetings in accordance with your instructions, but, so far, they have confined themselves to ambiguous threats and veiled attacks upon constituted authority."[25] Following another of Hylan's leads, Enright again came up empty-handed. In June the police investigated a socialist-run Sunday school in Brooklyn to determine "whether comparisons were made between the American and the Bolshevik forms of government in disparagement of the former, but nothing was learned to confirm such an assumption."[26] Notwithstanding these disappointments, Enright was proud of the work of the Bomb Squad, boasting, in his annual report for 1919, of the "closer and sustained cooperation between the Police Department of this city and the federal agents charged with the duty of suppressing radical activities . . ."[27]

The federal agents with whom the Bomb Squad cooperated most closely worked for the Bureau of Investigation. The Bureau, which later became the Federal Bureau of Investigation, had been set up in 1908, not, originally, to combat radicalism but rather to assist the Department of Justice in enforcing the antitrust laws. In 1910, when Congress passed the Mann Act to prohibit the transportation of women across state lines "for immoral purposes," the Bureau shifted its focus to prostitution and commercialized vice. After the United States entered the war, the Bureau also began to play a role in the enforcement of newly enacted prohibition statutes. Only three hundred agents strong, the Bureau was headed in 1917, as it had been since 1912, by A. Bruce Bielaski, a former Secret Service agent.

The Bureau had begun its surveillance of radical groups even earlier than 1917, and it stepped up this aspect of its operation during the war. Then the bomb scares in the spring of 1919 transformed a rearguard action into an all-out war. A jittery Congress came up with a special allocation of half a million dollars, a large sum for the time. To spend the money, Palmer created the position of Assistant Attorney General in charge of anti-radical activities, and appointed his friend, Francis P. Garvan, to the office. Palmer also found an aggressive new Chief to replace Bielaski in the Bureau of Investigation: William J. Flynn (then head of the Secret Service), whom Palmer considered "the greatest anarchist expert in the United States."[28] Flynn immediately instructed all agents to launch "a vigorous and comprehensive investigation of anarchistic and similar classes, Bolshevism and kindred agitations advocating change in the present form of government by force and violence, the promotion of sedition and revolution, bomb throwers and similar activities."[29] At a June council of war, Palmer, Garvan, Flynn, and their aides decided to establish a General Intelligence Division within the Bureau.

To head the Division, they selected J. Edgar Hoover, a twenty-four-year-old Department of Justice employee whose zeal, single-mindedness, and bulldog determination had, within a short time, greatly impressed his superiors. Hoover had joined the Department in 1917, after having put himself through the law program at George Washington University by working as a clerk at the Library of Congress during the day while taking classes in the evening. Before long he was appointed a Special Assistant to the Attorney General. Hoover was not inclined, then or later, to understate the threat of radicalism. "Civilization faces its most terrible menace of danger since the barbarian hordes overran West Europe and opened the dark ages," he claimed in 1920, and added, for good measure, that radicals "threaten the happiness of the community, the safety of every individual, and the continuance of every home and fireside. They would destroy the peace of the country and thrust it into a condition of anarchy and lawlessness and immorality that pass imagination."[30]

The project dearest to Hoover's heart was the development of a master file of left-wing organizations and individuals, a file as comprehensive as he could make it. By 1919 more than half the Bureau of Investigation's field force was covering radical activities, and every agent's report, sent from anywhere in the country, was summarized and "carded alphabetically in the radical index." Within a matter of months Hoover's Division could boast that its index contained 80,000 such entries "covering the activities of not only the extreme anarchists but also the more moderate radicals." The system, Hoover thought, had distinct advantages: "At a moment's notice a card upon an individual, organization, or a general society existing in any part of the country can be obtained and a brief resume found on the card requested."[31]

Hoover attached such importance to compiling this index not only because it suited his compulsive nature but also because his Division, and the Bureau of Investigation, lacked statutory authority to take stronger action, at least against American citizens. The signing of the armistice had made it virtually impossible to invoke the wartime Sedition Act. Existing federal laws, Hoover remarked unhappily in August 1919, "were not sufficient to enable a successful prosecution . . . of American citizens actively engaged in agitation for the overthrow of the Government of the United States by force and violence."[32] Yet it was certainly possible—since, presumably, no one outside the Bureau would know about it—to keep citizens under surveillance, and to keep cards on them, cards "awaiting use as soon as adequate legislation is passed which will reach the activities of American citizens who fail to appreciate the benefits accorded by their government."[33] Until such a peacetime Sedition Act was passed, the Division could make its information available to the authorities in those states which had enacted measures to reach the activities of such unappreciative American citizens.

When it came to ridding the country of aliens, however, the federal government had broad authority under the Immigration Act of October 16, 1918. Recognizing this, Hoover devoted himself in 1919 to obtaining the evidence needed to initiate deportation proceedings against aliens who were anarchists or who believed in the violent overthrow of the government. Not yet the armchair bureaucrat, Hoover occasionally made personal forays into the field. In October 1919 he went to New York City to confer on Emma Goldman's forthcoming deportation hearing. Finding himself with a free evening, Hoover, accompanied by several Bureau agents, attended a mass meeting at the Central Opera House. More than 3,000 shouting, cheering radicals—"mostly of foreign extraction," Hoover reported—packed the hall. He added, somewhat ruefully, "None of the speakers over-stepped the line prescribed by law, though some of the persons in the audience who became over-enthusiastic did make remarks that were in violation of law."[34]

The young Hoover revealed, if only in embryonic form, two traits that would mark his long career: an imperial disregard for such legal niceties as search warrants, and a fascination, bordering on the perverse, with illicit sexual behavior (real or imaginary). Locating a Harlem warehouse in which Emma Goldman and Alexander Berkman had stored their belongings, Hoover, on the same October trip to New York, reported excitedly that he and his agents "were able to induce the person in charge to permit us to go over this material. . . . I found the expense accounts of the Goldman–Berkman group for many years back, together with scrap books which had been kept by that group. Valuable information was secured by me from this collection."[35] Not many months later, the two anarchists safely having been deported in December 1919, Hoover let his imagination run free in describing correspondence recently found in John Reed's possession. "On his person were found in addition some letters from EMMA GOLDMAN which proved to be rather spicy reading and show that Emma and John were friends of the most intimate hue."[36]

Hoover wrote this letter to a Colonel in the Army's Military Intelligence Division, which had also gone into the business of keeping radicals under surveillance, now apparently a growth industry. Entering the field later than either the Bomb Squad or the Bureau of Investigation, Military Intelligence quickly made up for lost time. In April 1917, when the United States entered the war, the Division consisted of two officers and two clerks, and had a budget of $11,000. Within a year, however, its Washington staff numbered in the hundreds and it employed an extensive field force. In August 1918 the War Department made Military Intelligence a coordinate division of the General Staff, thereby enhancing its authority and prestige. One of the Division's many responsibilities was to collect information "upon which may be based measures of prevention against activities and influences tending to impair our military efficiency by other than armed forces." The Foreign Influence Section had the task of studying "the sentiments, publications, and other actions of foreign language and revolutionary groups both here and abroad, in so far as these matters have a bearing upon the military situation."[37]

The Military Intelligence Division drew up elaborate contingency plans for putting down an insurrection. On May 2, 1919, the New York City office drafted "plans for the Protection of New York in case of Local Disturbances." The city was divided into eight battle zones, an "ethnic" map was prepared showing the most likely danger spots, and plans were made "to combine all the machine guns in the possession of the First Brigade into a Machine Gun Battalion with two motor trucks capable of carrying eight guns and crews." Even so, worried officials feared that there were too few men on call, that they were inadequately equipped, and that it took too long to assemble them. The National

Guard in New York City numbered only 6,000 officers and men, the office noted, and they were armed with inferior Remington rifles. "The stocks split with comparatively no provocation and at 'order arms' the bolts are very liable to fly open." Worse still, the armories were not properly guarded, so that "a determined and sudden rush on any given armory with bombs blowing in the door would result in the distribution of the arms and ammunition to the rioters hours before the men began to assemble."[38]

Military Intelligence officials viewed the threat of radicalism in much the same way as Palmer, Flynn, and Hoover. "These Bolsheviks have made up their minds to become troublesome, and it is advisable that we go after them, tooth and nail, and never let up until we have landed the leaders behind the bars," was how one officer explained the situation.[39] Although the Division sent its operatives to cover meetings, rallies, parades, and demonstrations, there were those who thought that more needed to be done. One special agent urged in January 1919 that Military Intelligence undertake a more systematic investigation of radicals, and "that where possible all of their meetings should be covered and stenographic notes taken of the speeches made; that under-cover operatives should be employed to obtain[,] discreetly, information as to their future plans and projects, and that the information thus acquired be forwarded to a central office for compilation." The information could then serve as "the basis of positive action."[40]

This modest proposal was the brainchild of Archibald Ewing Stevenson, a self-appointed superpatriot and the moving force behind the creation of the Lusk Committee, the fourth and final element in the machinery of the surveillance state. In his mid-thirties, Stevenson had graduated from New York University in 1904, had then taken degrees in engineering and law, and had later become affiliated with the National Vacation Bible School Association and with the conservative Union League Club. Radicals dismissed him contemptuously as "an ambitious and totally ignorant lawyer with strong capitalistic connections," but there was no denying his influence.[41] In 1918 Stevenson managed to position himself strategically, first as a special agent of the Bureau of Investigation and then in the Propaganda Section of the Military Intelligence Division.

The ink on the armistice of November 11, 1918 was hardly dry when

Stevenson submitted a memorandum to Military Intelligence entitled "Dangers of the Menace of the Bolsheviki Movement in the United States." Surveying the success of revolutionary movements around the world, and noting that the foreign-born in American cities constituted "a fertile field for the agitators of the Bolshevist movement," Stevenson warned that "a revolutionary move is in contemplation," indeed, that "there is an organized conspiracy to overthrow the present form of the American government and to establish in its place an industrial republic modeled after that now attempted in Russia."[42] Stevenson soon came up with a stratagem to avert such a disaster. State law, he reported, authorized the Attorney General of New York to conduct "secret investigations," even when no criminal charges had been made, and, even better, to subpoena witnesses and require them to produce all relevant papers and correspondence. Stevenson had checked with the Attorney General, who was prepared to use these extraordinary powers to investigate radicalism, but only if formally requested to do so by Military Intelligence. Stevenson proposed that the Division make just such a request and, moreover, that it offer to share the information in its files with the state investigators.[43]

Stevenson's superiors turned him down flat. To Colonel John M. Dunn, the Acting Director of Military Intelligence, the plan was suspect on four counts. First, such an investigation "would be protracted and somewhat vague in purpose" and would only serve to publicize the radical movement; a better strategy was to employ "the conspiracy of silence." Second, the inquiry might move into areas "not germane to an investigation of strictly *revolutionary* movements and might conceivably touch partisan issues to the embarrassment of the Government and the delight of the Bolsheviki." Third, "much of the information in the Division's files is of the hearsay variety which we would not like to communicate to persons outside of duly authorized Federal agencies. There would be too great a risk of Military Intelligence becoming identified publicly with repressive measures in the realm of politics." Finally, it would be unfair to the Department of Justice, and "impolitic and unwarranted" besides, for an agency of the federal government to urge a state official to conduct an investigation that was national in scope.[44]

Shortly after his plan was rejected, Stevenson was forced to sever his connection with Military Intelligence. In January 1919, testifying before a Senate Committee, he embarrassed the War Department when he charged that sixty-two men and women (including such prominent reformers and educators as Jane Addams, Lillian D. Wald, Oswald Garrison Villard, Charles Beard, David Starr Jordan, and Frederic C. Howe) were all radicals. As a tide of indignation rolled in, Secretary of War Newton D. Baker repudiated Stevenson by asserting that the list contained the names of some people of "exalted purity of purpose, and lifelong devotion to the highest interests of America and mankind." The Secretary also said, mistakenly as it turned out, that Stevenson "has never been an officer or an employee of the Military Intelligence of the War Department."[45] In any event, Stevenson had overstayed his welcome in the Military Intelligence Division.

But he was not one to lick his wounds silently, at least not for long. Since Military Intelligence would not ask the Attorney General of New York to undertake the needed investigation, Stevenson, and his friends in the Union League Club, turned directly to the state legislature, which responded, in March 1919, by creating a Joint Committee to Investigate Seditious Activities. The Committee carried on its work for a year.[46] Stevenson, as assistant counsel, remained its guiding genius, although it was officially headed by Clayton Riley Lusk, a newly elected state senator. Lusk, who held a law degree from Cornell University and had practiced law in Cortland since 1902, described his committee with a refreshing directness. Its goal was repression, he said, but "repression carried on by and with the consent of the vast majority in the interests of that majority." Lusk thought that "a reasonable and wise repression of revolutionary activities tends towards the maintenance of law, order and peace in the community."[47]

By June 1919 agents of the Lusk Committee had fanned out across the state, and were issuing reports from out-of-the-way villages and from obscure hamlets as well as from large metropolitan centers. In New York City Stevenson masterminded a series of spectacular raids. The Russian Soviet Bureau, the Rand School of Social Science, the Russian branch of the Industrial Workers of the World, the offices of radical publications—all were raided, their files seized, their supporters hustled off to be questioned. The Committee worked closely with the Police Department's Bomb Squad. Commissioner Richard Enright bragged that his men and Lusk's "planned and executed a determined movement against the anarchists in this city, many successful raids being made upon their headquarters and anarchist meetings."[48] The Committee also cooperated with the Bureau of Investigation; in fact, Lusk's chief investigator, Rayme W. Finch, was a former Bureau agent.

Archibald Stevenson was not content merely to spy on radicals, raid their headquarters, and seize their membership lists. He wanted to prosecute them, and for statutory authority he turned to Article XIV, § 160–162 of the state's penal code. Enacted in 1902, those sections outlawed "criminal anarchy," which was defined as "the doctrine that organized government should be overthrown by force or violence, or by assassination of the executive head or of any of the executive officials of government, or by any unlawful means. The advocacy of such doctrine either by word of mouth or writing is a felony." An "advocate" even included someone who "voluntarily assemble[d]" with or joined a group teaching the doctrine. The law also stipulated that individuals could not claim a constitutional privilege against giving evidence in such cases, so long as their own testimony was not used against them. That is, witnesses could be granted immunity but were required to tell everything they knew about others. Conviction carried a maximum penalty of ten years in prison. One staff member exulted, "It is difficult to conceive of a case of Bolshevism that cannot be brought within the provisions of the foregoing Article."[49] In August 1919 two Finnish anarchists, Gus Alonen and Carl Paivio, were indicted for having published an article entitled "The Activity of the Rioting Masses" in their magazine *The Class Struggle.* The chief witness against them was Archibald Stevenson. The two were convicted in October and sent to Sing Sing.

By then the machinery of surveillance was fully operative. That is not to suggest that its parts always functioned smoothly or were perfectly synchronized. There were occasional overlapping and duplication of effort between the Bomb Squad, the Bureau of Investigation, the Military Intelligence Division, and the Lusk Committee. There were even occasional disagreements and jurisdictional conflicts. On the whole, however, the system of surveillance accomplished exactly what it was supposed to: keeping the government informed about what was going on. William J. Flynn, the Chief of the Bureau of Investigation, exaggerated only slightly when he remarked, "There is not an anarchist haunt in this country that is not under Federal or local surveillance."[50] The reports that were filed about Abrams, Steimer, Lipman, and Lachowsky—about the meetings they attended, the speeches they made, the letters they wrote, the picnics they went on—were similar to reports filed about thousands of people who held political views of which the government disapproved.

## The World of the Undercover Agent

"I have been reflecting on our clique of anarchists," began the undercover agent's report. "They are indeed, the world's riff-raff. None with whom I have become well acquainted are normal but I presume if they were normal they would not be anarchists." The informant was a woman who had spent almost three months infiltrating a group of anarchists in Greenwich Village. Fidgeting uncomfortably at the lectures they apparently enjoyed so much, she was also subjected to nonstop talk about their love lives. Her patience finally exhausted, she vented her anger in her report. One of the anarchists was a drunkard, she commented, while another was "dangerously insane," and a third was "neurotic and sickly sentimental." There was also a "lazy, sentimental egotist who would do anything for money," and "an impossible young Jew, also a drunkard," and two who were "abnormal in their moral life and both are drunkards." Others were even more dissolute, including one who "has the reputation among the anarchists of being able to be 'intimate' with more men in a day than any woman."[51]

This Bureau of Investigation agent is identified only as "BB." Her report, although blunter than most, is by no means atypical. The Bureau had made a decision "to obtain the services of confidential investigators who could establish relations with the leading radicals and anarchists and who could become members of societies under investigation."[52] These undercover agents, however, were breaking relatively new ground in 1919. Inexperienced, gullible, poorly prepared, they were often hired simply because they happened to be in the right place at the right time. They had not yet learned, as federal agents later would, how to use bureaucratic jargon to disguise their likes and dislikes. To the contrary, their reports were biased and opinionated, and they virtually bristled with moral judgments.

Undercover informants commonly detested the radicals with whom they were required to mingle. Forced by the nature of their work to befriend these people, the agents could, as "BB" did, let their superiors know just what a sacrifice they were making. After sitting quietly through a meeting at the Manhattan Lyceum, an agent of the Lusk Committee expressed his indignation: "This convention is a continuous slander, insinuation and ridicule of the Government of the United States. Why should this convention be permitted? . . . Give these Russians the treatment which they were accustomed to under Czar Nicolas. From my observation of the matter I am sure that it is not one to be handled with kid gloves."[53] Government agents were offended by the radicals' deliberate avoidance of patriotic displays. A Military Intelligence agent, returning from a socialist rally, reported that "not a note of patriotic American music was heard at this great meeting, which, for the sentiments uttered, might have been held in Bolshevik Russia."[54] To an informant of the Bureau of Investigation, it seemed that radicals were stuck in a groove of fault-finding. He finally remarked in exasperation that one had "made a long speech in which he criticized everything, everywhere."[55]

What offended the agents was not merely the radicalism but the lifestyle that invariably accompanied it, a lifestyle that seemed shockingly immoral. Informants' reports rarely failed to mention that the young women were "practitioners of free love," that So-and-so was the "common law wife" of Such-and-such, or that the men preferred to wear their hair long and the women theirs short.[56] Men at a radical hall, an agent observed, were accustomed to "swearing something awful in the presence of the ladies" and, what was worse, in the presence of "little children age about 7 & 8" so that "their little mouths even are full of curses what they hear from the others."[57] After visiting the Ferrer Colony in Stelton, New Jersey, agents of the Lusk Committee sounded as if they had been to Sodom and Gomorrah, although, unlike Abraham, they did not plead with the Almighty to spare the place. "They teach the children sex hygiene and explain to them all the organs of the body. The boys and girls live in the same dormitory and take their baths at the same time," a scandalized agent told Archibald Stevenson. "As you walk through the colony, you will see a full grown mother with just a night dress on leading a boy and girl absolutely nude. This is a common scene." With morality "left to the wisdom of the individual," it was no wonder that "no church is there or anything like one."[58]

To spy on Yiddish-speaking Jewish radicals, the government, for obvious reasons, sought to recruit Jews. But this was not always possible, and, again as in the case of "BB," some agents voiced blatantly anti-Semitic sentiments. After a debate sponsored by anarchists, one informant said, " 'Question time' was the usual riot of prejudiced Jews shrieking pointless questions or making speeches under the guise of questions."[59] Observing a May Day rally in which three hundred Jews participated, a Military Intelligence agent reported, "The English language was rarely spoken before and during the meeting, and there was about the hall a distinctly foreign atmosphere, to say nothing of the odor which suggested a close proximity to a garlic garden and a gafilter [*sic*] fish."[60] The most vituperative such remark was made by an undercover informant for the Lusk Committee who had infiltrated an anarchist group. "Those damned kikes have a strong hold and I feel I must work not only night but day and night to help kill this movement now and quick."[61]

Undercover agents had to know enough to engage convincingly in conversations about radicalism. They had to be able to think on their feet, to tell small lies that would lull their prey into a false sense of security. One agent, wanting to leave a meeting early, described the excuse he used to make his getaway. "I told the boys I had to go home on the 9 P.M. train and could not stay out all night as I had to work next day. This appealed to them."[62] Agents pricked up their ears whenever someone made an extreme or outrageous statement, as for example, when two anarchists passed an American flag and one said, "Look at that bastard," and the other chimed in, "We will tear down that son of a B flag tonight."[63] Engaged in deadly serious work, informants tended to take everything literally, rarely recognizing a humorous remark for what it was. An agent who attended a class in public speaking solemnly reported that the instructor "taught us, if we should ever be in a prison about to be shot, how to say, Long Live the Revolution, so they would be able to hear us on the outside."[64]

The temptation to overdo it was difficult to resist, as even the Bureau of Investigation admitted when it stated, for internal consumption only, that "the tendency of many informants is to exaggerate their reports."[65] Partly this may have reflected the agents' own self-interest. Since they were on the government's payroll, they understandably wanted to justify their continued employment, and how better than to inflate the activities of the radicals? But the exaggeration may also have resulted from the informants' subconscious need to feel good, or at least better, about what they were doing. Their work, to a considerable extent, involved a betrayal of people who had taken them into their confidence. It is reasonable to assume that such work created feelings of guilt which could be alleviated by a conviction that the deception and double-dealing were justifiable because the radical threat was so menacing.

Agents in the early days of surveillance often took an informal, improvisational approach to their jobs. One Military Intelligence officer, finding it impossible or inconvenient to cover a rally held on behalf of political prisoners, filed a lengthy report anyway, explaining, "My informant is my wife who attended the meeting with some friends, out of curiosity. She was personally thoroughly disgusted with the affair."[66] Systematic mail interception was still unknown, but an investigator for the Lusk Committee made his own extemporaneous arrangements. Attending a meeting in Brooklyn, he noticed that two men had left to mail some bulky packages. So he went to the nearest post office, told the night foreman he was a Committee agent, waited for an hour until a mailman brought in the packages, and opened them. They were addressed to persons being held at Ellis Island, and contained copies of two radical publications. The agent took a copy of each, and the rest were impounded.[67]

To avoid arousing suspicion, undercover agents sometimes accepted leadership positions in radical organizations. The agents' supervisors regarded this practice as undesirable but unavoidable. They apparently were troubled by the possibility that agents would have to commit illegal acts to preserve their cover, but could come up with no acceptable alternative. In one case, the Bureau of Investigation explained, an informant had served as recording secretary of a radical group and then had acted as temporary chairman, a position that rotated among members. "It is almost imperative on the part of our informant to take his regular turn acting as temporary chairman," an official commented. "To do otherwise would serve to direct the open suspicion of the other members against himself. The informant in question has been directed at all times to refrain from provocative work of any nature," the report continued, and had already turned down assignments "which might savor of this sort of work."[68]

The opposite possibility—that an agent would go over to the radical side, either for political or personal reasons—caused government officials even more worry, and with good reason. The Lusk Committee hired an operative who briefly succeeded in obtaining a position as Emma Goldman's private secretary. She reported what she overheard in the office, the names of contributors, and the like. To establish her credibility, she went bar-hopping in Greenwich Village with her newfound comrades, and even pretended, as she put it, to be "smitten" by one of them. Soon, however, a different tone began to creep into her reports. After listening to Goldman talk about her experiences in the State Penitentiary in Jefferson City, Missouri, the agent commented, "if all Emma says is true Jefferson's Female Dept. needs help most pitifully." When the Lusk Committee dropped her like a hot potato, she responded, "As I am by nature sincere and as I am fond of Goldie and sorry for Sasha it is as well that I am no longer forced to deceive my comrades." The activities which at first had been a means of establishing her credibility had come to have attractions of their own. "I can get all the liquor I want, and the lovin has just come to me sort of natchurl." But Goldman had already decided it was too risky to employ someone whom she did not know, and after a week dismissed her, "with the hope that you may develop into a free and independent woman earnestly desirous to take your place in the great human struggle."[69]

Such turnabouts were rare but by no means unknown. Another woman employed as an informant by the Bureau of Investigation announced that "she had decided to marry one of the members of one of the radical organizations." Rayme W. Finch, later the Lusk Committee's chief investigator but still, at the time, a Bureau official, met with her, and evidently talked himself blue in the face trying "to discourage this young woman from her contemplated step, but to no avail." Angry and disappointed, Finch attributed her decision not to a political conversion but to her fear of spinsterhood. "Incidentally, she is, in appearance, unattractive, undersized, and in the thirties, and I believe one of the motives prompting her to marry is the fact that the radical she will marry is a steady worker with an income of about $40 a week, and at last she has an opportunity to marry." Despite her defection, Finch explained that women often were effective agents because men were more likely to confide in them and "the leaders make it a point to have women present at all times as an added attraction to keep the men interested . . ."[70]

In one elaborate operation, a man, not a woman, had to play the central role. In December 1919 a Bureau of Investigation agent named Joseph McDevitt arrived in New York City, accompanied by a shadowy figure, one Hajek (whose first name was variously given as James, or George). Hajek, who had once been a Bureau agent in Philadelphia and who may have had a tenuous connection with the British Secret Service, went under the alias of Max Potocki and claimed he was a Polish count. Not only had he established contact with anarchists in New York City, but one of them, a young woman named Minna Lowensohn, had fallen in love with him. An inventive individual, Hajek concocted cloak-and-dagger stories the Bureau found irresistible. He claimed, on one occasion, that the anarchists corresponded with each other by "using a secret ink, which all of them carry about their person in a bottle marked 'eye wash', and that . . . when they arrive at Ellis Island they are permitted to keep this liquid inasmuch as they claim that their eyes are in such condition that they will go blind without the use of it."[71]

With McDevitt (pretending to be an Irish nationalist, "Joseph Mackin") sticking to him like glue, Hajek set the stage for attempting to exploit a woman's love. He rented an elegantly furnished apartment on West 88th Street. A Dictograph was conveniently hidden in the dining room, "especially for the purpose of having these radicals come here." He got Lowensohn to introduce him and McDevitt to her friends in the movement, and for several weeks they frequented the anarchists' favorite watering places. One was a Greenwich Village restaurant whose decor McDevitt found striking; he reported, "the tops of the tables are painted red; the curtains upon the windows were red paper; . . . Everything in the room is red." Hajek further ingratiated himself by "spending money lavishly on theatre parties, presents, dinners, taxicabs." Meanwhile, he continued his deception of Minna Lowensohn.[72] After a few months the anarchists came to suspect Hajek. Lowensohn loyally defended him, at first, but eventually she learned the truth.

The purpose of the charade was to discover who was responsible for the appearance of a periodical called *The Anarchist Soviet Bulletin* and of several inflammatory leaflets, all of which had been widely distributed in New York City and elsewhere. The investigation eventually centered on a man named Hippolyte Havel, of whom more shortly, but the Bureau also believed that four other radicals were involved. Hajek himself, the bogus count, thought that "Abrams and Lachowsky, now under sentence, were both members of the Anarchist gang, who publish the Anarchist Bulletin and the circulars."[73] Top officials in the Bureau's New York office had suspected for some time that "this is the work of the Mollie Steimer, Jake Abrams, Hyman Lachowsky and Samuel Lipman quartet of revolutionists."[74]

## J. Edgar Hoover and the Anarchists

The first issue of *The Anarchist Soviet Bulletin* appeared in April 1919. Printed on a single page, it consisted mainly of an appeal "To The Workers, Farmers, Soldiers and Sailors!" The war, it said, had not been fought for noble purposes, but to make the United States safe for capitalism and the world safe for reaction. Furthermore, President Woodrow Wilson had gone to the Paris Peace Conference not, as he claimed, to form a League of Nations but to form "a league of the WORLD'S THIEVES AND MURDERERS," and to "unite the governments of the world against the marching SOCIAL REVOLUTION of the WORLD'S WORKERS!" The circular called on Americans to organize "anarchist soviets" to prepare for the moment when "we will DO IT—by beginning to TAKE OVER the FACTORIES, MINES and FARMS of America." In the meantime members of the armed forces should "SEIZE the wire cables and ASK your brother soldiers in Russia to stop being MURDERERS and momentarily arrest all their officers and WITHDRAW from Russia." Making the grandiose if wildly improbable claim that anarchist soviets had already been organized by soldiers and sailors in San Francisco, by steelworkers in Pittsburgh, by department store workers in New York City, and even by farmers in South Dakota, the editors asserted that 650,000 copies of the *Bulletin* had been distributed and that this was only the beginning.[75]

Printed at the bottom of the leaflet was the statement: "Issued Unperiodically by The American Anarchist Federated Commune Soviets." In fact, the *Bulletin* appeared on a monthly basis for the rest of the year, and before long it had begun to justify, if not actually advocate, revolutionary violence. Since capitalists employed "clubs, blackjacks, machine guns and revolvers to drown in blood the demands of the workers!", the only sensible response, from the anarchists' perspective, was to reply in kind. "We shall fight against our oppressors and enslavers with every weapon possible. The blood spilled will fall on their heads!"[76] Addressing their enemies directly, as if to make their threats more credible, the editors angrily told the rich and powerful to abdicate. "But if you refuse, if you will attempt to keep yourselves in power by murder and bloodshed, THEN YOU WILL BE MADE TO PAY THE PRICE FOR IT!" Borrowing a famous line from Shelley's "The Mask of Anarchy," and modifying it only slightly, the editors exulted: "We are MANY—You are FEW!"[77]

By the fall of 1919 it seemed to many observers, not anarchists alone, that American workers were about to "Rise like Lions after slumber/ In unvanquishable number." In September the nation's 365,000 steelworkers went on strike, and in November 400,000 coal miners, defying a federal injunction, walked out. Taking note of the industrial turmoil, *The Anarchist Soviet Bulletin* urged workers to strike not merely to obtain higher wages but rather "to take possession of every industry in the country, and run it for our own interest." This would require "general strikes everywhere, with the ultimate aim and purpose of overthrowing the entire present society, based on economic slavery, suffering and want—and in its place establish the Workers' Commune Soviets!" Refusing to mince words, the editors wrote impetuously, "Start by seizing factories and industries . . . United in Workers' Commune Soviets march away to the warehouses and take whatever you need—for it is yours, you have produced it and to you it rightfully belongs!"[78]

The most significant article, however, had appeared in the August issue and was entitled "Anarchism and Bolshevism." This subject, it began gingerly, was not an easy one to discuss in a publication "which has for its main purpose to agitate for the overthrow of capitalism and its supporting institutions." The author nevertheless proceeded to assert that "the fundamental difference between Anarchism and Bolshevism is nothing else but the difference between Centralization and Decentralization." Although Lenin's government was committed to abolishing capitalism, "still it only wishes to replace it and is replacing it wherever it can, with the same Centralized functioning organ—the State, that is the government." Decision-making in Russia, while no longer in the hands of the capitalists, was now the province of government officials, the article contended, which meant merely that one form of oppression had replaced another. The conclusion was plain: "Bolshevism stands for new slavery—Centralized Government. Anarchism stands for Decentralization—for real freedom."[79]

This indictment of Soviet Russia, which later became an article of faith among anarchists, was as yet considered heretical. Certainly Emma Goldman and Alexander Berkman were not ready to write off the Soviet experiment, and neither were such anarchists as Jacob Abrams and Hyman Lachowsky, not to mention the socialist Samuel Lipman. Mollie Steimer was the only one of the original four who appears to have had anything to do with *The Anarchist Soviet Bulletin.* "We formed a new group and published the Anarchist Bulletin," Steimer recalled, and it was as an emissary of this group that Steimer had her first encounter with Goldman, who had been released from the penitentiary in September. Steimer later recalled the incident for Goldman's benefit. "Here we had our first 'argument' because our paper carried an article criticizing the heads of the Russian government. You and Sasha thought that we were unjust in our attitude and that the R. G. ought not be compared with other govs. etc."[80]

Joining Steimer in putting out the *Bulletin* were several other young anarchists: Ethel Bernstein, a twenty-one-year-old dressmaker who had emigrated from Russia in 1911 (and who was Samuel Lipman's lover); Arthur Katzes, a twenty-two-year-old pressman who had emigrated from Russia in 1914; a man named William Winters; and Marcus Graham, a twenty-six-year-old Rumanian Jew. Graham had come to the United States in 1907. He worked as an egg candler, and then as a cutter in the garment industry. In 1917 he fled to Toronto, where, taking the name "Robert Parsons," he published a Yiddish-language antiwar anarchist paper. By January 1919 he had returned to the United States, for in that month an agent of the Military Intelligence Division reported a speech by one "Marcus" that was strikingly similar to articles that later appeared in the *Bulletin* (of which, in fact, Graham was editor). According to the agent, the speaker asserted "that the people ought to go out on a general strike until all the 'political prisoners' are free and that we tear the locks off the jails and seize all the food that is stored in the warehouses and the money that is in the banks; as it belongs to the people as they earned it."[81]

Another individual who was connected with the *Bulletin* was Hippolyte Havel. Wherever he was and whatever he was doing, Havel was the focus of attention. His bizarre appearance, his temper tantrums, his incessant talk—all commanded the spotlight. So did his ability to hold his liquor. One of his best friends said that Havel "was a determined drinker. To drink much and often was a part of his code of honor."[82] A government agent, distinctly less friendly, thought that Havel "is the worst looking type of a man I have ever seen in my life—repulsive to look upon and ridiculously dressed." Yet even the agent conceded that there was something fascinating about the man. With his "stubby mustache and thick long mixed gray hair combed back over a bald spot on the top of his head," his enormous black horn-rimmed glasses, his bright red cravat, and his "light colored checkered suit with spats and cheap shoes," Havel "attracts the attention of everyone walking along the street, people turn and look after him."[83]

When asked about his national origin, Havel was likely to reply, "Cro-Magnon." In fact, he had been born in Bohemia in 1869, and had lived, at various times, in Prague, Zurich, Paris, London, and Vienna. Meeting Emma Goldman in London in 1899, he had a brief affair with her, accompanied her to an anarchist congress in Paris, and returned with her to the United States in 1900. Havel settled in Chicago, where he edited several anarchist periodicals, but then moved to New York City. In 1919 he was living with Polly Holladay, who owned a restaurant in Greenwich Village.[84] He was also being observed by undercover agents of the Bureau of Investigation who picked through his overcoat pockets while he was asleep, copied names from his address book, and even tore out a page to obtain a handwriting sample. They also recorded his coarser statements, such as: "This country is nothing but a garbage can and all talk about patriotism or Americanism is bullshit. . . . This country is the rottenest of all; it must be destroyed."[85] But just when they had begun to believe that Havel was the editor of *The Anarchist Soviet Bulletin,* one of the anarchists scotched the notion, telling an agent that "he is no more the editor of the SOVIET BULLETIN than you are. He only wrote one article for it—that is just more of HAVEL's talk."[86]

The *Bulletin*'s continued distribution drove J. Edgar Hoover and other government officials to despair. Reading the September issue, Hoover remarked angrily, "It again gives utterance to the typical anarchistic doctrines and appears to be more vicious than the previous issues." Hoover remained full of hope, however, that "a clue may be able to be obtained as to the place of publication of the literature of the American Anarchist Commune Soviets."[87] The Bureau of Investigation painstakingly tracked down every clue, however faint. Agents scurried about the streets of Chicago, Baltimore, New York, and other cities, trying to trace the *Bulletin,* only to learn that there were numerous printing establishments, "particularly among the Hebrews," any of which could have been responsible. An agent in Paterson, New Jersey, following what he thought was a red-hot lead, interrogated a five-year-old girl who told him that she and her seven-year-old friend had found "three of the above mentioned leaflets, and they not knowing contents of same handed one to a civilian passing who at a glance advised them to destroy this literature which they obeyed and received from him two pennies." Trailing the two suspicious characters further, the agent ascertained that "they entered a little candy store. They were eating candy when they came out."[88]

Equally worrisome to the government were two leaflets, written and distributed by the same group of radicals who issued the *Bulletin.* If anything, the language in these leaflets was more intemperate, the threats more direct. The first, entitled "Constitutional Day. What It Means To Us-Workers!", satirized the plans being made by conservative groups to mark the anniversary, on September 17, of the day on which the Constitutional Convention of 1787 had completed its work. Such a commemoration was fitting, the anarchists observed sarcastically, for the document had always been used to protect capitalists who murdered militant workers and to imprison labor's champions. After mentioning the Haymarket riot of 1886 and the Homestead strike of 1892, the leaflet continued, "Neither shall we ever forget the brutal 'unconstitutional' tortures inflicted upon Jacob Schwartz, and which resulted in his death!" The lesson the anarchists drew "is that capitalism uses the 'constitution' of the U.S. as a cloak to protect by violence and murder our slavery!" The leaflet concluded with intentionally provocative statements: "Their press, church and government, together with their holy 'constitution' can all go straight to hell! . . . Down with all constitutions, governments, capitalism, churches and synagogues!"[89]

The second circular, "Arm Yourselves!", was even more inflammatory. It appeared in October and condemned the New York City police for having broken up a demonstration called to protest against the blockade of Soviet Russia. Contending that a "murderous pogrom" had been carried out by "mounted police murderers," the leaflet continued: "Since the government has czaristically-russianized its methods in clubbing and murdering you whenever you raise your voices in protest against injustice or dare to go out on strike, there remains for you the workers only one thing left, and that is to: ARM YOURSELVES!" Not only were workers exhorted to "ARISE AND START TO FIGHT BACK," but for the first time threats were made against officials who were involved in the prosecution of anarchists: Alexander I. Rorke, an Assistant District Attorney ("this dirty scoundrel HIMSELF"); James J. Gegan, head of the Bomb Squad; and Bartow Sumter Weeks, a New York Supreme Court Judge. The leaflet said they "may as well drop their 'high positions' for they will HAVE TO PAY the price for EVERY WORKER KILLED OR WOUNDED!" A frightened Justice Weeks asked for police protection. An armed guard was posted outside his Park Avenue apartment. The newspapers reported that "practically the entire city was closely guarded last night against anarchist bomb throwers."[90]

The authorities did more than just guard the city. The Bomb Squad and the Bureau of Investigation, cooperating closely, rounded up the anarchists, one by one. In April Marcus Graham was arrested in Paterson, New Jersey, and copies of the *Bulletin* were found in his suitcase. He spent two weeks in the county jail, and two more weeks on Ellis Island. He was finally freed on $1,000 bail, while the government proceeded to seek a warrant of deportation (which would be issued in November). From prison Graham had written to a comrade, explaining that he "was pulled by police here. . . . one Federal bull telling me he will make me talk—hell—they will."[91] William Winters was indicted in October on the charge of sending "Arm Yourselves!" through the mails, and he then disappeared. Ethel Bernstein and Arthur Katzes were arrested on September 30, at two o'clock in the morning, when a policeman noticed them stuffing copies of the *Bulletin* into mailboxes along East 99th Street. Charged originally with disorderly conduct, they were then arraigned under the state's criminal anarchy law; at the same time, the machinery of deportation was set in motion. J. Edgar Hoover took a personal interest in the matter, since, in his view, they had "been a considerable source of trouble."[92]

But it was Mollie Steimer whom Hoover stalked most relentlessly. She had actually been arrested earlier in the year, but with Harry Weinberger's help had slipped out of the government's net. She was one of 164 people taken into custody in March in a Bomb Squad raid on the Russian People's House, a social center on East 15th Street. None of those arrested had been doing anything wrong, and nearly all of them were quickly released. All, that is, but four who were aliens and admitted to being anarchists. One of them was Mollie Steimer (another was Arthur Katzes). She was taken to Ellis Island and remained in custody for five days while Weinberger attempted to obtain her release.[93] He finally succeeded, but only by promising to produce her for the immigration authorities whenever they wished. By September 1919, however, the Bureau of Investigation had concluded that Steimer was too dangerous to remain at large, and Hoover had decided it was time to act.[94] Let us, for a moment, follow the government agents as they follow Mollie Steimer.

On September 17, at five-thirty in the afternoon, Detective Walter Culhane and two other policemen were walking along Canal Street, in lower Manhattan, near the intersection of Lafayette Street. They noticed that leaflets were being thrown from the roof of 245 Canal Street. The leaflets turned out to be the September *Anarchist Soviet Bulletin* and "Constitutional Day. What It Means To Us-Workers!" Disturbed by what they had found, the policemen entered the building and started up the stairs. "On the way up," one account stated, "they met a demure looking young woman coming down the stairs. She said that she knew nothing of the circulars. She had got into the wrong house, she said, and was leaving."[95] But one of the detectives, thinking she looked familiar, asked, "Aren't you Mollie Steimer?" She admitted her identity, was arrested for disorderly conduct, and charged "with intent to provoke a breach of the peace."[96] She was interrogated at the station house by Assistant District Attorney Rorke, who had a particular reason to be disturbed because he and Justice Weeks had received copies of the same leaflets in the mail. Steimer refused to answer any questions and was locked up in the Tombs.

She spent the night in jail and appeared in City Magistrate's Court the next day. One newspaper reported: "When requested to plead she said she had no interest in the proceedings—the court might do as it pleased."[97] The hearing was attended by two Bureau of Investigation agents, Frank Faulhaber and Mortimer J. Davis, and by Sergeant Gegan himself. When it adjourned, the three men, and other officials, went into an anteroom "where an informal questioning of Mollie Steimer took place." Gegan asked, "Mollie, did you throw these circulars off the roof?" She answered, "Yes, I did; I am responsible for that circular and I stand by every line in it." She also admitted that she had distributed the same circulars at the corner of Sixth Avenue and 42nd Street "because it was the heart of the laboring section where many workers pass daily."[98] Although Steimer refused to say who had printed the leaflets, the agents deduced that their "make-up and wording," as well as the "reference to the case of Jacob Schwartz, who was known only locally," indicated that "the circular is the work of either Steimer and her associates or the work of some of the Russian Jewish element in this city who are totally in sympathy with the doctrines and belief of the Steimer, et al, group."[99]

Steimer's bail was set at $500, a sum, Agent Davis reported, that Gegan considered ridiculously low. Bureau officials, concurring, declared that "this woman is a menace to the community and . . . if possible, means should be devised whereby she be placed under a heavy bail bond. . . . She is of the type who have absolutely no respect for law and order. I, personally, have seen her openly defy the court and on several occasions refuse to leave her seat in the courtroom, when a band outside was playing the national anthem."[100] When Harry Weinberger did, in fact, post the $500 bail, Gegan, again according to the Bureau report, "then took up the proposition of having Miss STEIMER shadowed upon her release, but due to the fact that there were no agents at this office to be spared, the Police Department decided to take care of this themselves."[101]

"She appears to be courting deportation," a report added, and J. Edgar Hoover quickly intervened to see that the courtship succeeded. Obtaining affidavits from Gegan and the others who had elicited Steimer's "informal" anteroom confession, Hoover offered his opinion of the leaflet and also explained his strategy. "This circular breathed in every sentence with open advocation of violence and anarchy. I immediately took the matter up with the immigration authorities in this city and was able to convince them that in view of the fact that she had renewed her activities and had circulated such a vicious pamphlet that she had broken her parole and for that reason should only be at large upon a large bond, which amount I named as $15,000. The immigration authorities concurred in my recommendation."[102] While Bureau officials feared that even the large sum of $15,000 could be raised by Steimer's friends and supporters, it "will at least make a sufficient dent in their financial resources to warrant the action in this case."[103]

On October 2 Commissioner General Anthony Caminetti, following Hoover's advice, authorized Ellis Island officials to take Steimer into custody on a $15,000 bond. Bureau of Investigation agents now thought all avenues of escape were closed; when Steimer appeared at City Magistrate's Court on October 7, she would either be convicted on the disorderly conduct charge and jailed, or else "it will be advisable to apprehend her on the deportation warrant at that time."[104] That day agents Davis and Faulhaber made their second appearance in the courtroom, only to find that Harry Weinberger had gotten a postponement. The Bureau of Immigration official was present, as planned, "armed with a deportation warrant." But a hurried conference with Assistant District Attorney Rorke, who was prosecuting Steimer on the disorderly conduct charge, led to a change in plans. The officials decided to delay serving the warrant until after the trial, "as it is very likely Miss Steimer will receive the full penalty (six months) after which time the deportation warrant can be served upon her."[105]

Three days later, on October 10, Steimer turned up as a visitor in another courtroom, the one in which Gus Alonen and Carl Paivio, who had been arrested on the Lusk Committee's initiative, were being tried under the New York State criminal anarchy statute. The judge was none other than Bartow Sumter Weeks, and the prosecutor Alexander I. Rorke. Agent Davis happened to be there, too, and he reported that when the judge entered the courtroom, "Mollie Steimer refused to rise. She was immediately taken into custody by court attendants and taken into the private chambers of Justice Weeks."[106] After an hour or so, the judge, having learned her identity (although she had refused to give her name), brought Steimer before the bench and proceeded to lecture her. "I am informed that you are one of the most pronounced abhorrers of this Government, have been convicted under the Espionage Act, and are now out under bail. You shall not be successful in an effort to pose as a martyr. I will let you go, although you deserve to be cited for contempt. You will not be allowed to enter this Court again except as a prisoner."[107]

That was on a Friday. On Monday, October 13, two Bomb Squad officers who were trailing Steimer were rewarded for their patience. Patrolmen Louis Herman and Jerome Murphy observed her as she (and two of her comrades) deposited envelopes in a mailbox at the corner of Broadway and 17th Street. The policemen dropped a marker into the mailbox, so that the letters could be identified. When the box was opened, the marker was lying on top of envelopes addressed to Alexander I. Rorke, Archibald Stevenson, and James J. Gegan. Each envelope contained a copy of "Arm Yourselves!" Steimer was seized on October 18, taken to police headquarters, and jailed. She was charged now with violating Section 211 of the United States Criminal Code by mailing material "of an indecent character and of a character tending to incite arson, murder and assassination." Arraigned on October 20, she was held on $5,000 bail.[108]

The decision to prosecute her on this charge was not lightly made. A federal offense, it was handled by United States Attorney Francis G. Caffey's office, which was careful to clear things with J. Edgar Hoover. Informed of the plan to indict Steimer, Hoover assured one of Caffey's assistants, Ben Matthews, "that his proposed action would not in any way interfere with the deportation matter."[109] In fact, the deportation warrant which Hoover had obtained earlier in the month now acquired new importance. On October 23 Agent Davis and Sergeant Gegan were thrown into a panic when they learned that the judge "who today heard pleadings in the Post Office case against Mollie Steimer, consented to permit Harry Weinberger to have the bail of $10,000 which he personally advanced to cover subject in her case under the Espionage Act, to apply also to the present case, thus Miss Steimer was permitted to go one bail for two cases. Sergeant Gegan asked if something could not be done by this Department to keep Miss Steimer confined, as the Sergeant stated she would no doubt probably prepare another circular immediately upon her release."[110]

Davis and Gegan put in an emergency call to Ellis Island, asking the authorities to deliver the deportation warrant to the federal courthouse where Steimer's motion for bail reduction had just been heard. As a Mr. Jones of the Ellis Island staff set out for the city, the officials stalled, trying to detain Steimer until he arrived. But she finally left and "we did not attempt to detain her." Harry Weinberger remained, however, and, according to Davis, he asked, "You have no more warrants to serve to Mollie, have you?" Davis explained, "I evaded a direct reply."[111] Eventually Mr. Jones showed up with the deportation warrant, and three policemen "went to the vicinity of Miss Steimer's home to await her arrival." At seven o'clock that night she appeared and was immediately placed under arrest. Shown the deportation warrant, Mollie Steimer shrugged. "Oh, that's the same old thing."[112]

Booked at police headquarters, she spent another night in jail and was taken to Ellis Island the next day. By then, still free on $10,000 bail pending the appeal of her fifteen-year sentence under the Sedition Act, Steimer was facing a disorderly conduct charge in City Magistrate's Court for which she was under $500 bail; she was under a federal indictment for violating the postal laws (for which bail had originally been set at $5,000); and she was being held for deportation as an alien anarchist with bail, at J. Edgar Hoover's request, set at $15,000. Emma Goldman, who commented that "the entire machinery of the United States Government was being employed to crush the slip of a girl," might have added that the machinery of the state and city governments was being employed for the same purpose.[113] Mollie Steimer arrived at Ellis Island on October 24, 1919. "Since then," she said much later, "I never saw the streets of N.Y. any more."[114]

## Frederic C. Howe: Social Reform and the Surveillance State

The immigration authorities had detained Mollie Steimer once before, in March, but the Ellis Island to which she was now returned was a changed place, and from her perspective, changed for the worse. The change had come about largely because Frederic C. Howe, Commissioner of Immigration at the Port of New York since 1914, had resigned in September 1919, and had been replaced by an official considerably less sympathetic to alien detainees. Howe, a generous and humane man, had devoted himself to improving conditions for the aliens being held on the Island. By 1919, however, as a result of the wartime suppression of dissent, he had lost his reformer's faith in the benevolence of the state. To hold an official position, he began to believe, was to be unavoidably implicated in the very evils he had spent a lifetime fighting. The realization drove Howe to the brink of a nervous breakdown. So he resigned, thereby preserving his own sanity but making things considerably more difficult for Mollie Steimer and other alien anarchists.

Throughout a long career in government, Howe's tolerance, his sympathy for the underdog, and his faith in social improvement typified what was best in urban progressivism. Howe had wanted to be a reporter, but decided he first had to know more about American history and government. So in 1889 he entered the Johns Hopkins University to study for a Ph. D. in political science (Woodrow Wilson, at the time, was on the faculty). Howe received his doctorate in 1892 and moved to New York City. Unable to find work as a journalist, he took a law degree, but felt "mentally soiled" when a law firm relegated him to debt-collecting. He moved to Cleveland, where he became a fervent supporter of Tom L. Johnson, who was elected Mayor on a reform ticket in 1901. Johnson greatly admired Henry George—"The single tax had come to him like Paul's vision on the road to Damascus," Howe reported—and it was under Johnson's tutelage, Howe said, that "the possibility of a free, orderly, and beautiful city became to me an absorbing passion." Elected to the city council and later the Ohio Senate, Howe fought for public ownership of municipal power facilities, for lower streetcar fares, and for tax reform.[115]

His confidence in the American system prevented Howe from succumbing to exaggerated fears of radicalism. He recalled that when Emma Goldman visited Cleveland she had expected to be barred from speaking, only to be told by Tom Johnson, "I would not stop you if I had the power to do so, and nobody else has any such power." Free to speak, Goldman was, in fact, left nearly speechless when Johnson added, "I have always admired Prince Kropotkin, and I agree with a great deal of what he says."[116] Howe's own commitment to freedom of expression was recognized in 1911, when, having left Cleveland and returned to New York City, he was asked to direct the People's Institute at Cooper Union, where he conducted "a free forum for discussion of questions of the day." Living on West 12th Street, on the edge of Greenwich Village, Howe naturally got to know the Village radicals, including the *Masses* editors—Max Eastman, Art Young, Floyd Dell, and John Reed—all of whom would later stand trial under the Espionage Act.[117]

In the summer of 1914 Woodrow Wilson appointed Howe Commissioner of Immigration at the Port of New York. Handed an opportunity "to ameliorate the lot of several thousand human beings," Howe lost no time in putting his theories to the test. Since "the evils usually ascribed to the badness of people are social in their origin," he reasoned, the thing to do was to create a pleasant, hospitable environment. A new look came to Ellis Island. "Everything suggestive of a prison has so far as possible been eliminated," Howe declared. A wall that used to separate men and women, even married couples, was broken down, and the high iron screen separating aliens from visitors was removed. Benches and swings were placed on the plaza. Handball courts were built, and calisthenics classes offered. A social hall was opened, and supplied with foreign-language newspapers. Sunday afternoon concerts were arranged, and plans were made to add folk dancing in the evening. The lawns, which had always been off limits, became play areas for the children. "Live babies were more precious than live grass," Howe said, and he took "a good deal of satisfaction in seeing the lawns trampled under foot." When problems arose, Howe simply talked to the aliens who were being held on the Island. He found that "there was never a controversy that was not allayed by a friendly conference."[118]

These changes infuriated powerful politicians and old-line bureaucrats, who thought Howe was overly solicitous and branded him "a half-baked radical, who has free-love ideas."[119] As a veteran of many reform battles, Howe probably expected this hostility from entrenched interests. What he did not anticipate was that the government would launch its own wartime campaign to suppress freedom. In October 1915 Howe wrote that "war preparations and emphasis upon militarism is national suicide to all the things I am interested in."[120] Three years later he believed that his fears had tragically come true. Writing to Lincoln Steffens in 1918, Howe said that he had always admired historical figures—Voltaire, Diderot, Tom Paine—"who emphasized the big liberties." Having witnessed "a nation wide and widely approved crusade" against all who spoke their minds, "it seems to me to be the most crushing disappointment of all. I can't find comfort in the thought that America wants to be rid of everybody but the drab ones." The deception practiced by the government, he added, had the effect "of making me physically sick."[121]

By 1919, as the government stepped up its campaign against radicals and dissenters, Howe's was one of the few voices of reason crying out in a wilderness of repression. "The way to progress is through freedom of discussion. The false falls by its own weight, while the truth lives because of its essential rightness," he affirmed. "The countries in which revolution has come are the countries that have endeavored to suppress such liberties."[122] But even as he was speaking, the Bureau of Immigration and the Department of Justice, employing the Immigration Act of October 16, 1918, had begun to round up radical aliens and ship them to Ellis Island. Howe spent the winter with Wilson and the American delegation at the Paris Peace Conference. When he returned to Ellis Island in February 1919, he found that men and women were being held on the basis of testimony that "was so flimsy, so emotional, so unlegal in procedure that my judicial sense revolted . . ."[123]

It was Howe who helped make possible Mollie Steimer's release from Ellis Island after her arrest, in March 1919, at the Russian People's House. It was Howe who saw to it that aliens were treated decently. "Before Howe came back no visitors were allowed to see any of the men, not half enough bedding was furnished, and there were only two shower baths . . .," one detainee said. "Today you find a great difference . . . conditions are in general improved since Mr. Howe came back to take charge."[124] And it was Howe who was consequently denounced as "a bolshevist sympathizer," and accused of having turned Ellis Island into "a Socialist hall, a spouting-ground for Red revolutionists, a Monte Carlo for foreigners only, a club where Europe's offscourings are entertained at American expense and given the impression that government officials are subject to their impudent orders."[125]

Even as he tried to ameliorate the aliens' lot, Howe began to experience corrosive doubts about the government and the things his official position required him to do. "I became distrustful of the state. It seemed to want to hurt people; it showed no concern for innocence; it aggrandized itself and protected its power by unscrupulous means. It was not my America, it was something else." Doubt soon turned to hatred. The government's war on dissenters "made me hate in a way that was new to me. I hated the Department of Justice, the ignorant secret-service men who had been intrusted with man-hunting powers; I hated the new state that had arisen, hated its brutalities, its ignorance, its unpatriotic patriotism." Hatred eventually turned to self-reproach. "I was officially part of the system. I was part of this government, very much a part, for I was the custodian of hundreds of persons whom I knew to be innocent."[126]

Self-reproach inevitably turned to acute despair. Howe's autobiography, *The Confessions of a Reformer,* describes, however obliquely, a man suffering from clinical depression with paranoid features. "I had rarely lost a night's sleep in my life; now I could not sleep. And I began to be afraid. The telephone became to me an evil thing. I felt a sense of oppression in that I was not doing what the crowd demanded; the fact that I was aiding men and women in their legal rights in an orderly way gave me little comfort. . . . For months I lived in a state of fear. I feared something impending, something mysterious that hung over me." He especially feared the "ruthlessness" of government agents (who, indeed, were filing negative reports on him). "I brooded over these fears, over the hostility of the bureau, of the island, of the press." One evening, at dinner with friends, a psychiatrist on the faculty of Johns Hopkins suddenly said to him, "Howe, you're sick. I wonder if you know it." He added, "You have been living through a conflict that can only be gotten rid of through the confessional," and recommended that Howe quickly find a way "to get it all out of your system."[127]

Howe did not seek the services of a priest, or even a therapist, but he otherwise followed his friend's advice. In his autobiography he recalls another dinner, this one at the exclusive Cosmos Club in Washington, attended by high-ranking government officials. Speaking with an intensity that is easily imagined, Howe stunned the assemblage. "Now that it's over, suppose we all tell the truth. Every one of us has done something he is ashamed of. We have violated our principles, done cruel things. All of us have been lying in some way or other. And many of us have been cowards." His *mea culpa* was met with a chorus of denials, he reported, but he immediately began to feel better. Having taken the first step, Howe still had to take the second: extricating himself from the position that was the root of the problem. Early in September 1919, back at Ellis Island, Howe symbolically burned his bridges behind him. "I sent for my personal correspondence. I gathered together records of aliens and personal-interest stories that I had been collecting for five years, and which I had planned to use in a book. I sent for a porter, and together we carried them to the engine room, where I consigned them to the flames. 'I will end that chapter forever,' I thought. Then I sat down and wrote my resignation to the President."[128]

"I left with a feeling of exhilaration," Howe reported, and no wonder. He signed on as director of a reform group working for government ownership of the railroads, and he bought an old farm on Nantucket where he spent his summers. Howe's former duties were assumed by Byron Uhl, who had spent twenty-seven years in the immigration service on Ellis Island. Acting Commissioner Uhl was one of Howe's severest critics. Shortly after taking over, he let members of a congressional committee know exactly what he thought of his predecessor. Had

Howe tried to turn the Island into a place where every alien could "do as he pleased?" "That was the impression created upon me, sir." Had the Island actually become a "gambling house and a forum for radical expression and anarchist speeches?" "Well, I wouldn't be justified in saying that it became such, but there were privileges granted, which, if they had not been curtailed, would probably have brought about that result." Having saved Ellis Island from this fearsome revolutionary prospect, Uhl launched his own version of a Thermidorean reaction. Guards were supplied with nightsticks (though Uhl would have preferred revolvers). Men and women were rigidly segregated. The "iron mesh or net" was restored to separate the aliens from their visitors and prevent the passing of "any kind of weapons, bombs, or pistols or knives." The lawns, presumably, were again off limits.[129]

On October 24, 1919, six weeks after Uhl replaced Howe, Mollie Steimer was taken to Ellis Island. Under the new dispensation, she was segregated from other aliens and kept in isolation, even at mealtime. An urgent note, scribbled to Harry Weinberger on the day of her arrival, managed to convey her indignation: "I wish to have a personal interview with you on very important matters. Would you please come down to the Island to see me as soon as possible?"[130] Steimer (and two other detainees) fought back by declaring a hunger strike on Saturday, the 25th. She recalled, "Sunday, October 26th A.M., we all felt fine, just a little weak. The matron came in and asked me whether I would eat, for otherwise I might get sick. I told her to notify the Commissioner that if anyone of us got sick the Commissioner would be held responsible." Informed that she was being kept in isolation because that was now the law, "I replied that aside from the law which men made, they also ought to reason and be *men*, not beasts!"[131]

Weinberger told the press of her ordeal, reporting, "Miss Steimer weighs about seventy-five pounds and this may mean death to her." He added that her pulse was weak, she was running a fever, "and there is the very grave possibility that something serious may happen." Headlines in the New York *Call*, a socialist newspaper, blared: "MOLLIE STEIMER MAY DIE FROM HUNGER STRIKE."[132] The authorities were sufficiently concerned to ask Emma Goldman, who was visiting the Island on a matter relating to her own deportation proceeding, to meet with Steimer and try to talk some sense into her head. But Steimer's hunger strike lasted for the four days she spent on Ellis Island. On October 30 she was convicted on the disorderly conduct charge stemming from her distribution of the "Constitutional Day" leaflet, was sentenced to six months in the workhouse, and was removed from the Island. From the workhouse, on November 6, she asked Weinberger to abandon his efforts to obtain her release, for "no sooner will I come out, than the government officials will trial me on the Criminal Anarchy charge." She wanted to "avoid much trouble for my people." She reported that she had regained her health, and signed the letter, "Yours for a world without oppressors."[133]

By the time Weinberger had received this letter, another of his clients, Steimer's codefendant Hyman Lachowsky, was incarcerated on Ellis Island. He was seized on November 7 when, for a second time, government officials raided the Russian People's House on East 15th Street, a raid timed to coincide with similar actions in more than a dozen cities. The People's House was a political, social, and educational center where Russian immigrants congregated to talk politics, to study, and "simply to be where they could meet other Russians, speak the Russian language, find Russian books and newspapers to read."[134] One eyewitness described what happened on the evening of November 7. "We were attending classes, some of us; others reading newspapers, smoking and talking. Then—the Cossacks!"[135] Books and files were seized, and furniture was smashed. People were roughed up, shoved down staircases, and beaten with blackjacks. Newsmen reported hearing "heavy thuds as of clubs descending on human flesh," and seeing people wearing bandages which "were heavily blood-stained."[136]

Hyman Lachowsky was among those who were arrested. Beaten with a blackjack and bundled off in a patrol wagon, he was served with a deportation warrant and taken along with forty other Russian aliens to Ellis Island. Harry Weinberger later described meeting him there. "I saw Mr. Lachowsky about two days after the raid, with his head all bandaged, his head having been opened in three or four places by being beaten over the head with blackjacks at the time of the raid. . . ."[137] Arthur Katzes was also taken to the Island, as was Ethel Bernstein. Composing a short account of her "Detention in Hell," she declared, "What a mockery! How these brutes act in the name of 'justice'! What conception they have of 'justice'!"[138] Both would be deported in December, on the *Buford,* the ship that carried Emma Goldman, Alexander Berkman, and 247 other aliens to Russia. Weinberger had sought permission for Ethel Bernstein to make a visit to her home, under armed guard if necessary, to pack her belongings, but Byron Uhl rejected the idea.

When he failed to convince the authorities to accept a reduction in the $10,000 bail set for Hyman Lachowsky, Weinberger took the case to court. He hoped that the judge would rule on a humane basis, he told Emma Goldman, adding bitterly, "but then, what is humanity to law."[139] He probably omitted the question mark on purpose. If the excesses committed in the name of the newly formed surveillance state had driven a social reformer like Frederic C. Howe to resign in angry protest, it is not difficult to imagine their effect on the more radical Weinberger.

In a real sense, his work on the anarchists' behalf was only beginning. If, as Weinberger reported, he had met Lachowsky two days after his arrest, it would have been on Monday, November 10, 1919. He would then have returned to his office to learn that the Supreme Court, that same day, had handed down its decision in *Jacob Abrams et al.* v. *United States.*

1. Jacob Abrams, 1910

2. Mollie Steimer

3. OPPOSITE: Jacob and Mary Abrams, with friends, reading *Der Shturm*, 1917

4. Samuel Lipman, 1916

5. *Frayhayt* Group, 1918

1. Hyman Lachowsky
2. Mollie Steimer (?)
3. Jacob Abrams
4. Sam Adel
5. Hilda Adel
6. Mary Abrams
7. Zalman Deanin
8. Sonya Deanin

6. Jacob Abrams and Jacob Schwartz, 1916

7 and 8. Two views of the funeral of Jacob Schwartz,
October 1918

9. OPPOSITE: Mary and Jacob Abrams, moments before entering prison, December 1919

10. Henry DeLamar Clayton, Jr.

11. Harry Weinberger, Hilda and Sam Adel, and niece

12. ABOVE: John Lord O'Brian

13. RIGHT: Francis Gordon Caffey

14. Oliver Wendell Holmes, Jr., 1922

15. Louis D. Brandeis

16. LEFT: John H. Wigmore

17. BELOW: Zechariah Chafee, Jr.

18. Samuel Lipman, Hyman Lachowsky, Mollie Steimer, and Jacob Abrams at the time of their deportation, 1921

19. Jacob Abrams, Ethel Bernstein, and Samuel Lipman in Russia

20. Senya Fleshin, Mollie Steimer, and Samuel Lipman in Russia

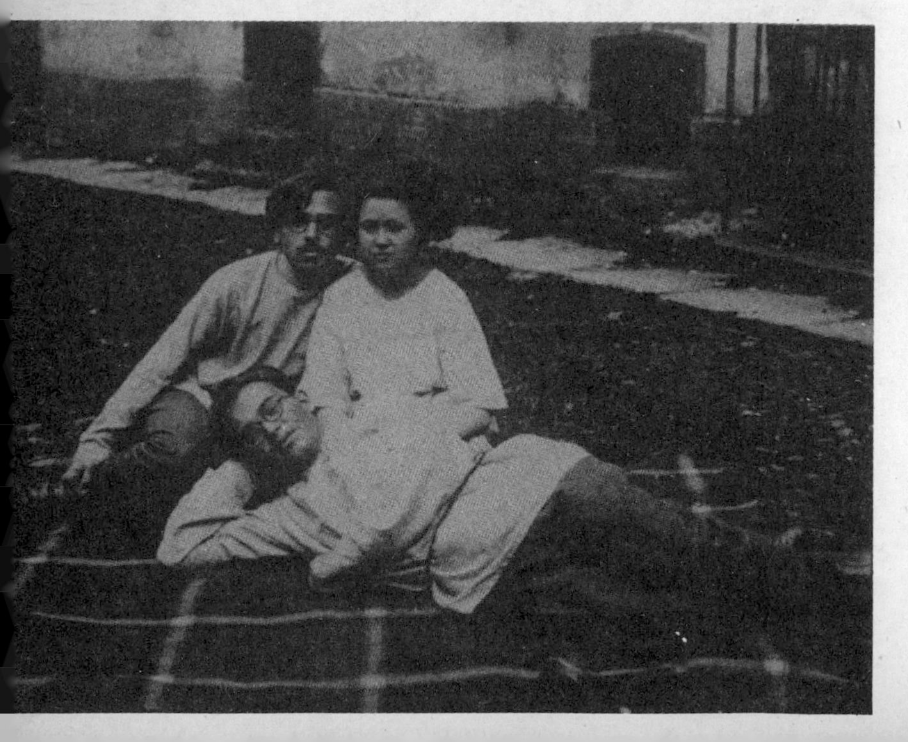

# 6

# The Supreme Court

## Conservatism and the Court

On Tuesday, October 21, 1919, just before noon, the nine Justices of the Supreme Court emerged from the room in the Capitol in which they donned their robes, and, led by Chief Justice Edward D. White, marched solemnly across the corridor to the courtroom where the day's calendar awaited them. After some preliminary formalities, the Justices heard motions regarding petitions for writs of certiorari in two cases involving railroad lines. Then the Court turned to the first of three Espionage Act cases on the docket, that of Joseph V. Stilson and Joseph Sukys. Members of the Lithuanian Socialist Federation in Philadelphia, they had published an anti-war newspaper and circulars, in Lithuanian, that had led to their conviction for conspiracy to obstruct the draft. Their appeal, however, focused entirely on procedural questions relating to the judge's conduct of the trial and his charge to the jury. The second case raised more substantive issues. It involved Peter Schaefer and four other men who put out the Philadelphia *Tageblatt,* a German-language newspaper. They had been convicted for publishing "false reports and statements with intent to promote the success of Germany and obstruct the recruiting and enlistment service of the United States."[1]

At two o'clock the Justices took their customary thirty-minute recess for lunch, and later in the afternoon the third Espionage Act case, *Jacob*

*Abrams et al.* v. *United States,* was called. Harry Weinberger made an opening statement in behalf of the "plaintiffs in error," as the anarchists were now legally known. Then Assistant Attorney General Robert P. Stewart started to argue the opposing case for the government. Before he could finish, however, the four o'clock hour of adjournment arrived. So he continued his presentation on Wednesday, and Weinberger, as was customary, made the concluding statement. Believing he had made a good impression, Weinberger wired his assistant, Jerome Weiss, "The argument here looks good for a favorable decision."[2]

Weinberger misread the Justices' reactions, perhaps because all or most of the questions were asked by Oliver Wendell Holmes, Jr., and Louis D. Brandeis, the two Justices, and the only two, who were sympathetically inclined. (This is necessarily conjecture, since, at the time, oral arguments before the Court were not transcribed.) But if the other seven members of the Court had indeed remained silent, or nearly so, their silence reflected anything but agreement with Weinberger. To the contrary, their values, convictions, experiences, and legal training led them to believe that anarchists posed a threat that called for the sternest countermeasures. Dedicated to upholding the rights of property, and devoted, as one legal historian has put it, to preserving "civil order," these seven Justices were not about to extend First Amendment protection to the kind of leaflets that Jacob Abrams and the others had distributed.[3]

The Chief Justice, Edward D. White, had a practical acquaintance with treason, having himself once taken up arms against the government. Born and brought up in Louisiana, on his family's sugar plantation, he was sixteen years old, a student at Georgetown College in Washington, when the Civil War broke out. White immediately returned home and volunteered to serve in the Confederate Army. Captured by Union forces in July 1863, he spent several months in prison before being paroled. When the war was over, White turned his attention to the law. He was admitted to the Louisiana bar after one year's study with a lawyer. Success then followed political success as he moved from the state Senate, to the state Supreme Court, and then, in 1888, to the United States Senate. In 1894 President Grover Cleveland surprised everyone by nominating him for the United States Supreme Court. White was not Cleveland's first choice, or, for that matter, his second or third, but Cleveland's preferred nominees, all New Yorkers, had either declined or had their candidacies shot down by New York Senator David Bennett Hill. Cleveland finally decided to outfox Hill by nominating a Senator, knowing that senatorial courtesy would require even Hill to vote for confirmation. White was an opponent of the administration's tariff program, so Cleveland was as anxious to remove him from the Senate as to install him on the high court.[4]

Just as White's appointment in 1894 served President Cleveland's ulterior purposes, his elevation to the Chief Justiceship in 1910 served President William Howard Taft's. To Taft, apparently, the most important consideration was that the new Chief Justice be the right age. Since Taft wanted to be appointed Chief Justice, after completing his term or terms as President, he wanted to select someone who was young enough to last until he was himself ready, but old enough to retire (or expire) when that time came. Accordingly, the fifty-three-year-old Taft bypassed the logical contender, forty-eight-year-old Justice Charles Evans Hughes, and selected the sixty-five-year-old White. (White died in 1921, and he was succeeded, slightly behind schedule, by Taft.) White never much liked writing opinions, for reasons best described by his biographer: "He found that he could write only when pressing the first finger of his right hand against the right side of his nose. Holding the pen between the second finger and his thumb, he had to bend until his nose nearly touched the paper, and should the first finger slip from his nose, the pen would drop from his hand."[5]

A stickler for the letter of the law, White was often insensitive to the actual effects of his rulings. In 1910, for example, the Court decided a case involving a government disbursing officer who had committed the petty crime of making false entries in a wage book but who had been sentenced to fifteen years at hard labor, wearing the ball and chain. The Court overturned the sentence on the grounds that the Constitution prohibited "cruel and unusual punishment," but the Chief Justice dissented, holding that this language referred only to "inhuman methods of causing bodily torture."[6] A comfortable member of a governing elite, White regarded radicals as wrong-headed and dangerous. Speaking to the annual banquet of the American Bar Association in 1914, he said that when he thought of "the infinite opportunity afforded those who misguidedly or with intentional wrong preach the destruction of our institutions under the guise of preserving freedom, a great dread comes to me that possibly some day in the future the forces of evil, of anarchy, and of wrong may gather such momentum as to enable them to overthrow . . . the constitutional institutions which the Fathers gave us and deprive us of the blessings which have come from their possession."[7] A man who loved formality, White greeted each of the Associate Justices, in order of seniority, by saying, "Good morning, Mr. Justice," and each, in turn, replied, "Good morning, Mr. Chief Justice."

The first of his brethren whom the Chief Justice greeted each morning was Joseph McKenna, who had been appointed to the Court in 1898. McKenna, whose family had moved to California when he was a youth, had completed a two-year course at Benicia Collegiate Institute, had studied law for a year, and had then appeared before a judge who asked him some questions and anointed him a lawyer. Entering local Republican Party politics, McKenna began a slow climb through the ranks that in 1884 led to his election to the House of Representatives. He served four terms, voting a hard-line Republican policy, and earning a well-deserved reputation as a friend of the Central Pacific Railroad. He also made the right friends, one of them fellow Representative William McKinley. Eventually McKenna reaped the rewards of his long, faithful political service. In 1891 he was appointed to the Ninth Circuit Court of Appeals, despite some sentiment that he lacked the necessary legal qualifications. In 1897, with his good friend McKinley in the White House, McKenna was appointed Attorney General and nine months later was chosen for the Supreme Court.

Recognizing his own limitations, McKenna, according to one scholar, "spent some time in New York at the Columbia University Law School in a feeble attempt to ready himself."[8] Ready or not, McKenna came to Washington, and in twenty-seven years on the Court he would be the author of 656 opinions. Unlike White, he had no difficulty in writing, only in expressing himself clearly. His biographer maintains that "he was regarded as somewhat slow in his mental processes, confused in his logic and lacking an easily definable legal philosophy . . ."[9] Another writer has characterized that philosophy as "erratic empiricism." "His mind uncluttered by the complex dicta of legal scholarship, McKenna tended to decide each case individually as it came before the Court, mostly on the basis of the application of 'common sense.' "[10] In his spare time McKenna played golf at the Chevy Chase Country Club, or hunted on a private estate owned by the president of the Pennsylvania Railroad.

McKenna's reaction to the Abrams case can be surmised from the opinion he later wrote in the Schaefer case (which, we have seen, immediately preceded *Abrams* on the Court's docket). McKenna's majority opinion upheld the convictions of three of the five men associated with the Philadelphia *Tageblatt.* The provisions of the Espionage Act were "not excessive nor ambiguous," McKenna said, but "were directed against conduct—speech or writings—that was designed to obstruct the recruitment or enlistment service or to weaken or debase the spirit of our armies causing them, it might be, to operate to defeat and the immeasurable horror and calamity of it." The fractured syntax aside, McKenna's aversion to those who claimed that the Constitution protected such speech was apparent. "A curious spectacle was presented: that great ordinance of government and orderly liberty was invoked to justify the activities of anarchy or of the enemies of the United States, and by a strange perversion of its precepts it was adduced against itself." However "coarse" and "vulgar" the pro-German articles, they might "chill and check the ardency of patriotism and make it despair of success and in hopelessness relax energy both in preparation and action." Worse still, McKenna feared, the morale of American soldiers "could be weakened or debased by question or calumny of the motives of authority."[11]

McKenna owed his appointment to William McKinley, but it was Justice William Rufus Day, elevated to the Supreme Court by Theodore Roosevelt, who devoted himself to keeping McKinley's memory green. The two men had been intimate personal friends, and Day never completely got over the shock of McKinley's assassination. In September 1901, when it still seemed McKinley might recover from the gunshot wounds inflicted by Leon Czolgosz, an alleged anarchist, Day implicitly equated such acts of terrorism with anarchism. "The advocates of its awful tenets must be kept from our shores; its principles must be torn, root and branch, from every foot of our domain, until its adherents learn that to attack the government through its highest official is one of the most heinous of crimes, sure to meet with swift and terrible retribution. Let there be no nook or corner of the civilized world in which it can hide and call itself safe." About a year later, on the anniversary of McKinley's death, Day declared, "This tragedy, which fills our hearts with grief, has a lesson for the living, and calls upon lawmakers and law enforcers for all that legislation and courts can do for the suppression and punishment of those who teach or practice the dreadful tenets of this code of lawlessness and ruin."[12] In January 1903, four months after making this speech, Day was nominated for the Supreme Court. Every year thereafter, on McKinley's birthday, he wore a carnation and brought eight more for his brethren.[13]

His lasting sorrow gave Day a serious mien, but it cannot be said that he had ever been a happy-go-lucky type. Even at the age of seventeen, a classmate at the University of Michigan pictured him as "running an undertaker's establishment and driving the hearse himself."[14] Day received a bachelor's degree after two years of study, read law for a year, and then took courses at the Michigan law school for another year. In 1872 he was admitted to the Ohio bar, and for the next twenty-five years he practiced law in Canton, Ohio, where McKinley also had a law office. In 1897 his best friend, now President, brought Day to Washington, first as Assistant Secretary and then as Secretary of State. Day later headed the American delegation to the peace conference following the Spanish-American War, and in 1899 was appointed to the Sixth Circuit Court of Appeals. There he remained for four years, until Roosevelt named him to the high court. Although he would serve until 1922, Day's biographer notes: "Like most of his contemporaries, he accepted the twentieth century with a certain reluctance."[15]

Those words also describe the two Justices appointed by President Taft—Willis Van Devanter and Mahlon Pitney—both of whom sorely begrudged the modern era. Van Devanter, who had been educated at the Cincinnati Law School, had made himself a behind-the-scenes power in Republican politics in Wyoming. He had served on the Eighth Circuit Court of Appeals from 1903 until 1910 when Taft chose him for the high court. Pitney, a Princeton graduate, had served briefly in the House of Representatives. Appointed to the New Jersey Supreme Court in 1901, he went on to hold the highest judicial post in the state, that of Chancellor, and took his seat on the Supreme Court in 1912. Van Devanter traced his ancestry to a Dutch settler who emigrated to America in 1662; Pitney was named for his paternal greatgrandfather who had fought in the Revolutionary War. Both men had sons who saw combat duty in World War I, and, as Van Devanter worriedly reported to his own son, the younger Pitney had been wounded by shrapnel which "penetrated his foot inflicting a bad wound and splintering some of the bones."[16]

Both men were rock-ribbed conservatives. Van Devanter worried that "it is in the air to reach out for *something new,*" so that "things are likely to be done which will not stand the test to which all things in real life must come sooner or later. Government cannot be maintained nor businesses be successfully conducted on the principle of the sailor who thinks any port looks good in a storm."[17] Less given to such sententious utterances, Pitney was known, if not universally loved, for his hostility to trade unions. In 1902, in a case involving a strike by New Jersey glassblowers, Pitney had upheld a sweeping injunction which not only forbade picketing and boycotting, but even barred union members from "addressing" scab workers "against their will, and thereby causing them personal annoyance, with a view to persuade them to refrain from such employment." The dissenting Justices said Pitney's decision was founded on outdated English cases "which bear the distinct impress of feudal law and custom."[18] When Progressives made a futile attempt to block Pitney's confirmation, the president of the National Association of Manufacturers, noting that he "comes from the kind of stock of which just and fearless judges are made," expressed indignation at the prospect that any Senator would vote against Pitney "because of the protest of labor agitators!"[19]

Mahlon Pitney would write the Supreme Court's decision in *Pierce et al.* v. *United States,* an Espionage Act case that was argued a month after *Abrams.* Four Albany socialists had been convicted for having circulated a pamphlet, entitled "The Price We Pay," in the summer of 1917. Written by Irwin St. John Tucker, an Episcopal clergyman, the pamphlet condemned conscription, and asserted that despite the rhetoric about democratic war aims "this war began over commercial routes and ports and rights" and was being fought to "determine the question, whether the chambers of commerce of the allied nations or of the Central Empires have the superior right to exploit underdeveloped countries." The indictment charged, in part, that these were "false" statements. To Justice Pitney the charge seemed eminently well founded, for, he thought, "there was lawful evidence of the falsity of the statements." What kind of evidence? "Common knowledge (not to mention the President's Address to Congress of April 2, 1917, and the Joint Resolution of April 6 declaring war, which were introduced in evidence) would have sufficed to show at least that the statements as to the causes that led to the entry of the United States into the war against Germany were grossly false; and such common knowledge went to prove also that defendants knew they were untrue."[20] Through this feat of judicial legerdemain, First Amendment safeguards vanished if speakers disagreed with official policy or with whatever Pitney considered "common knowledge."

The Justice, however, who was most intensely biased against all dissenters, particularly the kind of dissenters who were represented in the Abrams case, was James Clark McReynolds. The first of Woodrow Wilson's appointees, he was, at fifty-seven, the youngest member of the Court. Born in Kentucky, McReynolds had attended Vanderbilt University and had then studied law at the University of Virginia. He had received his degree in 1884, after which he practiced law in Nashville for nearly twenty years. Appointed Assistant Attorney General in 1903, he soon gained a reputation for vigorous enforcement of the antitrust laws. When he left government service in 1907, McReynolds moved to New York City. He backed Wilson's candidacy in 1912 and was named Attorney General in the new administration. But his unbridled temper and haughty manner alienated the congressmen and officials with whom he had to deal. Wilson, wishing to eliminate this source of friction and place an antitrust man on the bench, appointed him to the Supreme Court in August 1914.

A man of strong likes and even stronger dislikes, McReynolds, according to Taft, was "fuller of prejudice than any man I have known."[21] He expressed those prejudices in snide comments and in unseemly behavior. Once, when an attorney, a woman, appeared before the Supreme Court, McReynolds snapped, "I see the female is here again."[22] When the Court overturned the conviction of Socialist leader Victor Berger on the grounds that the trial judge had made disparaging comments about German Americans ("their hearts are reeking with disloyalty," for example), McReynolds dissented; he noted that the judge had directed his remark "towards certain malevolents from Germany, a country then engaged in hunnish warfare and notoriously encouraged by many of its natives who, unhappily, had obtained citizenship here."[23] McReynolds said contemptuously that blacks were "ignorant, superstitious, immoral and with but small capacity for radical improvement."[24] Harold Laski once commented that "McReynolds and the theory of a beneficent deity are quite incompatible."[25]

McReynolds was a consummate anti-Semite: he loathed Jews for the fact that they were Jews, and he made his feelings known. The appointment in 1916 of Louis D. Brandeis—the "Hebrew," McReynolds called him—was a source of unrelieved grief. For a time, McReynolds would ostentatiously leave the conference room when Brandeis began to speak; he stood outside the door and did not reenter until Brandeis was done. In 1921, when Taft, the new Chief Justice, asked when it would be convenient for the Justices to dine with the Attorney General, McReynolds replied, "Anytime, My dear Chief Justice. I do not expect to attend, as I find it hard to dine with the *Orient.*"[26] According to Brandeis, in this instance perhaps not the most objective reporter, Oliver Wendell Holmes referred to McReynolds as "a savage, with all the irrational impulses of a savage. Holmes says he isn't civilized—he is a primitive man."[27]

A clue to the thoughts that may have been running through James Clark McReynolds' mind when Harry Weinberger appeared on behalf of Jacob Abrams, Mollie Steimer, Samuel Lipman, and Hyman Lachowsky is provided by a comment he made to Holmes about another case the Court heard that same October term of 1919. In *Evans* v. *Gore,* the Court was asked to rule on a recently passed measure that required federal judges to pay income taxes. Although the Justices all voluntarily filed tax returns, the majority held that the law was unconstitutional. Holmes dissented, arguing that the Constitution did not make judges a privileged class, and he was joined by Brandeis. McReynolds, evidently believing that Brandeis had persuaded Holmes to dissent, wrote a message on the opinion Holmes circulated asking him whether he had ever thought "that for four thousand years the Lord tried to make something out of Hebrews, then gave it up as impossible and turned them out to prey on mankind in general—like fleas on the dog for example."[28]

For some unexplained reason, the fellow Justice whom McReynolds treated the most unkindly, and the one whom he hurt the most, was not Brandeis but John Hessin Clarke. Although Clarke had none of McReynolds' mean-spiritedness, the two men had much else in common: both had bolted the Democratic Party in 1896 in reaction to William Jennings Bryan's nomination and had supported the "Gold Democrats"; both had represented major railroads, McReynolds the Illinois Central and Clarke the Nickel Plate and Erie lines; both had been appointed to the Supreme Court because Wilson regarded them as sound on the issue of trusts. But while McReynolds would remain on the Court for twenty-seven years, Clarke stayed for only six. Appointed in 1916, he resigned in 1922, primarily because he found the work wearying but also because of McReynolds' unrelenting hostility. True to his nature, McReynolds pointedly refused to sign the Court's farewell letter. Clarke later commented that McReynolds was "too much of a grouch to have a good opinion even of himself."[29]

Of all the Justices, Clarke's outlook was probably closest to Woodrow Wilson's. Taking an expansive view of government's power to regulate the economy, Clarke favored workmen's compensation and child labor laws. He also held a favorable view of labor unions, and was prepared to uphold the right to strike and march on picket lines. A supporter of Wilson's foreign policy and the war, Clarke told his old friend Secretary of War Newton D. Baker that he felt privileged to have had a chance to witness "the great part which our beloved country has had in the salvation of the world."[30] When the armistice was signed in November 1918, Clarke complimented the President on his "clear vision," and, on retiring from the Court, devoted himself to campaigning for United States affiliation with the League of Nations and membership in the World Court.[31]

But like other Wilsonians, Clarke drew the line sharply when it came to tolerating radical agitators. In 1901, as a successful attorney in Youngstown, Ohio, he had written an article deploring "the obnoxious, supercilious 'philosophy' of the 'reds' . . . accompanied by the most brutal expressions of the spirit of murder. . . . Their doctrines are most dangerous and should find no room for culture or spread in this free and enlightened government." Clarke's views never changed, his biographer notes, and he always demonstrated an "instinctive hostility to violent change or extreme radicalism in any form. Revolutionary talk, no less than revolutionary acts, was repulsive to him." The very strength of his commitment to the President's war aims may have made Clarke especially unsympathetic to Jacob Abrams or anyone else who denounced Wilson as a hypocrite. In any event, Clarke had a "deep-seated emotional distaste for the exaggerated, violent talk of the radical fringe. . . . He could not shed the prejudice, widely shared by his class of the progressive elite, against the unwashed, ill-mannered Socialists and Anarchists."[32]

All things considered, there was little reason for Harry Weinberger to be sanguine as he took his seat in the Capitol courtroom on October 22, 1919. For the most part, the men before whom he had been pleading had been placed on the Supreme Court not because of their legal attainments but for reasons having to do with personal friendship or political service. Holmes and Brandeis excepted, the Justices' belief in property rights was matched only by their fear of radicalism, and their view of the First Amendment was summed up in Edward D. White's comment that freedom of speech was "subject to the restraints which separate right from wrong-doing."[33] The subtitle of a biography of the Chief Justice—"Defender of the Conservative Faith"—describes the Court as accurately as it does the man.

## Oliver Wendell Holmes and the Clear and Present Danger Standard

The Justice who listened most attentively to the contending presentations by Harry Weinberger and Assistant Attorney General Robert P. Stewart may have been Oliver Wendell Holmes, Jr. Seven months earlier, in March 1919, when the Court had decided the first Espionage Act cases that came before it, Holmes had formulated the "clear and present danger" standard. That standard was consistent with everything that Holmes, in a legal career spanning fifty years, had written about the relationship between law and human nature, and about the proper balance between social order and individual rights. The clear and present danger test, in its original form, was not at all solicitous of the rights of dissenters. Between March and November, as we shall see, Holmes's thinking would undergo a significant change, and the Abrams case would play a central role in that change.

The son of a famous father, Holmes had grown up in a Beacon Street home at which Theodore Parker, Wendell Phillips, and Ralph Waldo Emerson ("Uncle Waldo" to the young Oliver) were frequent visitors. Holmes had entered Harvard in 1857, but even before his graduation in 1861 he had joined an infantry regiment to fight in the Civil War. In October 1861 the twenty-year-old Holmes suffered a chest wound at the battle of Ball's Bluff, the bullet narrowly missing his heart and lung. At Antietam in September 1862 he was shot through the neck. In May 1863, at the second battle of Fredericksburg, he was hit by shrapnel which splintered his heel and nearly cost him a leg. Eventually he was able to rejoin his regiment, and when he left the Union Army in July 1864 it was as a Lieutenant Colonel. Returning to Boston, Holmes took a law degree at Harvard, and entered practice. In 1882 he briefly held a professorship at Harvard Law School, but resigned in December, after only a term, to accept a position on the Supreme Judicial Court of Massachusetts. Explaining his decision, Holmes wrote that one could not "without moral loss decline any share in the practical struggle of life" or opt for "the less manly course."[34] In 1899 Holmes became Chief Justice of the Massachusetts Court, and in 1902 President Theodore Roosevelt appointed him to the Supreme Court.

In 1881 Holmes had published *The Common Law.* The book's famous dictum—"The life of the law has not been logic: it has been experience"—was Holmes's elegant way of saying that laws necessarily embody people's values; as those values change, so do laws. Laws, he said, "correspond with the actual feelings and demands of the community, whether right or wrong." Moreover, Holmes thought, since people are not fundamentally altruistic, laws, which reflect people's needs, cannot be founded "on a theory of absolute unselfishness." He continued, "At the bottom of all private relations, however tempered by sympathy and all the social feelings, is a justifiable self-preference. If a man is on a plank in the deep sea which will only float one, and a stranger lays hold of it, he will thrust him off if he can. When the state finds itself in a similar position, it does the same thing." Starting with these premises, Holmes concluded that in the event of a conflict between individual rights and national welfare only one outcome is possible: "No society has ever admitted that it could not sacrifice individual welfare to its own existence. If conscripts are necessary for its army, it seizes them, and marches them, with bayonets in their rear, to death."[35]

If laws reflect prevailing values, and if those values are subjective and self-centered, it is especially important, Holmes thought, for the administration of justice to be as objective and impartial as possible. Judges and juries should concern themselves with the acts people commit, not with their reasons for committing them. The law should not even inquire into "the degree of evil in the particular person's motives or intentions." Intent, in legal terms, did not refer to what a person wanted to happen but only to "what a man of reasonable prudence would have foreseen." However difficult the quest, courts must always search for a "general objective standard," not for "internal phenomena of conscience." Holmes stated his conclusion bluntly: "Moral predilections must not be allowed to influence our minds in settling legal distinctions."[36]

Three of his early Supreme Court decisions illustrate how the views expressed in *The Common Law* shaped Holmes's approach to reconciling the claims of liberty and order. *Patterson* v. *Colorado* (1907) involved a newspaper which had published articles and cartoons attacking the manner in which the Supreme Court of Colorado was handling a case while it was still pending. A judge had found the newspaper in contempt, and the state defended the citation on the grounds that freedom of speech cannot "be carried to such an extreme as to impede, embarrass, or justly influence the due and orderly administration of justice, or prejudice the rights of litigants in pending cases." Holmes agreed. "When a case is finished, courts are subject to the same criticism as other people," he wrote, "but the propriety and necessity of preventing interference with the course of justice by premature statement, argument or intimidation hardly can be denied." Holmes was satisfied that the grounds upon which such contempts were punished were "impersonal." It made no difference whether or not the newspaper's statements were "true," Holmes added, for the constitutional provisions protecting free speech, while barring prior restraint, "do not prevent the subsequent punishment of such as may be deemed contrary to the public welfare."[37]

The second case, involving a far more severe abridgment of individual freedom, also originated in Colorado. In 1903 the Western Federation of Miners went on strike and the state was plunged into industrial warfare. Governor James H. Peabody declared a state of emergency, imposed martial law, and called in the militia. On March 30, 1904, Charles Moyer, a union leader, was arrested and held without bail or a trial until June 15. The issue before the Supreme Court was whether Peabody had deprived Moyer of due process of law by locking him up for two and one-half months when the courts were functioning. Writing for a unanimous Court in *Moyer* v. *Peabody* (1908), Holmes held that "due process of law depends on circumstances. It varies with the subject-matter and the necessities of the situation." Since the Governor had the right to call in the militia, and even to order the soldiers to "kill persons who resist," he surely had the right to apprehend those he considered dangerous, so long as the arrests were made "in good faith and in the honest belief that they are needed in order to head the insurrection off." Holmes then rephrased what he had written in 1881 about marching conscripts off to war: "When it comes to a decision by the head of the State upon a matter involving its life, the ordinary rights of individuals must yield to what he deems the necessities of the moment."[38]

The third case arose when, on a summer's day in 1911, Mrs. Stella Thornhill went swimming in the nude because, she claimed, it was good for her rheumatism. She was a resident of Home Colony, an anarchist community on Puget Sound, where behavior such as hers had become a source of considerable controversy. When Mrs. Thornhill was fined sixty-five dollars, another resident, Jay Fox, wrote an editorial entitled "The Nude and the Prudes" in the community's paper, *The Agitator.* Fox condemned the opponents of nude swimming, and was indicted under a Washington statute which made it a misdemeanor "to encourage or advocate disrespect for law," in this instance the law against indecent exposure. Tried in January 1912, he was convicted and sentenced to two months in prison. In May 1915 a unanimous Supreme Court upheld the decision, with Holmes again writing the opinion.[39]

Holmes began by quoting excerpts from Fox's editorial, especially those sections urging the "free spirits" to boycott the "few prudes" who "got into the community and proceeded in the brutal, unneighborly way of the outside world to suppress the people's freedom." Holmes concluded that "by indirection but unmistakably the article encourages and incites a persistence in what we must assume would be a breach of the state laws against indecent exposure." By interpreting "disrespect" to mean "manifested disrespect, as active disregard going beyond the line drawn by the law," Holmes sidestepped the issue of whether the statute could be invoked against someone simply for criticizing the laws. "It does not appear and is not likely that the statute will be construed to prevent publications merely because they tend to produce unfavorable opinions of a particular statute or of law in general." Again echoing *The Common Law,* Holmes explained that "we have nothing to do with the wisdom of the defendant, the prosecution, or the act. All that concerns us is that it cannot be said to infringe the Constitution of the United States."[40]

Writing to friends in the years between *Fox* v. *Washington* and the wartime Espionage Act cases, Holmes referred scornfully to softheaded social reformers who failed to realize that order would always come before liberty, the state before the individual. To many, Holmes may have appeared cynical, but surely he preferred to think that he possessed a realistic understanding of human nature. It was not his fault, as he put it, that "man's destiny is to fight."[41] In November 1915 he asked an acquaintance, Dean John Wigmore of the Northwestern University Law School, "doesn't this squashy sentimentality of a big minority of our people about human life make you puke?" Holmes said he was thinking of several groups: those who condemn "the sensible doctor and parents who don't perform an operation to keep a deformed and nearly idiot baby alive—also of pacifists—of people who believe there is an upward and onward—who talk of uplift—who think that something particular has happened and that the universe is no longer predatory. Oh bring in a basin."[42]

In the summer of 1918 Holmes explained his view of free speech, a view to which forty years of reflection had led him. A nation would protect itself against the expression of dangerous opinions, he said, as readily as it would against the spread of smallpox. "Free speech stands no differently than freedom from vaccination," he told Judge Learned Hand. "The occasions would be rarer when you cared enough to stop it but if for any reason you did care enough you wouldn't care a damn for the suggestion that you were acting on a provisional hypothesis and might be wrong."[43] In a letter to Harold Laski, Holmes succinctly restated the same argument: "My thesis would be (1) if you are cocksure, and (2) if you want it very much, and (3) if you have no doubt of your power—you will do what you believe efficient to bring about what you want—by legislation or otherwise. In most matters of belief we are not cocksure—we don't care very much—and we are not certain of our power. But in the opposite case we should deal with the act of speech as we deal with any other overt act that we don't like."[44]

This was how Holmes saw things when, late in January 1919, the first three Espionage Act cases—*Schenck, Frohwerk,* and *Debs*—came before the Supreme Court. Arguing each case for the government were the Special Assistants to the Attorney General, John Lord O'Brian and Alfred Bettman. The Court unanimously upheld all three convictions, and Holmes wrote all three opinions. *Schenck* was decided on March 3, *Frohwerk* and *Debs* on March 10. Although the facts in the cases were substantially different, the clear and present danger standard which Holmes formulated to justify the ruling in *Schenck* also served as the basis for the two other decisions.

Charles T. Schenck was the general secretary of the Socialist Party in Philadelphia. In August 1917 he and his comrades had arranged to mail a leaflet to men whose names were listed in the newspapers as having passed their draft board physical examinations. The leaflet was printed front and back; the statement on one side was entitled "LONG LIVE THE CONSTITUTION OF THE UNITED STATES," and on the other "ASSERT YOUR RIGHTS!" Both attacked conscription as a repudiation of the freedom guaranteed by the Constitution. "A conscript is little better than a convict," began the most famous sentence. "He is deprived of his liberty and of his right to think and act as a free man." As many as 15,000 copies of the leaflet may have been printed, although not all were mailed. Schenck and four others were arrested and charged with conspiring to "obstruct the recruiting and enlistment services of the United States." The trial, which was held in December 1917, lasted four days. The judge directed the jury to acquit three of the defendants for lack of evidence. Schenck and Dr. Elizabeth Baer, a member of the Party's executive committee, were found guilty; he received a six-month sentence, she ninety days. Both remained free on bail until the Supreme Court upheld their convictions.[45]

Holmes's opinion, after quoting some of the leaflet's more quotable passages, offered a summation of the theme: "It denied the power to send our citizens away to foreign shores to shoot up the people of other lands, and added that words could not express the condemnation such cold-blooded ruthlessness deserves, &c., &c., . . ." Those who mailed the leaflet must have intended it to have an effect "and we do not see what effect it could be expected to have upon persons subject to the draft except to influence them to obstruct the carrying of it out." Conceding that in time of peace the defendants would have been within their rights in publishing the leaflet, Holmes continued, "But the character of every act depends upon the circumstances in which it is done. The most stringent protection of free speech would not protect a man in falsely shouting fire in a theatre and causing a panic. . . . The question in every case is whether the words used are used in such circumstances and are of such a nature as to create a clear and present danger that they will bring about the substantive evils that Congress has a right to prevent. It is a question of proximity and degree." The "clear and present danger" test, therefore, was first used not to protect speech but rather to limit it, and the most brilliantly persuasive expression that ever came from Holmes's pen—"falsely shouting fire in a theatre and causing a panic"—was employed to justify the limitation.[46]

Inasmuch as the anti-draft circulars had been mailed to a select group of men who were preparing to enter the armed forces, the Schenck case seemed at the time, and later, to offer an example of speech that indeed constituted a clear and present danger. But the transcript of the trial, the reports of the federal agents who arrested Schenck and his co-workers, and the correspondence of Francis Fisher Kane, the United States Attorney who decided to prosecute the case, suggest that the case was not as clear-cut as Holmes thought.

To begin with, Kane admitted that he "was already familiar with" the side of the leaflet entitled "LONG LIVE THE CONSTITUTION," which the Socialists had been distributing for some time, and did not believe it violated the Espionage Act.[47] While the leaflet asserted that conscription was unconstitutional and unjust, it did not call on anyone to violate the law but rather to change it through the orderly processes of government. Readers were urged to "join the Socialist Party in its campaign for the repeal of the Conscription Act. Write to your congressman and tell him you want the law repealed. Do not submit to intimidation. You have a right to demand the repeal of any law. Exercise your rights of free speech, peaceful assemblage and petitioning the government for a redress of grievances. Come to the headquarters of the Socialist Party, 1326 Arch Street, and sign a petition to congress for the repeal of the Conscription Act."[48] Holmes admitted that this side of the leaflet "in form at least confined itself to peaceful measures such as a petition for the repeal of the act."[49] Yet he nevertheless offered it as an example of speech that poses a clear and present danger.

It was the other side of the leaflet—the side entitled "ASSERT YOUR RIGHTS!"—which moved Kane to action. He reported that it "contained printed matter that was entirely new to me, and which in my judgment was clearly an appeal to violate the provisions of the conscription law."[50] Yet this second tract, while certainly more impassioned, contains no such appeal. Of its two most "extreme" statements, one was quoted—somewhat incorrectly—by the Bureau of Investigation agent, Frank L. Garbarino, who first brought the leaflet to Kane's attention; and the other was quoted—also somewhat incorrectly—by Oliver Wendell Holmes in his decision. Garbarino quoted the leaflet as follows: "In lending tacit or silent consent to the conscription law, in neglecting to assert your rights, you are (whether knowingly or not) helping to condone and support a most infamous and insidious conspiracy to abridge and destroy the sacred and cherished rights of a free people."[51] The leaflet, however, said "unknowingly," not "knowingly." Holmes, for his part, quoted the leaflet as follows: "If you do not assert and support your rights, you are helping to deny or disparage rights which it is the solemn duty of all citizens and residents of the United States to retain."[52] The leaflet had actually placed "deny and disparage rights" in quotation marks, because, to justify the argument that people had the right to express opposition to the draft, it had, a few paragraphs earlier, quoted the Ninth Amendment: "The enumeration in the Constitution of certain rights[,] shall not be construed to deny or disparage others retained by the people." Ironically, some of the words Holmes thought constituted a clear and present danger were taken directly from the Bill of Rights.

The trial record shows that few inductees ever received the circular and that none who did, and who testified, were influenced by it. It is not clear exactly how many circulars were actually mailed, or delivered, in August 1917. Once the postal inspector discovered the circulars, he impounded 610 other envelopes which, he suspected, contained them. The envelopes were easily detected, since they were addressed in distinctive handwriting styles, were mailed in batches from a few post offices, and were thin enough so that—even without being opened—their contents could be made out. At the trial, the prosecution called as witnesses eleven men to whom the circulars had been sent. Eight of them, however, had never received the circulars; one man had been handed the envelope by the United States Attorney in September, had opened it, but had not read the circular; seven others saw the envelopes for the first time in December when they took the witness stand, at which point they were handed the envelopes and opened them. Under cross-examination they stated, predictably enough, that the circulars would not have led them to violate the draft law. Only three of the prosecution's witnesses had received the letters in the mail in August. Each of them did the same thing: the first forwarded it to the postal authorities, "stating that I didn't think such literature should be sent through the mail"; the second said, "it caused me to go out of my way to bring the people that sent it around to the attention of the proper authorities"; and the third (whose name had been wrongly listed in the newspapers) reported, "and then I went and had a conversation with an attorney and I brought it to Mr. Kane."[53]

Of course, one can be guilty of conspiring to violate a law even if the conspiracy fails. As Holmes pointed out, "we perceive no ground for saying that success alone warrants making the act a crime."[54] But in the case of a conspiracy to violate the Espionage Act, as Holmes had stated, the elements of "proximity and degree" were crucial. The trial hardly demonstrated that the Socialist Party's circular created a "clear and present" danger of bringing about "the substantive evils that Congress has a right to prevent." Holmes would have rendered the facts in *Schenck* far more accurately—but far less memorably—had he written, "The most stringent protection of free speech would not protect a man in falsely advising theatregoers that a 'no smoking' ordinance deprived them of their rights, and causing the audience to turn him in as a troublemaker."

If the clear and present danger standard had to be stretched to accommodate *Schenck,* it had to be stretched even further in *Frohwerk.* Jacob Frohwerk had published a number of articles in the Missouri *Staats Zeitung* from July to December 1917, for which he had been tried under the Espionage Act and sentenced to ten years in prison. In his decision upholding the conviction, Holmes paraphrased the anti-war themes of the articles "to the general effect that we are in the wrong and are giving false and hypocritical reasons for our course. . . ." Holmes conceded that much of what Frohwerk had said was entirely proper even in wartime. "We do not lose our right to condemn either measures or men because the Country is at war." Besides, in *Frohwerk,* unlike *Schenck,* "it does not appear that there was any special effort to reach men who were subject to the draft."[55]

The problem, Holmes said, was that Frohwerk's attorneys had failed to submit a "bill of exceptions," so the Supreme Court had no way of knowing how strong the Government's evidence was. On the basis of the record before the Court, which was admittedly inadequate, "it is impossible to say that it might not have been found that the circulation of the paper was in quarters where a little breath would be enough to kindle a flame and that the fact was known and relied upon by those who sent the paper out." Elaborating on his view of free speech, Holmes added that the First Amendment "cannot have been, and obviously was not, intended to give immunity for every possible use of language." He now gave a somewhat different example than he had given in *Schenck:* no one could suppose "that to make criminal the counselling of a murder within the jurisdiction of Congress would be an unconstitutional interference with free speech."[56]

Holmes's decision in the Debs case revealed even more clearly the restrictive nature of the clear and present danger doctrine. Socialist leader Eugene V. Debs had given a speech in Canton, Ohio, in June 1918, in which he attacked all capitalist wars, and claimed "the purpose of the Allies is exactly the purpose of the Central Powers." Debs also said that working men and women always bore an unfair burden in wartime, and he praised the courage of the many socialists who had been persecuted by the government. As Holmes noted, however, "the main theme of the speech was socialism, its growth, and a prophecy of its ultimate success."[57] Indicted under the Sedition Act, Debs stood trial in federal district court in Cleveland in September. He was found guilty, among other things, of attempting to cause insubordination in the armed forces and of attempting to obstruct military recruitment. He was sentenced to a ten-year prison term. None of this surprised Debs, who had told a sympathizer, "I am expecting nothing but conviction under a law flagrantly unconstitutional and which was framed especially for the suppression of free speech."[58]

In his opinion for the Court Holmes summarized what Debs had said at Canton, but cited two additional pieces of evidence. The first was Debs's statement to the jury: "I have been accused of obstructing the war. I admit it. Gentlemen, I abhor war." The second was the St. Louis platform of the Socialist Party, adopted in April 1917, which called for "continuous, active, and public opposition to the war, through demonstrations, mass petitions, and all other means within our power." Evidence that Debs accepted this view of his duties when he made his Canton speech, Holmes wrote, "is evidence that if in that speech he used words tending to obstruct the recruiting service he meant that they should have that effect." Moreover, the jury had been instructed not to find Debs guilty "unless the words used had as their natural tendency and reasonably probable effect to obstruct the recruiting service, &c., and unless the defendant had the specific intent to do so in his mind." In *Debs* Holmes offered no analogies to shouting fire in a theater or to counseling murder. Claiming that the constitutional issue had been settled in *Schenck,* he did not even ask whether Debs's speech created a "clear and present danger"; the "natural tendency" and "reasonably probable effect" of his words were all that mattered.[59]

While writing the opinion in *Schenck,* Holmes said that the case had "wrapped itself around me like a snake in a deadly struggle to present the obviously proper in the forms of logic—the real substance being: Damn your eyes—that's the way 'it's' going to be." He had recently reread John Stuart Mill's *On Liberty,* Holmes added, and perhaps he was influenced by Mill's argument that speech could properly be limited when—and only when—it caused "harm" to society. Opinions "lost their immunity," according to Mill, "when the circumstances in which they are expressed are such as to constitute their expression a positive instigation to some mischievous act." The opinion that all corn dealers are starvers of the poor, Mill explained, could be printed in a newspaper but not "delivered orally to an excited mob assembled before the house of a corn dealer" or even "handed about among the same mob in the form of a placard."[60]

Holmes may have thought that the clear and present danger standard made a similar distinction, but his formulation, as historian Fred D. Ragan has pointed out, served nevertheless "as a negative or restraining device rather than as a positive, libertarian or permissive rule." The Oliver Wendell Holmes who wrote the Court's decisions in *Schenck*, *Frohwerk*, and *Debs* was the Civil War veteran, the legal theorist, and the jurist who thought that individual rights must yield when society felt threatened, who sneered at the squashy sentimentality of those who denied that the universe was predatory, and who drew a comparison between laws prohibiting certain kinds of speech and laws requiring vaccination against smallpox. As yet, Holmes was "quite insensitive to any claim for special judicial protection of free speech."[61]

## Holmes and the Libertarians

Shortly after the Supreme Court handed down the Debs decision, Holmes received a letter from Judge Learned Hand. The two men had begun to correspond the previous June, after a chance meeting on a train as each was traveling to his summer home, Holmes to Beverly Farms, Massachusetts, and Hand to Cornish, New Hampshire. They had started to talk about "Tolerance" ("that rarest of the gods," as Hand once termed it) and continued their discussion in an exchange of letters. "Opinions are at best provisional hypotheses, incompletely tested," Hand had written at the time, ". . . they are never absolutes. So we must be tolerant of opposite opinions or varying opinions by the very fact of the incredulity of our own." Hand proposed a standard of "direct incitement" that was extraordinarily protective of free speech: only "direct advocacy" of unlawful acts could be punished; all other speech, no matter how critical of government policies, would be protected. He had earlier applied this "absolute and objective test" in deciding that *The Masses* could not be barred from the mails.[62]

Now, in late March 1919, Learned Hand resumed his dialogue with Holmes. Writing about Debs's conviction under the Espionage Act, Hand claimed that "the thing against which the statute aims is positive impediments to raising an army. Speech may create such by its influence on others' conduct." But speech only violated the Act "when the words were directly an incitement." In effect, Hand was saying, whatever Debs's intent may have been, and whatever the effect of his speech, his conviction should have been upheld only if he had directly incited his listeners to violate the law. Holmes replied on April 3, saying, "I don't quite get your point," and adding that he could not see any difference between Hand's direct incitement test and his own clear and present danger standard. Inasmuch as Hand agreed that certain kinds of speech could violate the statute, Holmes wrote, "I don't know what the matter is, or how we differ so far as your letter goes." This uncharacteristically obtuse response, according to constitutional lawyer Gerald Gunther, indicates "the primitiveness of Holmes's first amendment thinking at that time."[63]

Hand, who respected and admired Holmes, always phrased his disagreements in a gentle, indeed deferential, manner. But a more harshly worded stricture appeared in the May 3 issue of *The New Republic*, which carried an article entitled "The Debs Case and Freedom of Speech" by Ernst Freund. A highly regarded scholar, Freund had taught at the University of Chicago for twenty-five years, first on the political science faculty and later at the law school. He had written standard works on administrative law, legislative standards, and the police power. In 1916 he had served as president of the American Political Science Association. Freund was also a prominent reformer, an advocate of workers', women's, and immigrants' rights. Jane Addams said that he "never once failed to be sensitive to injustice and preventable suffering."[64] So he brought impressive credentials to the task of criticizing Holmes's view of the First Amendment.

The Debs decision, Freund began, "raises inevitably the question of the freedom of agitation in war time." Holmes's clear and present danger standard, however, did not provide a satisfactory answer. "To know what you may do and what you may not do, and how far you may go in criticism, is the first condition of political liberty; to be permitted to agitate at your own peril, subject to a jury's guessing at motive, tendency and possible effect, makes the right of free speech a precarious gift." The Debs ruling illustrated "the arbitrariness of the whole idea of implied provocation." Freund airily dismissed Holmes's famous argument in Schenck. "Yet Justice Holmes would make us believe that the relation of the speech to obstruction is like that of the shout of Fire! in a crowded theatre to the resulting panic! Surely implied provocation in connection with political offenses is an unsafe doctrine if it has to be made plausible by a parallel so manifestly inappropriate." Freund pointed to France (and even Germany) where the law did not penalize implied provocation, but "only direct provocation which has reference to some definite and particular criminal act."[65]

Freund's view, therefore, resembled Learned Hand's: both believed that the clear and present danger standard was too vague, and both feared that juries, swayed by hysteria, would be overly anxious to convict dissenters. Freund, moreover, surely favored Hand's direct incitement test over Holmes's less precise standard. But in some respects Freund was willing to go even further than Hand. The war had such widespread support, Freund thought, that even those who directly incited opposition to the draft or called for a curtailment of military production were unlikely to cause any harm. As Freund wrote, "The peril resulting to the national cause from toleration of adverse opinion is largely imaginary; in any event it is slight as compared with the permanent danger of intolerance to free institutions." Those who were jailed would invariably be those, like Eugene Debs, who had the courage of their convictions. To brand Debs a felon, Freund wrote, was to "dignify the term felony." The sensible thing to do was to ignore such critics, for suppression only strengthened them. "Toleration of adverse opinion is not a matter of generosity," Freund concluded, "but of political prudence."[66]

Learned Hand read Freund's essay with undisguised delight. "Your article in last week's 'New Republic' was a great comfort to me," he wrote to the Chicago law professor on May 7. "I had supposed that in holding such views about the Espionage Act I was in a minority of one in the profession, and that is rather too slim a party to carry a banner.

You express my own opinion much better than I could myself and in your distinguished company I shall take heart of grace to believe I am right, even with the whole Supreme Court the other way." Grateful to find someone else who viewed the First Amendment more or less as he did, Hand, if anything, overstated the similarity between Freund's view and his own. But he did express quite clearly his dissatisfaction with Holmes's failure to understand what was at stake. "I own I was chagrined that Justice Holmes did not line up on our side; indeed, I have so far been unable to make him see that he and we have any real differences and that puzzles me a little."[67]

Holmes, as might be imagined, reacted quite differently to Freund's article. On May 12 he composed a letter to Herbert Croly, the editor of *The New Republic*, justifying the Court's rulings while, at the same time, expressing reservations about the wisdom of the Espionage Act prosecutions. The constitutional question had been decided in *Schenck*, Holmes wrote, "and so all that was needed in the Debs case was to refer to that decision." Moreover, Holmes said, restrictions on speech "were proper enough while the war was on. When people are putting out all their energies in battle I don't think it unreasonable to say we won't have obstacles intentionally put in the way of raising troops—by persuasion any more than by force." Yet Holmes also admitted to certain nagging doubts. "I hated to have to write the Debs case and still more those of the other poor devils before us the same day and the week before. I could not see the wisdom of pressing the cases, especially when the fighting was over and I think it quite possible that if I had been on the jury I should have been for acquittal . . ." Although still insisting on the law's constitutionality, Holmes added, "But in the main I am for aeration of all effervescing convictions—there is no way so quick for letting them get flat." Holmes said that he had written the letter "only to ease my mind." Then, having written it, he decided not to mail it. Instead he sent a copy to Harold Laski, with the comment that Freund's article was "poor stuff."[68]

A similar ambivalence appears elsewhere in Holmes's correspondence. To one acquaintance Holmes complained that the Debs case had caused "a lot of jaw about free speech," and to another he wrote, "If a man thinks that in time of war the right of free speech carries the right to try to impede by discourse the raising of armies I am content to ignore his intellect and say you will find that you had better not monkey with the buzzard."[69] But it was one thing to believe that Debs's conviction was justifiable under the clear and present danger standard, and quite another to believe that he should spend ten years, or, for that matter, any time at all, in prison. Between March and June 1919 Holmes returned to the same themes: he "greatly regretted" having to write the Espionage Act decisions, he was sorry the government had "pressed them to a hearing," he feared that federal judges "have got hysterical about the war," he hoped the President "might do some pardoning."[70]

It was in this somewhat unsettled frame of mind that Holmes read Zechariah Chafee's article, "Freedom of Speech in War Time," in the June issue of the *Harvard Law Review.* Chafee, a professor of law at Harvard, conceded that the First Amendment did not protect all speech. The problem was to determine "where the line runs" between speech that is protected and speech that is not. In the Espionage Act cases, he said, Holmes had missed a "magnificent opportunity" to indicate where to draw that line. The clear and present danger standard, Chafee explained, only suggests that "certain plainly unlawful utterances are, to be sure, unlawful." Citing Holmes's sentence about falsely shouting fire in a theatre and causing a panic, Chafee offered a rejoinder. "How about the man who gets up in a theater between the acts and informs the audience honestly but perhaps mistakenly that the fire exits are too few or locked. He is a much closer parallel to Schenck or Debs." What was required, Chafee concluded, was not "the multiplication of obvious examples" but rather "the development of a rational principle."

Chafee suggested that Holmes, without fully realizing it, had already discovered such a rational principle; he merely had to construe his clear and present test to mean what Learned Hand had meant by direct incitement in *Masses.* Holmes had said, in *Schenck,* that the question was whether words create a clear and present danger "that they will bring about the substantive evils that Congress has a right to prevent"; and this, Chafee thought, "substantially agrees with the conclusion reached by Judge Hand." Speech should be unrestricted, Chafee argued, "unless it is clearly liable to cause direct and dangerous interference with the conduct of the war"; the line should be drawn "close to the point where words will give rise to unlawful acts." If by substantive evils were meant overt acts of interference, "then Justice Holmes draws the boundary line very close to the test of incitement at common law and clearly makes the punishment of words for their bad tendency impossible." Of course, Chafee admitted, this is not the way Holmes had construed the clear and present danger test in *Debs* (otherwise "it is hard to see how he could have been held guilty"), but what was to stop him from construing it that way in the future?

To help Holmes along, Chafee made the following argument: "The true meaning of freedom of speech seems to be this. One of the most important purposes of society and government is the discovery and spread of truth on subjects of general concern. This is possible only through absolutely unlimited discussion, for, as [Walter] Bagehot points out, once force is thrown into the argument, it becomes a matter of chance whether it is thrown on the false side or the true, and truth loses all its natural advantage in the contest." Conceding that government had other purposes, such as the preservation of order, and that "unlimited discussion sometimes interferes with these purposes," Chafee nevertheless insisted there was a "social interest in the attainment of truth" and that "truth can be sifted out from falsehood only if the government is vigorously and constantly cross-examined." As if directing his message to one reader, and one reader only, Chafee buttressed his argument by quoting "the judge who had done most to bring social interests into legal thinking." Oliver Wendell Holmes, he noted pointedly, had once criticized judges who "have failed adequately to recognize their duty of weighing considerations of social advantage."[71]

Not only did Holmes read the article, but he met Chafee during the summer of 1919 when Harold Laski invited them for tea. Laski was himself much taken by the article—"we must fight on it," he told Chafee. "I've read it twice, and I'll go to the stake for every word"—and had already recommended it to Holmes.[72] So we may assume that free speech was one of the topics of conversation that afternoon. By then, it seems clear, Holmes had begun to reconsider his original view of the subject, the view expressed in *Schenck, Frohwerk,* and *Debs.* While he still thought that a nation at war was going to restrict speech, he did not believe that it was necessary, or desirable, for Eugene Debs or other "poor devils" to go to jail. While the national interest might call for limitations on speech, those limitations had to be weighed against the social interest in obtaining the truth. Holmes had been led to this reconsideration by the criticisms he received from Learned Hand, Ernst Freund, and Zechariah Chafee, and also, perhaps, by other authors he was reading.

Holmes used to jest that he would hate to appear before his Maker on the Day of Judgment and have to confess that he had never read Plato, or, for that matter, any other important writer. Actually, he had little to fear. Holmes had a lifelong reading habit, one that provided him immense satisfaction. His taste ran to history, biography, philosophy, and the classics, but he also read novels, plays, and poetry, and he sometimes took up a book of prints or paintings. Two of his friends, Laski and Sir Frederick Pollock, regularly recommended authors, whom Holmes would often dutifully read. During the spring and summer of 1919, as always, Holmes's reading was eclectic, but much of it dealt with free speech and, more particularly, with the nature of truth and with the punishment of dissenters. Although there is no way of knowing for certain what effect any of these works had on Holmes, it is striking that, apart from his work on the Court, his reading focused on the issues posed by the Espionage Act cases.

Early in April Holmes received a copy of James Ford Rhodes's *History of the Civil War* (1917) from Rhodes's sister, who happened to be a friend of the Justice. The volume, an extremely handsome one, with fifteen tinted, fold-out maps, represented an abridgment and reworking of material from Rhodes's older three-volume history, published between 1895 and 1904. Although Holmes told Laski and Pollock that he loathed reading about the Civil War, he found the book "most interesting and well done," "a real work of art."[73] A passage on page 68 could not have failed to catch Holmes's eye. After describing the battle of Ball's Bluff, at which, it will be remembered, Holmes was wounded, Rhodes quoted a letter written by Oliver Wendell Holmes, Sr., about the Union casualties: "I have a stake in this contest, which makes me nervous and tremulous and impatient of contradiction. I have a noble boy, a captain in one of our regiments, which has been fearfully decimated by a battle and disease and himself twice wounded within a hair's breadth of his life."[74] That noble boy, now, more than a half century later, a Supreme Court Justice, would surely have been interested in the rest of what Rhodes had to say.

And what did the eminent historian have to say about civil liberties during the Civil War? While praising Abraham Lincoln's merciful nature and "the greatness of his character and work," Rhodes came down hard on his willingness to abridge free speech and suspend the writ of habeas corpus. Notwithstanding the unpatriotic speeches of Southern sympathizers, the "still more dastardly writing" in newspapers, and the disloyal talk in streets and hotels "where prudence and restraint were cast to the winds," Rhodes thought that the Lincoln administration had gone too far in suppressing freedom, and that, indeed, Lincoln "stands responsible for the casting into prison of citizens of the United States on orders as arbitrary as the lettres-de-cachet of Louis XIV." In measured language Rhodes concluded, "For my own part, after careful consideration, I do not hesitate to condemn the arbitrary arrests and the arbitrary interference with the freedom of the press in States which were not included in the theatre of the war and in which the courts remained open."[75]

On completing Rhodes, Holmes next turned to Harold Laski's *Authority in the Modern State* (1919). The twenty-six-year-old Laski, who was then teaching at Harvard, had struck up a friendship with Holmes several years earlier. He dedicated his new book to Holmes and Felix Frankfurter, "the two youngest of my friends." A study of three nineteenth-century French political theorists (Bonald, Royer-Collard, and Lamennais), the book opened with a chapter, 100 pages in length, which argued that the authority of the state should not extend over the minds of its citizens. As Laski put it, "Where the conscience of the individual is concerned the state must abate its demands, for no mind is in truth free once a penalty is attached to thought." In defending his view that freedom of thought should be "absolute," Laski emphasized the importance of what he termed "the saving grace of experiment." He also maintained that the quest for truth was an ongoing process: "the discovery of right is, on all fundamental questions, a search, upon which the separate members of the state must individually engage."[76]

When Holmes was not reading Laski, he was often reading books Laski suggested. Indeed, Laski did more than recommend Graham

Wallas's *The Life of Francis Place;* he sent Holmes a copy in May, "with my love."[77] Wallas was a professor of political science at the London School of Economics. His biography of Place, the early-nineteenth-century British reformer and Chartist, was first published in 1898, and revised in 1918. Wallas described at some length Place's bitter struggle against the stamp tax on newspapers, which had been imposed in a wave of reaction that swept over England in 1819. By the 1830s hundreds of newspapers were being prosecuted each year for failure to pay it, and many editors had gone to jail or were in hiding. (The tax was lowered in 1846, but not repealed until 1855.) Wallas also described the persecution of one of Place's friends, Richard Carlile, "the well-known martyr of free speech, [who] had lately spent six years (1820–26) in Dorchester gaol." Carlile had defended agricultural workers who had set stacks of hay and wheat on fire to protest against their impoverished conditions. In the ensuing controversy over "rick-burning," Place insisted that Members of Parliament had themselves used more incendiary language in letters to the newspapers, but the government pressed the case "and Carlile received the savage sentence of two years' imprisonment and a heavy fine."[78]

What seemed "savage" to Graham Wallas might have seemed rather civilized to Eugene Debs facing ten years in jail, not to mention Jacob Abrams, who faced twenty. Holmes's feeling that, whatever the constitutionality of the Espionage Act, those convicted under it ought to be pardoned may well have been reinforced by another, more famous book he read that year. "I blush to say I never read Locke's treatise on Government," Holmes wrote to Pollock late in August. Pollock replied "you must certainly read" at least the second Essay on Civil Government, if not the first. Even before receiving Pollock's letter, he had read both.[79] As he came to John Locke's discussion of executive prerogative, did Holmes pause to think about the sentences handed out under the Espionage Act? Locke wrote, " 'Tis fit the ruler should have a power, in many cases, to mitigate the severity of the law, and pardon some offenders: for the *end of government* being the *preservation of all,* as much as may be, even the guilty are to be spared, where it can prove no prejudice to the innocent." Perhaps an analogy Locke employed may have struck a familiar chord in Holmes; "a strict and rigid observation of the laws may do harm," Locke said "(as not to pull down an innocent man's house to stop the fire, when the next to it is burning)."[80]

Holmes read other authors besides Rhodes, Laski, Wallas, and Locke that spring and summer. A topic that strongly attracted him was one central to Chafee's and Laski's arguments for free speech: the search for truth. He read Sir Charles Waldston's *Truth*, a book, he decided, he did not much like.[81] On the other hand, he was surprised at how much he enjoyed F. S. Marvin's *The Century of Hope*, an overly sanguine survey of developments in Europe and America since 1815. "I like to read an optimistic, hazardously generalizing book of that sort," Holmes commented. "Even though I can't follow it with entire belief, it stimulated hope."[82] Undoubtedly, he noted the epigraph on Marvin's title page: "Truth justifies herself, and as she dwells/ With Hope, who would not follow where she leads?"[83]

One day in April, after returning from Court, Holmes reported to Laski that "I toyed with books on etching and got a snooze. . . . *Inter alia* I looked at some of Goya's Miseries of War. They grow more terrible with familiarity."[84] Goya's *Los Desastres de la Guerra*, depicting war as pillage, rape, and torture, filled with terrifying and fiendish images of mutilation, starvation, and death, consists of eighty prints. Each has a brief caption, and it may not be unreasonable to suggest that Holmes lingered especially long over the next to last print, depicting what appears to be the corpse of a beautiful woman about to be interred, with the caption, "*Murio la Verdad,*" or "Truth has died"; and perhaps even longer over the last, depicting the same woman, her eyes suddenly open, rays of light flashing from her visage, with the caption, "*Si resucitara?*" "Will she live again?"

By October 1919 Holmes had begun to view the issue of free speech differently than he had in March. He had not accepted Learned Hand's "incitement" test, or Ernst Freund's still more libertarian outlook, or even the theoretical arguments advanced by Zechariah Chafee and Harold Laski. But his reading of history, biography, and political philosophy had made Holmes more sensitive to the value of free speech as a means of getting at the truth, to the importance of experimentation, and to the need to treat dissenters mercifully, or, as Locke had said, "to mitigate the severity of the law." Holmes expressed his view in a letter to Harold Laski. "I fear we have less freedom of speech here than they have in England. Little as I believe in it as a theory I hope I would die for it and I go as far as anyone whom I regard as competent to form an opinion, in favor of it. Of course when I say I don't believe in it as a theory I don't mean that I do believe in the opposite as a theory. . . . When you are thoroughly convinced that you are right—wholeheartedly desire an end—and have no doubt of your power to accomplish it—I see nothing but municipal regulations to interfere with your using your power to accomplish it."[85] Holmes wrote this letter on October 20, the day before the Supreme Court heard argument in the case of *Abrams et al.* v. *United States.*

## The Decision

When Harry Weinberger stood before the Court and began his oral presentation, he could not have known of Oliver Wendell Holmes's recent intellectual odyssey. But even if he had been able to read the Justice's mind, it is unlikely that he would have tailored his argument to suit Holmes's emerging view. Weinberger wished to use the Abrams case to defend an even more libertarian construction of the First Amendment than Holmes or, for that matter, any of his critics were prepared to endorse. In September, when he had finished working on his fifty-one-page brief, the lawyer wrote: "I think the point is put up to the Supreme Court pretty straight as to whether or not you have the right to criticize the President and the policies of the Government."[86]

Weinberger began by claiming that the evidence at the trial did not support a guilty verdict on any of the indictment's four counts. The first and second counts had charged the defendants with conspiring to publish scurrilous and abusive language about the form of government of the United States, and language designed to bring the form of government into contempt and scorn. But all Abrams and the others had done, Weinberger insisted, was to criticize government officials, and "the right to criticize is the foundation of our Government." The third and fourth counts alleged that the anarchists had conspired to "incite, provoke and encourage resistance" to the United States in the war against Germany, and to advocate curtailment of essential production, with the intent of hindering the prosecution of the war. Weinberger maintained, as he had throughout the trial, that they had intended only to oppose intervention in Soviet Russia and that they were not in the least sympathetic to Germany.[87]

Earlier, Weinberger had asked Abrams' advice "as to the position we should take in arguing on the Russian question. My present inclination is to stand and justify the position taken by you, be the result thereby good or bad. But, of course, I do not want to take that kind of position in my brief without having you consider the matter."[88] Abrams evidently agreed with Weinberger, for the brief, while conceding that the leaflets were "intemperate" and "inflammatory," added, "but it was a public discussion of a public policy in reference to a country with which we were not at war, and against which country the use of troops has never been legal." In fact, Weinberger observed, prominent politicians and respected publications had recently called Wilson's policy of intervention "stupid and ignorant" and denounced it as "loathsome hypocrisy," statements at least as extreme as those made by his clients. Since they had not intended to interfere with the war, but rather to arouse opposition to intervention against Soviet Russia, they were wholly within their rights. As Weinberger wrote, "The discussion of public questions is absolutely immune under the First Amendment to the Constitution, when that is the only intention in the discussion."[89]

Then Weinberger moved to a more general, and fundamental, point: the Espionage Act, as modified in May 1918, was unconstitutional, he said, because the Founding Fathers had sought to guarantee "the unabridgeable liberty of discussion as a natural right." This liberty, he added, could not be snuffed out even in wartime, for if the government could restrict speech on the pretext of safeguarding the public welfare, then "it can be taken away in peacetime on the same pretext." Weinberger offered his own view as to where the line should be drawn: not, as Holmes said, when speech creates a clear and present danger of producing an illegal act; not, as Hand believed, when speakers directly incite listeners to commit an illegal act; not even, as Chafee thought, "close to the point where words will give rise to unlawful acts." Weinberger relied on a statement of Thomas Jefferson's, one the Virginian had admittedly made in discussing religious toleration, not free speech: "It is time enough for the rightful purposes of civil government for its officers to interfere when principles break out into overt acts against peace and good order." Overt acts could be punished, Weinberger conceded, but speech itself must be "perfectly unrestrained." In Weinberger's view "absolute freedom of speech is the only basis upon which the Government can stand and remain free."[90]

Weinberger's brief was ready a month in advance. The government did not file its answer until five days before the Court was to hear the case. Originally, in March 1919, the brief had been assigned to Alfred Bettman and John Lord O'Brian, who had been instrumental in the enactment of the Sedition Act and its enforcement. But they had resigned in May, when the War Emergency Division closed up shop. One wonders what might have happened had they remained in the Department of Justice. Both men, but especially Bettman, had devoted their last months in office to urging the President to pardon, or commute or reduce the sentences, of those convicted under the Espionage and Sedition acts. Bettman feared that continued repression would only give wider exposure to radical doctrines. He also argued that "it is time for us to get over a spirit of intolerance which was necessary as a war measure but is no longer justified or American; that if our institutions cannot stand a little radical talk they are surely weak in the affections of the people."[91] On March 14, four days after the Supreme Court handed down its decision in the Debs case, Bettman noted, "The Jacob Abrams et al. case represents a type of agitation to which the term 'Bolshevism' is today generally applied. It is not an absolutely clear case, and, in view of the whole present situation, I believe it would be well not to force this case to an early hearing, but to postpone the question of advancement for the time being."[92]

With the resignations of Bettman and O'Brian, other, less benevolent views came to prevail. Robert P. Stewart, an Assistant Attorney General, was placed in charge of preparing the brief and oral argument in the Abrams case, and he was aided by an attorney named W. C. Herron. They would come up with arguments that had never been used before, even at the trial, arguments that would be echoed in the Supreme Court's majority opinion. Nothing more graphically illustrates Stewart's outlook than his response to Weinberger's desperate last-ditch effort to keep the anarchists out of jail by arranging instead for their deportation to Soviet Russia.

In May 1919 Weinberger wrote to Attorney General A. Mitchell Palmer in an effort to strike such a deal. Referring to the leaflets that Abrams had distributed, Weinberger conceded that "the language is extreme, but the purpose is merely to arouse public opinion on the Russian question. . . . By no stretch of the imagination can this case be considered as one that was pro-German or intended in any way to aid Germany in the war."[93] In June the case was rescheduled for October. In August Weinberger met with Palmer, told him, "I felt much encouraged after my talk with you," and added that his clients, as aliens and anarchists, would of course be deported. Meanwhile, "Their release at this time would I am sure have a very good effect on the people of the East side. They have already been in prison three months, suffered beating by the police and lived for a year under the cloud of a sentence."[94] Through a mutual friend, Weinberger urged Ray Stannard Baker, the veteran Progressive journalist, to intervene on the radicals' behalf.

On September 23 Baker responded by writing to Palmer. He had no sympathy for the defendants' views, Baker said, "but it seems to me that such a punishment for a group of foolish youths, scarcely more than of age (with one exception) for an act of political agitation which in peace times would have passed unnoticed, is excessive." Such unwonted severity creates martyrs, Baker added, and drives radicals underground. "I suppose tens of thousands of people have heard of these foolish Russians and have read their circulars to tens who would have known anything about them if they had either been let alone, or else shut up, during the war emergency, for a few months." To Baker, the thought of sending a twenty-one-year-old "girl" to the penitentiary for such a paltry offense for fifteen years "seems a kind of monstrosity." Palmer replied on September 29, noting simply that nothing could be done other than "to carry the case to completion."[95]

Palmer's letter was prepared by Assistant Attorney General Robert P. Stewart, who explained, "They are anarchists, and so state in their testimony. Apparently they are proud of their adherence to anarchistic doctrines and are typical supporters of the proletarian republic or Bolsheviki government in Russia." The defendants had been properly convicted of "the stealthy circulation" of pamphlets which tended to bring the government into disrepute, and so "the case is a case of first [importance] involving portions of the Espionage Act which have never been heretofore considered by the Supreme Court . . ." There was no reason to drop the case, Stewart continued. "I believe this offense must be carefully distinguished from political agitation as we recognize such agitation to be lawful. The actions and declarations of these defendants, in my judgment, called for the overthrow of the present form of Government, which they denominate a government of the capitalists and by the capitalistic class."[96] Abrams, writing in opposition to Russian intervention, had actually "called upon all of the workers in this country to oppose this action, by a revolution, if necessary."[97] Stewart thereby introduced a new consideration into the case: the issue was no longer merely whether the anarchists had intended to interfere with the war, or disrupt essential production, but whether they had favored the overthrow of the government.

Stewart's brief picked up where his letter left off. Not only did Abrams, Steimer, Lipman, and Lachowsky advocate curtailment of munitions production, the Assistant Attorney General contended, but "there is nothing in their own testimony to rebut the inference that they intended in the leaflets . . . to advocate resistance to, and overthrow of that form of government by force." Their true purposes were easily deduced; "they were all Russian aliens, none of them had made any attempt to become a citizen of the United States of America, because, it may be presumed, they despised its form of government" and because their "true and loyal allegiance was, not to the Government of the United States of America, but to the Soviet Government of Russia." To dispel any remaining doubts, Stewart added his own gloss to the language in the Yiddish leaflet calling for a general strike, "meaning that a general strike of all workers should be had in order to stop the production of munitions, and to overthrow by force the form of government of the United States as by law established."[98]

Stewart's version of constitutional history was the polar opposite of Weinberger's. Stewart claimed that the First Amendment had been designed to "fix the liberty of the press. . . . What such liberty was at the time of the adoption of the Constitution, that it shall continue to be, no more, no less." But in eighteenth-century America, he went on, "no liberty of the press was conceived of which included the unlimited right to publish a seditious libel. No claim of that sort was ever made by any respectable person." Weinberger went about as far as it was possible to go in protecting speech; Stewart, in rehabilitating the doctrine of seditious libel, would have allowed Congress, using "the power of self-preservation," to make any attack on the form of government unlawful.[99] Reading the opposing briefs, one cannot be sure the two lawyers were talking about the same Constitution.

Stewart made a final point: if, as *Schenck* held, the Espionage Act was constitutional, then the Sedition Act must also be constitutional. If speech that created a clear and present danger of obstructing the recruiting service could be restrained, then speech that created such a danger of curtailing war production could also be restrained. The government's brief pointed out that the leaflets had been distributed in August 1918, "at a critical period of the war when the Nation needed the concentration and cooperation of all its forces of men and material to reach the result which it happily attained." The leaflets, moreover, "were circulated in the largest city and port in the country," where vital goods were being manufactured, and were distributed by "devoted adherents" of the Soviet government, "itself a government established and maintained by force."[100]

The Supreme Court handed down its decision on November 10, 1919. John Hessin Clarke wrote the majority opinion, joined by all the other Justices except Holmes and Brandeis. Clarke based his ruling on narrow, procedural grounds. Since the defendants' contention that their leaflets were protected by the First Amendment "is definitely negatived" by *Schenck*, the only question before the Court was "whether there was some evidence, competent and substantial, before the jury fairly tending to sustain the verdict." Moreover, since the sentences under the four counts of the indictment did not exceed that which could have been imposed under any single count, "the judgment upon the verdict of the jury must be affirmed if the evidence is sufficient to sustain any one of the counts." Free therefore to ignore the more problematical first and second counts (which dealt with language designed to bring the government into disrepute), Clarke held that "much persuasive evidence was before the jury tending to prove that the defendants were guilty as charged in both the third and fourth counts of the indictment (which dealt with language designed to provoke resistance to the government and to curtail war production).

To support this, Clarke either quoted selectively from, or paraphrased, the leaflets. He not only cited one of the lines in the Yiddish leaflet which had been mistranslated—"Workers, Russian emigrants, you who had the least belief in the honesty of *our* Government"—but even italicized the mistranslated word, and added, for good measure, "which defendants admitted referred to the United States Government," without indicating that Abrams had admitted this on the witness stand only after Judge Clayton, as we have seen, had virtually put the words in his mouth. Clarke quoted the most extreme language in the leaflets, ignoring the more cautious statements which were inconsistent with his interpretation. He did not mention, for example, Samuel Lipman's postscript to the English leaflet which began, "It is absurd to call us pro-German. . . ."

The quotations were designed to show that the defendants had indeed intended to interfere with the war. Adopting the usual distinction between motive and intent, Clarke reasoned that it was no defense to argue that the anarchists had only sought to prevent injury to Soviet Russia. "Men must be held to have intended, and to be accountable for, the effects which their acts were likely to produce. Even if their primary purpose and intent was to aid the cause of the Russian Revolution, the plan of action which they adopted necessarily involved before it could be realized, defeat of the war program of the United States." If they wanted their appeal "not to aid government loans and not to work in ammunition factories" to be heeded, then, in a legal sense, they "intended" to interfere with the war.

Clarke labored mightily to apply the Court's clear and present danger standard to the Abrams case. Borrowing Assistant Attorney General Stewart's arguments, indeed coming close to adopting the same language, Clarke observed that the leaflets were "circulated in the greatest port of our land, from which great numbers of soldiers were at the time taking ship daily, and in which great quantities of war supplies of every kind were at the time being manufactured for transportation overseas." Clark also alluded to the *Schenck* rule by pointing out that the leaflets had been distributed "at the supreme crisis of the war" and had amounted to "an attempt to defeat the war plans of the Government

. . . by bringing upon the country the paralysis of a general strike." Even his characterization of the defendants as "intelligent" and having had "considerable schooling" may have reflected the same purpose.

Clarke borrowed from Stewart, too, in discussing the defendants' revolutionary objectives. Clarke quoted the lines "The Russian Revolution cries: Workers of the World! Awake! Rise! Put down your enemy and mine! Yes friends, there is only one enemy of the workers of the world and that is CAPITALISM." He then explained, "This is clearly an appeal to the 'workers' of this country to arise and put down by force the Government of the United States. . . ." To clinch his argument, Clarke then quoted from "the additional writings found in the meeting place of the defendant group and on the person of one of them." So Samuel Lipman's "Revolutionists! Unite for Action," although never printed or circulated, was exhumed. The sentence, "Know you lovers of freedom that in order to save the Russian revolution, we must keep the armies of the allied countries busy at home"—which Clarke chose to italicize—was offered as proof of "the purpose to throw the country into a state of revolution if possible and to thereby frustrate the military program of the Government." Similarly, after quoting from another unpublished statement, Clarke concluded that "the defendant alien anarchists" had wanted to excite "disaffection, sedition, riots, and, as they hoped, revolution, in this country for the purpose of embarrassing and if possible defeating the military plans of the Government in Europe."[101]

This last point aside, insofar as Justice Clarke's decision was based on the belief that the Supreme Court should ordinarily defer to the findings of a jury, on the use of selective quotation as a means of determining a document's meaning, on the classical distinction between motive and intent, and on the application of the clear and present danger standard, it was quite consistent with the position that Oliver Wendell Holmes had taken in *Schenck*, *Frohwerk*, and *Debs*. Clarke's *Abrams* opinion, in November, was very much like one Holmes might have written eight months earlier.

## The Dissent

Perhaps that is why, shortly after circulating a draft of his dissent in the Abrams case, Oliver Wendell Holmes was visited at his home by three of his brethren. The story of this pilgrimage to 1720 I Street was related to Dean Acheson, who was Louis Brandeis's clerk, by Stanley Morrison, who was Holmes's. Willis Van Devanter, Mahlon Pitney, and a third Justice whose identity Acheson could not recall, accompanied by Holmes's wife, Fanny, entered the Justice's study. "They laid before him their request that in this case, which they thought affected the safety of the country, he should, like the old soldier he had once been, close ranks and forego individual predilections. Mrs. Holmes agreed. The tone of the discussion was at all times friendly, even affectionate. The Justice regretted that he could not do as they wished. They did not press."[102] It is likely that at some point in the discussion Pitney said, "I think there was a case for the jury," since that is the comment he jotted on the dissent Holmes circulated.[103] Holmes, who had anticipated this pressure to go along with the majority, and had commented that he would "perhaps be persuaded to shut up, but I don't expect it," stood his ground.[104] As he later told a friend, "I thought as I was given the Debs case and some others when the convictions were upheld, it was my duty and my right to state my opinion as to the limit."[105]

Louis D. Brandeis told Holmes, "I join you heartily & gratefully. This is fine—very."[106] The opinion to which Brandeis referred consists of twelve paragraphs; the first ten are unremarkable, but the eleventh and the twelfth are among the most eloquent in the annals of American law. The first paragraph summarizes the charges in the four counts of the indictment; the second summarizes the English leaflet, "The Hypocrisy of the United States and Her Allies," (reprinting in full the postscript beginning "It is absurd to call us pro-German"); and the third summarizes the Yiddish leaflet, "Workers—Wake Up!!" Holmes either quoted the leaflets directly or else paraphrased them. He also commented that the Yiddish leaflet used "abusive language" and engaged in "some usual tall talk."

In the fourth paragraph Holmes said that "no argument seems to me necessary" to show that the leaflets did not support either of the first two counts of the indictment, and continued, "What little I have to say about the third count" (conspiring to encourage resistance to the United States) "may be postponed until I have considered the fourth" (conspiring to incite curtailment of production of things necessary for the war). "It seems too plain to be denied," Holmes said, that the remarks directed at munitions workers and the advocacy of a general strike "do urge curtailment of production of things necessary to the prosecution of the war." For such advocacy to be criminal, however, the Sedition Act "requires that it should be 'with intent by such curtailment to cripple or hinder the United States in the prosecution of the war.' It seems to me that no such intent is proved."

Having raised the issue of intent, Holmes devoted the fifth and sixth paragraphs to defending his interpretation. He conceded that "the word intent as vaguely used in ordinary legal discussion means no more than knowledge at the time of the act that the consequences said to be intended will ensue" but that "when words are used exactly, a deed is not done with intent to produce a consequence unless that consequence is the aim of the deed." In other words, Holmes argued that the word "intent" in the statute required that just such an aim be present. An act is not done with the "intent" to produce a particular consequence, he went on, "unless the aim to produce it is the proximate motive of the specific act, although there may be some deeper motive behind." The Sedition Act should "be taken to use its words in a strict and accurate sense." Otherwise, Holmes pointed out, an "absurd" situation would result: "A patriot might think that we were wasting money on aeroplanes . . . and might advocate curtailment with success, yet even if it turned out that the curtailment hindered and was thought by other minds to have been obviously likely to hinder the United States in the prosecution of the war, no one would hold such conduct a crime." Then, almost apologetically, he remarked, "I admit that my illustration does not answer all that might be said but it is enough to show what I think and to let me pass to a more important aspect of the case."

That aspect was the First Amendment protection of freedom of speech, which Holmes addressed in the seventh and eighth paragraphs. He asserted that in the Schenck, Frohwerk, and Debs cases "the questions of law that alone were before this court . . . were rightly decided." He adverted to the example he had given in *Frohwerk:* just as Congress could punish speech persuading to murder, it "constitutionally may punish speech that produces or is intended to produce a clear and imminent danger that it will bring about forthwith certain substantive evils that the United States constitutionally may seek to prevent." In restating the clear and present danger standard, however, Holmes modified it significantly, by changing "present" to "imminent" and by adding the critical qualifying word "forthwith." The power to restrict speech would necessarily be greater in wartime because of the special dangers involved. But "Congress certainly cannot forbid all effort to change the mind of the country." Even during a war "the principle of the right to free speech is always the same," which is to say that only "the present danger of immediate evil," or an intent to bring it about, warrants restriction. No such danger was present in the Abrams case, Holmes said. "Now nobody can suppose that the surreptitious publishing of a silly leaflet by an unknown man, without more, would present any immediate danger that its opinions would hinder the success of the government arms or have any appreciable tendency to do so." Admitting that the law could properly punish speech made "for the very purpose of obstructing" the war, Holmes concluded: "So I assume that the second leaflet if published for the purposes alleged in the fourth count might be punishable."

By now Holmes had circled back to the question of intent, and resumed the discussion in the ninth and tenth paragraphs. "I do not see how anyone can find the intent required by the statute in any of the defendant's words." The crucial document was the Yiddish leaflet, and "it is evident from the beginning to the end that the only object of the paper is to help Russia and stop American intervention there against the popular government—not to impede the United States in the war that it was carrying on." To "attempt" to do something required an "actual intent." "To say that two phrases"—the lines addressed to munitions workers and the call for a general strike—"taken literally might import a suggestion of conduct that would have interference with the war as an indirect and probably undesired effect seems to me by no means enough to show an attempt to produce that effect." Returning to a consideration of the third count, which he had earlier postponed, Holmes wrote, "I think that resistance to the United States means some forcible act of opposition to some proceeding of the United States in pursuance of the war. . . . For the reasons that I have given I think that no such intent was proved or existed in fact."

In the eleventh paragraph, Holmes wrote:

> In this case sentences of twenty years imprisonment have been imposed for the publishing of two leaflets that I believe the defendants had as much right to publish as the Government has to publish the Constitution of the United States now vainly invoked by them. Even if I am technically wrong and enough can be squeezed from these poor and puny anonymities to turn the color of legal litmus paper; I will add, even if what I think the necessary intent were shown; the most nominal punishment seems to me all that possibly could be inflicted, unless the defendants are to be made to suffer not for what the indictment alleges but for the creed that they avow—a creed that I believe to be the creed of ignorance and immaturity when honestly held, as I see no reason to doubt that it was held here, but which, although made the subject of examination at the trial, no one has a right even to consider in dealing with the charges before the Court."

Unlike Justice Clarke's majority opinion, which conceded that the anarchists were intelligent and well-educated, Holmes, to demonstrate the absence of a clear and present danger, belittled the anarchists, their beliefs, and their leaflets (as he had earlier, when he referred to a "silly leaflet by an unknown man"). Moreover, Holmes virtually admitted that he dissented, at least in part, because he believed that the long prison sentences were indefensible. Although the appropriateness of the sentences was not before the Court, it was a very real issue to the Justice who had wanted, and expected, Eugene Debs to be pardoned, who had been reading about the years spent in Dorchester gaol by Richard Carlile, the friend of Francis Place, and who perhaps recalled John Locke's advice that "even the guilty are to be spared, where it can prove no prejudice to the innocent."

Holmes's final paragraph discussed the connection between freedom of speech, the search for truth, and the value of experimentation. Reading Laski, Chafee, and Hand, he had been mulling over that connection for many months.

> Persecution for the expression of opinions seems to me perfectly logical. If you have no doubt of your premises or your power and want a certain result with all your heart you naturally express your wishes in law and sweep away all opposition. To allow opposition by speech seems to indicate that you think the speech impotent, as when a man says that he has squared the circle, or that you do not care whole heartedly for the result, or that you doubt either your power or your premises. But when men have realized that time has upset many fighting faiths, they may come to believe even more than they believe the very foundations of their own conduct that the ultimate good desired is better reached by free trade in ideas—that the best test of truth is the power of the thought to get itself accepted in the competition of the market, and that truth is the only ground upon which their wishes safely can be carried out. That at any rate is the theory of our Constitution. It is an experiment, as all life is an experiment. Every year if not every day we have to wager our salvation upon some prophecy based upon imperfect knowledge. While that experiment is part of our system I think that we should be eternally vigilant against attempts to check the expression of opinions that we loathe and believe to be fraught with death, unless they so imminently threaten immediate interference with the lawful and pressing purposes of the law that an immediate check is required to save the country. . . . Only the emergency that makes it immediately dangerous to leave the correction of evil counsels to time warrants making any exception to the sweeping command, "Congress shall make no law abridging the freedom of speech." Of course I am speaking only of expressions of opinion and exhortations, which were all that were uttered here, but I regret that I cannot put into more impressive words my belief that in their conviction upon this indictment the defendants were deprived of their rights under the Constitution of the United States.

Holmes had again reformulated the clear and present danger test so as to permit speech unless "an immediate check is required to save the country." So defined, the standard surely would not support the conviction of Abrams, Steimer, Lipman, and Lachowsky, but neither would it uphold the convictions of Charles T. Schenck, Jacob Frohwerk, or Eugene Debs. That is why one scholar has claimed that Holmes's dissent transformed "the phrase 'clear and present danger' from an apology for repression into a commitment to oppose authority," and another has noted that it "did at last provide a real basis for regarding clear and present danger as a speech-protective doctrine."[107]

Holmes soon had second thoughts about his view that the jury had no basis for finding the defendants guilty on the fourth count. "I think it possible that I was wrong in thinking that there was no evidence on the Fourth Count," he wrote on December 14. But Holmes never doubted that his interpretation of intent was correct. "I still am of opinion that I was right, if I am right in what I devoutly believe, that an actual intent to hinder the U.S. in its war with Germany must be proved." Insisting that "the only object of the leaflets was to hinder our interference with Russia," Holmes only regretted that he had not "developed this in the opinion. But that is ancient history now."[108] To Harold Laski, Holmes explained that "I assumed, but I ought to have made it clearer," that it was "necessary that the overt act laid should be proved to be done with intent to forward a conspiracy to interfere with the war with Germany," not merely to block intervention in Russia.[109]

Laski hardly required convincing. He remained a lifelong admirer of Holmes's dissent, that "fine and moving" statement, that "landmark of noble courage," which "has a special niche in the temple of fame," and was "superior either in nobility or outlook" to anything Holmes had ever written.[110] Laski's view was widely shared, especially in Cambridge, Massachusetts. Roscoe Pound, Dean of Harvard Law School, told Holmes that the dissent was "a document of human liberty" worthy of a Socrates, a Milton, or a Mill.[111] Zechariah Chafee nearly depleted his store of superlatives, talking of Holmes's "magnificent exposition of the philosophic basis" of the First Amendment, and praising the "enduring qualities" of his reasoning.[112] Learned Hand assured Holmes that he was "greatly pleased with your dissent in the Abrams case, especially with the close which, if I may say so, was in your very highest vein."[113]

To Chafee, however, Hand expressed some reservations. "I must say, however, that on the facts it seems to me very questionable whether the [majority] decision was not correct. At first, upon reading the opinion, I was quite sure the majority was wrong, but the distinction seems to me pretty tenuous between the purpose to encourage resistance to the United States and merely to prevent the United States from overthrowing the Bolshevik party." But Hand added, "Nothing could be more needed than Justice Holmes's opinion. I am delighted that it appeared." Although Holmes had begun moving in the right direction, Hand still preferred his own direct incitement test. "I do not altogether like the way Justice Holmes put the limitation. I myself think it is a little more manageable and quite adequate a distinction to say that there is an absolute and objective test to language. I daresay that it is obstinacy, but I still prefer that which I attempted to state in my first 'Masses' opinion, rather than to say that the connection between the words used and the evil aimed at should be 'immediate and direct.' "[114]

Meanwhile, Learned Hand received an unsolicited message from John M. Ryan, the Assistant U. S. Attorney who had prosecuted Jacob Abrams and the others. The message, Ryan informed Hand, came from Judge Henry DeLamar Clayton. Ryan had sent Clayton a newspaper clipping about the decision upholding the conviction "in the case of the Bolshevists . . ." The judge replied, "I have always thought that the case of the U. S. vs. Prober, Abrams and others, would be affirmed and it was gratifying to have this news from you. Why is it that such people, who have avowed themselves to be anarchists and said in open court that they knew they could not be naturalized, can not be deported, or is the purpose of the Department of Justice to put them in prison instead of deporting them?"[115] Clayton wanted Hand to know that "after December I will have very little to do in Alabama, and if my services are needed in New York I can come."[116]

On November 10, the day the Court handed down its ruling, Jacob Abrams and Samuel Lipman were residing in New York City, Mollie Steimer was in the Workhouse where she had begun to serve her six-month sentence on a disorderly conduct charge, and Hyman Lachowsky was being temporarily detained on Ellis Island following the raid, a few nights earlier, on the Russian People's House. The Court's mandate, requiring defendants whose convictions had been upheld to turn themselves in, normally arrived thirty days after the ruling. Facing the prospect of twenty years in prison, Abrams and Lipman decided to jump bail. As Lipman later wrote, "We were given 30 days to prepare for prison, but we didn't need so much for 3 days after the decision we are far from New York."[117] By November 14 they had made their way to New Orleans, where they planned to board a steamer for Mexico, and from there set out for Soviet Russia.

# 7

# The Response

## Flight and Arrest

It was evening when Jacob Abrams and Samuel Lipman arrived in New Orleans. They rented a room in a boardinghouse on Canal Street, using the assumed names of "Mr. Stone" and "Mr. Green," and they contacted a comrade, Peter Ysasi, who was supposed to help them make arrangements to get to Mexico. Through Ysasi, they soon fell in with John J. Ballam, a leading Boston communist, who was also planning to flee the country. The thirty-year-old Ballam, the editor of the *New England Worker,* had already served a year in jail for violation of the Espionage Act. For the past month he had barely managed to stay a step ahead of the Boston police. A wanted man, he had been indicted under the Massachusetts anti-anarchy act for having incited the violent overthrow of the state government.

Despite the use of aliases and the other precautions the fugitives must have taken, their whereabouts became known to agents of the Bureau of Investigation within twenty-four hours. As agent Edward T. Needham reported, "On November 15th, Informant Guzman advised this office that he had information from Peter Ysasi to the effect that three Russian fugitives from New York had arrived in New Orleans the previous evening and were expecting to catch the S. S. *Mexico* on the following day for Progreso, Mexico, and that he would keep the office advised of their actions."[1] From November 16 to 28, Guzman regularly filed reports about Abrams, Lipman, and Ballam and their efforts to arrange an escape. Although their identities were as yet unknown to him, Guzman provided a description of the three men, and on November 29 he finally "obtained the name of one of the Russians, Jacob Abrams." He also reported that José Cortes, a crew member on the *Mexico,* was to help them steal aboard the steamer, which was planning to leave that very day.

On further inquiry, Agent Needham learned that the departure was to be postponed, at least until Monday, December 1. That afternoon "two employees of the Columbia Storage Battery Company called at this office and stated that they had been repairing the wireless aboard the S. S. *Mexico* and from the action of the crew, they judged that possibly some ammunition was to be smuggled into Mexico aboard this steamer and they further stated that the boat was expected to leave at 9:00 P.M. on the first." So at eight o'clock that evening Needham and two other agents "went to the Napoleon Avenue Street Ferry, and after crossing the Mississippi River to the Standard Oil Docks, where the *Mexico* was taking on oil, boarded the ship." The agents ordered the crew members on deck and questioned them. Then Needham and the ship's First Officer began a systematic search of the vessel. Climbing down a hatchway to the forward hold, they "*discovered the three Russians stowed away.*" Almost as an afterthought, Needham reported that "the search for ammunition developed nothing." The three fugitives were taken into custody, as was José Cortes.

Only when Abrams and Lipman were questioned at the Bureau's office did Needham discover the reason for their getaway attempt. Abrams admitted that he was facing a twenty-year prison term, and that "upon learning that the Supreme Court had confirmed his sentence he left New York with the intention of leaving the country." Abrams was willing to "tell anything of his past, but . . . would not tell anything on anyone else and would not implicate or testify against anyone for aiding him to escape." He denied even knowing Cortes. "After several hours of questioning," Needham said, "it was clear that no information could be obtained from this man." Like Abrams, Samuel Lipman explained why he was fleeing, but "also refused to make any statement other than that concerning himself." Ballam said that he had met Abrams and Lipman in New Orleans, that they had made all the sailing arrangements, "that he had frequently heard them mention a man by the name of *Cortes,* also that he knew it *cost $100.00 for them to be place*[*d*] *aboard the ship*—to whom this money was paid he did not know." Cortes, a twenty-five-year-old Mexican, denied knowing anything about the arrangement.[2]

On December 2 Washington was informed of the arrests, and the next day the story hit the newspapers. The New Orleans *Times-Picayune* wrote that the capture of the "three international leaders of the Bolsheviki" was "one of the most important catches . . . since the United States government declared war on the Reds." Abrams and Lipman, the paper added, "speak English fluently and impressed their captors as highly educated men." The Boston *Globe* informed its readers that Ballam "is said to have belonged to the gang suspected of plotting to send bombs in Christmas packages to high officials throughout the country." The New York *World* explained that "government agents had been watching the three leaders closely since they arrived in New Orleans," and that, in all, they had "made nine efforts to get out of the country."[3]

The newspapers also reported that the four men had been taken to the city's Parish Prison and were being held without bail, Abrams and Lipman as fugitives, Ballam and Cortes for conspiring to aid their escape. Lipman later recalled that conditions in the jail were "filthy."[4] Abrams added another complaint. He told Harry Weinberger that he and Lipman were locked up in a cell with condemned men, who "face the rope and it is not very comfortable to be with them in one place because you feel your self all day the shadow of death."[5] Cortes was later released, and Ballam was apparently extradited to Massachusetts, but it took three weeks to arrange for Abrams' and Lipman's return to New York City.

Federal authorities did not want them transferred until after December 10, when the Supreme Court mandate requiring their surrender was to be handed down. Then United States Attorney Francis G. Caffey's office, acting on instructions from Attorney General A. Mitchell Palmer, insisted that Weinberger pay for the two men's transportation from New Orleans, and also for the round-trip fare of guards "to see that they do not make [a] second effort to abscond."[6] When Abrams and Lipman objected to being moved at their own expense, Weinberger asked the

Assistant United States Attorney in New Orleans to "bring them to New York with or without their consent."[7] On December 18 Weinberger wired $550 to New Orleans. Only then did Abrams and Lipman, accompanied by three guards, board a train for New York City. They arrived at Pennsylvania Station on the afternoon of December 22, were met by a federal marshal with a bench warrant for their arrest, and were taken to the Tombs.

There they were reunited with Hyman Lachowsky, who had surrendered on December 16, after he had prepared a statement for the press. He observed that "Mr. Justice Holmes and Mr. Justice Brandeis have said that I had as much right to give out these leaflets as the United States had to issue its own Constitution." Lachowsky continued, "When my country, Soviet Russia, takes her equal place among the Nations of the world, recognized by all the Nations of the world, Russia will demand my freedom." He was willing to be deported to Russia, he added, but if the United States wanted the disgrace of keeping him in jail, "I am willing to be that sacrifice in the hope that by it, the true liberty-loving heart of America will awaken from its deadly sleep caused by the Espionage Law under which I was convicted."[8]

His comrades also issued statements as they prepared to enter the penitentiary. Abrams said that his imprisonment would not break the spirit "of the brave men and women that fight for freedom" but would encourage thousands more "to enlist in the Revolutionary Ranks, and make starvation and slavery a thing of the past. Long live the spirit of international Brotherhood. Long live Soviet Russia."[9] Lipman, whose sweetheart, Ethel Bernstein, had been deported on the *Buford* the day before he got to New York City, was equally unrepentant. He said that he had not changed his opinion of President Wilson's Russian policy, and still regarded intervention as "the most inhuman, most brutal act of the U.S." The policy of deporting alien radicals only "proves the weakness of the Throne. One strong storm and it will go to pieces. The imprisonment of agitators is a failure, for we do as much propaganda in prison as outside." He promised to fight tyranny and oppression "wherever I will be, and as long as my red blood will flow in my veins."[10]

On December 26 the three men were transferred from the Tombs to the federal penitentiary in Atlanta, Georgia. Although they had been sentenced originally to the Maryland State Penitentiary in Baltimore, the place of confinement was now changed by Federal District Judge John C. Knox. He may well have acted at the prisoners' request, or at least their lawyer's, for on December 17 Weinberger had informed Lachowsky "that you will probably be taken to Atlanta instead of to the Baltimore Prison, which is, of course, what you and Abrams and Lipman desire."[11] Judge Knox also had to decide another crucial question: would Abrams and Lipman be required to forfeit their $10,000 bail bonds, and their $1,000 appeal bonds, for having attempted to escape?

Had their attempt succeeded, of course, forfeiture would have been automatic. That is why their decision to jump bail had met with Mollie Steimer's sharp disapproval and, perhaps, why Lachowsky had not joined them. The escape scheme had been discussed for months, discussed, indeed, so matter-of-factly that in August an undercover agent had picked up rumors "that they are planning to return to Russia, and 'jump' their bail bonds here."[12] In November 1919 Steimer could no longer try to dissuade Abrams and Lipman, since she was in the Workhouse on Blackwell's Island, serving a six-month sentence for disorderly conduct. But she had made her opposition known from the start. When Abrams first broached the idea, Steimer recalled, "I pointed out that when people placed their confidence in us: 4 unknown workers, advancing 40 thousand dollars to bail us out, we cannot and must not deceive them."[13]

Since, in fact, the escape attempt had failed, United States Attorney Caffey had to request the District Court to order forfeiture of the bonds. Judge Knox, while seemingly disposed to grant such an order, took the matter under advisement to give Weinberger time to submit evidence "showing that none of the collateral put up was owned by the defendants."[14] Weinberger explained that Abrams and Lipman were wage earners who could not possibly have raised the requisite bail out of their own slender resources. He also submitted an affidavit from Lipman's aunt, Ida Fishman, stating that she had provided $5,000 for her nephew; $2,000 of that amount was hers, but she had borrowed the rest from friends and relatives. To Caffey's consternation, the judge granted the attorney's motion to remit the forfeiture. On December 29, with considerable satisfaction, Weinberger informed Abrams that "Judge Knox ordered the return of the forfeited bonds."[15]

This was the first letter Harry Weinberger wrote to Jacob Abrams in the Atlanta penitentiary, but not the last. In December 1919 Weinberger still expected to obtain a commutation of the sentences on condition that Abrams and the others accept deportation to Soviet Russia. "We can probably get a pardon and have you all sent to Russia," he assured Lachowsky, and he concluded a letter to Abrams "with my best hope that the New Year will see you on your way to Russia and out of Atlanta."[16] Weinberger could not have foreseen that Abrams, Lipman, and Lachowsky would languish in Atlanta for nearly two years, or that Mollie Steimer, once her six-month term was up, would be incarcerated in the State Penitentiary in Jefferson City, Missouri, for as long. As the four convicted radicals settled down to the daily grind of prison, the echoes of the case began to reverberate through the legal community.

## John H. Wigmore: "Freedom of Thuggery?"

Within that community, Oliver Wendell Holmes's minority opinion met with anything but universal approval. One law review article branded the dissent "most unfortunate and indeed deplorable," termed its point of view "a positive menace to society and this Government," and predicted that radicals would "send it out as propaganda to their fellows, thus destroying in large measure the beneficent result of the conviction." The author was "unable to conceive how a man with the antecedents, education, learning, attainments and experience" of Holmes could have written the *Abrams* dissent.[17] Others objected to Holmes's interpretation of "intent." People "must be held to intend, if not the usual consequences of their acts, certainly the necessary means to their objectives," another writer said.[18] Even if Abrams and the others had wanted to block American intervention in Russia, they must have known that a decrease in munitions production would "necessarily, in and of itself, have constituted a hindrance to military operations against Germany." One of Holmes's critics, while proclaiming his commitment to toleration, nevertheless maintained that "legal toleration pushed to its ultimate conclusion becomes impotence, self-destruction. We may not believe that the truths we hold are immutable, but for some of them at least we must stand ready to fight."[19]

The sharpest attack on the dissenting opinion, however, appeared in an article in the March 1920 issue of the *Illinois Law Review.* Entitled "Abrams v. U.S.: Freedom of Speech and Freedom of Thuggery in War-time and Peace-time," it was written by John H. Wigmore, one of the most widely respected legal scholars in America. Wigmore was a graduate of Harvard Law School, class of 1887, and one of the founders of the *Harvard Law Review.* He had spent three years teaching Anglo-American law at Keio University in Tokyo, where he became fluent in Japanese (his biographer claims Wigmore could read or speak about a dozen languages, including Russian and Arabic), and where he also acquired an abiding respect for Japanese culture. In 1893, after his return to the United States, Wigmore, at the age of thirty, accepted a professorship at Northwestern University Law School in Chicago. A prolific writer, with a special interest in criminal law and legal history, Wigmore was best known for his four-volume *Treatise on Evidence,* published in 1904–1905. In the course of a long career he would write forty-six books or case-books, edit thirty-eight books, and compile sixteen volumes on the law of the Tokugawa Shogunate. Roscoe Pound, who taught at Northwestern from 1907 to 1909, later commented, "No one is more fertile in good ideas than Wigmore, and really he is worth careful reading and careful reflection after reading, and I guarantee will yield great results when so read and reflected upon."[20]

Wigmore became Dean at Northwestern in 1901, and a year later, when the law school moved into new quarters, he invited Oliver Wendell Holmes, who had just been nominated for the Supreme Court, to speak at the ceremony. Holmes accepted the invitation, "for the purpose," as he put it, "primarily of pleasing Wigmore. . . . and giving him a puff."[21] Indeed, the two men had been friends for many years, and shared a warm regard for each other. Wigmore told Holmes, "I venture to regard you as our greatest American or English analyst and jurisprudent," and if Holmes was not quite so effusive, he nevertheless considered Wigmore "a very deserving and quite superior man," and praised one of his early efforts as "a first rate piece of work."[22] When Wigmore published a highly flattering essay, "Justice Holmes and the Law of Torts," in the *Harvard Law Review*, Holmes responded, "Your kindness brought tears to my eyes."[23] On one of the rare occasions when he publicly disagreed with Holmes, Wigmore apologized good-naturedly in advance, and afterward thanked the Justice for not taking offense. Wigmore quipped that his disagreement "made me feel like a hound" but that "the public presumption will be that I am hopelessly wrong, anyhow."[24] As late as March 1917 Holmes wrote, "I have to repeat to you what a constant joy your friendship has been to me and with what pleasure I follow each of your achievements."[25]

Wigmore was also acquainted with Louis D. Brandeis, and thought highly of him. They had first met in Boston in 1889, when Brandeis hired Wigmore, then a young lawyer, to do research on legal problems. Later Brandeis encouraged Wigmore to return to the United States from Japan so that he could take a position teaching law and aid in the "scholarly scientific work" being done by "progressive" legal scholars.[26] Wigmore had mixed feelings about Brandeis's nomination for the Supreme Court, or so it would appear from a cryptic letter he wrote to Holmes. "I have long loved and admired Brandeis. He gave me my first genuine retainer. But to seat him on the outer edge of the Washington woolsack is something like giving Brutus the vacant place of Paul or Ulpian among the Five Splendid Prudentes. However, I would rather see an excess in this direction than another excess in the other direction."[27] Holmes replied that he had known Brandeis for years, "and he always has made on me the impression of a good man, as well as one always bringing fresh suggestions and a hopeful attitude toward the future that seems characteristic of his race."[28]

In 1916 Wigmore, who had termed Germany a "moral outlaw" for carrying on submarine warfare, applied for an officer's commission in the Reserve Corps of the Judge Advocate General's Office.[29] In July 1917, three months after the United States declared war on Germany, he was assigned to active duty. Taking a leave of absence from Northwestern, Wigmore went to Washington as an aide to General Enoch H. Crowder, rising, eventually, to the rank of Colonel. According to a friend, Wigmore, during his nearly two years in Washington, "worked as if the outcome of the war depended on him alone. To him it was a time for action, and discussion became taboo. What many others viewed as grey was black to him." An associate recalled, "He was in a colonel's uniform; and his pride in it was evidenced by his abrupt correction of anyone addressing him as Dean. He fully radiated the military tradition; and he bore himself as a soldier." The Colonel even composed a song, "We'll See Them Through!," which he called "a marching song for the National Army," and for which John Philip Sousa provided the orchestration.[30]

Wigmore's patriotic fervor shaped his attitude toward the treatment of conscientious objectors. Those men who were willing to accept noncombatant status, he advised, should remain on bases in the United States. Inasmuch "as they refuse the risks, so they should be denied the glory of serving even near the front." But those men who, for whatever reason, refused to accept noncombatant status would have to take their medicine, although the dose would depend on whether they were religious objectors or radicals. "Some of these men are merely I.W.W. and other kinds of trouble makers, and must be shut up for the duration of the war; while the really conscientious ones can be let off with one year; the minimum should be one year to avoid giving slackers any hope of an easy sentence." Above all, Wigmore condemned the notion that a man who had religious scruples against accepting noncombatant duty should be furloughed ("an open invitation to slackers to profess scruples," he snapped) or, even worse, discharged ("simply an abandonment of the Government's entire rights over him," he called it.)[31]

In the Judge Advocate General's Office Wigmore worked on matters relating to military and industrial mobilization. One of his most important assignments, however, was to supervise the "voluntary" registration of 13 million men between eighteen and forty-five years of age in September 1918. Fearing that as many as one million men would slip through the Selective Service net, Wigmore met in August with representatives of the Committee on Public Information. Arrangements were made for placing advertisements in every newspaper, for assigning "4-minute men" to address theater audiences, and for displaying posters in all post offices and railroad stations. After consulting with the CPI's advertising division in New York City, Wigmore was considerably reassured. "The men present represented enormous concentration of publicity machinery. The most devoted, energetic spirit was exhibited, together with a great pride in being called in to assist the Provost Marshal General in this enterprise."[32]

Publicity, however, was only the half of it. Wigmore also wanted local draft boards to "list every house" and "account for every individual." Moreover, on the day of registration, "to catch the slacker class, the American Protective League should be asked to direct its members in each locality to offer their services to the Local Boards."[33] Wigmore believed that every man of draft age should not only carry a draft card with his signature on it, but also wear a metal button, visible to all, as a recognizable means of identification. "The psychological effect of knowing beforehand that such marks of fulfillment of obligation would be imposed would be a most powerful element in forcing a complete registration," he said. "Men would not dare to hold back with such a prospect ahead."[34] Although this proposal was not adopted, the success of the draft registration put Wigmore's fears to rest and, he later said, provided "the greatest thrill that I have ever had."[35]

So ardent a patriot could not countenance radicalism any more calmly than he could pacifism. Impatient with those who failed to appreciate the virtues of American capitalism, Wigmore vented his anger at "the ephemeral literature of the extreme socialists" which, he thought, was leading young people "into doubting all sorts of fundamentals."[36] His conservatism, no less than his support for the war, found expression in his *Illinois Law Review* article. Although he never mentioned Holmes or Brandeis by name, referring only to the "minority of two," Wigmore took dead aim at what he considered the "dangerous implications" of the dissent.

Wigmore began by denouncing the Bolshevik regime. Its leaders, he said, were "unscrupulous men" given to "cruel and ruthless terrorism." These "shrewd assassins" wanted to foment revolution everywhere, "to upturn all other civilized countries into the same seething ruin of anarchy." In 1918, he continued, revolutionary efforts were under way in the United States. "They were engineered by alien agents, who relied primarily on an appeal to the thousands of alien-born and alien-parented of their own races earning a livelihood in this country." Jacob Abrams and his associates, Wigmore pointed out, "had lived in this country for from five to ten years, without applying for naturalization." Anarchists by their own admission, they had distributed circulars urging a general strike by munitions workers. Wigmore then quoted some of the more extreme language from the leaflets. But he also used three sentences from the drafts of two other leaflets which had been found in Lipman's and Abrams' possession, without indicating (as Justice Clarke did in his majority opinion) that these documents had never been distributed or even printed. On this tenuous basis, Wigmore concluded that Abrams and the others had called for concrete actions: "(1) a concerted general strike, or cessation of work; (2) particularly by workers in war-munitions factories; (3) with such armed violence that the American troops remaining in the United States would be kept at home to oppose this violence and to preserve civic order."

Turning next to the way in which the minority opinion had interpreted the leaflets, Wigmore wrote that the dissent "is shocking in its obtuse indifference to the vital issues at stake in August, 1918, and it is ominous in its portent of like indifference to pending and coming issues." After briefly summarizing Holmes's interpretation of "intent" and his view of "present danger," Wigmore commented that "argument is useless" because "you cannot argue with a state of mind." The facts, he thought, were incontrovertible. To Wigmore, for example, it was a "fact" that the war had begun because "a ruthless military caste had inspired the German nation to dominate the world by force, at any cost of life, treasure, honor, and decency." It was similarly a "fact" that "the whole spirit and conduct of the German cause, from start to finish, was the egoistic brutal will to bruise, smash, and destroy every other interest, however worthy in itself, which interfered in the slightest with the most trifling will of the German."

Other "facts" related to the actual military situation in the spring and summer of 1918. The war "was going against civilization," Wigmore reminded his readers. After a series of German offensives, "the darkness was settling" and the future looked "gloomy." Then American troops arrived, 300,000 of them every month, in June, July, and August. While the German advance was halted, the war could be brought to a victorious conclusion only if American soldiers received adequate supplies. Munitions workers in the United States, however, could not produce the needed weapons quickly enough. "The supply never equalled the need, until the end of September," Wigmore wrote, ". . . the feverish tension was unbroken. There was danger in a single day's lapse at a single factory or a single work-bench." At this moment of maximum peril, "Abrams and his band of alien parasites" attempted to "cripple our fighting men. Every load of rifles less meant more hopelessness for the cause of world-morality and world-safety." Such behavior was not merely "a plain offense against the law," but "cowardly and dastardly."

As for the minority opinion, Wigmore added, it was not merely "obtuse," but "blind to the crisis—blind to the last supreme needs of the fighters in the field, blind to the straining toil of the workers at home." It would not do to say, as Holmes did, that there was no danger in "the surreptitious publishing of a silly leaflet by an unknown man," because, Wigmore argued, "what is lawful for one is lawful for a thousand more." If malcontents had a right to publish such leaflets, "every munitions factory in the country could be stopped by them." Nor did Wigmore believe that such leaflets could be justified by references to a search for truth. Munitions workers who were persuaded by the leaflets might well go out on strike, so even if the "truth" ultimately won out, its victory "would be too 'ultimate' to have any practical value for a defeated America." The minority opinion, "if it had made the law as a majority opinion, would have ended by our letting soldiers die helpless in France."

Wigmore then proposed a different way of interpreting the free speech guarantees of the First Amendment. He began by asking whether freedom of speech meant "that those who desire to gather and set in action a band of thugs and murderers may freely go about publicly circulating and orating upon the attractions of loot, proposing a plan of action for organized thuggery, and enlisting their converts, yet not be constitutionally interfered with until the gathered band of thugs actually sets the torch and lifts the rifle?" Since the answer had to be "No," the question was how to draw the line so that "Freedom of Speech does not become identical with Freedom of Thuggery." In time of war, Wigmore thought, the answer was easy, for freedom of speech was properly suspended. In such an emergency, all rights "become subordinated to the national right in the struggle for national life." To illustrate his point, however, Wigmore offered an example of speech that would almost certainly have failed Holmes's clear and present danger test: If an individual encountered a company of soldiers on their way to the front, and told them they were fighting in a bad cause, "the state would have a moral right to step promptly up to that man and smite him on the mouth."

In peacetime, too, Wigmore thought the line between speech and thuggery was easily drawn. Free speech meant the "unlicensed ventilation of the most extreme views, sane or insane, on any subject whatsoever." But that did not include the right to advocate what was illegal. One could say anything "to help change public opinion and the law by the usual methods," but one could not "exhort" anyone to "do a specific act which would have consequences deemed by the legislature to be deleterious to the commonwealth." Suppose, Wigmore said, a statute made it a crime to invite a friend over for a drink; and suppose that a man "circularizes his friends arguing for the folly of such a restriction and urging them to come to his house for the purpose." Would the circular enjoy constitutional protection? "Certainly not," Wigmore answered. Just as certainly, the man would have a right to argue for a change in the law. "That is all that the right of freedom of speech exists for, in the last analysis."

Wigmore concluded by condemning the excessive "tenderness" lavished on freedom of speech. Was it not apparent, he asked rhetorically, that the United States already had "an irrevocably established free trade in every blasphemous, scurrilous, shocking, iconoclastic, or lunatic idea that any fanatical or unbalanced brain can conceive?" Wigmore thought that "there is no opinion, however false and absurd in itself, or however nauseous to orthodox hypocrisy by its very truth, that cannot be uttered and reiterated and blatantly paraded with legal impunity." The real danger was not that the government would suppress dissent, but that a "misplaced reverence" for free speech would be used to protect the "treacherous thuggery" of "impatient and fanatical minorities—fanatically committed to some new revolutionary belief, and impatient of the usual process of rationally converting the majority." If the minority opinion in the Abrams case was ever to carry the day, "little indeed would be safe from licensed turbulence."[37]

Praise for Wigmore's article came from far and wide. United States Attorney Francis G. Caffey called it to the attention of Robert P.

Stewart, the Assistant Attorney General who had prepared the government's brief in the Abrams case for the Supreme Court.[38] Stewart found it "of absorbing interest" and, in turn, urged the United States Attorney in Chicago to pass the "masterly article" along to the appropriate appellate judges.[39] From Washington, Secretary of War Newton D. Baker informed Wigmore that he had read the article "with infinite delight and complete sympathy," and said he agreed that the problem was not one of "suppression" but rather "overindulgence."[40] Another lawyer, a resident of Hawaii, complimented Wigmore on his "brilliant and logical" analysis. "I do not think that anybody except a Wigmore can put things so succinctly and clearly."[41] These encomiums were, perhaps, still a source of pride to Colonel Wigmore when, on May 30, 1920, he donned his uniform to march with the Evanston Post of the American Legion in the Memorial Day parade.

In his article Wigmore had cited Edmund Burke's *Reflections on the Revolution in France* to demonstrate that, in 1789 as in 1918, a revolutionary nation posed a threat to its neighbors, and to support the argument that rights depended not on abstract concepts but on actual circumstances. "I flatter myself that I love a manly, moral, regulated liberty," Burke had said, and Wigmore quoted the remark approvingly.[42] Wigmore's critique of Holmes, like Burke's of the National Assembly, was grounded in fundamental conservative principles. Where Holmes talked about relativity, freedom, and experimentation, Wigmore talked about continuity, order, and stability. Where Holmes welcomed a certain turbulence in public affairs, Wigmore favored uninterrupted tranquillity. Holmes searched for a standard that would preserve the individual's right to freedom of speech even while protecting society against a "clear and present danger." Wigmore accepted a formula that extinguished free speech in time of war, and that left it flickering dimly in time of peace. Wigmore could well have quoted another remark of Burke's: "What is liberty without wisdom, and without virtue? It is the greatest of all possible evils; for it is folly, vice and madness, without tuition or restraint."[43]

## Sir Frederick Pollock and the Common Law

"Wigmore in the *Ill. Law Rev.* goes for me *ex cathedra* as to my dissent in the *Abrams* case," Oliver Wendell Holmes wrote to his good friend, Sir Frederick Pollock, on April 25, 1920. "You didn't agree with it," he continued, referring to his dissent, "but Wigmore's explosion struck me (I only glanced at it), as sentiment rather than reasoning—and in short I thought it bosh. He has grown rather dogmatic in tone, with success. . . ." Pollock replied, "I was sorry to see Wigmore carried away by the panic mongers. His reasons amounted to saying that it is wrong to criticize an indictment for murder because homicide is a very dangerous offence and many murderers are very wicked men."[44] Shortly thereafter, the October issue of the *Law Quarterly Review,* an influential British journal, carried an article by Pollock endorsing Holmes's dissent. Pollock had come around to siding with Holmes's view of the Abrams case, but not out of any sympathy for dissent in wartime, much less for the defendants' viewpoint. Rather, he had become convinced that the conduct of the trial and the severity of the sentences violated common-law "principles of justice" to which he was strongly attached.

Holmes and Pollock had first met in England in 1874, when Holmes was thirty-three, Pollock twenty-nine. "There was no stage of acquaintance ripening into friendship," Pollock later said; "we understood one another and were friends without more ado."[45] That friendship, which would last for more than sixty years, was founded on a pleasant convergence of interest and outlook. Both men were "deeply engrossed in the origin and development of the English Law," and both approached the subject in comparative and historical perspective.[46] But where Holmes was known best for his judicial opinions, Pollock gained recognition chiefly as a scholar, teacher, and editor: Corpus Professor of Jurisprudence at Oxford from 1883 to 1903; founder and for many years editor of the *Law Quarterly Review;* and co-author, with Frederick W. Maitland, of the magisterial *History of English Law before the Time of Edward I* (1895). He was also the author of the standard works on contracts and torts, two volumes which, according to one of his admirers, "showed students and practitioners that English law was no mere collection of precedents and statutes, but a system of principles and rules which were logically coherent, and yet eminently practical, because they were the product of the long experience of the race."[47] Pollock had assumed the baronetcy, a hereditary title, on the death of his father in 1888.

Sir Frederick Pollock, Bart., as he was known thereafter, was a devout believer in the common law. His reverence was such that he frequently resorted to religious terminology in discussing it. As early as 1890, in his *Oxford Lectures and Other Discourses,* Pollock wrote, "So venerable, so majestic, is this living temple of justice, this immemorial and yet freshly growing fabric of the Common Law, that the least of us is happy who hereafter may point to so much as one stone thereof, and say, The work of my hands is there."[48] Two decades later Pollock was no less worshipful. In the first of his Carpentier Lectures at Columbia University in 1911, he said, "We are here to do homage to our lady the Common Law; we are her men of life and limb and earthly worship." The lectures, later published as *The Genius of the Common Law* (1912), concluded that the particular virtue of the common law "is that Freedom is her sister, and in the spirit of freedom her greatest work has ever been done."[49]

His faith in the common law predisposed Pollock to favor freedom of speech. Persecution for the expression of ideas rested on two propositions: "that the alleged dangers are real, and also that legal restraints will effectually provide against them," neither of which he thought was true. Pollock denied that "the publication of certain opinions is dangerous to society," or that restrictive legislation is "fitted to attain the desired end." In an 1882 essay, entitled "The Theory of Persecution," Pollock claimed that England was none the worse for having followed a permissive policy. "The foundations of morality have not been weakened; the practice of it has not ceased; respect for the law has not diminished; society is not on the brink of dissolution."[50]

Even so, the only dissenters whose rights Pollock defended were those who "used decent language and otherwise conformed to the ordinary law of the land." Common sense as well as the common law called for "the observance of good manners," and protected only the "sober and serious expression of heterodox opinions." When a belief is held strongly enough, "gross and wanton attacks upon it will presumably give widespread offence and pain, and it may be fair enough to punish them without requiring proof that individuals have been in fact offended." For example, the law should allow criticism of Christianity to be voiced, but it should not "suffer the Christian religion to be assailed with gross and indecent vituperation." In addition, Pollock asserted, the law "is not without resources in the face of rebels and public enemies." Martial law was one such resource, and so were less extreme "measures of temporal police, often perfectly just and necessary."[51] Those resources would be most liberally employed in wartime. In May 1917 Pollock wrote to Holmes, "My private opinion is that there is no liberty of the subject in time of war within the realm."[52]

To Pollock, a man of profoundly conservative inclinations, war itself was harmful chiefly because the men who fought and died were, on the whole, "of better type than the unfit and unwilling." As he told Holmes, "My complaint against war is not that it kills men but that it kills the wrong ones, taking an undue proportion of the strong and adventurous and leaving too many weaklings and shirkers, thus working a perverse artificial selection of those who are least fitted to adorn or improve the commonwealth."[53] Pollock had no patience with radical nostrums. "Mankind being what they are," he said, every plan to create a socialist utopia "would work out (if at all) only to a pretty despotic oligarchy, none the better for a disguise of philanthropic formulas."[54] The proof, he thought, was to be found in Soviet Russia. "There seems to me quite an appreciable chance that the civilized world may have to fight the Bolsheviks one day," Pollock eventually concluded. "—it would have been comparatively easy to suppress them immediately after the war, but we puttered about . . ."[55]

Pollock's view undoubtedly owed much to his son John's harrowing experiences in revolutionary Russia. John Pollock had gone to Russia in 1915, at the age of thirty-seven, to administer relief to war refugees. He kept up this work after the Bolshevik Revolution, but by the summer of 1918 he began to fear that the Soviet authorities were planning his arrest, even his murder. So he adopted an alias, Ivan Pollak-Ulanda, and, to complete the disguise, "grew a fine beard and cultivated a Boston accent." He pretended to be a theatrical producer, while continuing, so he claims, to work in behalf of children made homeless by the war. John Pollock believed that the documents collected by Edgar Sisson, and later published by the Committee on Public

Information as *The German-Bolshevik Conspiracy,* proved that Germany "practically owned" Lenin's government. If anything, the younger Pollock outdid Sisson in his loathing for the Bolsheviks who, he said, were merely a "gang of cut-throats." "There is not a sentiment dear to civilised beings, not an aspiration fruitful of good in the world, not an ideal to raise and purify, that they do not pollute and violate. Mammon and Might are their two gods; deceit, crime, corruption, and brutality their offerings upon the altar."[56] In February 1919, much to the relief of his worried father, he quietly made his way across the border. Pollock cabled Holmes: "Jack safe Finland escaped Bolsheviks."[57]

So it is understandable that Sir Frederick Pollock's initial reaction, when he read the Supreme Court's decision in the Abrams case, was one of disagreement with his old friend. Writing to Holmes in December 1919, he argued that the leaflet written in Yiddish, "which was issued in time of active war," said, in effect: "Hostilities against the Bolsheviks are a crime against all workers, therefore if the U.S. includes any such hostilities in its military operations it is the duty of all workers to resist by (1) stopping or curtailing the production of munitions, (2) active rebellion, so as to cripple the military power of the U.S. altogether." Consequently, Pollock believed, the Supreme Court majority was on firm ground in holding that there was evidence to go to the jury, at least on the fourth count of the indictment: conspiring to incite and advocate curtailment of production of things "necessary and essential to the prosecution of the war." Pollock added, however, that, "as a matter of policy, I believe there were many leaflets of much the same kind distributed in this country on which it was not thought useful to prosecute any one." He also agreed with Holmes that the first three counts of the indictment could not be sustained, and that "the monstrously excessive sentence" could not be justified.[58]

A few months later, however, Pollock moved much closer to his friend's viewpoint, influenced primarily by reading an article by Zechariah Chafee in the *Harvard Law Review* which supported Holmes's interpretation of intent. On June 3, 1920, Pollock told Holmes he now thought that the Sedition Act required the government to prove that the intent to interfere with the conduct of the war was "a specific intent in fact, and not an intent imputed to the defendant by way of inference from what ought to have been his knowledge of probable consequences." Pollock condemned "the dangerous importation of 'presumed to intend probable consequences' into the trial of offences where a specific intent is required to be proved."[59] On this interpretation, even the fourth count of the indictment was unsupportable. Defending this proposition in the October *Law Quarterly Review,* Pollock approved the dissent while, at the same time, expressing his deep distaste for radical agitators.

Pollock began by labeling the defendants "a half-dozen of hare-brained young Russian anarchists," and by noting that their leaflets had not "produced any effect whatever." But he attributed their convictions largely to the atmosphere in which the trial was held and to the prejudice of Judge Henry DeLamar Clayton. The trial, Pollock said, was apparently marked by "a singular disregard of judicial fairness and of the principles of justice respected, as a rule, by American and English tribunals alike." It could hardly have been otherwise, Pollock continued. "Spy mania was, it would appear, in the air of New York in 1918, and Judge and jury may be presumed, as the most charitable explanation of their conduct, to have been suffering from an acute form of truculent panic. . . ." Judge Clayton cross-examined the defendants "quite in the fashion of sixteenth-century State trials," and "charged the jury without any reference to the specific offences created by the statute." What was more, he handed down unpardonably heavy sentences. "For a similar offence in England the usual sentence would be imprisonment for six months, or twelve at the outside."

Then Pollock turned to the issue of intent. He conceded that any attempt to curtail munitions production would, on its face, appear to hinder the United States in prosecuting the war against Germany. So "even if the only thing the defendants wanted to hinder was the production of munitions to be used against the Soviet Government," the jury might well find an intent to hinder the war. But Pollock now believed that the usual definition of intent applied only to acts that were inherently "harmful" but not to those that were "indifferent." One could not attack another person with a dangerous weapon, and claim, in defense, that the intent was not to inflict bodily harm. "But the doctrine that a man is presumed to intend the natural consequences of his acts will not carry so far as to dispense with proof of a particular intent where that intent is expressly specified as an element in a new criminal offence by the statute creating that offence." Since the Sedition Act created the new offense of interfering with the war, a specific intent to interfere with the war was needed to gain a conviction.

Yet Pollock did not think that Abrams and the others should necessarily have gone scot-free. "It does not follow that the defendants might not have been properly visited with some other reasonable and moderate correction as offenders against the peace of the State of New York, if not of the United States." Criticism of the government was permissible, Pollock said, but only "provided that information is not given to the enemy, nor obstruction offered to executive operations." Whether such criticism "may contain matter punishable as a seditious or otherwise criminal libel, are again other and distinct questions." Pollock concluded on an uncharacteristically personal note, "Right or wrong, a man whose son narrowly escaped with his life from the Bolsheviks only a year and a half ago can hardly be biassed by any personal sympathy with the Soviet Government or its adherents." No "honest and reasonable" person could believe that the Soviet government was a workers' republic. "But I am not prepared to regard such belief as in itself a criminal offence, or to abandon the elementary rule of justice that every case must be tried and determined according to what is laid and proved."[60]

Pollock, while concluding that "on the whole, the dissent . . . appears to me to have been correct," was considerably more restrained than some other writers in law reviews, who praised Holmes's "courageous voice," and said that the "stirring words" of his dissent constituted "a landmark in the law" which were sure to find a place in the category of "literary and judicial classics."[61] Nevertheless, Pollock's prestige was such that Harry Weinberger sent a copy of the article to Assistant Attorney General Robert P. Stewart, who responded dryly that it "reflects a tolerant attitude on a question that I had thought the English viewed quite differently."[62] Weinberger sent Pollock a copy of a pamphlet, "Sentenced to Twenty Years Prison," recently published by the Political Prisoners' Defense and Relief Committee. Pollock reported to Holmes that he had received "a lurid pamphlet" issued by a "seemingly not very wise" defense committee.[63]

However lurid the pamphlet, Pollock thanked Weinberger for sending it to him. "Much of it is in my opinion neither judicious nor relevant," he commented on February 5, 1921, "but that is not your business or mine." Pollock then explained that a few months earlier, "some men were charged and summarily convicted before a police magistrate at Shields for importing seditious (Bolshevik) literature, seemingly as part of an organized plan. Sentence, six months. Notice in London press a brief paragraph in small print. I doubt if the local papers gave it much more. Such are our old fashioned ways in this effete monarchy where we still believe in the common law."[64] The letter nicely illustrates Pollock's approach to free speech; one did not try agitators in a boisterous, circus-like atmosphere and put them away for the better part of their lives; one tried them summarily in a sober, dignified manner and, if convicted, put them away for six months.

## Louis D. Brandeis: Thinking Through the Subject

In February 1916, commenting on Louis D. Brandeis's nomination to the Supreme Court, Justice Oliver Wendell Holmes predicted that he would agree with Brandeis "oftener, a good deal" than with any other Justice.[65] That prediction was surely borne out in the area of free speech. Yet if the two Justices usually arrived at similar conclusions in these cases, they did so for different reasons. Those differences were not yet evident in November 1919, when Brandeis joined Holmes's dissent in the Abrams case. They surfaced in 1920, however, when the Supreme Court decided three civil liberties cases. In two of them, *Schaefer* v. *United States* and *Pierce* v. *United States,* both handed down in March, Holmes concurred in Brandeis's dissents; in the third, *Gilbert* v. *Minnesota,* decided in December, Brandeis dissented but Holmes did not. By then Brandeis had so drastically reformulated the clear and present danger standard, even as it had been applied in the Abrams dissent, that Holmes told him, "I think you go too far."[66]

Louis Dembitz Brandeis was born in Louisville, Kentucky, in 1856. His parents were Jews who, a few years earlier, had emigrated to the United States from Prague. Brandeis attended Harvard Law School, receiving his LL.B. in 1877, and went on to establish a highly successful legal practice in Boston. In the 1890s, having acquired a considerable fortune, he took up the causes that led him to be known as "the people's lawyer." Brandeis challenged an imposing array of powerful, entrenched interests, among them the Boston Elevated Railway Company, the Boston Consolidated Gas Company, the Metropolitan and Prudential Life Insurance companies, and the New Haven Railroad. Relentlessly exposing what he considered to be their greediness, inefficiency, or actual mismanagement, Brandeis tried to force these corporations to bring down prices for consumers, and in many cases he succeeded. Brandeis soon gained national prominence. In 1908 the Supreme Court upheld the argument he advanced in behalf of the constitutionality of Oregon's ten-hour law for women. In 1910 he helped organize the campaign to unseat Secretary of the Interior Richard A. Ballinger, who had turned over Alaskan coal deposits to private interests and who was eventually forced to resign.

In 1912, as an advisor to Woodrow Wilson, Brandeis became an architect of the New Freedom, the Democratic candidate's program to break up, or at least to limit, concentrations of economic power. To support Wilson's proposals for banking reform, Brandeis wrote a series of articles attacking the monopolistic power of the great investment banking houses. Published in 1914 as *Other People's Money,* the articles exemplified Brandeis's hostility to what he called the "curse of bigness." They also illustrated his belief that a process of empirical investigation could expose the facts of economic life, and that "the facts, when fully understood, will teach us." Giving those facts the widest possible publicity, he continued, would remedy social evils. For all his emphasis on data-gathering, however, Brandeis also demonstrated a gift for trenchant expression. "The goose that lays golden eggs has been considered a most valuable possession. But even more profitable is the privilege of taking the golden eggs laid by somebody else's goose. The investment bankers and their associates now enjoy that privilege. They control the people through the people's own money. . . . The fetters which bind the people are forged from the people's own gold."[67]

In that same paragraph Brandeis condemned "vast fortunes," which, he said, were "regrettable," were "inconsistent with democracy," were "unsocial," and "seem peculiarly unjust when they represent largely unearned increment." Comments such as these earned Brandeis an unwarranted reputation for radicalism and led to a chorus of outrage from conservatives when Wilson, in January 1916, submitted his name as a Supreme Court nominee. This vehement response had other sources as well. One prominent attorney, who in fact supported the nomination, explained that Brandeis was unpopular with members of the Boston bar because he was "an outsider, successful, and a Jew," and because he had "none of that spirit of playing the game with courtesy and good-nature which is part of the standard of the Anglo-Saxon. He fights to win, and fights up to the limit of his rights with a stern and even cruel exultation in the defeat of his adversary." To former President William Howard Taft, the thought of Brandeis on the Supreme Court was a "nightmare," but to reformers and progressives it was "good to think that there will be at least one Judge on the Supreme Court Bench who sets humanity above all else." In May the Senate Judiciary Committee confirmed Brandeis's nomination, as did the Senate, on June 1, by a vote of 47 to 22.[68]

Five days later Brandeis took his seat on the Court. Over the years he and Holmes would so often take the same side that one observer claimed they had "achieved a spiritual kinship."[69] Yet the two men, even while developing a close friendship, held dissimilar views of law and society. Where Holmes had little faith in social improvement, Brandeis was an avid reformer. Where Holmes was most comfortable dealing with ideas, Brandeis was consistently attracted to facts. As Holmes once remarked, Brandeis "always desires to know all that can be known about a case whereas I am afraid that I wish to know as little as I can safely go on."[70] If Holmes was usually reluctant to invalidate statutes, it was because he thought that the Constitution allowed wide latitude for experimentation. Brandeis, less the detached observer, was more likely to uphold statutes because he agreed with their purposes. One of Brandeis's clerks said he had "an extraordinary faith in the possibilities of human development," a statement that would hardly have described Holmes, who thought it generally the case that power prevailed over reason.[71]

These differences in outlook, inclination, and temperament produced divergent attitudes toward freedom of speech. In 1919 Brandeis had accepted Holmes's formulation of the clear and present danger standard, voting to sustain the convictions in *Schenck, Frohwerk,* and *Debs,* and dissenting in *Abrams.* Much later, in a conversation with Felix Frankfurter, Brandeis admitted having second thoughts about Holmes's interpretation. "I had not then thought the issues of freedom of speech out—I thought at the subject, not through it," Brandeis said, adding, by way of explanation, "Of course you must also remember that when Holmes writes, he doesn't give a fellow a chance—he shoots so quickly."[72] Brandeis's chance to think through the subject came in 1920, when he wrote the dissenting opinions in three cases arising out of wartime restrictions on freedom of expression. Although he relied on the clear and present danger standard, Brandeis actually refashioned it and, in so doing, grounded free speech in a very different set of principles. In place of Holmes's emphasis on the relativity of all truths, the desirability of experimentation, and the benefits to be derived from a free clash in the marketplace of ideas, Brandeis substituted his own concern for factual certainty, social reform, and the democratic process.

As we have already seen, *Schaefer* v. *U.S.* was argued on October 21, 1919, the same day as *Abrams,* and the majority opinion upheld the Espionage Act convictions of three men associated with the Philadelphia *Tageblatt,* a German-language newspaper. But while the Abrams decision was handed down in only three weeks, the Schaefer case was not decided until March 1, 1920. Brandeis, therefore, had a good deal of time to reflect on the issues involved. His dissent, in which Holmes joined, represented a first step toward refining the clear and present danger standard. Brandeis now declared that it represented "a rule of reason" which could be "applied correctly only by the exercise of good judgment."

Good judgment, in turn, required "calmness" on the part of the trial jury. In deciding whether speech could be curtailed, Brandeis wrote, a jury had wide latitude but not unlimited discretion. If the words in question "were of such a nature and were used under such circumstances that men, judging in calmness, could not reasonably say that they created a clear and present danger that they would bring about the evil which Congress sought and had a right to prevent," the trial judge had an obligation to withdraw the case from the jury. Brandeis then asserted, "In my opinion, no jury acting in calmness could reasonably say" that any of the articles cited in the indictment created a clear and present danger of obstructing recruiting or promoting the success of the nation's enemies.

To prove his point, Brandeis did two things which Holmes had not done in the Abrams case. First, he argued that documents had to be judged in their entirety rather than "by culling here and there a sentence and presenting it separated from the context." He therefore incorporated in his dissent the complete texts of four of the most important *Tageblatt* articles (of the fifteen cited in the indictment). Just as the prior practice of selecting key phrases or sentences made such documents seem more inflammatory than they actually were, Brandeis's tactic made them seem less pernicious. Second, Brandeis turned to the original source—in this case, an article, in German—printed in the *Tageblatt.* Finding that the government's translation was faulty, he printed, in parallel columns, the German text and the translation. He thereby disproved the government's claim that the *Tageblatt* had tacked a new sentence onto a dispatch which it had copied and, in so doing, had published a "false" report. Brandeis, who was fluent in German, commented, "Evidently both the jury and the trial judge failed to examine the German original."[73]

Later, reflecting on his dissent, Brandeis said that one reason he had quoted extensively from the documents was to "put it all out, let the future know what [we] weren't allowed to say in the days of the war and following."[74] But Brandeis wished to do more than set the historical record straight. He wanted to make it clear that wartime prosecutions set a dangerous precedent for peacetime. "The constitutional right of free speech has been declared to be the same in peace and in war," Brandeis wrote. If that was so, and if such innocuous articles and "impotent expressions of editorial opinion" could be punished in wartime, they could also be punished in peacetime. That knowledge "will doubtless discourage criticism of the policies of the Government" and would "permit an intolerant majority, swayed by passion or by fear" to "stamp as disloyal opinions with which it disagrees." The convictions of the *Tageblatt* publishers would have a potentially chilling effect for they "not only abridge free speech, but threaten freedom of thought and of belief."[75]

A week later Brandeis wrote the dissent in *Pierce* v. *United States.*

As in *Schaefer,* he insisted on considering the document—in this instance, "The Price We Pay," an anti-war pamphlet distributed by four Albany Socialists—in its entirety. Where Justice Pitney, speaking for the majority, said, "It is too long to be quoted in full" and extracted the most vivid one and one-half pages, Brandeis countered, "The whole leaflet must necessarily be read," and he incorporated all seven and one-half pages. According to Pitney, the pamphlet's statement that the United States entered the war for selfish economic motives was "false," and the defendants knew it. Brandeis pointed out that the causes of war were complex, and that even "historians rarely agree in their judgment as to what was the determining factor in a particular war." Statements regarding the origins of a war necessarily involved "matters of opinion and judgment, not matters of fact to be determined by a jury." Moreover, Brandeis could find "not a particle of evidence that the defendants knew that the statements were false."

Brandeis also proposed a more precise application of the clear and present danger standard. The majority opinion held that it was up to the jury to decide whether the words "would in fact produce as a proximate result a material interference with the recruiting or enlistment service, or the operation or success of the forces of the United States." Brandeis found this unacceptable. Noting that the pamphlet was not distributed among soldiers and did not even counsel disobedience to the law, he argued that disloyalty and refusal of duty were such serious crimes that "it is not conceivable that any man of ordinary intelligence and normal judgment would be induced by anything in the leaflet to commit them and thereby risk the severe punishment prescribed for such offences." The Albany Socialists merely wanted to advance the cause of socialism, he added. There was not "a particle of evidence that these statements were made with intent to interfere with the operation or success of the military and naval forces."

Brandeis endeavored not only to broaden the range of speech protected by the First Amendment, but also to provide a convincing reason why speech deserved such broad protection. In *Abrams* Holmes had argued that free speech was necessary because truth would emerge from the conflict of opinions. In *Pierce* Brandeis subtly but significantly modified that idea. Free speech was necessary because decision-making in a democracy depended on the voters' right to hear all opinions,

Brandeis reasoned. "The fundamental right of free men to strive for better conditions through new legislation and new institutions will not be preserved, if efforts to secure it by argument to fellow citizens may be construed as criminal incitement to disobey the existing law—merely, because the argument presented seems to those exercising judicial power to be unfair in its portrayal of existing evils, mistaken in its assumptions, unsound in reasoning or intemperate in language."[76]

Brandeis amplified this view in his dissenting opinion in *Gilbert* v. *State of Minnesota.* The case involved a conviction under a state law that made it a crime to teach or advocate "that men should not enlist in the military or naval forces" or that citizens "should not aid or assist the United States in prosecuting or carrying on war with the public enemies of the United States." The statute was enacted in the spring of 1917, after the United States entered the war but before the federal Espionage Act was passed. In May 1918 Joseph Gilbert was indicted for a speech he had allegedly made nine months earlier, in August 1917 at Kenyon, Minnesota. According to seven witnesses who testified for the prosecution, Gilbert had said that "we were stampeded into this war by newspaper rot to pull England's chestnuts out of the fire for her," and that "if they conscripted wealth like they have conscripted men, this war would not last over forty-eight hours." The seven witnesses claimed that they could recall, word for word, the same ten sentences from Gilbert's speech. "Despite this remarkable feat of memory," one historian has noted, "none of the witnesses was able to remember anything else Gilbert had said."[77] The jury found Gilbert guilty and he was sentenced to a year in the county jail. The case eventually made its way to the Supreme Court, where it was argued on November 10, 1920—a year, to the day, after the *Abrams* decision was handed down—and was decided on December 13, 1920.

Since the case involved a state statute, there was no reason to assume that First Amendment limitations on the power of Congress to restrict speech were applicable. The majority opinion, written by Justice Joseph McKenna, indicated that the Supreme Court was prepared to give states the widest latitude in restricting speech. McKenna claimed that the Minnesota statute "may be supported as a simple exertion of the police power to preserve the peace of the State." It was not necessary to demonstrate that anything Gilbert said had created a clear and present danger to the conduct of the war; it was sufficient that his words might have caused his listeners to attack him. His remarks "were resented by his auditors" and were met with "protesting interruptions, also accusations and threats against him, disorder and intimations of violence." Moreover, McKenna added, Gilbert must have intended his speech to discourage recruiting, and must have known that the statements he made were untrue. Indeed, "every word that he uttered in denunciation of the war was false, was deliberate misrepresentation of the motives which impelled it, and the objects for which it was prosecuted."

The Gilbert case seemed to create an awkward problem for Brandeis. The First Amendment limits only what Congress may do; not until 1925 would the Supreme Court decide that freedom of speech and press were protected, under the Fourteenth Amendment, from impairment by the states. To Brandeis, however, this difficulty was easily overcome. He began his dissent by noting that the Minnesota statute, while passed during wartime, "applies equally whether the United States is at peace or at war." It therefore precluded the teaching of pacifism at any time, under all circumstances. Moreover, the prohibition was absolute and took no account of the speaker's motive or purpose. Since "the statute aims to prevent not acts but beliefs," it could even be used against parents who taught their children to hate war. "Thus the statute invades the privacy and freedom of the home. Father and mother may not follow the promptings of religious belief, of conscience or of conviction, and teach son or daughter the doctrine of pacifism. If they do any police officer may summarily arrest them."

Although the law in question was a state law, Brandeis went on, freedom of speech had implications that transcended the states' interests. The proper functioning of the federal government depended on citizens having access to all points of view and having a chance to convince others of their own beliefs. Freedom of speech, therefore, was a right which necessarily had constitutional protection. Elaborating on his argument in *Pierce,* Brandeis said, "The right to speak freely concerning functions of the Federal Government is a privilege or immunity of every citizen of the United States which, even before the adoption of the Fourteenth Amendment, a State was powerless to curtail.

. . . The right of a citizen of the United States to take part, for his own or the country's benefit, in the making of federal laws and in the conduct of the Government, necessarily includes the right to speak or write about them; to endeavor to make his own opinion concerning laws existing or contemplated prevail; and, to this end, to teach the truth as he sees it."[78]

Brandeis also proposed two important modifications in Holmes's clear and present danger standard. When the nation faced such a danger, Congress "may conclude that suppression of divergent opinion is imperative; because the emergency does not permit reliance upon the slower conquest of error by truth." Speech could only create a clear and present danger of producing a certain result, then, if it would produce that result before the deliberative process could have a fair chance to work. According to one authority, this reading confined the standard "to the status of an emergency exception to political deliberation."[79] In addition, Brandeis suggested that the Supreme Court could use the clear and present danger standard to set limits on legislative policy. As Samuel Konefsky has pointed out, the question was not only whether the standard had been correctly applied in a particular case, but also whether Congress had a reasonable basis for deciding that curbs on free speech were necessary.[80]

So it is understandable that Oliver Wendell Holmes told Brandeis that he had gone "too far" in his Gilbert dissent, and added, "I have marked McK.[enna's] Op.[inion] 'Concur in result on the record.' "[81] If Holmes was not prepared to accept Brandeis's reformulation of the clear and present danger standard, it was, perhaps, only fitting; after all, Holmes's Supreme Court brethren had been equally unprepared for his own reformulation of the standard from *Schenck* to *Abrams.* In Louis D. Brandeis's hands, the standard served several purposes: to prevent the states from restricting speech, to curb the power of Congress to restrict speech, and to set limits to juries' discretion. Moreover, Brandeis had raised issues that later would prove central to free speech cases: the importance of placing language in context, the need to protect a right of privacy, the danger that prosecutions would create a chilling effect, the application of First Amendment liberties to the states. Above all, Brandeis had demonstrated the connection between freedom of speech and the functioning of democratic government.

## The "Trial" of Zechariah Chafee, Jr., at the Harvard Club

"Word comes of the attack upon you for desiring to be free," Brandeis wrote to Harvard law professor Zechariah Chafee, Jr., on May 19, 1921. "You did a man's job. The persecution will make it more productive. By such follies is liberty made to grow for the love of it is re-awakened."[82] Brandeis offered these words of encouragement because Chafee was about to stand "trial" for the views he had expressed about the Abrams case. A group of conservative Harvard alumni, led by Austen G. Fox, had charged that Chafee (and several other faculty members) had acted improperly in supporting an amnesty petition for Jacob Abrams, and that an article Chafee had written on the case for the *Harvard Law Review* contained misleading statements. The Committee to Visit the Law School, made up of fourteen eminent Harvard Law School graduates, had asked Chafee to appear at the Harvard Club on May 22, 1921, to confront his accusers and to answer allegations that he was unfit "to be entrusted with the training of youth."[83]

Zechariah Chafee, Jr., came from a prominent and well-to-do Rhode Island family. He had attended Brown University, graduating in 1907 with a major in Classics. After working for three years in the family's iron business, which he came to regard as a "trap," he entered Harvard Law School, received his degree in 1913, and then joined an established Providence law firm. In the fall of 1916, at the age of thirty-one, he returned to Harvard as a faculty member. He began by teaching a course in equity, but his interest soon shifted to the problem of free speech. In November 1918 Chafee wrote an article for *The New Republic* which argued that speech should be free in wartime "unless it is clearly liable to cause direct and dangerous interference with the conduct of the war."[84] His June 1919 article in the *Harvard Law Review*, as already noted, came to Oliver Wendell Holmes's attention and led Harold Laski to introduce Chafee to the Justice. In July 1919 Chafee published another article in *The New Republic.* Tolerance, he claimed, was "the tradition handed down to us by Roger Williams and Thomas Jefferson." In fact, Roger Williams was one of Chafee's ancestors.[85]

In 1920 Chafee became still more deeply involved in the defense of civil liberties. With his friends Lawrence G. Brooks, a Boston lawyer, and Felix Frankfurter, a Harvard colleague, Chafee worked on preparing a brief in behalf of two aliens, William and Amy Colyer, members of the Communist Party, who had been arrested in the Palmer raids on radicals and were being held for deportation. The judge who heard the case, George W. Anderson, ruled that there was no statutory basis for deporting alien communists. He also blasted agents of the Bureau of Investigation for trampling on individual rights.[86] In May Chafee was one of twelve lawyers and law professors who, under the auspices of the National Popular Government League, published a *Report Upon the Illegal Practices of the United States Department of Justice.* Harshly condemning the January raids—the wholesale arrests, the violations of due process, the breaking and entering without warrants—the *Report* declared: "Workingmen and workingwomen suspected of radical views have been shamefully abused and maltreated."[87]

His interest in the Abrams case would bring Chafee some very unwelcome notoriety. At the urging of Harry Weinberger, he agreed to sign a recommendation for amnesty, and he persuaded four Harvard colleagues—Frankfurter, Francis B. Sayre, Edward B. Adams (the Law Librarian), and Dean Roscoe Pound—to add their names to it. Weinberger had their signatures reproduced on petitions, along with a statement endorsing executive clemency on the grounds that "the expression of opinion on the Russian Question by Jacob Abrams, was the honest expression of a Russian citizen on Russian intervention," and that there had been "no intent" to help Germany or hinder the United States. Since Abrams was willing to be deported, "the United States could in no way be injured by an amnesty at this time." The petitions, which were widely circulated, also included a plea from Weinberger which said, "if you agree with Roscoe Pound, Edward B. Adams, Felix Frankfurter, Francis B. Sayre and Z. Chaffee, Jr., [sic] all of Harvard University, that these four Russians should be given immediate amnesty, sign this recommendation and return to me . . . to be forwarded to the President of the United States."[88]

On April, 21, 1920, when he learned that Chafee and the others had signed the amnesty petition, J. Edgar Hoover decided that this was a job for the Bureau of Investigation. He instructed one of his agents to compile "as complete a resume as you have upon each of these subjects." He sent another investigator to Providence to dig up whatever he could on Chafee, but the agent reported only that he "comes from a very wealthy family in Providence," and that none of his relatives "were ever known to be connected to any radical organizations." Nevertheless, the Bureau's dossier on Chafee continued to expand as a result of his activities in the Colyer case. Reports on him were filed under the heading "Attorney for Radical Organizations."[89]

Chafee was not, of course, the attorney for Jacob Abrams, but portions of his article in the April issue of the *Harvard Law Review* read as if he were. In fact, Chafee relied partly on information he obtained from Weinberger. Responding to a letter from Chafee, Weinberger complained about the jury's bias and the judge's intolerance, and said that the accounts of the trial published in the socialist newspaper the *Call* were reliable. Moreover, while conceding that Jacob Schwartz had died of pneumonia, Weinberger attributed his weakened condition to his mistreatment by the police. "There is no question in my mind that the beatings for hours, when the boys and the little girl would not tell where the leaflets were printed, was the cause of Schwartz's death." Weinberger also explained that Samuel Lipman was not permitted to see his "sweetheart," Ethel Bernstein, before she was deported on the *Buford.* "They never had an opportunity to say good-by," Weinberger wrote, and added that the telegram Lipman had sent her after she sailed "will go down in history as a great heart message." ("Though time and distance separate us, my love goes out to you over the waves," Lipman had wired. "The humanity and heart of the world may yet demand that we be reunited by my deportation to Soviet Russia, where you are going.")[90]

Chafee's article was entitled "A Contemporary State Trial—the United States Versus Jacob Abrams et al." Twenty-seven pages in length, it began by telling the story of the distribution of the English and Yiddish leaflets in August 1918, and included the texts of the leaflets. "One prisoner died before trial, but the others were indicted," Chafee wrote. They were tried before Henry DeLamar Clayton, who was summoned from Alabama "because of the crowded condition of the local docket. This was his first Espionage Act case." Chafee noted that Abrams had purchased the printing press, that Lipman and Schwartz had written the leaflets, and that Lachowsky and Steimer had distributed about 9,000 of the 10,000 copies printed. Chafee also wrote, "There was no evidence that one person was led to stop any kind of war work, or even that the pamphlets reached a single munition worker."

Chafee contended that there were two possible "theories of guilt," the first illegitimate and the second legitimate, and that as a result of Judge Clayton's rulings the defendants had most likely been convicted on the former. The crucial count of the indictment, Chafee noted, required proof of an intent to interfere with the war against Germany. The first theory of guilt held that the sending of American forces to Siberia was part of a broader strategic operation against Germany; consequently, any opposition to the expedition could hinder the war effort. But on this theory, Chafee pointed out, anyone who opposed intervention in Russia could be indicted under the Sedition Act, and even the government refused to advance such a claim. The second theory, "the only legitimate basis for conviction," held that armaments were vital to carrying on the war; therefore, any call for a strike of munitions workers could interfere with its conduct. The trial record led Chafee to think it was "highly probable that the jury convicted the defendants on just the other theory, for trying to hinder the Russian expedition." It was the judge's duty to warn the jury "against the Russian theory of guilt, and confine their attention to the pro-German theory." Yet Judge Clayton never made the distinction clear. Rather, he confused the issue, and in cross-examining the witnesses actually applied the Russian theory. It was therefore "very probable" that the convictions rested on "an erroneous theory of guilt."

Chafee then addressed the issue of whether there had been sufficient evidence to find the defendants guilty on the proper theory. Conceding that several sentences in the Yiddish leaflet called on munitions workers to strike, Chafee argued that radicals used such language ritualistically. Their words should not be taken at face value, he said. "The Yiddish leaflet is more specific and calls for a general strike, which can no more be kept out of a radical pamphlet than King Charles's head could be barred from Mr. Dick's Memorial. We ought to hesitate a long while before we decide that Congress made such shop-worn exuberance criminal." In addition, Chafee argued, whatever the circular said, "it is open to question whether an incidental portion of a general protest which is not shown to have come dangerously near success really . . . amounts to advocating." Chafee went on to attack the prosecution for using unpublished leaflets to demonstrate an intent to interfere with the war. "What one man jots down and refrains from printing is very weak proof of what several other men intended when they printed something else."

As he concluded his account of the trial, Chafee could barely contain his indignation. He commented on the way the confessions had been gotten. "The army sergeants deny threats and force, but the charges of brutality are disquietingly specific and sincere. The defendants and their counsel also insisted, but not so convincingly, that Schwartz's fatal illness resulted from the violence of one soldier . . ." He noted that the anarchists could not have received longer sentences "if they had actually conspired to tie up every munition plant in the country and succeeded." He also remarked on a judge "who jests with the lives of men," and quoted Judge Clayton's supposedly humorous comment that the defendants had never "produced" anything but agitation. In a footnote Chafee observed, "Abrams and Lachowsky bound books, Lipman produced furs, Rosansky produced hats, Molly Steimer produced shirt waists, Judge Clayton produced the Clayton Act."

Turning next to the Supreme Court decision, Chafee defended Holmes's argument that the word "intent," as used in the Espionage Act, required not merely a general knowledge that certain results would follow from certain acts, but the specific aim that those results should follow. It was not sufficient to say that one who intended to curtail munitions production for any purpose "must know that fewer munitions will hinder the war and therefore must *ipso facto* intend to hinder the war." Such an interpretation, Chafee wrote, would make every strike, for whatever purpose, illegal in wartime. Freedom of speech "is to be unabridged because it is the only means of testing out the truth," Chafee argued. He further contended, "The state must meet violence with violence, since there is no other method, but against opinions, agitation, bombastic threats, it has another weapon—language."

In his final paragraph Chafee avoided any qualifying phrases, writing, "The systematic arrest of civilians by soldiers on the streets of New York City was unprecedented, the seizure of papers was illegal, and the evidence of brutality at Police headquarters is very sinister. The trial judge ignored the fundamental issues of fact, took charge of the cross-examination of the prisoners and allowed the jury to convict them for their Russian sympathies and their anarchistic views." Maximum sentences were imposed for the distribution of "the silly futile circulars of five obscure and isolated youngsters, misguided by their loyalty to their endangered country and ideals, who hatched their wild scheme in a garret and carried it out in a cellar. . . . The wife of one prisoner has been deported to Russia without even a chance for farewell, while he and his friends are condemned for their harmless folly to spend the best years of their lives in American jails." And then, hammering home his disapproval: "The whole proceeding, from start to finish, has been a disgrace to our law, and none the less a disgrace because our highest court felt powerless to wipe it out."[91]

The publication of Chafee's article infuriated a group of conservative Harvard alumni. One of them, seventy-one-year old Austen G. Fox, had graduated from Harvard Law School before Zechariah Chafee was born. A wealthy Wall Street lawyer, Fox had played a leading role in the fight to prevent the confirmation of Louis Brandeis's nomination to the Supreme Court. Fox was joined in his crusade against Chafee by another Law School graduate, Robert P. Stephenson, who had learned, to his dismay, that the law professor had sent galleys of his Abrams article to Weinberger in advance of publication. To Chafee this seemed only proper, since, as he told Stephenson, "it was for his use in obtaining an amnesty from the President, which my work on the article convinced me to be an act demanded by justice."[92] Stephenson could not have found this explanation reassuring. In May 1920 Chafee told a friend that Stephenson was "hot on my trail."[93]

As the trail grew still hotter, two more Harvard Law School graduates—United States Attorney Francis G. Caffey, and John M. Ryan, the Assistant Attorney who had handled the Abrams case—joined the hunt. In June 1920 Chafee, who was revising the article for publication in his book, *Freedom of Speech,* wrote to Caffey asking if he could consult the stenographic minutes of the trial. Caffey gave his consent, but added that the Abrams article "impressed me as unfair in your statement of the facts, in your reliance upon sources unworthy of credence, and in your failure to seek information from the most obvious source." It would not be sufficient, Caffey said, to correct errors before the book was published. A correction should also appear in the *Harvard Law Review*.[94]

When Chafee arrived at Ryan's office to examine the trial record, he was surprised to find that Robert P. Stephenson was already there. Ryan reported that he and Stephenson "had a long talk with Chafee in which we pointed out specifically the inaccuracies and misstatements of fact that appeared in his article." They especially "took him to task . . . for assuming that the testimony of the defendants in reference to the alleged 'third degree' treatment they received after their arrest was true." In all, Chafee made three visits to Ryan's office, but the Assistant United States Attorney was not particularly impressed. "Professor Chafee strikes me as a man who assumes facts without investigating them. I do not think he has much power of analysis," Ryan reported. "He has the conceit and egotism of the school-master, yet is quite humble in the manner of expressing his opinions."[95]

Reading the trial record, listening to Ryan's explanation (and taking notes on it), and seeking, perhaps, to mollify his critics, Chafee blue-penciled the article before publishing it as a chapter in *Freedom of Speech*. The book appeared in December 1920. Although his view that the convictions were unjustified remained unchanged, Chafee provided more information about the case and corrected a number of factual errors that had crept into the article: Schwartz had died before the trial, but had, indeed, been indicted; it was not Judge Clayton's first Espionage Act trial, but his first "prominent" one; Prober was not acquitted by the judge, but by the jury. Having learned from Ryan that Lipman and Ethel Bernstein were not married, but that she was "only a mistress," Chafee omitted any reference to the deportation of a defendant's "wife."

Also, the tone introduced in the book differed substantially from the article; the radicals, he now wrote, had been "captured," not "entrapped"; they were "young aliens," not "youngsters"; there were "charges" of police brutality, not "evidence." Chafee let his readers know what he thought of Abrams and his friends. "There is little of the heroic about these defendants and much that is repellent." The allegation that Schwartz died as a result of the third degree was "improbable," he wrote, adding that the Assistant United States Attorney, "who showed much consideration toward the prisoners, noticed no traces of violence on the morning after the arrest, and is convinced that none was used." Chafee retained the footnote about the defendants producing books, furs, hats, and shirtwaists, but omitted the gibe about Judge Clayton producing the Clayton Act. He also struck out the assertion that the whole proceeding had been "a disgrace to our law." On the galleys, next to the deleted sentence, Chafee wrote: "Omitted, thinking it better to let readers draw own conclusion though this was sound."[96]

There the matter might have rested had Chafee not been called to testify before a Subcommittee of the Senate Judiciary Committee, which had decided to investigate charges that the Department of Justice had resorted to "illegal practices" in arresting radical aliens during the Palmer raids. On January 22, 1921, three days before Chafee was to appear, John M. Ryan told Robert P. Stewart, the Assistant Attorney General who had argued the Abrams case before the Supreme Court, that Chafee had made several misstatements in his *Harvard Law Review* article and that it should be a simple matter to discredit him.[97] At the hearings, however, Chafee was not asked about the article. Instead, he was queried about his work in behalf of the Colyer case and the National Popular Government League. He also maintained that there was a difference between inciting violence, which state laws already prohibited, and advocating revolution, which, he thought, the First Amendment protected. "We should not punish opinions as opinions," Chafee argued, "but we should punish acts which incite to violence." Defending the petition he had signed in behalf of Jacob Abrams and the others, Chafee said, "I asked that those people be let out of prison and be deported to Russia. . . . I have no desire to see them remain in the United States. I thought that the sentence was too long. . . . I think Russia is the place for them."[98]

On February 9, two weeks after Chafee testified, a number of Harvard Law School graduates met in New York City. Over lunch they decided to prepare a formal list of charges against Chafee, and assigned the task, naturally, to Austen G. Fox. On February 12 Fox wrote to the Bureau of Investigation requesting any documents "that show Mr. Chafee's close association, or sympathy with anarchistic 'Reds.'" The letter was referred to J. Edgar Hoover, who merely forwarded a copy of Chafee's testimony before the Senate Subcommittee. In March, however, responding to an inquiry from Archibald G. Thacher, one of Fox's allies, Hoover wrote that Chafee had supported amnesty for Abrams and the others who were "at the very time of the circulation of this petition actively engaged in the distribution of literature advocating the overthrow, not only of our Government by force and violence, but of all our institutions.[99] Fox also turned to Caffey and his assistant Ryan, who prepared a memorandum listing the "misstatements of fact" in Chafee's article. But, Ryan explained, "due to having prosecuted the Abrams case, I did not care to do more than assist in collecting the facts."[100]

While Fox was building his case, Chafee found a crucial ally in Abbott Lawrence Lowell, the president of Harvard University. It would be hard to tell whether Lowell's intervention came as more of a surprise to Fox or Chafee. An arch-conservative, an aristocrat, and an anti-Semite, Lowell's prejudices had coalesced in 1916 when he joined Fox in opposing Brandeis's nomination to the Supreme Court. Yet he now told Fox that he was "an old-fashioned believer in the constitutional protection to individual rights."[101] Lowell wanted not only to protect the academic freedom of faculty members from external threats, but also to prevent a public squabble that could injure Harvard's reputation. On February 11, having learned of the New York luncheon, Lowell informed Fox that he "dreaded the undermining of principles under the stress of events: it is that which undermines institutions."[102]

Lowell failed to deter Fox, but he did steer the controversy into the safest possible channels. By early May 1921 Fox had prepared a thirty-two-page statement criticizing Chafee, which was signed by twenty Harvard alumni. On May 9, when it was presented to the Board of Overseers, Lowell, fearing any decision would be "uninformed and heated," managed to have the statement referred to the Committee to Visit the Law School. Chaired by Francis J. Swayze, of the New Jersey Supreme Court, the Committee's membership included Augustus N. Hand, who was a federal district judge, and Benjamin Cardozo of the New York Court of Appeals. The hearing was set for May 22. Chafee, who confessed that he was in "bad shape," contemplated resigning after the hearing. But soon he came to regard it as a "great opportunity to impress the iniquity of the Abrams trial on a group of influential men," especially after learning that Lowell would appear on his behalf.[103]

Twenty-six men showed up for the "trial" at the Harvard Club on a hot, muggy Sunday morning. Eleven of the fourteen members of the Committee to Visit the Law School were present. (One of the three absentees was John H. Wigmore, Dean of Northwestern University Law School.) Chafee was of course there, with his supporters: Lowell, Frankfurter, and Pound; so was Fox, with his: Caffey, Ryan, and Stephenson. The hearing lasted all day. Lowell easily disposed of Fox's first allegation, concerning the amnesty petition for Jacob Abrams. It turned out that the petition had not included the statements to which Fox objected when Chafee and the others signed it; those statements—that "the expression of opinion on the Russian question by Jacob Abrams, was the honest expression of a Russian citizen on Russian intervention," and that there was "no intent" to help Germany or hinder the United States—were added by Harry Weinberger, afterward, without the signatories' knowledge. Since Fox had a copy of the original petition, he had either knowingly made a false charge or had demonstrated a carelessness more significant than any he attributed to Chafee. Fox had no choice but to withdraw the charge.[104]

The discussion then turned to the *Harvard Law Review* article. Fox and Ryan presented a list of errors in the article. Chafee admitted he had made "a few slight unintentional mistakes" but insisted that "on the main contentions of my article I was not only honest but right." Adding that he "had no sympathy with the political and economic doctrines of these prisoners," Chafee said, "I can hardly imagine any persons with whom I should get along worse than with Abrams and his associates. My sympathies and all my associations are with the men who save, who manage and produce. But I want my side to fight fair. And I regard this Abrams trial as a distinctly unfair piece of fighting." Lowell, serving in effect as Chafee's lawyer, "asked whether anybody in the room thought that Judge Clayton had given the prisoners a fair trial. Nobody spoke."[105] In his summation Lowell explained that Chafee had already corrected the few unintentional errors in his book. Lowell also "declared that so long as he was President of the University no Professor should be disciplined without his consent." According to

Chafee, Fox "babyishly" refused even to respond to Lowell's closing argument.[106]

In the evening the eleven members of the Committee began their deliberations. They agreed unanimously that none of Chafee's statements in the article were "consciously erroneous." But on the question of whether the article "contained erroneous statements of fact which should not have been made, and having been made, should have been corrected in the Harvard Law Review," the Committee was divided. Chafee was exonerated by the narrowest possible margin, 6 to 5, with Benjamin Cardozo casting the deciding vote.[107] Informed of the outcome, Chafee was jubilant. He told Learned Hand that "with Lowell's energetic support, we threw the Wall St. invaders back with heavy losses."[108] He informed Brandeis that "we had a knock-down and drag-out contest all day last Sunday" which ended in a victory.[109] He described Lowell as "magnificent" and "splendid." Exultingly he told Holmes, "The fact that the President of the Harvard Law School Association had denounced the conviction and the sentences was a crushing argument." The President of the Harvard Law School Association, of course, was Oliver Wendell Holmes.[110]

As he was leaving the Harvard Club late that Sunday afternoon, Chafee told Francis Caffey that he would be willing to publish a note in the *Harvard Law Review* correcting the article. Lowell urged Chafee to drop the matter. A correction "would simply start talk," Lowell said, while "if nothing further is published, the talk will die out and what will be remembered is merely that you were attacked and vindicated."[111] But soon the Professor and the President switched sides. Chafee found it impossible to draft a satisfactory list of corrections that would not compromise his views. The attempt, he said, got him "thoroughly tangled up and bogged down."[112] He told Lowell that since "the mistakes were corrected in my book," it would be best to remain silent.[113] Lowell, however, had come under pressure from some of those who had voted against Chafee and who wanted the *Review* to publish a correction. In October 1921 Lowell suggested as much to Chafee. "If I were you, I should make it extremely short, simply saying that you found errors in a previous issue and desired to correct them, as follows. A mere statement of this kind would, I think, avoid criticism and really make clear to anybody who read it that in your opinion the errors were trivial."[114]

The November 1921 issue of the *Harvard Law Review* carried the report of the Committee to Visit the Law School, and a list of eight "corrections and statements." The list was prepared for Chafee by Edward H. Warren, the Acting Dean of Harvard Law School, who, while unsympathetic to Chafee's position, wished to heal the rift between the Law School and its alumni. The eight corrections were, in the main, the ones Chafee had already made in his book. One point, however, required the greatest tact, for one sentence still bothered Francis Caffey: "The whole proceeding, from start to finish, has been a disgrace to our law. . . ." Chafee had omitted the sentence from his book, but needed to say something about its inclusion in the article. This was the solution: "The author remains of the opinion that (a) the conduct of the trial by Judge Clayton was very unfair to the prisoners, and (b) that the sentences recommended by the prosecuting officers and imposed by the court . . . were much too severe. But the author did not intend to charge, and does not charge, that the prosecuting officers tried the case in an unfair manner." Before the corrections were published, Warren arranged a luncheon for the twenty signers of the anti-Chafee petition (but did not invite Austen G. Fox). Presenting a draft of the document, Warren talked about the future of the Law School, and courted the disaffected alumni with great success.[115]

Once, condemning the injustice done in the Abrams case, Chafee suggested that readers "see Morley's indignation at the 'thundering sentences' for sedition in India."[116] The reference was to the memoirs of John, Viscount Morley, who, as head of the India Office in 1908, had criticized the sentences (less severe than those handed down by Judge Clayton) imposed on agitators for Indian independence. Morley wrote, "We must keep order, but *excess* of severity is not the path to order. On the contrary, it is the path to the bomb."[117] That was Chafee's view precisely. The way to deal with radicals, he thought, was to permit them to speak their minds and give them a stake in society. He believed that "a savings bank account, a steady job, and plenty of good-humored toleration and friendly help and encouragement, will bring into harmony with our ideals all but a few heated theorists."[118] Libertarian in outlook though he was, Chafee had no sympathy for radical nostrums. He was, a friend wrote, "a conservative as regards the economic and political views."[119] But as the same friend, with the same libertarian and conservative inclinations, once said to Chafee, "It seems the hardest thing in the world to straighten out the honest conservative American mind on this question of free speech."[120]

As Chafee recalled it, he had tried to explain to the Committee to Visit the Law School why he had written the article that caused all the trouble. "I said that after studying the trial, I was so thoroughly convinced of the injustice done to the prisoners, that as I walked through the streets I kept thinking all the time that while I was enjoying the sunlight, these men and this woman were in prison for a large portion of their lives. I made up my mind that I would set down the truth about this trial for all time, so that others might realize the great wrong that had been done."[121] During all of 1920 and most of 1921, while the issues raised by the Abrams case occupied the thoughts of scholars, jurists, and theorists as diverse as Professor Zechariah Chafee, Jr., Justice Louis D. Brandeis, Sir Frederick Pollock, Bart., and Dean John H. Wigmore, "these men" and "this woman" remained in prison, where, in truth, they enjoyed very little sunlight.

# 8

# Prison

## The American Prison System

LATE IN OCTOBER 1919 Mollie Steimer was taken to the Workhouse on Blackwell's Island to serve her sentence for disorderly conduct. Six months later, at the end of April 1920, she was transferred to the state penitentiary in Jefferson City, Missouri. On the day after Christmas 1919, Jacob Abrams, Samuel Lipman, and Hyman Lachowsky left New York City for the federal penitentiary in Atlanta, Georgia. At the time, Steimer and Lipman were twenty-two years old, Lachowsky twenty-six, and Abrams thirty-three. They remained in prison until November 1921, when their lawyer, Harry Weinberger, finally gained their release on the condition that they accept deportation to Soviet Russia. They were only four of the hundreds of anarchists, socialists, draft resisters, and members of the Industrial Workers of the World who were jailed during and after the war.

As a report prepared for the American Prison Association in 1919 recognized, these political prisoners were misfits behind bars. Such offenders, the report said, "form a strange element that cannot be made to fit in among the others, for they may be wholly without criminal bent and intent, and therefore cannot be made subject to ordinary reformative influences." One goal of the prison, ostensibly, was rehabilitation. Yet no one believed that political offenders were going to be reformed. Moreover, the report added, radicals were bound to be a disruptive presence: when they broke prison rules they were regarded as martyrs, but when they accepted "every hardship or deprivation without a murmur" they only exposed the indefensible fact that "the non-criminal is made to fare exactly as the human dregs adjudged guilty of the most revolting offenses." Noting that prison regulations were drawn up "to meet the needs of the derelicts of society," not high-minded idealists, the report concluded that political prisoners should "be set apart from the common herd of evildoers." The recommendation was never seriously considered.[1]

The prisoners demeaningly referred to as the "common herd of evildoers," the "human dregs," and the "derelicts" were among the least educated of Americans, and, to a disproportionate degree, members of racial minority groups. Of the men who did time in the Atlanta penitentiary in 1920 and 1921, about 10 percent were illiterate, 40 percent had not finished elementary school, another 40 percent had received a grade school education, 8 percent had been to high school, and 2 percent had attended college.[2] At Leavenworth, in those same years, blacks, Mexicans, Indians, and Chinese made up 27 percent of the prison's population. In 1918 the various jails in New York City had custody, for some period of time, of 49,611 men and women; only 358 of them, fewer than one percent, had gone to high school or college.[3] Lacking education and resources, convicts, one sympathetic observer wrote, were "of a class that have no voice to articulate their wrongs in the public press."[4]

Prisons spent next to nothing to feed and clothe their inmates. The annual cost of maintaining a man in the Atlanta penitentiary in 1920 was $317.64, a mere 87 cents a day. Food came to 28 cents a day per person, and clothing to 10 cents. The meals, when not revolting, were unpalatable. One Atlanta inmate complained that "the hash, which often made the breakfast, was composed of fragments of gristle and refuse left on the prisoners' plates after dinner, mixed with potatoes and rancid grease."[5] A prisoner in Jefferson City, Missouri, reported that "the food that is served is not fit for a human being to eat and many men are made sick from the effects of the same." In Texas, investigators found that "the prisoners are fed with peas and beans infested with weevils and worms and also were supplied with strong and unwholesome meats."[6] When one prisoner, an anarchist and a vegetarian, asked for permission to purchase his own food, federal authorities turned him down with the comment, "This Department thinks it would be undesirable to permit this prisoner to put into effect his peculiar ideas on diet, and to subsist on nuts, fruits and raisins, even though purchased by himself."[7]

To cut costs even further, many prisons required inmates to work for private manufacturers. Typically, these companies paid a fee to the state for the privilege of using convict labor in prison workshops. "As late as 1923," historian David Rothman has pointed out, "40 percent of all goods manufactured in prison were made under the contract system and 60 percent of all prison goods were sold on the open market."[8] Captive workers could not complain about working conditions. They had to do what they were told, under threat of disciplinary punishment, and, of course, could not strike for better pay. In fact, two-thirds of the prisons did not pay convicts anything at all for their work. Where they were paid, daily earnings ranged from as little as one and one half cents to $1.50. Only nine states paid convicts 50 cents a day or more. Not until much later was the private contracting system abolished, and replaced by one in which the products of prison labor, such as license plates, were purchased by the state, or in which convicts were employed on public works projects.

When prisoners were not in the cafeteria or workshop they were in their cells. The typical cell in Atlanta was "a steel box about eight feet long by five wide, and seven or eight high. On one side, two cots two feet wide were hinged against the wall, one above another; they reduced the living space to a breadth of three feet."[9] Sometimes, three or even four convicts were confined in the same cell, and when that happened, as in the Eastern Penitentiary in Pennsylvania in 1923, each prisoner had less room "than a dead man has in his coffin."[10] Cells were equipped with a mattress and pillow (usually stuffed with straw), a washbasin, a stool, and an electric light bulb. There was also a toilet, although some of the older prisons provided only an uncovered bucket, which could be emptied once every twenty-four hours. Prisoners had no privacy, since guards could observe them either through the bars or peepholes. Cells were commonly infested with lice and bedbugs. Cockroaches crawled everywhere.

Time spent out of doors, in the prison yard, was strictly rationed.

Convicts ordinarily exercised for about an hour each day, and for longer periods on Saturday and Sunday afternoons. Motion pictures were shown often enough, largely because it was thought they promoted good discipline. "Properly censored films are a marvelous power for good," the authorities said. "Effort is made to select those that will develop the aesthetic sense and stimulate altruistic feelings." War films were especially favored. As one prison official wrote, "He must be dull indeed, who, after seeing pictures of our boys in a parade returning from deeds of valor, knowing that the Americans have fought for right, justice and humanity, is not stirred and thrilled by the National anthem."[11] Music was also employed "as a Means of Discipline." In one instance, a report to the American Prison Association explained, women who were shouting obscenities at each other quieted down when a supervisor began singing "The Star-Spangled Banner," moved on to "The Battle Hymn of the Republic," and came "in half an hour to 'Silent Night' and 'Stars of the Summer Night,' with that beautiful suggestive line, 'Sleep, my lady, sleep.' "[12]

Prison discipline, by its very nature, was arbitrary and despotic. The system encouraged inmates to curry the favor of guards who exercised absolute power over them. Infractions were so loosely defined—"shirking," "grimacing," "impertinence," "insolence," "laughing and fooling," or "staring at visitors," were all offenses—that guards, if they were of a mind to, could always find an excuse to punish a prisoner. Moreover, in the interests of maintaining control, a guard's word was always taken over a prisoner's, or, for that matter, over any number of prisoners'. Typically, guards were "petty tyrants of the worst type, sulky, sneering, malignant, brutal, and liars and treacherous into the bargain."[13] It could hardly have been otherwise, given the nature of the job and the unrestrained authority that went with it. One observer noted, "The pay is low, the hours long, the conditions of labor irksome, the personal danger considerable, and the prospects of promotion practically nil."[14] A federal commission, commenting on the problem of recruiting guards, reported "that it is impossible to secure any but the least competent."[15]

Prison discipline was not only capricious—it was also cruel. Prisoners were sometimes put in shackles and chains or forced to wear leg irons. They were also flogged. In 1923 a Joint Legislative Committee reported that in a South Carolina prison "women and men are stripped naked to the waist, men are sometimes entirely naked. The women have their arms placed in stocks while being whipped. . . . Men whipped in the basement of the hospital building have their wrists handcuffed and secured above their heads to a ring in the wall." The strap used to flog them was "a piece of smooth, pliable harness leather about a quarter of an inch thick, two inches wide and twenty inches long secured to a round wooden handle ten inches long." In the Michigan state prison the victim was blindfolded, his wrists and ankles restrained. He was stretched over a barrel, his back bared, and a piece of "stout linen cloth placed over the bare spot." He was whipped with a heavy leather strap, four inches wide, which had been soaked in water to make it pliable. The prison physician held the man's pulse "and gives the signal for the flogger to stop."[16]

But flogging was falling out of favor as a method of punishment. In 1920 the warden of the West Virginia penitentiary explained that "the whipping-post, buck and gag, the dungeon and water-cure, are not only unnecessary, but tyrannical and have no place in this enlightened age." Such techniques bred bitterness and resentment, he reasoned. But the "sentimental coddling" of prisoners was just as bad as treating them cruelly. The important thing was to instill military discipline, to train inmates "to act with others under orders, learn subordination and the habit of obedience." For those who refused to conform to prison routine, more brutal punishment was in order: "In some few cases for refusal to work, or insubordination, solitary confinement and being handcuffed in a standing position for a number of hours is not too severe, and will in practically every case make the man see the error of his way."[17]

And so the preferred form of punishment was the isolation cell, or what prisoners called the "pit," the "cooler," or the "dark hole." The cells varied from one prison to another, but not by much. Pitch black or perhaps only dimly lit, they resembled "a steel cage just big enough to enable the prisoner to stand upright."[18] There was no bed and no furniture but a straw mattress, or a wooden shelf, on which to sleep. There was no toilet, only a bucket for bodily needs. There were no regular meals, only bread and water. Sometimes the prisoner was handcuffed to the bars, as the West Virginia warden recommended, sometimes not. In one prison the cell was so cramped that the inmate "cannot bend his knees, he cannot lean against the bars, he cannot turn round; his hands are held tight against the sides of his body, and he stands straight, like a post, for a full day, on a little bread and water—and for as many days as the warden or the deputy sees fit."[19] The best-known prison reformer of the time, Thomas Mott Osborne, once had himself incarcerated, incognito, in Auburn and was put in the cooler. "I had never imagined anything so terrible," he reported. "At the end of only 14 hours confinement I came out feverish, nervous, completely unstrung." Osborne was overwhelmed by "the filth; the vermin; the bad air; the insufficient food; the denial of water; the overpowering, sickening sense of accumulated misery—of madness and suicide, haunting the place."[20]

The New York County Penitentiary for men on Blackwell's Island also had a dark hole. It was vividly described by Osborne's friend and biographer, Frank Tannenbaum. In 1914 Tannenbaum had been convicted of unlawful assembly for taking part in a demonstration against unemployment. He remembered the stifling confinement, and the hunger and thirst resulting from a daily allotment of two slices of bread and four ounces of water. Above all, he remembered the guard, "a tall, lanky, slim, pale-faced person, with a bald head, except for the fringe of yellow hair hanging loosely down the back of his head." His mouth hung open, and he had no teeth. His eyes "were just a little green and rather small." Every now and then, when a bird flew onto a window sill, providing a momentary distraction, he chased it away. He cursed at the prisoners, and dumped pails of cold water into their cells. In protest, the men would make a racket, and the guard "would rub his hands, open his toothless mouth, and shout above the din of the banging buckets against the iron doors, 'This is hell and I am the devil.' "[21]

## Blackwell's Island: The Workhouse

Blackwell's Island—later it would be renamed Welfare Island, and still later Roosevelt Island—is situated in the East River. The narrow strip of land extends alongside Manhattan for nearly two miles, from 50th

Street to 86th Street. Acquired by New York City in 1828, the island soon became a place for municipal prisons, hospitals, and storehouses. On the southern end stood the City Hospital and the New York County Penitentiary for men; in the central portion, the City Home and the Neurological Hospital; and to the north, the Metropolitan Hospital and the Workhouse for women. The Workhouse—nearly everyone still called it that even though its name had been changed in 1917 to the Correction Hospital—was opposite 70th Street. Built in the 1850s, it was a massive structure made of stone. There was a central area, which housed administrative offices, and two large wings, each with four tiers.

The south wing had recently been remodeled into hospital wards. Nearly nine of every ten women who entered the Workhouse required medical attention. More than two-thirds of the inmates had some form of venereal disease, or were treated as if they had. Inasmuch as there was no absolutely certain test for gonorrhea, "all prostitutes sent to the Department of Correction are required to take treatment for gonorrhoea for a minimum of thirty days."[22] About half of the inmates were drug users. They were kept in the hospital for two weeks, while drugs were slowly but inexorably withdrawn. The staff took pride in its ability to recognize the various ruses addicts employed to satisfy their craving. Some feigned attacks of hysteria, a staff physician reported, while others inflicted wounds on themselves. All addicts were "pathological liars" and "potential criminals," he said, adding that their addiction was "a pernicious habit and not a disease."[23]

The Superintendent of the Workhouse, Mary M. Lilly, was a woman of some distinction. A graduate of New York University Law School, where she received her degree in 1895, she was one of the first women admitted to the state bar, and later served as editor of the *Women Lawyers' Journal.* She was an officer in the City Federation of Women's Clubs, the Society for the Aid of Mental Defectives, and the Catholic Big Sisters. She was a widow, with one son who was a Major in the Army. In 1918 she had been elected to the State Assembly as a Democrat from a normally Republican district on Manhattan's Upper West Side. She was one of the first women elected to the state legislature. In the fall of 1919 Lilly was completing her first term and was engaged in a heated battle for reelection. On the day before the election the Citizens' Union alleged that she had violated both state and city codes by serving in the Assembly while holding the Superintendent's position at Blackwell's Island. On election day *The New York Times* carried her rebuttal under the headline, "Mrs. Lilly Upholds Her Two Salaries." She insisted that she had accepted the post at Blackwell's Island the previous June only after being assured that it was not a public "office" and therefore appropriate. The allegations, however, may have contributed to her defeat.[24]

When Mollie Steimer was taken to the Workhouse from Ellis Island on October 30, she had just concluded a hunger strike lasting four days, and she was so weak that Superintendent Lilly sent her directly to the hospital. There Steimer presumably followed the normal routine: a new inmate bathed, and was then "dressed in suitable capes and slippers and given a complete examination by physicians."[25] In residence was Dr. John M. O'Connor. The hospital had been attempting to hire female physicians, but thus far its efforts had proved unavailing. The examination completed, Steimer would have been issued regulation prison garb along with towels, a pair of shoes, soap, a toothbrush, and a comb. Since the second floor of the hospital was designated for patients with venereal disease, the third for drug addicts, and the fourth for "psychopathic" cases, she probably remained in one of the rooms on the ground floor.

On November 16 Steimer was transferred from the hospital to a cell in the north wing of the Workhouse. About two hundred women were incarcerated at the time, serving sentences ranging from five days to three years. Three-fourths were between eighteen and thirty years of age, and nearly two-thirds were recidivists. Some had been convicted of serious crimes, such as arson and robbery, others of lesser offenses: telling fortunes, violating the Sabbath laws, or being "incorrigible." Some were drug addicts who had not been convicted of a crime but had entered the Workhouse voluntarily in order to be cured, and in so doing had agreed to remain in custody for at least one hundred days. One inmate was a "harmless old woman aged eighty-three who had served six terms and is now here for a year for vagrancy."[26] The Department of Correction explained its system of assigning prisoners to cells: "The healthy and diseased are separated, colored prisoners are placed together on one tier, and self-committed drug addicts have a tier to themselves."[27]

When the steel door slammed shut behind her, Mollie Steimer found herself in a fairly large cell, one that measured thirteen feet, ten inches in one direction, ten feet, nine inches in the other, and was eight feet high. There was a window. There was a cot, which folded up against the wall, with a mattress and pillow. But there was no running water. "None of the rooms contain toilets or lavatories," an investigator reported. "The old unsanitary bucket is still in use." Since there were only 131 cells, inmates sometimes had to double up. Even so, "the antiquated, insanitary, unhealthful, and oft-times-condemned buckets are used under these crowded conditions." It was largely for this reason that the State Commission of Prisons condemned the Workhouse. "This prison, built nearly seventy years ago is probably one of the worst in the State and is a disgrace to this great City."[28]

During the daytime most of the women worked in the kitchen, the hospital, or the laundry. Others worked in the sewing room, where they supposedly "received a knowledge of industry which would enable them, should they so desire, to secure a good living in the industrial world."[29] In good weather inmates could spend one hour, from 5 to 6 P.M., in the yard. After dinner they were locked in their cells until the next morning. No outdoor work was provided, and yard time was restricted even on Sundays. The location of the Workhouse, near the Metropolitan Hospital and the road transversing Blackwell's Island, was "responsible for keeping the women indoors," or so it was claimed, "because women prisoners naturally attract more attention than men and are more apt to be subjected to the tormenting gaze of inquisitive people."[30] Inmates were permitted to have visitors once every two weeks.

But the prisoner in Cell 98, Mollie Steimer, never went to work, never got to exercise in the yard, and never was permitted to see her family. According to Superintendent Lilly's recollection, when Steimer arrived from the hospital on November 16, "I asked her to work. She refused and remained in her cell, and she has continuously since that date refused to work when asked." And so the institution's system of punishment came into play. A prisoner who broke a rule was deprived of privileges—no exercise, no visitors, no mail, no books or magazines—and was left alone, in her locked cell, all day and all night. The Department of Corrections noted, "It is peculiar about these women—

they dread being alone in a cell. The punishments indicated are greatly feared; quietly administered, they are much more effective than permitting any one of these women to play to the gallery while being dragged to the 'cooler,' feeling herself to be the heroine of a moving picture tragedy. Except in rare cases, isolation has been abolished." In those rare cases, however, the punishment was "confinement in isolation cells on the ground floor. The eight cells are of regular size with a grated and outside wooden door which prevents outside communication. There is a small window in the cell for light and air. Two of the cells are padded. While confined here women are given full meals, bed and blankets and all clothes but no shoes. There is an electric light in each of the cells."[31] Matrons made hourly rounds to check on the women's condition.

With Lilly maintaining that prison rules had to be obeyed, and Steimer insisting that they were arbitrary and illegitimate, an open clash was inevitable. When Lilly asked her why she had been sent to the Workhouse, Steimer answered, "Because I am fighting for freedom." Lilly countered, "If you think there isn't enough freedom for you in this country why don't you go to your own?" Unfazed, the prisoner replied, "Wherever I am there is my home, and there I shall do what little I can to change things for the better." Deprived of mail privileges, Steimer nevertheless tried to write her comrades a letter, which another inmate had offered to sneak out. As she was writing, explaining how to use a code, she caught a glimpse of Lilly's approaching shadow. The Superintendent snatched the letter away from her. Steimer tried to grab it back, and when Lilly would not let go, tore it to bits. "We struggled like a cat and mouse," Steimer recalled. "Where the mouse got so much strength as to defeat the cat, I don't know, but during the fight I broke her glasses and caused her fingers to bleed . . ."[32]

Mrs. Lilly soon had her revenge. The next day, Steimer recounted, "I was locked up in a cell facing the bureau of Lilly! This was a torture! To be caged and exposed to the observation of Mrs. Lilly the whole day long! Nothing to do, nothing to read . . ."[33] Steimer had brought a copy of Max Stirner's *The Ego and His Own* to the Workhouse, and had given it to the woman in the adjacent cell for safekeeping. Now she got the book back and tried to read while hiding it under her blanket. "The State always has the sole purpose to limit, tame, subordinate, the individual," Stirner (a pseudonym for Johann Kaspar Schmidt) had written, in a work first published in 1843. One wonders whether Steimer reached the page on which the author observed that prisons were designed so that prisoners could never forget, even for a moment, that they were, in fact, prisoners, because to forget "brings danger to the prison, and . . . must not even be permitted."[34] Under Lilly's unrelenting stare, Steimer could hardly have forgotten where she was.

On November 19 Mollie Steimer's mother came to see her. Lilly, sensing an opportunity to extract a pledge from the rebellious inmate in return for a restoration of visiting rights, claimed that she "went into her cell and asked her to give her word of honor that she would not try to send letters out surreptitiously. She refused to give her word. On this account her mother was not permitted to see her."[35] Steimer recalled the incident somewhat differently: Lilly told her she could see her mother, but only if she asked Lilly's pardon. Steimer was faced with a cruel dilemma, but "choking every feeling in me I told the matron that I have nothing to ask pardon for." To Steimer, a crucial principle was at stake. "If I should once submit and ask for pardon she will try more and more to belittle me."[36] To the authorities, an equally crucial principle was involved. When Harry Weinberger complained about the deprivation of privileges, the Commissioner of Corrections replied, "If she obeys the rules of the department she is entitled to and will receive certain privileges. If on the other hand, she wilfully disobeys and persistently defies the head of the institution, she forfeits all privileges."[37]

However stringent Lilly's behavior, Steimer's own account suggests that the Superintendent made the first conciliatory gesture. On Thanksgiving Day, November 27, as the inmates gathered to sing patriotic and religious songs, Lilly unlocked Steimer's cell door, "and putting her hand on my shoulder said, 'This is a great Thanksgiving day and I want to show you that we Americans are a great free people and I forgive you.' " She invited Steimer to attend the celebration and enjoy herself. But the younger woman wanted no part of any such truce. "You are a big hypocrite," she retorted. "Besides, to listen to these songs is no enjoyment for me." Despite the rebuff, Lilly nevertheless allowed Steimer to leave her cell, to eat in the dining room with the other prisoners, and to enjoy other privileges.[38]

This new arrangement lasted for only forty-eight hours, when the calm was shattered by a prison riot. On Saturday, November 29, Steimer reported, when the prisoners went to the dining room, they found that salt, not sugar, had been sprinkled on the meal of rice and raisins. They complained, but were told by the matron that the food was good enough to eat. "Thereupon the tin cups of hot 'coffee' as well as the rice and raisins started to fly in the air!" The prisoners, screaming uncontrollably, then raced through the Workhouse, smashing everything in their path. Steimer was stunned. "Never before have I seen people in revolt, and it was a painful experience for me," she later told Emma Goldman. "Human beings turned into wild beasts! The sight was frightful, the screams enough to turn one mad. The iron beds torn off the walls and thrown into the hall, the fire exti[n]guishers opened and the water coming from all sides, the electric lamps broken and while doing these things they screamed and cursed as I never imagined women could do. I was amazed, horrified. . . ."[39]

A few of the ringleaders, injured by the broken glass, entered Steimer's cell to be bandaged. That is where Lilly found them, and quickly concluded that the anarchist was responsible for the destructive rampage. "This is the result of the freedom I gave you," she snapped.[40] Her account of the riot indicates that she regretted the kindness she had shown Steimer and was determined not to permit any further erosion of discipline. "On November 29, 1919, there was a riot in the workhouse. The inmates broke windows, turned on the hose, wrenched the electric light fixtures, threw the tables and chairs about. I traced the instigation of this riot to Mollie Steimer, who preached her anarchistic doctrines to the inmates as they passed her cell. At the end of the riot the ringleaders took refuge in her cell. For this she with others were locked in their separate cells for twenty-four hours without breakfast."

The next morning, Lilly continued, Steimer "was still preaching anarchistic doctrines, shouting out through her cell door, in substance, there should be no prisons, for a person should be permitted to live in her own way, etc. She was thereupon placed in the 'cooler' for fifty-six hours. Her cell was searched and there was found a manuscript in her own handwriting containing anarchistic doctrine and a picture of Lenine. The 'cooler' is a dark cell isolated from the other cells and those confined are put on a bread and water ration."[41] Steimer's version was more graphic. As another woman was being dragged off to the isolation cell, she spoke out, shouting that only better conditions, not punishment, would prevent future riots. Approaching her, Lilly said, "Shut your mouth or you go with them!" "I repeat the dark hole won't stop riots and if you put these girls there I will go with them. Whereupon she ordered the police to 'take this one'. But the holes were already full and I was put into a padded cell, for insane inmates."[42] In protest, Steimer went on a hunger strike. After three days she was returned to her regular cell.

By then Steimer had served a little more than one month of her six-month sentence. She was again deprived of all privileges, and when Harry Weinberger complained, Lilly informed him that "until Mollie Steimer obeys the rules of this Institution I cannot allow her any privileges."[43] Not to be denied, Steimer again contrived to send and receive mail through another inmate. But Lilly suspected what was going on. She explained, "I had forbidden the introduction of newspapers into her cell, but, upon searching, found in January clippings of local newspapers containing articles of police raids on anarchistic meetings."[44] So the Superintendent decided the time had come to rid herself of her nemesis. On about February 1, 1920, she transferred Steimer to another cell, and assigned matrons to watch her around the clock. Fannie E. Smith now was responsible for her supervision, and responsible for nothing else. As she put it, "I have been obliged to give my entire time and attention to her."[45]

For Steimer, the minutes, hours, and days dragged by interminably. She discovered that even Harry Weinberger's letters were not being given to her when she found an envelope from his office, addressed to her, in the wastebasket. Furious, because "the worst criminal is entitled to the mail from her attorney," she asserted that it was "a shameful & brutal deed to keep a prisoner in absolute ignorance regarding her own matters."[46] The doctor had recommended that she be allowed an hour's exercise each day, "but those unreasonable creatures who 'run' the Workhouse, stopt it off! under the pretence that I refuse to work."[47] She was observed all day long by Fannie Smith, "an old maid whose pride was 18 years service at the Workhouse and the best trusted guard in the women's department."[48] In a letter smuggled out of the Workhouse to Harry Weinberger, Steimer wrote plaintively, "To be body guarded and kept in *constant* confinement *without any exercise whatever* is an aughful torture."[49]

She was still denied the privilege of having visitors, and barred from talking to the other inmates, but the prohibition could not be completely effective. It took some doing, but on several occasions Weinberger obtained a pass so that his assistant, Jerome Weiss, could meet with Steimer to discuss an amnesty appeal. On February 19, when she was taken to Ellis Island to be questioned by the immigration authorities, her mother and another friend met her at the ferry house and accompanied her on the trip over and back. In March Weinberger endeavored, with no apparent success, to have her taken, under guard, to an oculist because she was suffering "excruciating pain" in her eyes.[50] Steimer kept trying to talk to the other prisoners as they passed by her cell, Warden Smith reported, adding, "It is necessary that I be continually on watch to prevent it." Ordered to stop, Steimer was "most rebellious and impertinent, both in her words and in her actions." In eleven years as a matron, Fannie Smith concluded, "I have never had an inmate that was so unruly and caused me such trouble and continuous attention as Mollie Steimer."[51]

Her behavior was so exceptional that the New York City Department of Corrections, breaking its usual rule, mentioned her by name in its annual report. The 1919 report on the Workhouse stated, "Where an offender having a straight sentence repeats an offense, or the offense even for the first time is grave enough to warrant it, she is deprived of the five days allowed for good behavior on a given month. This punishment has never been inflicted a second month, except in the case of Mollie Steimer, the Bolshevist." Steimer, the report continued, "would not obey any rule, would not work, but with the aid of her lawyer demanded all kinds of law to be administered for her benefit. Through her attorney she asked for what she deemed her rights, but never for one moment did she admit that she owed a duty in exchange for these so-called rights."[52]

In April, as her six-month sentence drew to a close, Weinberger attempted to gain a two-week delay before Steimer was sent to the penitentiary in Jefferson City. He thought that allowing her to say good-bye to her mother, her brothers, and her friends before entering prison for fifteen years would be a humane act, especially since it would be virtually impossible for her relatives to make the trip to Missouri.[53] United States Attorney Francis G. Caffey thought otherwise. "I shall not interfere in any way with the due execution of the bench warrant when her term in the City prison expires," he told Weinberger.[54] So the lawyer wrote to Attorney General A. Mitchell Palmer, only to be informed that the Department of Justice "is without authority to interfere with the service of process of the Court."[55] Finally Weinberger turned to the United States Court for the Southern District of New York, where he had to appear before Judge John C. Knox. John M. Ryan, who as Caffey's assistant had handled the prosecution eighteen months earlier, argued against Weinberger's motion. To buttress his case, he submitted depositions from Lilly and Smith describing Steimer's rebellious behavior. Lilly claimed, "She absolutely refused to obey any rule or regulation of the institution and when questioned replies by preaching her anarchistic doctrine, and by preaching this doctrine to other inmates has caused them to be unruly at times."[56]

On April 24 Judge Knox denied the motion. He observed, "The conduct of the prisoner during her confinement at the Workhouse upon Blackwell's Island has been such that does not give rise to the hope or expectation that her conduct will be any better if I were now to stay for a short period the execution of her sentence for 15 years and to permit her in the meantime to remain in the City Prison. That she has none but herself to blame for deprivations of the privilege of seeing members of her family while on Blackwell's Island, is quite apparent from the affidavits before me . . ." Moreover, Knox added, Weinberger, not Steimer, was making the motion. "She, I understand, does not recognize authority of any kind and will not directly apply for any relief." Such an attitude "is not conducive to the extension of privilege." Whether or not she saw her family before leaving for Jefferson City was up to the United States Marshal.[57]

Released from the Workhouse on Thursday, April 29, 1920, Steimer was taken to the Marshal's office, where her family was, in fact, permitted to see her that afternoon and the next day. She boarded a train for Jefferson City, Missouri, on April 30. *The New York Times* reported that "unusual precautions" had been taken to prevent supporters from demonstrating in behalf of "the 20-year-old Red." Before leaving for the penitentiary, the newspaper reported, "the girl devoted herself to a tirade against cruelties she said she found on the Island."[58]

She would undoubtedly have had an easier time of it had she conformed to prison regulations. Mrs. Lilly could be callous and vindictive, but she could also show consideration to prisoners who were properly deferential. A reporter who visited the Workhouse a year later found that the inmates regarded her much as pupils did "a well-liked teacher. They did not scruple to stop the Superintendent and demand or complain, or entreat, but it was all done with a mingling of respect and amiability."[59] But there was nothing respectful or amiable about Mollie Steimer. Lilly considered her "the most obstreperous and uncontrollable" inmate she had ever seen.[60] From Steimer's perspective, however, to accept the terms set by her captors was to confess defeat. By internalizing their expectations, she would have truly been imprisoned, for she would have adopted a prisoner's mentality. But her rebellious stance also took a toll. As she later recalled, Superintendent Lilly "made it so hard for me that I was almost driven to insanity."[61]

## Atlanta: "Huge Walls of Stone . . . Tiny, Airless Cages"

In December 1919, when Abrams, Lipman, and Lachowsky arrived at the federal penitentiary in Atlanta, a forbidding sight greeted them. The prison, one of the nation's largest, stood "gray and massive behind its fence of tall iron pickets."[62] The penitentiary was located in the city's southeastern section, off McDonough Boulevard. The main building, constructed of granite cut from nearby Stone Mountain, had been completed in 1902. "There can be 750 prisoners accommodated here," the Atlanta *Constitution* gloated, "and always one more if necessary." With the addition of an east wing in 1915, and a west wing in 1918, the prison's capacity was more than doubled. The grounds, occupying 28 acres, were surrounded by a massive wall 4,178 feet long, varying from 2 to 4 feet in width, and from 28 to 37 feet in height. Armed guards were stationed in ten tall turrets. There were four cell blocks, each with five tiers. The Bureau of Prisons later described the institution as one of the "heavily barred-and-bolted, fortress-like walled bastilles which reflect the general nineteenth-century philosophy of prison design."[63]

The warden was Frederick G. Zerbst, who, at the age of forty-nine, had spent his entire career in prison administration. A native of Hanover, Germany, he had emigrated to the United States when he was eighteen years old. In 1895 he was appointed a guard in the newly established United States Prison Service, and over the years rose steadily through the ranks. In 1910 he was selected to be the only federal parole officer in the country, and, three years later, to be deputy warden of the federal penitentiary at Leavenworth, Kansas. He was appointed warden at Atlanta in March 1915, a post he held until mid-1921, when he returned to Leavenworth to supervise the narcotics section. It was said of Zerbst that although he was "a strong believer in dealing with prisoners according to the 'Golden Rule,' he nevertheless was a strong disciplinarian."[64]

In six years at Atlanta Zerbst brought about significant reforms. He introduced a system of paying prisoners a modest wage, which, he said with justifiable pride, had the effect of "building up self-respect and confidence to a degree heretofore largely lacking." A prison farm was set up in Panthersville, eight miles from the penitentiary. About one hundred men worked there, growing vegetables and caring for a dairy herd. Zerbst boasted that the convicts "are entirely on their honor, no armed guard whatever being employed on the farm." The warden eliminated compulsory chapel attendance. He also built new athletic facilities in the yard, where, he explained, "excellent baseball diamonds, tennis courts, hand-ball courts, basket-ball courts, and a variety of other methods of recreation and physical development are provided."[65] The Catholic chaplain certainly thought this was a major improvement. "There is no better cure for morbidness, despair, and moral depravity than clean, healthy sports, Sundays included," he wrote.[66]

In 1920 the penitentiary housed about 1900 prisoners. Thirty-three of them were serving life terms, and ninety were serving sentences of twenty years or more. About half of the inmates had been convicted of such offenses as counterfeiting, illicit distilling, larceny, robbery, murder and manslaughter, stealing United States mail, using or selling drugs, tax evasion, or running prostitution rings. But men were also in jail for other kinds of "crimes": thirteen for committing acts of sodomy or oral intercourse, one for furnishing liquor to an Indian, thirteen for mailing obscene material, one for piracy, and one for sinking a vessel in a navigable stream. The men came from every walk of life. According to the warden's report, the prisoners had been engaged in 187 different occupations. Many were farmers, workers, and clerks, but the prison had its share of blacksmiths, butlers, candy makers, chauffeurs, cowboys, fishermen, hucksters, lawyers, magicians, musicians, preachers, pugilists, and sailors. Only two of the prisoners, however, Abrams and Lachowsky, had been bookbinders, and only one, Lipman, had been a furrier.

By the time the three arrived, political prisoners were a familiar sight in the Atlanta penitentiary. The anarchist Alexander Berkman had already been there for nearly two years, after the Supreme Court had upheld his conviction for opposing conscription. Entering the penitentiary in February 1918, he was assigned to the cotton-duck mill, "working all the time on Singer sewing machine." He reported that prisoners were granted half an hour in the yard every afternoon, and as much as two hours on Saturdays and Sundays, "unless one is deprived of this as a result of punishment." Berkman was punished for having protested a guard's fatal shooting of a black convict, and also for having insisted on the right to "propagandize" the other prisoners. He spent thirty hours in the dark hole, suffering "the torture of gradual suffocation."[67] Then he was placed in solitary confinement, where, for seven months, he was denied books, newspapers, writing materials, or tobacco. When Harry Weinberger interceded on his behalf, the Superintendent of Prisons blandly replied, "If a prisoner in punishment is to have his tobacco, writing privileges, and books, there would be very little real punishment involved, especially to men of Berkman's type."[68] As Berkman put it, "Outside you try to economize time; here we are doing our best to kill it."[69]

Since Berkman was not released until early October 1919, he was imprisoned, for a time, with the socialist leader, Eugene V. Debs, whose speech against the war had led to his conviction under the Sedition Act. Transferred to Atlanta from a prison in Moundsville, West Virginia, in June, the sixty-four-year-old Debs would remain for two and one-half years, until Christmas 1921. Unlike Berkman, Debs did not break prison rules or antagonize the institution's authorities. Assigned to light chores in the prison hospital, he was never deprived of any of the usual privileges. Debs tried to put the best face possible on his incarceration, telling his brother, Theodore, in June 1920, not to worry because "the men here are as my brothers, and if you could but see how kind and loving these imprisoned souls are to me, you'd be touched to tears."[70] But the rigors of prison life nevertheless took their toll, and Debs, as his biographer, Nick Salvatore, points out, eventually succumbed to despondency and despair.[71]

Although Berkman and Debs were the best-known political prisoners to have been locked up in Atlanta, they were by no means the only ones. Louis Kramer and Morris Becker had served time there for the crime of distributing leaflets announcing a rally to oppose the draft. In December 1919 seven other men, besides Debs, Abrams, Lipman, and Lachowsky, were being held in Atlanta for violations of the Espionage Act. Some, like Debs, did easy time, but for others, like Berkman, it was harder. In one case, it was claimed, a guard had one of the radicals sent to isolation merely for waving to a fellow radical with his bandana. Another political prisoner wrote that Warden Zerbst had threatened, "I will put you in the hole, yes in the dungeon, for all the rest of your time and you will lose good time, too, where you will not see a God damn person, if I hear of you saying anything in favor of Socialism or against the war."[72]

The prison administration read and censored all of the prisoners' correspondence. During this period inmates were permitted to write one letter (or at most two) each week. A letter had to fit on two sides of a sheet of paper and could be sent only to a lawyer or to an approved list of relatives and friends. No limit was put on the number of letters that might be received. Censorship was a time-consuming task, since, in a typical year, the prisoners wrote about 125,000 letters, received nearly 175,000, and received 137,000 copies of newspapers. Inmates, of course, knew that their mail was being read by the prison censors. Lipman joked, "You know, I have enough secretaries in here—one opens my letters, the second reads them to be sure nothing injurious in them, the third brings it to my 'desk.' "[73]

What Lipman and his friends did not know was that the Bureau of

Investigation was also reading every letter they wrote and received. In January 1921 the agent in charge of the New York City office asked J. Edgar Hoover, in Washington, for authority to obtain copies of the letters "as no doubt considerable information can be secured concerning the movements of the radicals through this means."[74] Hoover readily gave his consent, directing the Bureau's Atlanta agent, Vincent Hughes, "that censorship be placed on all mail received and sent by . . . Jake Abrams, Lachowsky and Lipman."[75] Hughes then made the necessary arrangements with the penitentiary officials. (The Kansas City, Missouri, office made a similar arrangement with respect to Mollie Steimer's correspondence.) Making doubly sure that nothing would be left to chance, Hughes not only forwarded a copy of all the letters to the Bureau's New York office, but also sent another copy to Washington. He sent the first batch of letters on February 23, 1921, and was advised to continue the procedure "inasmuch as it is believed that valuable information will be secured thereby."[76]

The letters do indeed provide much valuable information, not about matters of concern to the Bureau of Investigation, but about the three men's experiences, thoughts, and feelings. All of them corresponded, naturally enough, with their lawyer, Harry Weinberger. Lachowsky wrote chiefly to his mother and two sisters, who lived on the Lower East Side; and to Rose Gordon and Rose Brownstein, two friends. Abrams wrote most frequently to his wife, Mary; to his sister, Manya, and her husband, Joseph Spivak; and to friends from the Bookbinders' Union. Lipman wrote long, soulful letters to Ethel Bernstein, who was by now in Russia, through her mother, who served as intermediary. He also wrote to his mother, Feige Lipczuk, who still resided in Pinsk, Poland. He was permitted to use Yiddish in writing to her, but even copies of those letters, duly translated into English, were kept on file. They were delivered only after the Bureau found that they "contain nothing of material importance."[77]

In discussing conditions in Atlanta, the three political prisoners tried to allay their friends' and relatives' anxiety by making light of their physical discomforts. Lipman, who had long suffered a problem with his vision, wrote that his eyes "were weak before I came here, and you wouldn't expect them to get stronger in prison, would you?"[78] He told Weinberger, perhaps only half in jest, "It is true that I am going blind, but why worry about one organ of my being, when the whole thing is shattered."[79] A vegetarian, Lipman explained how he managed on prison fare. "My food consists of a bowl of milk and bread three times a day, 7 days a week, 4 weeks a month, 12 months a year—it seems to be quite sufficient, as I gained weight since I am in here."[80] Abrams, referring to a dental problem, told his wife not to send the money needed to have three teeth replaced. "I wish I had the food to chew for the twenty nine teeth that I will soon have in perfect order."[81] Assigned at first to the laundry ("when I'll come out I will join the laundry union," he commented), Abrams was eventually put to work as a typesetter on the prison newspaper, "and that gives me much more freedom than before in other words back to my old work and not afraid to get twenty years (for printing)."[82]

In a few instances Warden Zerbst took care of problems that Weinberger called to his attention. He arranged for Lipman to be examined by an optometrist, and reported that he was "not suffering from any eye trouble, that cannot be remedied by proper glasses."[83] Even so, Lipman was transferred from sewing shirts to making rugs. The new work, he said, "is very easy in general and on my eyes in particular." He was working on Oriental rugs, Lipman told an aunt, adding, "if you need some for your Restaurant send an order to my firm. One of my friends when he sees me walking in the yard says 'There walks the Rug factory', the reason is because I am the only one on this work."[84] When Lachowsky was placed in a cell with a "crazy fellow, who tortures him," Weinberger asked Zerbst to arrange a transfer, and the warden promptly honored the request.[85] The three friends were eventually assigned to the same cell, an arrangement they understandably found much more to their liking.

They also tried to make the most of their time, to find even small pleasures in the few ways available to them. Lachowsky took advantage of the exercise period in the yard, telling his mother, "I am also getting Americanized. I know what is a base-ball game, I know who the crackers are."[86] In the evenings he was able to listen to recordings of operas and Russian folk songs. Lipman, reporting that "the warden promised to let in books so long as they weren't revolutionary," read widely in such fields as biology, geology, sociology, and economics.[87] Abrams obtained a banjo-mandolin, which he enjoyed learning how to play.

Also, as he slyly told his sister and brother-in-law, he went "to church every Sunday . . . I am being saved. You see since I came here I found that I have a little Jakele called a soul, and when I die this little one comes out and goes for trial again . . . and when it is all right it goes to heaven, so I go to church, so it means the little Jakele will have a clean record, so I will not get twenty years any more. You understand now."[88]

Yet sports, music, books, and chapel were no more than momentary diversions in the grinding monotony of prison life. As Lipman wrote, "The days are rather long, when a month begins it forgets to end—the everlasting, cursed monotony chokes me."[89] Lachowsky tried to explain to a friend how important letters were in relieving "for a few moments or sometimes for a few hours" the everlasting tedium. "The whole day is so long and one feels lonesome and monotonous and every one hopes for the mail hour, and when the hour comes every minute is like a century, and imagine how one feels after waiting the whole day and then—the guard who brings the mail passes by like a twenty century train— . . . and then we wait again and hope for to-morrow . . ."[90] "To write chapters on the life of a prisoner?" Abrams asked. "What interest can one find in reading, of physical deprivation, . . . of the long monotonous day, what attraction can one find in a letter when its contents is full of groans, dreams, desires and constant thought of the best friends on the outside."[91]

The three men reacted to prison life in somewhat different ways, the differences deriving, in part, from what they anticipated on their release. They had been in Atlanta for thirteen months when freedom became an actual rather than a hypothetical prospect. On January 30, 1921, as the Wilson administration was leaving office, Weinberger obtained a commutation of their sentences (and of Mollie Steimer's) to two years and six months, on condition "that they be deported to Russia and never return to the United States, or to require them to serve the sentences imposed."[92] So a definite date, June 27, 1922, had been set as the latest on which they would be released. "As the saying goes on here," Abrams wrote, "roll on you damned time, so I also say roll on you 1921 and bring June 27th 1922, yes that is the day I am waiting for and off I go to Russia."[93] Each of the men indeed knew that they would be going off to Russia, but each regarded the prospect quite differently.

Hyman Lachowsky, a slender, dark-complexioned man, just over five feet tall, with black eyes, black hair, and heavy eyebrows, was prisoner number 10420. His letters from Atlanta suggest that, on occasion, he became severely depressed, not only because he was imprisoned but also because he had lost his faith in human nature, a loss which, to a dedicated anarchist, could be devastating. He saw deceit and selfishness everywhere. "Yes everyone is fighting for his existence, for his and not more," he commented. "Why fool my self and say that I see light when I see darkness wretchedness etc."[94] The iron bars, he grieved, were his only friends, for the more he learned about people, the less he trusted them, and the more he preferred "to speak to the bars for I know that they (the iron bars) will not betray me."[95] He sometimes gave in to self-pity. "Yes, I long, I long, I long for the time when I loved every one. I long for the time when I believed everyone. I long for the time when I trusted everyone. If I could be the same now—but I can't."[96] He advised one anarchist, "Just look into the eyes of your class conscious friends and comrades and those who claim that they are building the society of happiness. Look into their hearts, look in a little more to their actions and you'll see hypocrisy lies deceit and so forth."[97] Once he could not bring himself to go outdoors with the other prisoners. While they were in the yard, he wrote, "I am sitting my head bent down, the teeth pressed together and don't say a word, as I would be angry with everyone."[98] He said he felt like a volcano, ready to erupt.

Lachowsky had no illusions about what to expect in Soviet Russia. When his friends insisted Russia was a land of freedom and equality, he replied, "Freedom! ha . . . ha . . . ha . . . ha . . . 'equality' Oh, Devil!"[99] He was in no hurry to be deported, he told Weinberger in July 1921, because "to me are all governments alike and it makes no different to me in what penitentiary I am."[100] On the other hand, he naturally did not want to remain in Atlanta "for to be a prisoner means to be a slave, a thing, and not a person but no one thinks that the prisoner is a free person, and I am not here by my own will where there I am a slave by my own will."[101] Reading reports of the Bolsheviks' suppression of anarchists, Lachowsky spoke of "the false altar of communism," and the Soviet "dictatorship over the proletariat." He did not expect to be happy in Russia, he wrote, adding, "I do not remember if I ever had a moment happiness."[102]

Jacob Abrams was prisoner number 10421. Never as despondent as Lachowsky, he undoubtedly exaggerated when he told his wife, Mary, that he was "healthy as a lion and cheerful as a child."[103] He sometimes grew angry when Mary neglected to write to him or seemed not to understand just how onerous prison life was, but his letters home more often had a friendly, bantering tone. "Yes, I nearly forgot to ask you did you go to see the Dempsey fight? Yes? You did? Fine. I expected you to go only fifty dollars a ticket, and I was sure that you will be at the fight."[104] Stoical about imprisonment, as about life, he said that suffering always preceded a new birth, and felt "that every day that I spend in here is as much necessary as the rain and sunshine for the blossoms development."[105] He told Mary that he was sustained by thoughts of "the new world, the world that I and you dream about."[106] She wrote to him, "True enough you have not been gone twenty years but we have literally lived through that length of time. But everything comes to an end, and so will our troubles someday."[107]

Abrams, like Lachowsky, heard about the persecution of anarchists in Russia, but refused to credit accounts printed in "the yellow prostitute press."[108] Even if the stories were partially true, he thought, there was a reasonable explanation: conditions in Russia remained so chaotic that some excesses were inevitable. He was not prepared to defend everything the Bolsheviks were doing—"I know it is long to keep men in prison, I know it is long to suppress freedom of speech and the press, I also know that it is a crime to interfere with the liberty of the individual"—but neither was he ready to denounce them.[109] "I am sure that Russia will be the promist land in the future," he said reassuringly.[110] He was not afraid of finding harsh conditions in Russia, he added. "What have I now that I shall be afraid of going to Russia . . . What is worse and what can be worse than to be bound between iron bars and stone walls. . . . is there any thing worst to be deprived of air and sunshine? . . . the best prison is a living grave."[111]

Samuel Lipman, prisoner number 10422, described himself as being five feet five inches tall, weighing 150 pounds, and having brown eyes, chestnut hair, and a light-brown complexion. He could not resist adding, "Other deformities, none! (The brains they tell me are not visible!)"[112] As a socialist rather than an anarchist, Lipman remained considerably more enthusiastic than his two friends about making a new life in Russia. Whatever mistakes the Bolsheviks had made, he never doubted that socialism would prevail, for "the absolute surrender of the greedy, selfish rule is imminent—The working class or the revolutionary movement may be suppressed, but never defeated."[113] Besides, he was desperately in love with Ethel Bernstein, who was already writing to him from Petrograd and Moscow. Suffering the sorrow that only the lovesick can suffer—he lamented that he was "being drowned in an ocean of longing"—he would have wanted to be reunited with her wherever she was. That she was in Russia was all the better. Confined in Atlanta, he nevertheless felt as if "my spirit is already in Petrograd."[114]

Ethel Bernstein wrote him glowing letters, portraying life in Russia as exciting but difficult. Shortly after arriving in Petrograd in January 1920, she said that, tired as she was, "Russia is not the place where you could rest." Food was scarce and the standard of living meager, she commented, adding quickly, "People have suffered so much and are still suffering, but for the revolution nothing is too hard." She had gone to the opera house to hear Chaliapin, and saw "plain workers" sitting in what had once been the Czar's private box.[115] From Moscow in December 1920 she wrote, "The art theatre is the most wonderful place in Moscow . . . the place was filled with workers, can you imagine what would your capitalistic friends say, to see the most wonderful theatre filled with working people."[116] In February 1921 Bernstein wrote about the death of Peter Kropotkin, explaining that his funeral "has been organized by the anarchist organization," but failing to mention that some of the anarchists had to be released from prison for the day in order to march in the procession.[117] Simply, eloquently, she expressed her love for Lipman, saying that she felt "miserable lonesome thinking where you are my Comrade, how you feel? . . . So time goes, and has passed already more than an eternity since we have seen each other. . . . If I could only be able to make you feel better, but I am so powerless, being so far away . . . I love you with all my soul."[118]

For Samuel Lipman, then, deportation to Russia had a personal as well as a political dimension. It was the waiting, the uncertainty, the disappointment when he did not hear from Ethel, that were the hardest to bear. Spring was the worst time. On May 2, 1921, he wrote to Ethel, "My craving to live in month of May is so strong, my longing to be embraced in the arms of my beloved, enveloped in the bright rays of the May sun is so intense, that I would rather be unconscious in the month of May, while in prison."[119] Admitting that there were many days "when my shattered nerves would not permit me to study," Lipman cried out in pain and loneliness, "I am or on the verge to go out of my mind."[120] He concluded one letter with the comment, "Ethel dear, if love should not be a mutual feeling, lovers would be victims. . . . My beloved, the bright Southern sun has enveloped all its victims alike, but inside is cloudy, frost, snow, storm, Your abnormal Lipman."[121]

As differently as Lipman, Abrams, and Lachowsky viewed the future, as devoted as they were to their books and music, as helpful as they found the warden on occasion to be, prisoners remained prisoners. They always had to toe the line, however arbitrarily it was drawn, or face punishment. The Atlanta penitentiary had the same kind of isolation cells as other American prisons, although they were located in a separate building, away from the regular cell blocks. In a year's time, about one prisoner in every five spent time in isolation, some of them more than once. There is no evidence that Abrams was so confined, but Lachowsky was on at least one occasion, and Lipman was three times.

"The first time, was in Feb. 1920," Lipman explained. "I was kept ten days in dungeon and then put in the second grade, which means taking away almost all the privileges. That time it was for saying to a guard. 'Did I ask you to speak to me?' He delivered a lecture of how I should behave & I kept on working, without paying any attention to him." The second time, Lipman continued, was on December 30, 1920. A deputy who had been reprimanded by Zerbst for his treatment of Eugene Debs "was mad as a dog and came running to the tailor shop, I was standing at my post working and Lachowsky having nothing to do at the time was near my rug 'factory' speaking to me. He jumped at Lachowsky, asking him why he is not in his place, and asked the guard in charge to report him. The next morning both of us were called in and put for three days in the 'Hole' (dungeon)." The third time,

Lipman said, was in July 1921, "for waving my hand to a prisoner in isolation." He again lost his privileges for thirty days.[122]

Lipman described these incidents in a letter to Harry Weinberger in November 1921, but it was not written from Atlanta. By then, the lawyer had arranged for the prisoners' early release and deportation. Lipman and his two friends were back on Ellis Island, awaiting the arrival of their comrade, Mollie Steimer, who had just spent eighteen months in the Missouri State Penitentiary.

## Jefferson City: Kate Richards O'Hare and Prison Reform

Mollie Steimer had never been to Missouri before she was taken to Jefferson City early in May 1920. Had circumstances been more auspicious, the visit might have had its attractions. Located on the southern bank of the Missouri River, Jefferson City is the state capital. A new capitol building had only recently been completed at a cost of $4 million. From its eight-columned portico, one enjoyed a splendid view, across the wide Missouri, of the beautiful bluffs of Callaway County. The population of Jefferson City was only about 14,500. Shoe manufacturing was a major industry, but the city's economic well-being rested on state employment, some of it provided by the Missouri State Penitentiary. When the prison had been built in the 1830s, it had housed only eighteen inmates. By 1920 the number had grown to 2,400, of whom 100 were women.

Unlike Atlanta and other federal penitentiaries, which operated under the civil service system, Jefferson City was run by a political appointee, the chairman of the Prison Board. William Rock Painter, without previous experience in penal administration, had been appointed to the position in 1917. A Missourian by birth, he had attended the Missouri School of Mines, had worked for a while as a civil engineer, but had then turned to journalism and politics. In 1894, at the age of thirty-one, he became editor and publisher of the *Daily and Weekly Democrat.* From then on, as one account said, "he accepted positions of honor and responsibility in his community." He also devoted much of his time to the Masonic Temple. His wife, Cora Herndon Painter, "for many years one of the outstanding club women of Missouri," held office in state chapters of the Daughters of the American Revolution and the Daughters of the War of 1812. In 1913 William Rock Painter was elected Lieutenant-Governor on the Democratic ticket and, after four years, was rewarded with the Prison Board chairmanship, a position he held through 1921.[123]

At the time, men convicted of federal crimes were sent to a federal penitentiary, but women were not. Until 1927, when the first federal reformatory for women was built in Alderson, West Virginia, such offenders had to be boarded at state institutions, where the majority of prisoners were men, and where most of the women had not committed federal crimes. The Missouri State Penitentiary in Jefferson City seemed to be the preferred location for female political offenders. It was where Emma Goldman was incarcerated from February 1918 until September 1919. It was also where Kate Richards O'Hare, a prominent socialist, served her Espionage Act sentence. She was imprisoned in April 1919, while Goldman was still an inmate, and they became close friends. O'Hare was freed in late May 1920, about a month after Mollie Steimer arrived. Harry Weinberger had taken the precaution of writing to O'Hare, "I hope that you will find Mollie a good companion, and that you will extend your sheltering wing to her."[124]

A more striking contrast between two women can hardly be imagined. Five feet, ten inches tall, O'Hare towered over the diminutive Steimer. O'Hare was forty-four years of age, the mother of four children, the eldest of whom, at seventeen, was not much younger than Steimer. There was nothing Russian, Jewish, or foreign about Carrie Katherine Richards O'Hare. Born on a 160-acre homestead in Kansas, she was raised by parents who were devout adherents of the Disciples of Christ, and she had thought, briefly, of becoming a missionary. After teaching elementary school in a small town in Nebraska, she worked in her father's machine shop. In the mid-1890s she became interested in socialism, and under the tutelage of Julius A. Wayland, editor of the *Appeal to Reason,* read some of the classic works of radical theory. She joined the Socialist Party in 1901. On New Year's Day 1902 she married Francis P. O'Hare, a Party organizer, and they spent their honeymoon on a socialist lecture tour.[125]

During the next fifteen years "Red Kate" became one of the Party's most prominent figures. Moderate in outlook, she rejected the use of violence, and dismissed the revolutionary stance of the Industrial Workers of the World as a "morbid phenomenon."[126] Through a gradual process of education, she believed, workers would come to see the advantages of a cooperative system and would elect socialists to office. She first tested this belief in 1910, when she campaigned for a seat in the United States House of Representatives from Kansas. A spell-binding orator, and tireless, she made hundreds of speeches, but received only 5 percent of the vote. In 1911 she began writing a column for a socialist periodical, the *National Rip-Saw*, which had 150,000 subscribers. She also served on the Socialist Party's National Executive Committee, and was its representative to the Second International.

In 1912 the O'Hares moved to St. Louis. Kate Richards O'Hare saw herself, and was apparently seen by others, as a responsible advocate of reform. Her socialist convictions notwithstanding, she was readily accepted by the city's political and cultural leaders. Rubbing shoulders with the upper crust, she joined many civic organizations and served as an officer in the Missouri Federation of Women's Clubs. In the winter of 1914–15, she was appointed to the city's Unemployment Committee. Working comfortably with politicians, clergymen, and municipal officials, she helped gather information and develop plans for public works. In 1916 she ran for a United States Senate seat from Missouri, but polled only 2 percent of the vote. An advocate of temperance reform, she looked toward a socialist future when "life will be clean, sane, secure and happy; and few will care to lose a single moment of it in drunken stupor."[127]

In keeping with the tenor of the era, her views regarding race and gender were entirely conventional. Not at all self-conscious about speaking to segregated audiences, she denied that racial integration had any place in the socialist scheme of things. "What is the solution of the race question?" she asked, and answered, "There can be but one. Segregation."[128] In the socialist commonwealth, "darkies" and "niggers" would be relegated to their own section of the country. As for women, they would marry and raise a family, for that was their "sacred" obligation. "Home is the logical location of womanly activity," she wrote, and marital love was "God's earthly messenger."[129] The "woman question" was fundamentally an economic one, O'Hare believed; it would be solved when capitalism was replaced by socialism. When women no longer had to work for starvation wages, they would not be forced to become prostitutes. Consequently, venereal disease ("the black disease of the brothel") would disappear.[130]

This was the eminently respectable woman who, in April 1917, undertook a speaking tour in defense of the Socialist Party's anti-war platform. Traveling from Florida to California, she spoke before one sympathetic audience after another, repeating much the same thing everywhere she went. She had given her standard speech about seventy-five times when, on July 17, she found herself in Bowman, North Dakota, addressing 125 people in the Cozy Theatre. For two hours she explained why workers and farmers had nothing to gain from the war. Since she spoke extemporaneously, no text of the speech exists. But the Army's Military Intelligence Division received a report about a speech she had given a week before, near Caldwell, Idaho, which, even allowing for the agent's bias, may have faithfully captured her oratorical style. Her critics, O'Hare said, claimed that socialism would take the child from its family, but it was conscription that had made the child "the chattel, the slave of the state." She went on, according to the report, "They say, 'Oh! Mrs. OHare, aren't you patriotic?!' and of course I answer, 'Y-E-S V-E-R-Y,' (with sneer and grimace). They say, 'Oh! Mrs. O'Hare, Dont you l-o-v-e y-o-u-r C-O-U-N-T-R-Y?' and I answer, 'yes, Y-E-S.' (with sneer and grimace). They say, 'dont you love your flag??' Then I say, 'Yes, yes, I love it too well to put it to dirty uses!' " She added, "The Government said, 'We need your boy to protect the profits of the Capitalist class, and your child is a slave, cannon fodder.' "[131]

On July 29, as she was waiting in a hotel lobby in Devil's Lake, North Dakota, O'Hare was served with a warrant charging her with discouraging enlistment by making "seditious and near treasonable statements" in her Bowman speech. Indicted under the Espionage Act, she was charged with having said "that any person who enlisted in the Army of the United States for service in France would be used for fertilizer, and that is all that he was good for, and that the women of the United States were nothing more or less than brood sows to raise children to get into the Army and be made into fertilizer." O'Hare, insisting that her words had been garbled, claimed that she had merely said that when the European governments and churches told women to give themselves to soldiers who were going off to war, so the soldiers might breed before they die, "the women of Europe were reduced to the status of breeding animals on a stock farm."[132] O'Hare posted the $1,000 bond, and awaited the trial, which opened in Bismarck, North Dakota, in December 1917.

The judge, Martin J. Wade, of Iowa City, had recently said that "a spirit of submission to all lawful authority" was "the highest form of patriotism."[133] Witnesses for the prosecution, only two of whom had attended O'Hare's speech, testified that she had made the "brood sows" remark. The defense countered that O'Hare was being framed because of a local squabble over political patronage. The witnesses against her, it turned out, were affiliated with a Democratic Party group which had recently lost control of the local post office to a Nonpartisan League faction. The new postmistress had entertained O'Hare on her visit to Bowman. So, the defense contended, Democratic politicians were scheming to oust the incumbent by associating her with a "disloyal" speaker. The judge refused to allow this line of argument. The jury found O'Hare guilty, and the judge, in passing sentence, said that he could not find that O'Hare had "ever paid a tribute to the American flag." He sentenced her to five years, commenting, "Every day she is at liberty she is a menace to the government."[134]

O'Hare remained at liberty for sixteen months, however, while her lawyers exhausted all avenues of appeal. On October 28, 1918—a few days after Judge Henry DeLamar Clayton sentenced Mollie Steimer and the other defendants in her case—O'Hare's conviction was upheld by a Circuit Court of Appeals. The Court declared that "there could be no more potent means of obstructing, or even defeating, a country in raising its forces for war . . . than a campaign of abuse calculated to inflame the ignorant or lawless against the operations of their duly constituted government, and to incite or encourage them to resistance."[135] An appeal was taken to the Supreme Court, but in March 1919 it denied a petition for certiorari. On April 15, 1919, the day after Eugene Debs was jailed, Kate Richards O'Hare entered the gates of the Missouri State Penitentiary.

The prospect of her imprisonment—for five years, at any rate—was not pleasing to Department of Justice officials. On April 12, 1919, John Lord O'Brian admitted to Attorney General Thomas Gregory that he was of two minds about the matter. "Mrs. O'Hare is a well-known lecturer, a well-educated, highly intelligent woman, but the suggestion of clemency in her case is complicated by the fact that ever since her conviction last October [*sic*] she has been lecturing almost daily, and some at least of her lectures have been in the nature of bitter attacks upon the administration of justice generally and our courts in particular."[136] Asking for time to consult with Alfred Bettman, O'Brian promised to have an opinion ready before the end of May, when he was planning to resign his position. On May 27 he suggested a commutation to eight months, but finally settled on six. O'Brian instructed the Pardon Attorney to prepare the necessary papers, and informed Gregory that there were "elements of aggravation which make me think it unwise to reduce the sentence lower than six months, one of them being the character of the attacks which this woman and her husband have repeatedly made upon Judge Wade, who presided at her trial."[137] In any event, O'Hare's sentence was not commuted until much later. She remained in prison not for six months, but for fourteen.

From O'Hare's standpoint, where she would be imprisoned and what work she would be doing were as important as how long her term would be. Although Judge Wade had sentenced her to the Missouri State Penitentiary, she hoped to arrange a transfer to the state penitentiary at Bismarck, North Dakota, the state where she had made her controversial speech. She also hoped to use her time in prison to compile a "case book on criminology," based on inmates' responses to a detailed questionnaire pertaining to their social and economic background.[138] To these ends, she conferred with the warden at Bismarck, with faculty members at the University of North Dakota, and with the Governor, Lynn J. Frazier. A member of the Nonpartisan League, Frazier offered a sympathetic ear, especially since he believed that "politics and spite work played the major part in the prosecution of this woman."[139] Disregarding appeals from state officials, the Department of Justice refused to authorize her transfer from Jefferson City to Bismarck.

Assuming the worst, O'Hare had approached the Psychology Department at the University of Missouri, and had met with the Governor of Missouri, who cordially promised to support her project. But when she was admitted to Jefferson City she was ordered to work in the sewing room, with the other women. The inmates filled out her questionnaires in the evenings, however, and she eventually collected nearly two hundred case histories. As she was preparing to leave the prison, officials removed the files from her cell and destroyed them. Unable to write the kind of book she had in mind, O'Hare managed, in various other ways, to expose the horrid conditions in Jefferson City: through letters to her family, some of which appeared in the socialist press and all of which were later published under the title *Dear Sweethearts;* through speeches she later gave in behalf of amnesty for political prisoners; and through her book, *In Prison* (1923), a powerful indictment of the existing system and a plea for reform.

A fastidious person, O'Hare was appalled by the filthy conditions she was forced to endure. The food in the cafeteria was enough to turn one's stomach: "The oatmeal and fruit were infested with worms, the macaroni filled with bugs, the beans inhabited by weevils, and the corn meal supported a thriving population of meal-worms." Moreover, O'Hare explained, "a decent degree of bodily cleanliness was impossible." Each inmate was provided with two garments, made of "the stiffest, coarsest, most raspy sort of brown muslin," one of which had to be worn for a week while the other was laundered. But the wash was done in wooden tubs and on wooden washboards, with too little soap, and wrung out by hand.[140] "There is nothing so degrading as dirt, and nothing so reformative as cleanliness," she wrote in December 1919. "I live in constant horror of loathsome disease germs, and I feel that months of scrubbing and bathing will be necessary to make me fit to live in decent society. The whole place reeks with every known vener[e]al disease."[141]

O'Hare's most gruesome experience involved her enforced proximity to a young woman, Alice Cox, who was dying of syphilis. She was an Indian who had been sentenced to twenty-five years for murder. The man she had murdered was a soldier who had raped her when she was seventeen years old. "From her throat to her feet," O'Hare wrote, "she was one mass of open sores dripping pus. I have seen her with her clothes so stiff with dried pus that they rattled when she walked, and I have seen live maggots working out of the filthy bandages about her neck." Told to bathe in a tub from which the young woman had just stepped, O'Hare refused. But O'Hare's cell was directly above Cox's. "Her open sores were never properly dressed, the stench was frightful, and the flies swarmed over her and then awakened us in the morning by crawling over our faces."[142] Emma Goldman, in the cell next to O'Hare's, confirmed this account. "Believe me it means torture for both of us to hear the suppressed groans and stifled sobs of that unfortunate creature. You can imagine what it means for us that a million flies crawl thro her open ulcers and then swarm over our faces and wake us up in the morning creeping over our lips." Mercifully, in February 1920, Alice Cox died.[143]

Jefferson City imposed an archaic rule of silence, calculated to cause inmates to cringe in fear. Prisoners were not allowed to speak to each other while they were in their cells, at work, or in the dining room. They could talk to each other only during the hour they were in the yard each day, and for several hours on weekends. In the shop a matron sat perched on a high platform, watching the women as they worked. Since "the most terrible punishments were inflicted" for breaking the rule, and since inmates were sometimes falsely accused of speaking, they kept their lips tightly drawn. In the cellhouse the rule was enforced arbitrarily and selectively by the trustee, a convict whom O'Hare described as a "negro stool pigeon." Prisoners who paid her off or who showed a "willingness to submit to sex perversions" could talk all they liked; others would be punished, and "the word of the ignorant, degenerate, vicious negro convict was law."[144]

Guards never ventured a kind, much less a gentle, gesture; to the contrary, they seemed to enjoy humiliating the prisoners. When a sewing machine needle accidentally pierced her fingernail, O'Hare reported, the matron "poured a little turpentine on it, bandaged it up with a little rag, and sent me back to the machine."[145] When her fifteen-year-old son, Richard, visited, he was not permitted to play his cornet for her. He had to stand outside the prison gates and play loudly enough so that his mother, her eyes brimming with tears, could listen to him through a window. In fourteen months, O'Hare later commented, she never once heard an inmate addressed courteously. The guards "either snarled at us, cursed us, or screeched at us, and those snarling, rasping, hateful voices still haunt my dreams."[146]

At first, O'Hare's cell was located directly across the corridor from the isolation cells. Once, a young black woman, whom O'Hare considered "quite plainly demented," was punished for having thrown a pail of hot water on another inmate. After a male guard beat her up, "the handcuffs were placed on her wrist, passed through the bars in the blind cell doors, and snapped on the other wrist. The bridle, a sort of gag . . . was placed in her mouth to prevent her screaming, and she stayed there ringed and bridled from early in the afternoon until about nine at night. She was taken down just before the lights were out for the night, and so far as I know was not hung up again." The woman spent fifteen days in isolation.[147] (As late as 1938, a report on the Missouri State Penitentiary, which by then no longer housed women, stated, "Men undergoing confinement for punishment purposes . . . may be cuffed up, neck high, to the grills for a period of one to three days.")[148]

As agonizing as she found prison, O'Hare did not hold Painter, the chairman of the Prison Board, to blame. On the contrary, she testified that he treated her with the utmost consideration, as he had Emma Goldman. Describing Painter as "exceedingly generous," Goldman said, "Both Kate and I would have a hard time here but for him."[149] O'Hare regarded him as "one of the kindliest, most humane prison officials in the country." She even said that she considered herself fortunate to be "under the care of a man like Mr. Painter. He has done all for me that I have asked and more."[150] Responding to O'Hare's urging, Painter made a number of improvements: shower baths were installed, the dining room was spruced up and meals were served while they were still hot, women inmates were permitted to use the prison library, ventilation fans were installed in the workshop, and the cells were whitewashed.

So by May 1920, when Mollie Steimer arrived in Jefferson City, conditions in the prison were not quite so primitive as O'Hare had first found them. In the remaining month of her sentence, the older woman did indeed take Steimer under her sheltering wing, as Harry Weinberger had requested. O'Hare wrote that "Mollie, the tiny four-foot, eighty-pound maiden" exemplified "youth that loves and hopes, gives and suffers for its ideals." She was heartsick that Steimer had been cast into a "disease-ridden pesthole and forced to live where mental, moral, and physical contamination was almost unavoidable."[151] Visiting his wife in prison, Frank O'Hare reported that Steimer "looked to me to be about the same size as my little thirteen year old daughter."[152] For her part, Steimer found O'Hare "a kind and fine character," and told her mother that O'Hare was "initiating" her into prison life.[153]

Steimer would spend the next eighteen months in a cell that was smaller than the one in the Workhouse on Blackwell's Island, but in other respects was less objectionable. The cells in the Missouri State Penitentiary were seven feet wide, eight feet deep, and seven feet high. There were steel bars in the front; the ceiling and the other walls were made of solid steel, and were, in the summer, too hot to touch. Each cell had a toilet, a sink with cold water, a small table, and a stool. A steel bunk was fastened to a wall, with straw for the mattress and pillow. Each inmate had her own cell, and could decorate it as she wished. Prisoners could receive packages of food from friends on the outside, or arrange to purchase groceries through the matron (so long as the food did not require cooking). There were no restrictions as to what prisoners could read. As Steimer wrote to her mother, "I can get reading and writing matter, food stuff, even bread (I can see you smile)."[154]

For nine hours each day Steimer and other prisoners worked at antiquated sewing machines in a long, narrow room, poorly lit and poorly ventilated. She was assigned a "task," a certain number of garments which had to be finished each day, and given a certain trial period in which to acquire the necessary speed. Since the "task" was always set at the level of the most skillful and experienced worker, it was not uncommon for prisoners to take work back to their cells, and spend an hour or so in the evening snipping thread ends. Making the "task" was crucial to the granting of privileges. A prisoner in class "C" was allowed to write one letter a week, and was paid fifty cents a month. After three months, if her work and behavior were satisfactory, she was placed in class "B," and could write two letters a week and receive seventy-five cents a month. After another three months she moved up to Class "A," which entitled her to write three letters a week and be paid a dollar a month. Any infraction, including a failure to make the task, meant demotion.

On Blackwell's Island Steimer had tried to buck the system, but in Jefferson City she did not. Perhaps, since she did not know exactly how many years of her fifteen-year sentence she would have to serve, she wanted to make things easier for herself, or perhaps she was simply worn down by the battle with Mrs. Lilly. Then, too, she wished to spare her mother unnecessary anxiety. After a week in Jefferson City she wrote to a friend, "I am now producing jackets for the capitalist state; and contrary to my expectations I made 50 of them on the 4th day. But the task required on the lot I am working is more than twice that amount. It is for the sake of my most wonderful Mother that I decided not to give the enemies a chance for further persecution, so far as work is concerned."[155] She reassured Fannie Steimer that she was being cooperative. "The prison officials assigned me to the factory where I am now working; and think of it, sweet mother, the matron who has charge of the shop told me that I am getting along fine and that my work is very nice! So there you are. This remark may serve as enough reason for you not to worry about me."[156]

Steimer may have been willing to make the task, but that does not mean she always did. By the summer of 1921 she had begun to experience difficulty seeing, and suffered from severe pains in her arm and shoulder. "Just now my eyes and my right arm give me a good deal of trouble, particularly my arm," she wrote to a friend in August. "I can not turn it without feeling a sharp pain in it. It often feels cold as if the blood does not circulate in it as it should."[157] At Harry Weinberger's request, Painter arranged for a medical examination and then reported that Steimer "was not seriously ill, only for a few days. She is alright now."[158] But years later Steimer, perhaps remembering times when she did not feel well, said, "In the penitentiary, the amount of work the prisoners were forced to render, was beyond my physical forces. I couldn't possibly produce the amount demanded of me and was punished by being locked up in the cell on bread and water."[159]

Cruelly confined, Mollie Steimer must surely have experienced moments of doubt, depression, and despair. Yet on August 22, 1920, on the eve of the second anniversary of her arrest, she could write to her family, "I feel so very happy these days that I must express my happy feelings toward you, my beloved ones. The reason for this outburst of joy you may well know. It is the world wide awakening of the working class! At no time during my life, so far as I can remember, have I ever felt such an intense joy, such a deep satisfaction, such inexpressible pleasantness as I feel now." Workers all over the world, she said, had refused to assist efforts to overthrow Soviet rule. "Two years ago, on the 22nd Day of August, this very day, a small group of us called upon the workers to strike against the United States and allied intervention in Russia, and we were imprisoned. Today millions of the workers will strike and the capitalist powers have to stand it. All they can do is say, 'Bah . . . it's unconstitutional.' At last our great hope, our beautiful idea of international workers solidarity for the common good of humanity, is coming true! We not only read about it, but see it, know it, and feel it. I just feel like embracing the whole world and crying out: 'Come—do not stop—keep marching on—and we shall be victorious.' "[160]

As the months passed, and the Bolsheviks stepped up their campaign against anarchists, Steimer expressed a more cautious view. By March 1921, reading that Russia had refused to admit six anarchists who had been deported from the United States, she told Abrams, Lipman, and Lachowsky (in the only letter she was allowed to write to them during her confinement), "Here is a revolutionary (a Workers government) comprised of individuals who were themselves once exiles and victims of autocracy—refusing entrance to rebellious workers who were born of the same soil, and whom the U.S. capitalist government has deported for the revolutionary activities; what justifiable reason can these 'idealists' give? Would these 6 anarchists stop the mental or economic progress of Russia? oh, no! But they may have said that they would resist a sort of discipline which spells sheer slavery."[161]

Yet despite her misgivings, she recognized that deportation to Russia remained the only alternative she had to imprisonment in America. In July 1921 she told Weinberger, "I will not avoid going to Russia because a severe persecution is carried on there against my comrades: the anarchists." Maintaining that all governments, capitalist or socialist, were oppressive, she said resignedly, "I know that I have a hard struggle ahead of me, that I will have to face privation in Russia and most likely, I will be persecuted for my belief in anarchism. But, I also know that in order to further the cause I love so dearly, the cause of real freedom and happiness for all,—I must be ready to suffer and sacrifice, and therefore I will not oppose my deportation to Russia."[162] As summer turned to fall and Steimer prepared to leave Jefferson City to rejoin her three comrades, she had only an inkling of the suffering that awaited them, and the many sacrifices they would have to make.

# 9

# Exile

## Wilson, the Political Prisoners, and Amnesty

If Woodrow Wilson had followed his first inclination, Abrams, Steimer, Lipman, and Lachowsky would not have gone to prison. Neither would Eugene Debs, Kate Richards O'Hare, or most of the other radicals who were jailed. The Supreme Court might never have ruled on the Espionage and Sedition Act convictions, because the cases would have become moot. Oliver Wendell Holmes would not have formulated the clear and present danger standard in *Schenck,* or reformulated it in *Abrams,* and Louis D. Brandeis would not have had to "think through the subject" of free speech. There would not have been an amnesty movement in behalf of political prisoners since there would not have been any political prisoners.

On November 19, 1918, a week after the signing of the armistice ending the World War, Wilson received a letter from Norman Hapgood, a well-known journalist, a former editor of *Collier's Weekly* and *Harper's Weekly,* and a loyal supporter. Hapgood had given a speech in Brooklyn to an audience which, he conceded, was "hot with enthusiasm for Lenin." Nevertheless, he said, "it occurred to me, as I listened to the indignation of these people over political imprisonment, that it might be more effective to pardon our political prisoners rather soon, voluntarily, than to wait until agitation makes the inevitable pardoning seem to be done under compulsion."[1] The President, intrigued, sent a note to his Attorney General, Thomas H. Gregory: "There is something in this suggestion of Norman Hapgood's. Do you think we could afford to act upon it?"[2] Gregory, considerably less intrigued, quickly snuffed out Wilson's interest. "We agreed that each application for pardon should be considered on its merits," he informed the President, adding, "Permit me again to suggest that these people are in no sense political prisoners, but are criminals who sided against their country; and, while the punishment meted out to some of them was more severe than it should have been, there are many others who are out on bond, have not been in prison for a single day, and who richly deserve substantial punishment."[3]

Replying to Hapgood, Wilson adopted Gregory's view as his own. "After minute inquiries," the President explained, "I must say that I do not think the men you refer to are in any proper sense political prisoners." Rather, they had "violated criminal statutes." Although each case would receive careful consideration, Wilson did not believe "that there is any justification for a general 'amnesty.' "[4] From then on, the administration always trotted out the same arguments: there were no political prisoners in America; individuals convicted under the Espionage and Sedition Acts were criminals; prison sentences, while sometimes unduly harsh, were for the most part well deserved; applications for pardon would be considered on a case-by-case basis; no general amnesty was justified.

In February 1919 Attorney General Gregory applied these principles to the Abrams case, which, to his annoyance, had been cited by the National Civil Liberties Bureau as a flagrant example of repression. Gregory denied that the case offered a good argument in behalf of amnesty. No one had been prosecuted for the "mere" expression of opinions, Gregory reasoned, but only for "the expression of opinions . . . under such circumstances as show a deliberate purpose of obstructing the conduct of the war." The facts in the Abrams case illustrated this crucial distinction, he added, because "one of the hand-bills distributed by these people urged munitions workers in this country to strike as a protest against the Russian intervention. This was at a critical period in the war when any reduction in the output of munitions of war might have had disastrous consequences."[5] As he prepared to leave office in March 1919—to be replaced by A. Mitchell Palmer—

Gregory reiterated that every conviction under the wartime statutes had required proof of "wilfulness and of an evil intent to hinder this country in the conduct of the war."[6]

During the spring and summer of 1919, while Wilson was attending the Paris Peace Conference, several well-known reformers, including Lincoln Steffens and Clarence Darrow, urged him to grant a general amnesty, and again the President was almost convinced. Steffens told Colonel Edward M. House, the President's advisor, that a policy of jailing radicals "is fighting Bolshevism in the Bolshevik spirit."[7] On June 28 House handed Wilson a memorandum supporting amnesty. On that same day Wilson wrote to Washington, telling his aide, Joseph P. Tumulty, to instruct the Attorney General and Postmaster General "that it is my desire to grant complete amnesty and pardon to all American citizens in prison or under arrest on account of anything they have said in speech or in print concerning their personal opinions with regard to the activities of the Government of the United States during the period of the war. It seems to me that this would be not only a generous act but a just act to accompany the signing of the peace." Then, however, Wilson added a crucial restriction: "I do not wish to include any who have been guilty of overt crimes, of course, but I think it would be a very serious mistake to detain anyone merely for the expression of opinion."[8]

Now it was Attorney General Palmer's turn to talk the President into taking a hard line. Like Gregory the previous November, Palmer insisted that "there are no persons in prison or under arrest on account of what they have said in speech or in print concerning their personal opinions with regard to the activities of the Government during the war." Only those who had been convicted "of some specific statutory crime which amounted to obstruction of the war" were in jail. Since amnesty was such an important issue, and "any general announcement would be widely misconstrued," Palmer urged Wilson to defer a decision until his return from Paris.[9] In July, with the President back in Washington, Palmer presented a more elaborate argument against amnesty, using the Debs case to illustrate his point. It was not yet time to commute the elderly socialist's ten-year sentence, Palmer said. Debs had been in prison "only a couple of months, is absolutely unrepentant, will not personally make any application for clemency, and a pardon now would be bitterly resented by a very large portion of the population who consider him a dangerous leader in the ultra-radical class war movement."

Palmer then argued that withholding amnesty would further Wilson's chief ambition: obtaining Senate approval of the Treaty of Versailles, with the provision for United States membership in the League of Nations. Opponents of the treaty, Palmer said, would seize on any suggestion of "too great leniency toward law violators" as an argument against ratification. Would it not be wiser, he asked, to wait until the Senate had ratified the treaty? Palmer promised to recommend the commutation of Debs's sentence, and those of other radicals, "at or about the time of the actual going into force of the treaty of peace."[10] On August 1, 1919, Wilson told Palmer that he agreed with him.[11] In the weeks that followed, Wilson expressed occasional concern over reports that Debs was being worn down by the harsh penitentiary regimen, only to be reassured by Palmer that he was "in splendid shape."[12] In September the President undertook an exhausting nationwide tour to rally public support for the League of Nations. Late that month he collapsed. He was rushed to Washington where, on October 2, he suffered a massive stroke, from which he never fully recovered. From then on, the fate of the political prisoners rested primarily with Attorney General Palmer.

So matters stood in November 1919, when the Supreme Court upheld the convictions in the Abrams case. Harry Weinberger immediately began working for his clients' release. He reminded officials in the Department of Justice that "these boys and this little girl" had been given fifteen- and twenty-year sentences even though they were "not pro-German but only pro-Russian." He admitted that their leaflets had been intemperate, but pointed out that other critics of intervention in Soviet Russia had used even stronger language.[13] To his friends, Weinberger predicted that "even clearer than the Debs case and the Kate Richards O'Hare case, the fight for amnesty can be swung around this case."[14] Since it involved alien anarchists, who were in any event subject to deportation after they had served their sentences, Weinberger based his appeal for their release on their willingness to leave for Russia immediately, a trade-off, he thought, that would be irresistible to those in authority.

One problem with this strategy was that Samuel Lipman—unlike Abrams, Steimer, and Lachowsky—was a socialist, not an anarchist, and therefore was not deportable under the Immigration Act of 1918. Although he was, of the four, the most anxious to get to Russia, some degree of subterfuge was needed to obtain the crucial deportation warrant. Those warrants were issued by the Bureau of Immigration, which was located in the Department of Labor. So the matter came before Louis F. Post, the Assistant Secretary of Labor. Ironically, he was the administration official most genuinely sympathetic to the plight of radical aliens. He devoted much of his time during the spring of 1920 to canceling deportation warrants for several thousand aliens who had been arrested in the Palmer raids, in cases where he determined that evidence had been illegally seized or that statutes had not clearly been violated. For his trouble, Post was denounced by Palmer for showing an "habitually tender solicitude for social revolution and perverted sympathy for the criminal anarchists of the country."[15] He was also brought before the House Rules Committee for impeachment proceedings, but exonerated.

In Lipman's case, however, Post was being asked to do the opposite of what radical aliens usually wanted. Not surprisingly, when Weinberger requested that he issue the warrant, along with those for the three anarchists, Post refused, on the grounds that Lipman could not legally be deported. "He positively denies that he is an anarchist and no affirmative evidence has been introduced by anyone showing that he is," Post wrote. His Department, he added, was obliged to act on the basis of evidence; "it is no part of its duty to deport anyone simply to evade operation of a criminal statute."[16] So in September 1920 Lipman had a special hearing before an immigration inspector, brought to Atlanta for the purpose, at which he claimed, falsely, that he was an anarchist. The charade acted out, Weinberger informed Post that the record showed that Lipman "comes under the deportation law" and a warrant was issued.[17]

A potentially more serious problem also confronted Weinberger: the reluctance of the radicals to petition for their release in the prescribed manner. The appeals system constrained them to compromise—to admit they had been wrong, to say they were sorry, to concede the government's right to judge them, and to promise to conduct themselves lawfully in the future. To Harry Weinberger, these were nominal compromises, well worth making, given the bleak alternative of spending fifteen or twenty years in prison. But to placate his clients, he agreed to file an application for "amnesty" not "pardon," and to include the sentence, "My sentiments are the same now as they were at the trial, and at the issuance of the leaflets."[18] This approach satisfied Abrams and Lipman, but not Hyman Lachowsky. He described himself as "always against begging," and said however the application was phrased, "it is a pardon just the same."[19] He signed the application reluctantly, so as not to jeopardize the release of his friends.

Mollie Steimer refused to cede even that much. The more she read the petition, she said, "the stronger I am opposed to it. The question to me is not so much how it is written but *what it is!* Since I am in the anarchist movement I constantly call upon the workers not to petition the government officials!—and if I were to do it now, it would be a deed contrary to my convictions." Nor did she wish to ask for her release "at a time when thousands of other political prisoners are languishing in the U.S. jails." Finally, she objected to giving her consent to deportation. While she did not mind going to Russia, "I am emphatically opposed to deportation. When the agents of brutality will send me out from the U.S., it will be by force and not because I will ever agree to be exiled."[20] Patiently, Weinberger explained that the application was "a demand for amnesty," not a request for pardon, that it did not retract her views about intervention, and that it could serve as "the opening wedge" to gain amnesty for other jailed radicals. By refusing to sign, he added, "you simply absolutely stop having anything done for the others who want it done. . . . It is not a weakening nor a crawling."[21] But Steimer never signed the application, even after Weinberger's formulation—"That Mollie Steimer, being willing to be deported to Soviet Russia, the United States could in no way be injured by an amnesty at this time"—was changed to conform more closely to her own view: "The United States could in no way be injured by an amnesty at this time for all political prisoners."[22]

Having persuaded three of the four prisoners to sign the necessary papers, Weinberger next turned to enlisting the support of people who, he hoped, had some influence with the administration. By the spring of 1920 he had made considerable headway, obtaining thousands of signatures for an amnesty petition. The signers—among them Floyd Dell, Oswald Garrison Villard, and Roger Baldwin—constituted a veritable Who's Who of the American left, but Weinberger was even more pleased to get the backing of George Creel, Ray Stannard Baker, Norman Hapgood, and Francis B. Sayre, all of whom had White House connections. When the petition from Cambridge, Massachusetts, signed by Zechariah Chafee and other Harvard Law School faculty members, was returned to Weinberger, the accompanying letter said, "The names I send you here are the finest in Boston."[23] By May Weinberger could inform Assistant Attorney General Robert P. Stewart that if there were time, and money, "we could get a million signatures or more."[24]

Weinberger, however, was unaware that Stewart was being subjected to pressure of a very different kind, from a source that proved considerably more influential. On April 18, 1920, J. Edgar Hoover, the Special Assistant to the Attorney General, came out flatly against releasing the four radicals. In Hoover's memorandum, fact and fancy were hopelessly entangled. Abrams, as a youth, had been associated with "the Russian terrorists," and in 1918 had been convicted of calling for a general strike of munitions workers, who "were openly advised to use violence in order that the American troops remaining in the United States at that time would be kept at home to oppose the violence." Lachowsky was "a self confessed anarchist" who distributed a circular "in which open advocation of violence appears." Lipman "was a leader of the anarchists in New York City and was an intimate friend of Emma Goldman." Steimer had corresponded with Goldman, Alexander Berkman, "and others equally notorious," and she had distributed a circular in which "certain individuals connected with the police force of New York City were named for assassination." The conclusion seemed inescapable: "I believe that the release of any of the persons . . . at the present time would be inimical to the best interests of the country, in that such action would but add impetus to the radical activities now being carried out in the United States."[25]

For a day or two, in the summer of 1920, Weinberger deluded himself into thinking he had extracted a promise from the Department of Justice to release the four prisoners. Early in August he spoke to Assistant Attorney General Stewart, and to the Pardon Attorney, James A. Finch. Weinberger then reported to an understandably impatient

Jacob Abrams that the two officials had been impressed by the number of signatures on the petition, that they were "favorably inclined" to let him leave the country, and "that an immediate recommendation will be made that you be amnestied." The arrangements, according to the lawyer, should take no more than ninety days. "This, of course, is really a guess on my part, but I think I am not far wrong. You should see yourself free and on your way out of the country before that time."[26] He then made the mistake of providing his version of events to *The New York Times,* which, on August 4, reported that Weinberger had been told that President Wilson would pardon the four on condition that they agree to deportation. The Department of Justice swiftly issued a denial, insisting that the case remained under review. On August 13 Weinberger lamely tried to reassure Abrams that the denial "really was not a denial," but merely an assertion that no final decision had been made. Weinberger wrote, "What they said was that they were going to recommend a pardon on the facts in the case as presented by me, but that they did not want you running around the country, posing as martyrs, but wanted to know about your deportation."[27] He still hoped to have Abrams and the others released within a few weeks.

But his hopes were without foundation. Department of Justice officials were, in fact, determined that Abrams and the others would not go free. This became evident when State Department officials, reading the original report in the *Times* and thinking that the four prisoners might be deported, asked the Attorney General whether it would be possible to work out an exchange for Americans who were being detained in Soviet Russia. J. Edgar Hoover informed the State Department that Stewart had not made any deal with Weinberger, but had only discussed "a possible recommendation to commute the various sentences to shorter terms."[28] Reporting on this exchange, another Department of Justice official wrote to Stewart, "As I recall, your opinion is that these people should not be permitted to accept deportation until they have served a substantial portion of their sentence."[29] On September 9 Attorney General Palmer explained that the application to commute the sentences would remain under consideration "for some time."[30]

Five days later Palmer and Stewart met with prominent labor leaders, among them Samuel Gompers of the American Federation of

Labor, all of whom favored a general amnesty. The Attorney General listened to what they had to say, but refused to budge from the position he had already staked out. He began by mentioning the "practical difficulties" connected with proclaiming a general amnesty, since "in nearly every one of these cases the person who is in prison now for violation of the Espionage Act was also convicted of some other offense"—such as conspiracy, or an overt act—"which might not come within the terms of the proclamation." This problem, Palmer said, justified the policy of considering each case individually, "upon its own facts." Of course, the "very severe sentences" handed down during the war would be reduced: twenty-year terms would be commuted to two to three years, and ten-year terms to one to two years. Pointing out that only 174 persons were in prison for having violated wartime statutes, Palmer noted that within three months 15 of them would be released, leaving fewer than 160 persons in jail. "That, I submit, in a population of 110,000,000 persons, does not indicate any severe oppression on the part of the Government," he concluded, but rather "a most careful discrimination between cases."[31]

During the fall of 1920 Harry Weinberger also attempted to gain an audience with Palmer in order "to answer, personally, any possible objection you may have to their immediate amnesty."[32] But Palmer turned him down, writing curtly, "A personal interview will not be helpful in the matter, since you state you desire it for the purpose of hearing my personal opinion. My recommendation will go to the President and cannot be disclosed to you."[33] In September and again in November Weinberger spoke to Assistant Attorney General Stewart, who reported that Palmer still had the case under consideration. Weinberger thought the administration would surely act, if not by Election Day, then by Thanksgiving, if not by Thanksgiving, then by Christmas. But by late January 1921, with Warren G. Harding's inauguration only six weeks away, nothing had been done. On January 21 Weinberger finally got to see Palmer, only to be told that the cases "have been written up by the Pardon Attorney and are now before me and will be given due consideration."[34]

Weinberger, as usual, wrote optimistic letters to the four imprisoned radicals, but Mollie Steimer, at least, had no illusions. On January 27 she wrote that she expected to remain in prison for some time. "I much rather prefer to face the bitter truth . . . than place hope in nothing! and from observing the deeds of Wilson and Palmer, I am convinced that they will leave their posts without granting amnesty to the Political Prisoners."[35] On February 8 an incredulous Weinberger learned that Steimer was right: the administration announced it had commuted the sentences to two and one half years, "on condition that they be deported to Russia and never return to the United States, or to require them to serve the sentences imposed."[36] Abrams, Lipman, and Lachowsky would have to remain in prison until June 1922, and Steimer until November 1922, since only the time she had served in Jefferson City, not the six months on Blackwell's Island, would be counted. Weinberger had gambled and lost. By agreeing to deportation, he had hoped to gain an immediate release; instead, deportation was made a condition merely for commuting the sentences.

For once, Weinberger wrote gloomy letters to Atlanta and Jefferson City. He had made a special trip to Washington, he reported, where he was told that Stewart "could do nothing" and that Palmer "would do nothing further in the matter."[37] Abrams replied that the sixteen months of imprisonment he now faced seemed "much longer than the twenty years." He had always assumed his original twenty-year sentence "would be on paper only," and so his time thus far in prison had "seemed short, but when it is a question of sixteen months, well that possibly I may have to serve."[38] Steimer's response struck a characteristic note. Her remaining twenty-one months, she declared, "do not bother me the least bit!" Dismayed that Weinberger had gone to Washington to request her release, she admonished him, "I do *not* want to ask for anything from Tumulty, Wilson, nor the new administration!" She was interested only in a general amnesty. "If not, I am determined to serve my term with a smile and am absolutely opposed to any individual appeals on my behalf!"[39]

Weinberger continued nonetheless to work for their release. He wrote to President Wilson, explaining that "the United States would in no way be injured if these Russians were freed and sent on their way home to their native country."[40] He wrote to Wilson's secretary, Joseph P. Tumulty, arguing that "their continued imprisonment makes justice a travesty."[41] He wrote to George Creel, the former head of the Committee on Public Information, who replied that he did not sympathize with their ideas but did not think they deserved the long sentences they had received.[42] He wrote to the President's friend, and later biographer, Ray Stannard Baker, only to be informed, "I have all along believed that these poor people should be set free and allowed to return to Russia. I have said so where I thought it would help. I think the only thing now to do is to take it up with the new administration."[43]

Weinberger also wrote to Norman Hapgood, urging him to apply "a little personal pressure" on Tumulty, without knowing, of course, that nearly two and a half years earlier Hapgood had gotten nowhere when he proposed that Wilson release all the political prisoners.[44] Hapgood, of all people, knew that amnesty was a lost cause. If his proposal had been rejected in November 1918—when the war had just been brought to a victorious conclusion, the President had been in full command, and the adoption of a benign policy had seemed a distinct possibility—what chance would an appeal in behalf of four Russian aliens have in February 1921? A sickly, embittered man, whose policies had recently been repudiated at the polls, was spending his final days in the White House, and he was being advised on the amnesty issue by an Attorney General who lacked any sympathy for imprisoned radicals. "I have no influence of the sort you speak of," Norman Hapgood told Weinberger on February 19, 1921, "and I doubt if anyone has."[45]

## Harding and Deportation

Two weeks later, Warren Gamaliel Harding moved into the White House. Prospects for amnesty under the new Republican administration, however, seemed no better than they had under Wilson. In July 1920, during the early stages of the presidential election campaign, Harding had said, "I believe in general amnesty for political prisoners, but the broad policy does not justify a hasty disposition of any case before it is considered on its merits."[46] By October, backing away even from this tepid endorsement, he commented that those who favored amnesty had succumbed to a "flabby sentimentality." Radicals who had broken the law, he added, were even worse than ordinary criminals. "The thief, or any ordinary criminal, is surely less a menace to those things which we all hold dear than the man or woman who conspires to destroy our American institutions."[47] After his election Harding told an amnesty delegation that, like Wilson, he would decide each case on its merits, "but that he would never as long as he was President pardon any criminal who was guilty of preaching the destruction of the Government by force."[48]

Harding's Attorney General was Harry M. Daugherty, whose attitude toward political prisoners made A. Mitchell Palmer's seem positively cordial. A lobbyist, a political fixer, and a patronage hound, Daugherty now presided over the Department of Justice—or, as one Democratic Senator labeled it, the "Department of Easy Virtue." Speaking before the American Bar Association in Cincinnati, Daugherty criticized those who clamored for the release of imprisoned radicals. "Those who do not believe in our Government and the enforcement of our laws should go to a country which gives them their peculiar liberty," he said.[49] Just as Palmer had urged Wilson to resist the pressure for amnesty, so Daugherty tried to stiffen Harding's backbone. For example, he warned the President that releasing Eugene Debs would reward "disloyalty, lawlessness, and defiance of the authority of the government."[50] But Harding went ahead anyway, commuting Debs's sentence so he would be home in time for Christmas 1921. Daugherty was more successful in his efforts to keep members of the Industrial Workers of the World behind bars. "Jurors have looked in their faces and heard their misguided defenses," the Attorney General said. "I am opposed to releasing any of them now. I would not desecrate Christmas time by giving them any relief."[51]

For three months Harry Weinberger failed to secure a sympathetic hearing for his clients. His requests for meetings during March, April, and May 1921 were snubbed, and his letters elicited frosty replies. But in June things finally began to turn in his favor. Since, under the terms of Wilson's commutation order, the four radicals were to be released in June (or, in Steimer's case, November) 1922, and then deported, Weinberger wanted merely to move forward the date of their release and deportation. To obtain this concession he promised that he would make arrangements to have the four admitted to Soviet Russia, and that he would obtain their consent to deportation. On June 27 Weinberger explained as much to Daugherty and to the Pardon Attorney, James A.

Finch. On June 29 Daugherty told Weinberger that on receipt of written statements that "it is their desire to be deported to Russia" and a proper showing that they would be "promptly deported to Russia if their sentences were commuted to expire at once, I might be disposed to recommend a commutation of their sentences in order that they might be deported."[52] To Weinberger, this represented the break for which he had waited so long.

His first promise—that he would obtain Soviet permission for the four radicals to enter Russia—was not an easy one to fulfill. By mid-1921 Soviet Russia had decided not to admit either immigrants or deportees from the United States (and the United States, in turn, had decided not to admit anyone from Russia). Charles Recht, the radical lawyer who had been involved in the *Masses* case in 1918, and who now represented Russia's legal interests in the United States, was quoted on July 7, 1921 as saying that "no exceptions are made" to Russia's policy of barring emigration from the United States.[53] The Bureau of Investigation, which kept careful track of these matters, and which maintained an ongoing interest in the fate of Abrams, Steimer, Lipman, and Lachowsky, reported that "the Soviet Government has consistently refused to receive any deportees from the United States, especially those who are known to be active anarchists and opposed to the present regime." Consequently, the Bureau concluded, there was "some doubt" that the sentences of the four would be commuted.[54]

But Weinberger prevailed on his friend Recht to forward a request to the Foreign Office in Moscow asking for a special exemption for his clients. The request, made on June 30, explained that the four radicals would be released "if Russia will cable me they will be admitted"; otherwise, they would have to serve nearly another year in jail.[55] As it turned out, Samuel Lipman's lover, Ethel Bernstein, was employed at the Foreign Office. Sending her a copy of the cable, Weinberger noted, "Now, it is up to you and the other friends to do your part."[56] Evidently they did. On July 22 Recht wrote to Weinberger, "I am directed by the Commissariat of Foreign Affairs of the Russian Socialist Federated Soviet Republic, through the representative in Esthonia, Litvinoff, to inform you that your clients, Mollie Steimer, Abrams, Lipman, and Lachowsky will be admitted into Russia if the American Government will release them from prison."[57]

Weinberger's second promise—to obtain the radicals' consent to deportation—was even more difficult to fulfill. Abrams and Lipman, of course, were only too happy to sign the statement the lawyer prepared for them. "I herewith consent to deportation to Russia and will take no legal steps to hinder or stop the same."[58] But Lachowsky balked at this further compromise of principle. Searching for a formula that would permit the anarchist to save face and yet get him out of the penitentiary, Weinberger proposed a modified draft. "I herewith state that I will not oppose deportation, though I will not consent to same." But Lachowsky replied that he would rather remain in the penitentiary than sign any such agreement. "I am opposed to be deported (though I will not try to fight deportation) not because I love so much the U.S. but I think that I have a right to live where I want."[59] Seizing on the parenthetical remark, Weinberger informed the Attorney General that while Lachowsky would not sign a statement on grounds of principle, "he will not fight deportation."[60]

As usual, it was Mollie Steimer who was the most inflexible of the four. Well aware by this time of her sensitivity on these matters, Weinberger broached the topic cautiously, merely asking how she felt about being deported to Russia. He told her that conditions there were such "that one should think twice before going there to live" and that "people of your belief are being jailed daily." He added, however, that "if you desire, you can sign the enclosed letters and return to me, or let me have your opinion on the subject."[61] On July 3 Steimer thanked Weinberger for taking an approach which, she said, shows "you are earnestly thinking of my well being." Still, she could not see her way clear to signing a statement. "I do not give my consent to deportation and therefore I will not choose any place to be deported to. The government of the United States will send me out of here by force, and it will naturally send me to the land where I was born, which act I will not oppose."[62] Three days later she made the same point. "I hold that the world belongs to each individual equally alike, and that though born on a different part of the earth,—I have just as much moral right to live in the United States as has any American native. However, I shall take no legal steps to stop my deportation, because I have had enough experience in the capitalist courts to convince me that justice can not be found there!"[63] As he had in Lachowsky's case, Weinberger reported to Daugherty that Steimer would not consent to her deportation, but would not seek to prevent it.

Having gotten all he was going to get from Steimer and Lachowsky, Weinberger kept up his entreaties to Washington during the summer and fall, telling Finch, the Pardon Attorney, that "each minute seems like a year" to prisoners who know they are to be set free but do not know exactly when.[64] Yet whenever it seemed that the final obstacle to their release had been overcome, another, Hydra-like, arose in its place. First, the State Department, as it had the previous summer, raised the possibility of exchanging the four radicals for American citizens who were being detained by the Soviet authorities. But, as J. Edgar Hoover reported, other arrangements were made to obtain the release of the "four Americans who are now in Russia."[65] Then Weinberger had to make sure that Mary Abrams could be deported with her husband and would be allowed to enter Russia. This, too, was arranged, much to the relief of Jacob Abrams, who told Weinberger, "You surely understand what it will mean for me and her if it shall happen that she shall have to go back."[66] Finally, the government decided, almost as an afterthought, that the deportees should pay the cost of their voyage, an added indignity which, at this late date, Weinberger was not disposed to contest, even though he had assumed all along that they would be deported at the government's expense.

It may well have been President Harding himself who decided, on impulse, to make the deportees pay their own way. By early October 1921 Harding had the Attorney General's recommendation for immediate commutation of the remainder of their sentences on his desk. Harding drafted a document granting Abrams, Steimer, Lipman, and Lachowsky a presidential "pardon" on condition that they be taken from the penitentiary to a ship on which they would "secure passage to Russia at their own expense." This document made its way to the Pardon Attorney, James A. Finch, who, on October 6, explained to Daugherty that he had serious reservations about it. Observing that Harding had agreed to a "*pardon,*" Finch said, "These prisoners are self-confessed anarchists of a most vicious and dangerous type, and yet the President pardons them, thus making them as guiltless before the law as though they had never offended, restoring every civil right and privilege and placing them on the same standing before the law as the very best citizens of our country, and this is done without a period of probation, but with the certainty that if they remain in or return to this country they will beyond doubt become a menace to our institutions."

Moreover, Finch thought, it was a bad idea to make them pay their own way, because if they were unable to, they could not be deported. The government, he noted, "can well afford to bear the expense of their transportation after being placed on the ship, in order to be rid of them, and that, in fact, it would be a wise thing to do from an economical standpoint rather than pay for their support in the penitentiary during the balance of their terms." Worse yet, if they boarded ship at their own expense, "some shrewd lawyer" might obtain a writ of habeas corpus that would allow them to remain in the United States pending a decision as to the legality of their deportation warrants. Finally, Finch believed, a provision must be included to prevent them from returning to Canada or Mexico, and then entering the United States where "their pardon would completely prevent their being apprehended and returned to the penitentiary."

Finch now faced a dilemma: while he was reluctant to prepare a warrant in accordance with Harding's directions, neither did he wish to disregard them. He recommended that Daugherty omit the provision requiring the deportees to pay their own passage. "My suggestion is that the sentences in these cases be commuted to expire at once upon condition, as to each, that the prisoner be immediately deported, and never to return to this country, and upon the further condition that if he does so return the pardon therefore becomes null and void and of no effect, and he is to be immediately apprehended and returned to the penitentiary and there to serve the unexpired portion of his sentence."[67] The Attorney General, in turn, transmitted Finch's memorandum to Harding, urging him to make the necessary changes since "you want to have the assurance that these violators are put on a ship for deportation."[68]

On October 10 Harding replied to Daugherty, acknowledging that Finch was right. The President admitted that the language he originally used "is the result of perhaps too hasty action. . . . Of course I want it impossible for them ever to return. It is a case of unhappy expression rather than mistaken intent." He explained that he would rewrite his endorsement to comply with Finch's suggestions. "I am delighted to get rid of these people. I never really intended to use the word 'pardon.' When I found these folks were anarchists I was so glad to get rid of them that I scratched out the endorsement in undue haste." Nevertheless, Harding still thought that it would be preferable for them to pay their own expenses; if this was not "practical," however, then the government should foot the bill.[69]

Writing to Weinberger on October 12, Daugherty omitted any mention of the possibility that the government would pay the expenses. Instead he dangled the prospect of freedom, provided that the lawyer accept this last condition. The cases were before the President, Daugherty declared, "and he has expressed a willingness to commute their sentences upon condition that they be at once deported to Russia, never to return to this country, and provided also they bear the expense of their transportation to that country. If you can arrange this latter detail, action will be promptly taken."[70] Tempted by this offer, Weinberger readily agreed to pay the transportation costs. On October 17 Daugherty told Harding that Weinberger "states under date of October 14, 1921, that transportation for the applicants will be provided." To prevent any last-minute legal shenanigans, the deportation warrants would not be delivered to the four radicals "until they are safely on board ship for deportation and after they have secured transportation at their own expense for their return to Russia."[71] On the basis of this understanding, the sentences were finally commuted on October 18.

Within ten days Abrams, Lipman, and Lachowsky had been taken from Atlanta to Ellis Island, there to await a ship bound for Soviet Russia. Abrams and Lipman were so eager to leave that "we do not give a *damn* for the 'favorable' conditions here. And choose the bad conditions of Russia. We are children of the slums, and to be hungry is our specialty."[72] On October 28 Lipman told Weinberger that he wanted to sail on the very first ship. "Is that clear? I can't make it any clearer. I got enough of your damn country believe me."[73] On November 3 Mollie Steimer arrived from Jefferson City, by way of Chicago. She had threatened not to leave the penitentiary if railroad workers went on strike, as it seemed they might, and she would have had to ride on a train operated by scabs. The strike, however, was called off. She also denounced the latest requirement: that the deportees pay their own expenses. The provision, she said, "is so resentful to me that I would much rather remain in the penitentiary for the next year than make any reply to the servants of the Iron Heel."[74] Weinberger had acquiesced without consulting her, she declared, and the lawyer indeed assumed responsibility for the decision.

He also assumed responsibility for making the four radicals' last days in the United States as comfortable as possible, under the circumstances. He interceded with the Ellis Island authorities to obtain reasonable visiting privileges for relatives, although "mere friends or acquaintances" were barred.[75] Weinberger tried, without success, to persuade officials to allow Lachowsky to leave the island (under guard) to visit his mother, who was too ill to visit him, and to allow Abrams to visit his sister, Manya, who was bed-ridden, even though, as Abrams said, "under conditions my sister is I doubt if I will ever see her again."[76] Weinberger booked passage on the S. S. *Esthonia,* which was scheduled to depart for Libau, Latvia. Third-class accommodations cost $150 a passenger, but he collected $185 for each of the deportees so they could travel second-class, explaining to those from whom he solicited funds that while the "little group of valiant fighters" were willing to travel third-class, they had been through so much in prison and faced such a bleak November voyage that they deserved something better.[77] Weinberger also helped arrange a farewell dinner at Allaire's Restaurant on November 21, two days before the departure date.

On November 1, about the time the four deportees were arriving at Ellis Island, Lincoln Steffens wrote a letter to Warren Harding's Postmaster General, Will H. Hays. Three years before, Steffens had urged Woodrow Wilson to offer a generous amnesty to political prisoners, and now he again pleaded for "not only a cautious picked gingerly amnesty, but the broadest, most generous declaration of pardon that has ever been declared in any country at any time."[78] The administration's action in the Abrams case was hardly what Steffens had in mind. The four radicals had not been pardoned. Wilson had already commuted their sentences on condition that they agree to accept deportation and never return to the United States, on pain of serving the remainder of their fifteen- and twenty-year terms; now Harding shortened their sentences by a matter of months on the further condition that they obtain permission to enter Soviet Russia and agree to pay their own passage.

Harry Weinberger was later criticized for accepting these terms, but he had little choice. As alien anarchists, Abrams, Steimer, and Lachowsky were deportable under the Immigration Act of 1918. The question was not whether they would be deported, but when. As a socialist, Lipman could have put up a legal battle against deportation, but he wanted to go to Russia to be reunited with Ethel Bernstein. Weinberger could have refused to meet the expense of deportation, but how was he to know that the administration was bluffing on this point? After two years of having his hopes raised and disappointed countless times, Weinberger can be excused if he thought he had done his best for his clients.

Certainly they thought he had. On the morning of November 23, before leaving Ellis Island, Lipman wrote to Weinberger, praising his "ability as a lawyer and sincerity as a man of ideals." Thanking Weinberger for his "laborious and continuous work in our behalf since the day of our arrest, i.e. Aug. 23, 1918," Lipman expressed the hope that Weinberger would continue his good work, for "in the struggle you will find joy. I wish for the day when you will be proud of your native country—but until then—do not give up!"[79] Jacob Abrams, too, wrote to Weinberger that morning. "I know you to be a man first and the lawyer after. I also believe that you are a liberty loving man for you could not carry on your legal work in defending those that fight for it if it would be a matter of dollars and cents only." Abrams concluded with the "hope that in the near future we will not need lawyers to defend the human rights."[80]

## November 23, 1921

It was noon, on the Wednesday before Thanksgiving, when the ferry from Ellis Island docked at a "bleak, freight-scattered pier" in South Brooklyn. Mollie Steimer, Jacob Abrams, Hyman Lachowsky, and Samuel Lipman, accompanied by five guards, were on board. Harry Weinberger was there to greet the deportees and lead them aboard the S. S. *Esthonia,* a ship of the Baltic-American line, bound for the Latvian city of Libau, a port on the Baltic Sea. As the party walked up the gangplank, the sixty friends and relatives who had already boarded the ship to say farewell burst into applause, but "the cheers which had been planned for them died away, as the crowd realized that it was probably seeing them for the last time." Mary Abrams, who would be accompanying her husband, was of course on hand. So were Steimer's mother and sisters; Lipman's aunt, Ida Fishman; and Lachowsky's mother, who, unable to walk, was carried on a portable bed.[81]

Lunch was served to the deportees, their guards, and their guests, among whom were such prominent anarchists as M. Eleanor Fitzgerald, Harry Kelly, and Stella Ballantine, Emma Goldman's niece. According to one newspaper report, "The only decoration on the table was a small silk American flag which occupied a vase in the center of the table."[82] The decorous departure of the *Esthonia* contrasted sharply with the frenzied arrangements surrounding the sailing of the *Buford,* at the height of the Red scare in December 1919, Weinberger told Robert E. Todd, who had recently taken over as Commissioner of Immigration. He was especially grateful, Weinberger said, for "the dinner arrangement on board the boat, which allowed these young people to see their friends in such a way that the business of the deportation was a little taken off until it almost seemed like a mere leaving for Europe."[83]

But in a public statement Weinberger expressed his indignation at what had happened to "this little girl" and "these young boys." They had been convicted for having "raised their voice of protest by leaflets against the illegal and unconstitutional use of the United States troops in Russia without a declaration of war," and then they had been imprisoned even though Justices Holmes and Brandeis "said they had as much right to do what they did as the United States had to issue its own Constitution." The United States should be ashamed of "its deportees, its political prisoners, the troops in labor struggles, always against the workers, its regimented minds, its Mooney cases, its Sacco-Vanzetti case, and now four Russian deportees."[84] Writing to Emma Goldman and Alexander Berkman, Weinberger said bitterly, "Black reaction is in the saddle, fear is in the hearts and minds of men, conscience is dead."[85]

In the tradition of radicals being sent to Soviet Russia, the deportees prepared statements claiming that they were not sorry to be leaving the United States, calling on workers to continue their struggle "until the reaction of America is wiped off the continent," and promising to return "when you have become a free nation." Mollie Steimer said, "Goodbye, all of you. I hope that America will be freer in the future than it is today. I wish to say that I hope I shall live to see the toiling masses realize the overthrow of the present capitalistic system. I believe they can establish it best by direct action instead of by the ballot."[86] Adding that "the present system brings to the workers: wars, starvation and unspeakable misery," she thought that it could not be long before workers around the world "will establish a new form of society that will be based on the principles of Anarchist Communism."[87] Standing on the deck, waving to her comrades as the ship moved off, Steimer "cried out 'Hurrah for the Anarchistic Russia' and the crowd on the pier called out, 'Hurrah for the Soviet Government.' "[88]

This exchange was reported by a Bureau of Investigation agent, one of three who had boarded the *Esthonia* and had "ascertained the presence of the four deportees." The agent's report included the observation that the deportees' sympathizers were "mostly women and there were hardly any English spoken among them."[89] The agents undoubtedly paid close attention as immigration authorities asked the deportees if they understood that, under the terms of the commutation, they would be arrested and made to serve the remainder of their original sentences if they ever tried to return to the United States. Not until nearly two weeks later did federal agents finally breathe a collective sigh of relief. Sending a newspaper account, presumably of the ship's journey, to J. Edgar Hoover, an agent remarked, "This report certainly contains 'sweet music' in that we will not have to be concerned over the activities of these individuals for some time."[90]

At three o'clock, as the *Esthonia* pulled away from the pier, the passengers could see—as a publicity brochure for the Baltic-American Line put it—"picturesque hilly Staten Island, crowded inshore with beautiful residences amongst shady trees and beautiful shrubbery, its shores lined with large docks crowded with steamers of all sizes." The ship, the brochure went on reassuringly, was entirely safe, for lifeboats were "all in A-1 trim and ready for immediate launching." Besides, there was a "Submarine Bell, which gives warning when the ship gets into shoal water or near any submerged object." The ship used a wireless to stay in touch with the shore and with passing steamers. Its hospital was staffed by "professional looking surgeons and trim looking nurses." Second-class passengers slept in comfortable cabins equipped with two double-decker beds. During the days and evenings they enjoyed a Promenade Deck, a Smoking Room, and a Ladies' Parlor, all of which rivaled first-class accommodations "in luxury and comfort."[91]

All in all, the eleven-day voyage to Libau was a pleasant one, more pleasant, undoubtedly, than the voyages to America that Jacob Abrams and Hyman Lachowsky had made in 1908, that Mary Abrams had made in 1911, or that Samuel Lipman and Mollie Steimer had made in 1913. "While on the Atlantic we enjoyed wonderfully well," Steimer wrote to Weinberger. "The weather was beautiful most of the time. None of us suffered from sea sickness. We were out on the deck getting in the pure air of which we prisoners were badly in need. While in the cabin we read together . . . thus you can see that all was well so far as the boat was concerned."[92] They reached Libau on December 4, and Riga, near the Russian border, on December 10, where they sent a cable: "Weinberger. Reached Riga. Greetings. Deportee."[93]

There they remained for a few days, held by the Latvian authorities while arrangements were made for their entry into Russia. Under the headline, "Reds Without a Country," *The New York Times* reported that the deportees "are in a concentration camp at Riga awaiting permission of the Soviet Government to enter Russia."[94] Mollie Steimer recalled that "during this period we had neither sleep nor food." At last, on December 15, they arrived in Moscow, "extremely tired and cold."[95] They were taken to the Foreign Office, where, Lipman reported, they received a warm welcome. They were given rooms in a hotel for new immigrants, and told they would receive a bread and soup ration until they found work.

By coincidence, the deportees had been in Riga at the same time as Emma Goldman and Alexander Berkman, who were, however, traveling in the opposite direction. Goldman and Berkman had left Russia after two years, bitterly disillusioned with Bolshevik rule. They were hoping to get to Sweden, and, from there, to whatever country might take them in. They had arrived in Riga from Moscow on December 5, with their friend, Alexander Shapiro. Berkman wrote in his diary that night, "Big and clean city . . . Bourgeois feeling atmosphere. Well fed horses. Pleasant jingling bells. People well dressed, well fed middle class."[96] The three anarchists remained in a residence occupied by the Soviet consulate. On December 22 they started on their journey to Reval, where they could find a ship to Sweden, but were immediately arrested by the Latvian police. They were held until December 30 while their papers and belongings were examined. On January 2, 1922, they reached Reval, where they boarded a steamer for Stockholm.

Neither of the two groups of radicals, one heading east, the other west, was aware of the other's presence in Riga. Yet even if, by chance, they had met and talked, it would not have made a difference. Berkman and Goldman would have warned the deportees that in Russia they would find the "collapse of everything the Revolution was fought for."[97] Steimer and Lachowsky might have agreed, but would probably have replied that they wanted to see for themselves, that they might be of help to the beleaguered Russian anarchists, and that, besides, they had nowhere else to go. Abrams would have conceded that much was wrong in Soviet Russia, but that mistakes were to be expected under the difficult circumstances confronting the Soviet leadership. Lipman, thinking chiefly of his imminent reunion with Ethel Bernstein, would not have listened. As Harry Weinberger later told Goldman, "They would probably have gone on their way for we learn not from the experience of others, but each one of the human race learns by their own travail and even sometimes the burnt child does not fear fire."[98]

## Lenin, the Cheka, and the Anarchists

"So long as the state exists there is no freedom. When there is freedom, there will be no state."[99] The words are not Peter Kropotkin's or Emma Goldman's, though they conceivably could have been. The words are rather from Vladimir Ilyich Lenin's *The State and Revolution,* which appeared shortly before the October 1917 revolution. As the statement suggests, anarchists and Bolsheviks disagreed chiefly about means, not ends. Anarchists wanted to destroy the state immediately; Communists wanted to use it to secure the gains of the revolution, and then allow it gradually to wither away. As Lenin said, "We do not at all differ with the anarchists on the question of the abolition of the state as the *aim.* We maintain that, to achieve this aim, we must temporarily make use of the instruments, resources and methods of state power *against* the exploiters, just as the temporary dictatorship of the oppressed class is necessary for the abolition of classes."[100] Consequently, the anarchists, a small but influential faction, backed the Bolshevik-led overthrow of the Kerensky government.

This shaky coalition, however, soon came apart. Each step Lenin took to consolidate power in November and December 1917—such as creating a Soviet of People's Commissars made up exclusively of Bolsheviks, affirming the right of each nationality to set up an independent state, and nationalizing banks and the land—offended his erstwhile allies. Worse yet, from the anarchists' perspective, the Bolsheviks used their control of the First All-Russian Congress of Trade Unions, meeting in Petrograd in January 1918, to bring the shop committees—autonomous bodies through which workers had gained a voice in running the factories—under centralized authority. Then, in February 1918, Lenin presented the Treaty of Brest-Litovsk for approval, leading one prominent anarchist to declare, "It is better to die for the worldwide social revolution than to live as a result of an agreement with German imperialism."[101] As historian Paul Avrich has written, "By the spring of 1918, the majority of anarchists had become sufficiently disillusioned with Lenin to seek a complete break, while the Bolsheviks, for their part, had begun to contemplate the suppression of their former allies, who had outlived their usefulness and whose incessant criticisms were a nuisance the new regime no longer had to tolerate."[102]

The agency that would carry out the suppression was the Cheka, although this was far from its original purpose. In December 1917, fearing a general strike by government employees, Lenin established a commission to examine ways "of combating such a strike by the most energetic revolutionary measures."[103] Its official title was the "All-Russian Extraordinary Commission (for Combating Counter-Revolution, Speculation, Sabotage, and Misconduct in Office)," but it was known generally as the Cheka, the "Extraordinary Commission." Over the next four years the Cheka was transformed into a secret police force. Operating throughout Soviet Russia, it employed a quarter of a million men, many of whom were undercover agents. Proudly surveying the results, an official declared that "there is no sphere of our life where the Cheka does not have its eagle eye."[104]

The Cheka had the authority to arrest suspects without necessarily charging them with a crime, and to detain them indefinitely. There were no effective limitations on what it could, and did, do. The Cheka tortured prisoners to make them confess to crimes, or, sometimes, merely to make them suffer. Victims were branded, stoned, and mutilated. There were instances in which "water was poured on naked prisoners in the winter-bound streets until they became living statues of ice . . . the living would be buried for half an hour in a coffin containing a decomposing body . . . a rat [was placed] into an iron tube sealed with wire netting at one end, the other end being placed against the victim's body, and the tube heated until the maddened rat, in an effort to escape, gnawed its way into the prisoner's guts."[105] The Cheka was both judge and jury, empowered to try prisoners secretly, without their knowledge, without counsel, and without witnesses. Dispensing arbitrary "justice," the Cheka, in some instances, also acted as executioner.

To head this operation, Lenin chose a veteran revolutionary, Felix Dzerzhinsky. Forty years old, he had spent eleven years in Czarist prisons or exile in Siberia, time enough to develop an implacable hatred of those whom he considered enemies of the Revolution. "My purpose compels me to be merciless and I am firmly resolved to pursue it to the end," he wrote in May 1918, and a few months later added, "We are soldiers at our fighting posts. . . . My will is for victory and despite everything, despite the fact that a smile rarely breaks on my face, I am sure of the victory of the mission and the movement for which and in which I live and work."[106] The mission of the Cheka often kept Dzerzhinsky at his desk twelve to eighteen hours a day, seven days a week. Zealously devoted to the Bolshevik cause, he lived a simple Spartan existence while overseeing the activities of his vast enterprise.

Soviet authorities claimed that there was a huge difference between "ideological" and "criminal" anarchists. The former were regarded as respectable, if misguided, revolutionaries, the latter as riffraff, whose erratic behavior jeopardized the stability of the Bolshevik government. From the Cheka's standpoint, the Moscow anarchists who organized the "Black Guards" early in 1918 fit squarely in the second category. Indeed, although most members were anarchists, others appear simply to have been adventurers. Arming themselves with rifles and grenades, the Black Guards requisitioned fashionable bourgeois residences and other property for themselves. When an anarchist band seized an automobile (which belonged, ironically, to Raymond Robins, who would later testify at the Abrams trial), the Cheka had the pretext it needed. On the night of April 11–12, 1918, it struck in force, raiding twenty-six anarchist centers in Moscow. Most of the anarchists surrendered without a fight, but at the "House of Anarchy," the headquarters of the Moscow Federation of Anarchist Groups, guns began blazing away. Twelve Cheka agents were killed, and about forty anarchists were killed or wounded. Shortly thereafter anti-anarchist raids were carried out in Petrograd and other cities. Anarchists were taken to prison, and some of their publications were temporarily shut down.

As militant Russian anarchists became increasingly disillusioned with Lenin's government, they resorted increasingly to violence. On September 25, 1919, a self-styled group of "Underground Anarchists," together with other disaffected revolutionaries, set off a bomb at the headquarters of the Moscow Committee of the Communist Party while a meeting was in progress. Twelve people were killed, fifty-five wounded. The perpetrators, whose act was repudiated by other anarchists, then announced that they had inaugurated an "era of dynamite." The Cheka responded swiftly, capturing and executing two of those responsible. Then it proceeded to round up hundreds of anarchists, many of whom it summarily tried and convicted. "We do not persecute Anarchists of ideas," Lenin insisted (to a visiting Alexander Berkman) by way of explanation, "but we will not tolerate armed resistance or agitation of that character."[107]

Those whom Lenin approvingly termed anarchists of ideas were, for the most part, anarchists who put aside their misgivings to support the Soviet government. Many anarchists simply could not bring themselves to oppose a "workers" regime—whatever the warning signs of centralization—which was fighting desperately for survival against the combined forces of counter-revolutionary Whites and Allied armies of intervention. In 1918, 1919, and 1920 it was still possible for anarchists to disapprove of particular Bolshevik policies while defending the revolutionary experiment itself. Many anarchists fought in the Red Army, and some held government positions, even in the Cheka. Aleksandr Ghe, for example, who had sharply criticized some of Lenin's policies, served as chairman of the Cheka in the northern Caucasus until January 1919, when he was killed by White forces in the battle for the city of Kislovodsk. As late as the summer of 1919, therefore, Lenin could declare that many anarchists were "becoming the most dedicated supporters of Soviet power."[108]

In late 1920, however, the fragile truce between Lenin and the pro-Soviet anarchists was broken. As the Red Army beat back the White forces, the Bolsheviks were free to move against the anarchists, whose support was now less vital. For their part, anarchists were no longer willing, for the sake of revolutionary solidarity, to keep their grievances to themselves. In November 1920 the Red Army attacked the forces of Nestor Ivanovich Makhno, the anarchist leader in the Ukraine, whose guerrillas had played an important part in defeating the White Army led by General Denikin. Moreover, the Cheka began rounding up anarchists who had not heretofore been harassed. By February 1921, when Peter Kropotkin died, many of the leading anarchists were already incarcerated in Moscow's Taganka and Butyrki prisons. Those who were still at liberty would allow Kropotkin's funeral arrangements to proceed only after the Cheka agreed to release seven of their comrades to serve as pallbearers. One of the seven, Aron Baron, delivered a eulogy, after which he and the others were returned to jail.

The bloody suppression of the Kronstadt rebellion in March 1921 snapped the remaining ideological strands connecting anarchists and Bolsheviks. The rebellion originated in February, when workers in Petrograd, suffering from a shortage of food and fuel, went on strike. Demanding much more than the provision of adequate supplies, they called for a revival of the autonomous factory committees, for freedom of speech, for an end to the Cheka's excesses, and for the release of anarchists and other political prisoners. "The workers and peasants need freedom," read one proclamation. "They don't want to live by the decrees of the Bolsheviki: they want to control their own destinies."[109] In March sailors and workmen from the nearby Kronstadt naval base, on Kotlin Island, joined the strikers. Faced with this internal threat, Lenin dispatched 50,000 soldiers to crush the mutiny. In the ensuing battle, which began on March 7 and lasted for ten days, 600 insurgents were killed, 1,000 were wounded, and 2,500 were taken prisoner. Thousands more fled across the ice to Finland. Following the Kronstadt revolt, the Cheka launched an anti-anarchist campaign that made its earlier efforts seem mild by comparison. "The time has come," Lenin said, "to put an end to opposition, to put the lid on it; we have had enough opposition."[110]

Like lightning bolts illuminating the night, these events enabled Emma Goldman and Alexander Berkman to see the repressive nature of the Soviet regime. As late as March 3, 1921, Berkman was still writing, from Petrograd, that "the New World is being built in the unique land of but recent Tsarism."[111] Two days later he and Goldman pleaded with the Soviet authorities to create a commission to settle the Kronstadt dispute peacefully. On March 7, to the two anarchists' horror, the battle began. Berkman wrote in his diary, "Days of anguish and cannonading. My heart is numb with despair; something has died within me. The people on the streets look bowed with grief, bewildered."[112] By the spring, even as they urged Lenin to call off the "systematic man-hunt of anarchists," Goldman and Berkman had resolved to leave Russia at the first opportunity.[113] "I am trying desperately to get out now that I have come to the conclusion that the situation here is utterly hopeless as far as anarchist activities are concerned," Goldman wrote that summer.[114] She said wistfully, "How we used to dream of the wonderful thing come true in Russia. But like all dreams there is an awakening which is hard to bear even for the strongest of us. . . ."[115]

At some point late in the summer of 1921, the Soviet authorities decided to permit political dissidents to leave the country, and even to provide them with passports and the necessary funds. The Bolsheviks may have acted to offset the discomfiture resulting from two well-publicized incidents. The first occurred in July. Thirteen anarchists in Taganka prison went on a hunger strike, which lasted for eleven days, timed to coincide with the gathering in Moscow of representatives to the first congress of the Red International of Trade Unions (Profintern). Responding to criticism from a number of the delegates, Trotsky declared that "considerations of revolutionary expediency" would make it possible to release anarchists on condition that they emigrate.[116] The second incident occurred in September, when the Cheka murdered two prominent anarchists, Lev Chernyi and Fanya Baron, who were being held on a counterfeiting charge. Subjected to a mounting barrage of criticism, Lenin ordered the immediate release of many anarchists, provided only that they agree to leave Russia. So the departure of

Goldman and Berkman in December 1921 was part of a larger exodus of anarchists, few of whom ever returned. As Goldman said, the choice before them was exceedingly stark: "either remain in prison or get out."[117]

That choice was not unlike the one that the American government had offered Abrams, Steimer, Lipman, and Lachowsky. Of course, radicals in the United States enjoyed legal rights that were conspicuously absent in Soviet Russia, where there were no public trials with an opportunity to face one's accusers, no defense attorneys such as Harry Weinberger, no appeals from rulings of the Cheka, and certainly no eloquent dissents by jurists such as Oliver Wendell Holmes. But having provided important procedural safeguards, the United States then treated dissidents as though they were criminals, to the point of denying, as Attorney Generals Palmer and Daugherty did, that there even were any "political" prisoners. In Russia, on the other hand, dissidents were left to the mercies of the secret police. Once in prison, however, their special status was recognized. Anarchists, Mensheviks, and Left Socialist Revolutionaries were usually not lumped together with common criminals. They were placed in separate cells, given special privileges, and permitted to elect delegates to present their grievances to prison officials. They were considered "people temporarily isolated from society in the interests of the Revolution and their conditions of detention should not bear a punitive character."[118]

Both Russia and the United States decided that anarchists could no longer be tolerated. The solution, in both countries, was to induce them, under threat of prolonged imprisonment, to go elsewhere. One difference, however, was that Russia subsidized the expense of deportation; the United States made its deportees pay their own way. While Russian officials stated openly that deportation was a policy justified by considerations of revolutionary expediency, it is unlikely that American officials, even privately, thought that deportation was a policy justified by considerations of capitalist expediency. Thoughts and actions which were branded "counter-revolutionary" in one country were branded "revolutionary" in the other. Ironically, while the United States shipped most of its anarchists to Russia, at least one exiled Russian anarchist, Mark Mratchny, found haven in the United States.

Toward the end of March 1921, not long after the suppression of the

Kronstadt uprising, Emma Goldman wrote to a friend in New York City. News had reached her in Petrograd that Harry Weinberger had gotten the Wilson administration to commute his clients' sentences to two and one half years. "We have heard that Mollie and the boys had their sentences reduced and we are glad of it. I am especially glad that H. W. did not succeed as completely as he had hoped—to have them released at once. . . . Please beg him from me to lay off a bit. Abrams and friends are all right where they are, believe me. Certainly better than their alternative, get me?"[119] Her advice was not heeded, and perhaps could not have been. Now, in December 1921, Goldman and Berkman arrived in Riga, as did Abrams, Steimer, Lipman, and Lachowsky. Goldman wrote to Weinberger, "We missed your young clients who I fear will not be very grateful for having been taken out of Atlanta and Missouri and sent to the Russian Penitentiary." Then she added ruefully, "But I suppose they wanted the change themselves."[120]

## Into Russia . . . and Out

Their initial impressions of Russia were mixed, their initial reactions guarded. "I suppose that you would like to know how I feel being in Russia?" Steimer wrote to Weinberger on December 20, 1921, five days after her arrival in Moscow. "To be frank, I must tell you, that a feeling of sadness had enveloped me. . . . At present I am listening to the experiences and views of those who lived here during the Revolution. My intention is to work, to study,—and to observe for myself."[121] Lipman recounted, "I walk around the streets of Moscow in search of evidence of the revolution," but in general "one could hardly find concrete evidence of 1917. . . . Dissatisfaction seems to be general, as there is not enough food. . . . On the whole it is a hard task to run a country by a new experiment—it's much easier to criticize."[122] Of the four deportees, however, Lipman alone remained in Moscow. The others went their separate ways, Lachowsky and Abrams by choice, Steimer by necessity.

Hyman Lachowsky was the first to leave. In his last prison letters, written in September and October, Lachowsky had confessed to a loss of faith in anarchism. "I think I am the most wretched person in the world for idealistic I am not," he wrote to a comrade; "a life which you dream of will never be. I can not see it any more." He had once shared such a belief, he added, "but it was thousands of years ago," and he signed his letters, "your pessimist."[123] So it was not surprising that he sought peace and quiet in Russia. As Steimer explained, Lachowsky "was unhappy in Moscow. Being a good printer, he decided to go back to his home town, Minsk, where he hoped to find work and peace of mind."[124] In 1927 Samuel Lipman paid him a brief visit. Lachowsky had gotten married, Lipman reported. "One could call him, in the full sense of the word, apolitical with some petty bourgeois ways. He is working and raising a son, by the way a very nice boy."[125] After that, Lachowsky fell completely out of touch with his old friends.

Mollie Steimer spent nearly two years in Russia. Shortly after her arrival, she met a young anarchist whose name was Simon Fleshin and they fell in love. Three years older than Steimer, Fleshin had emigrated from Russia to the United States in 1910, and had become involved in the anarchist movement in New York City, working in the office of Emma Goldman's *Mother Earth.* In 1917, in the full flush of revolutionary ardor, Fleshin had returned to Russia, where he plunged into anarchist activities in Petrograd and Kharkov. By the time he met Steimer, he had been arrested by the Cheka on three separate occasions, most recently in June 1920, when he had been seized in a raid on an anarchist bookstore in Kharkov, and was released only after going on a hunger strike which lasted for a week. In 1922 Fleshin and Steimer helped to organize a campaign to aid their imprisoned comrades. Fleshin spent the month of August in northern Russia, visiting anarchists who had been sent into exile or who were being held in concentration camps.

Among other things, Fleshin and Steimer tried to get warm clothing, food, and books to these unfortunate people, and so they had to negotiate with the officials who were in charge of the camps. The officials, however, no longer worked for the Cheka. In February 1922 that agency had been superseded by the State Political Administration, known as the GPU. Where the Cheka had been autonomous, the GPU was a branch of the Commissariat of Internal Affairs. Where the Cheka could impose extra-judicial sentences, the GPU, according to Lenin, was supposed to observe "greater revolutionary legality." But the GPU was soon equipped with a crucial weapon which it could, in fact, wield at its own discretion: administrative exile. In August 1922 it was authorized to order the exile of anyone who was engaged in "counter-revolutionary activity." The offender could be exiled for up to three years, and could either be sent to a remote place inside Russia or else deported. Soon this authority extended to "persons whose presence in a certain place appears, from their activity, their past, or their connection with criminal circles, dangerous from the point of view of safeguarding the revolutionary order." Felix Dzerzhinsky directed the GPU, as he had the Cheka.[126]

In the fall of 1922 Steimer and Fleshin were staying in a Petrograd apartment. On the night of November 1 they were arrested by the GPU and taken to headquarters. After being held for two days, Steimer was finally questioned about her work in behalf of "an underground organization" which was aiding imprisoned anarchists and which had "connections with Europe and America." She protested that it was not an "underground" organization, but one that went about its work openly. Asked why she had been corresponding with Goldman and Berkman, she started to argue with her inquisitor about the meaning of the expression "counter-revolutionists." She explained, "But the man is so narrow-minded and one-sided, that I saw no sense in discussing with him and left the room." Fleshin also refused to answer any questions about their organization. They were taken from the GPU's Inner Prison to the House of Preliminary Detention, where they remained for more than two weeks. Some of the other twenty-seven people who had been arrested at the same time were then released, but Steimer and Fleshin were not. On November 17 they were sentenced to two years' exile to Obdorsk, Siberia. In protest, they declared a hunger strike. The following day they were released on condition that they remain in Petrograd and agree to appear before the GPU.

When they did, they were asked "to sign an understanding that they would not participate in any Anarchist work." They refused, and were told that they would have only themselves to blame "if, after a while, we shall again arrest you and exile you to Siberia."[127] The GPU, however, also offered to provide them with passports so they could leave the country. "We accepted the latter proposition," Fleshin said, but protests on their behalf by French anarcho-syndicalist delegates to the Red Trade Union International Congress, which was then meeting in Moscow, gained them a reprieve. On December 4, 1922, Steimer wrote to Alexander Berkman, explaining (in a code in which "Japan" stood for "Russia") that the government *"has deliberately framed up idealists* and seeks not only to send innocent people to the gallows, but to blacken their names and the movement to which these sincere rebels have given their lives."[128]

The events that finally led to Steimer's and Fleshin's deportation from Russia began on July 9, 1923, again in the early morning hours, when GPU agents appeared at their door. When it was opened, "7 men rushed in wild fashion, pointing their revolvers at us. They ordered us both to lift our hands up. We were searched, then told to show the place we occupy." The GPU conducted a three-hour search of the apartment, confiscated anarchist literature, and took them to the Inner Prison, located on Gorokhovaya Street. In all, the GPU raid in Petrograd netted forty-one anarchists. On July 11 Steimer was questioned about her activities, and her work on behalf of anarchist prisoners. Her interrogation was not unlike the one conducted in New York City, nearly five years earlier, by officials of the Military Intelligence Division. "You are an Anarchist?" "Yes." "You are having Anarchist gatherings?" "I refuse to answer." Steimer described the conditions under which she was held: "They were dreadful days and nights. Those tiny bits of dark holes which are called cells there, are actually full of insects: lice and bed-bugs. All the while one is forced to scratch and pick. . . . I thought I'd go mad. I never slept during these 4 days and 4 nights we spent there." On July 13 she was transferred to the House of Preliminary Detention, on Shpalernaya Street, where conditions were considerably better.

Ever since the Revolution, "politicals" in Soviet prisons had been granted certain privileges that were denied to "criminals." But by 1923 the GPU had embarked on a campaign to eliminate this special consideration. Consequently, as Steimer related, she "was placed in the criminal corridor and in criminal conditions." For breakfast she was given a cup of hot water and a pound of bread; for lunch, and again for supper, "a cup of watery, grayish-looking, stinking soup and a piece of meat which is so hard and smells so badly that it is impossible to eat it." She was allowed a fifteen-minute exercise period, and had to obtain special permission to receive visitors. On July 21, at a hearing, she protested against the denial of political status, and wrote to the GPU demanding "political" conditions: two hours of exercise daily, the right to have visits, the use of the prison library, and better food. Her request was denied on July 26, and she was also "threatened with the dark hole" for having waved to another prisoner. On July 27 she declared a hunger strike, in which she was joined by Fleshin and three other prisoners.

After three days she was offered political conditions, but was told that one of the other hunger strikers, her friend, Maria Veger, would not receive the same privileges. Steimer indignantly refused to end her hunger strike. "I was locked up in the cell without anybody interfering with me. Each day the nurse passed by, and looking in through the hole in the door, she inquired how I was. . . . On the 3rd of August the head doctor entered my cell. I was then unable to walk and there was a terrible evil odor coming from my mouth. I was so weak that I had difficulty in lifting my hands or head and could not keep my eyes open." The doctor told her she could hold out for another day, and then would be force-fed in the hospital.[129]

But on August 4, apparently as a result of the doctor's report, her demands were met. She and Fleshin remained in prison until August 26, when a GPU official came to the House of Preliminary Detention and read their sentences: expulsion from the Russian Socialist Federated Soviet Republic forever. Steimer later wrote that she and Fleshin were offered a choice: three years in the infamous Solovetsky Islands concentration camp, or deportation from Russia, "to be shot when returned."[130] Understandably, they chose deportation. Exactly a month later, on September 26, they were handed their passports, visas, and tickets for sea passage. They sailed from Petrograd for Stettin, Germany, on September 27, 1923. To Emma Goldman, who met the two deportees in Berlin, it seemed "incongruous" that Steimer, who had been "persecuted and imprisoned then deported from America for her ideas, should now be deported from the so called Workers Republic."[131]

To Steimer, it did not seem incongruous at all. In 1924 she wrote two articles for *Freedom*, an anarchist journal published in London.

"On Leaving Russia" appeared in January, "The Communists as Jailers" in May. The Communists, she declared, had turned into "the most reactionary, most brutal and autocratic rulers, who care for nothing but the maintenance of their power." The censorship, the secret police, the political surveillance, the concentration camps—all went beyond anything that existed in the United States. Russia had been turned into "a great prison where every individual who is known not to be in full agreement with the Communists is spied upon and booked by the 'G.P.U.' (Tcheka) as an enemy of the government." Yet, she recalled, when she had left New York City in November 1921, "my heart was light"; now, leaving Russia, she felt "deeply grieved." Indeed, she added honestly, "never have I felt so depressed as since I have been sentenced to exile from Russia." As an anarchist, she expected to be persecuted in capitalist America. But she had not expected, in revolutionary Russia, to be "scoffed at and ridiculed by the prison administration as well as by the higher authorities."[132]

By 1925 Steimer had left Berlin and, with Fleshin, had moved to Paris. It was there, in October, that she received a letter from Jacob Abrams. He had been working in a steam laundry in Moscow, and, after four years, had grown increasingly restless and dissatisfied. It was time to leave Russia, he told Steimer. "I got stale, sitting on one place. I got to refresh myself." Several months earlier, he had contemplated moving to Mexico, but his friends had advised against it. He had thought of moving to England, but did not know anyone in that country who could help him obtain a visa, and he was not sure whether he would be able to move to France. So he had decided to revert to his original plan and go to Mexico, primarily because it "is very easy." Someday, he expected, "I will be once more in Russia and because I know it, I want to get a little more world experience." In the meantime, to feel that he was "able to be useful to society and as well as for my own knowledge I got to drink again and again from the bitter cup."[133]

Jacob and Mary Abrams left Russia for Paris on November 15, 1925, arriving about ten days later. They stayed with Steimer and Fleshin, but the visit was a brief one. Alexander Berkman, who was collecting first-hand reports about the repression of dissidents in Russia, hoped that Abrams would remain in Paris long enough to provide some current, firsthand information. Learning that he intended to remain only a short time, Berkman urged Fleshin, "at least take down in writing all that Abr. has to say. We could use it for our Bulletin etc." A somewhat perturbed Berkman pointed out that Mexico "will still remain where it is if he will delay for 2 weeks."[134] But the Abramses had booked passage on a ship which was scheduled to leave for Havana on December 4, 1925.

On November 23, 1925, the fourth anniversary of the sailing of the S.S. *Esthonia,* Steimer was undoubtedly thinking of her imminent reunion, however short it turned out to be, with Abrams. Samuel Lipman, who was still in Moscow, was also thinking of his fellow deportees. To mark the occasion, he recorded his memories: "A rainy, cold, late autumn day in New York, many eyes, and tears, and oceans of feeling. It is getting dark—'Estonia' whistles, we are off. It was four years ago to-day. Four years, four long years."[135] During those years Lipman had married Ethel Bernstein, and their son was born in 1924. To cheer himself up when he was tired or depressed, he would look at the volume of Edgar Allan Poe's poetry Steimer had given him in 1922 with the inscription, "To dearest Soul Lipman . . . From Mollie."[136] In November 1925 he told Steimer and Fleshin that he "would like to see you myself, with my own eyes, speak to you & be near you, at least for a short time."[137] They were so close geographically, he said, and yet so far apart politically.

Those political differences eventually ended the friendship. Lipman wrote only two letters to Steimer in 1926, and none in 1927. He wrote a final letter in 1928, characteristically enough on August 23, the tenth anniversary of their arrest in East Harlem by the Bomb Squad. Writing partly in English and partly in Russian, Lipman observed, "Ten years have flown by since that evening, historic for us." He thought that "it would be interesting to know if we all noted this night or only I." Recalling "that nightmarish night," and "that well-knit group of enthusiasts-revolutionaries," he could not help being "involuntarily struck by our present dispersion, not in a geographical sense but mainly in a political one." Lachowsky was in Minsk and had become apolitical; Abrams was in Mexico City and had apparently "moved away from atheism"; Steimer was in Paris and had remained a dedicated anarchist.

As for himself, Lipman reported, he had applied for membership in the Communist Party. From 1925 to 1927, he explained, he had gone through "a period of doubts, struggle with my own self & debating." But "since 1927 I definitely decided to join the Communist party, but decided to wait one year and see if I will not change again my mind. About two months ago I filed my application and expect to be in the party within about three months. Of course it is very possible I should not be accepted but this will be only a formal matter, morally the moment I filed my application I am a member of the party ideologically." Having obtained a degree in agricultural economics, he now had a "highly paid position" and a "prestigious title" as chairman of the Department of Economic Geography at a university. He nevertheless thought it would be impossible to remain in Russia if his application was not approved. "If I will not be accepted most probably I will leave U.S.S.R. In U.S.S.R. to be outside of an organization means to be dead politically, by the way this is true not only of U.S.S.R."[138] Lipman's decision surely came as a disappointment to Steimer, though not, perhaps, as a surprise. As she put it, he "always was a Marxist."[139]

During Steimer's hunger strike in Petrograd in August 1923, a GPU agent had tried to get Fleshin to persuade her to end it. When Fleshin refused, the official snapped, "Steimer thinks that [it] is the American Government she is dealing with, and that whatever she asks will be complied with. . . . None of that!" Steimer later commented, "He spoke as if the brutal methods of the American police were tenderness itself compared with what he and his comrades intended to do."

If officials in the United States were not notably more tender than Russian officials in their treatment of anarchists, they were certainly more scrupulous. The Bureau of Investigation, unlike the Cheka and GPU, could not convict and sentence dissidents, or impose the penalty of administrative exile. In the United States, moreover, anarchists who were native-born citizens enjoyed a degree of legal protection unknown in Russia. But these important reservations aside, the American government treated many alien anarchists in much the same manner as the Russian government treated most anarchists. Neither government wanted them dead, but rather, in Lipman's telling phrase, "dead politically." By holding out deportation or exile as the only alternatives to imprisonment, both governments accomplished their mission.

EPILOGUE

# A Reunion in Mexico City

ON DECEMBER 16, 1941, the *Serpa Pinto,* out of Lisbon, docked at Vera Cruz, a port on the Gulf of Mexico. Among the passengers were Mollie Steimer and Senya Fleshin, traveling as a married couple, "Marthe" and "Simon Flechine." "As we drew in, Abrams was there—on a small boat waiting for us," Steimer recalled; "his warm and most friendly greeting meant new hope and a new life for us." Abrams and his wife, Mary, had been in Mexico City since 1926. Steimer and Fleshin would stay with the Abramses for several months, until they could find their own home. Since Fleshin had worked as a professional photographer for many years, they planned to open a studio. "We prefer to work by ourselves, just the two of us," Steimer explained.[1]

More than eighteen years had passed since Steimer and Fleshin had been deported from Russia. They had spent the early years of their exile in France, but not, it appears, happily. Steimer felt isolated, cut off from effective political action (although she did help raise funds for "Anarchists and Anarcho-Syndicalists Imprisoned and Exiled in Russia") and she resented being dependent, in any degree, on contributions from affluent sympathizers. In 1929, after six years in Paris, they moved to Berlin, where Fleshin was employed in an established photography studio, and where Steimer, according to Emma Goldman, threw herself into the anarchist movement. "That fills her life," Goldman said. "She really has no interest in anything else. Her one regret is that we do not have such mass demonstrations as the Nazis, or the Communists, street fights and arrest. That would be fuel to her fire." Goldman feared that Steimer, whom she loved dearly, was as "narrow and fanatical" as always.[2]

Early in 1933, after Hitler assumed power, Steimer fled Berlin. Unable to obtain a visa for Spain, she spent a few weeks in Holland, and then went to France, where she was joined by Fleshin. She tried to continue her work on behalf of imprisoned Russian anarchists, but the French government kept her under close surveillance and barred her from attending political meetings. "The circumstances under which we are forced to live, make life utterly meaningless," she wrote in 1935, and she added that all the world had become "nothing but a great big prison."[3] Steimer watched despairingly as the civil war in Spain devoured that nation's anarchists, and as the Nazis stepped up their campaign against German Jews. When the Second World War engulfed Europe, she and Fleshin considered joining Abrams in Mexico, but were unable to obtain visas. By May 15, 1940, however, they had decided to remain where they were. As German divisions swept through France, Steimer explained, "We both decided: *to stay here* and share the fate of those near us, and of the people in general." There was "such indescribable distress and destruction" that "the human beings (who are *still human*) should stand by each other, and if the worst should come, well one dies only once."[4]

Eight days later, on May 23, Steimer was arrested by the French authorities and sent to the concentration camp at Gurs, located at the base of the Pyrenees. She was seized, perhaps mistakenly, perhaps not, as a "German Jew," and like thousands of other "enemy aliens" was interned by a panic-stricken government reeling under the Nazi assault. As one account explains, "The official targets in all this were enemy aliens, but Jews were caught in the nets like other foreigners, and their Jewishness seems to have compounded their vulnerability."[5] The camp to which she was sent had been built in 1939 for refugees from the Spanish civil war, but by 1940 it was being used chiefly for German Jews. In the distance inmates could see the imposing snow-capped Pyrenees. But inside the camp, one prisoner recalled, "There were neither trees nor shrubs. Wherever one looked there was nothing but barracks behind barbed wire. . . . People died like flies, mostly of dysentery."[6]

Steimer was held in Camp de Gurs for seven weeks, during which time she was not permitted to communicate with Fleshin, who wrote that "the agony of waiting is awful."[7] She later described the hardships she endured. "Imagine 60 women in a thin wooden barrack which is no more than 3 meters wide and not even 30 meters long, sleeping on the floor on straw mattresses." The camp was infested with rats. A little cold water was available for a few hours a day. "No need to talk of sanitary conditions. They do not exist." At night it was freezing cold. "The food is not bad enough to die from starvation, but good enough to result in scurvy, and every other possible disease." For a time, she was housed with other political suspects, suffering even worse conditions. "There we had *no* light, *no* mattresses, *no* water, and *no* right to buy anything at all."[8]

Toward the end of July Steimer was released, perhaps because she was able to prove that she was a Russian, not a German, citizen. She boarded a train which took her to Toulouse, where, at the railroad station, she met Fleshin, entirely by chance. He had been trying to reach Gurs, and one can imagine their emotions as they caught sight of each other. Afraid to return to Paris, which by then had fallen to the Nazis, they moved to a small village in Clermont, in central France, an area controlled by the Vichy government. Each month they applied and received permission to remain, but they were never granted work permits. Their expenses were paid by friends, and they lived with a Catholic family "who acted as our protectors."[9] Again, they dreamed of leaving, but as Steimer wrote in August 1940, "Leaving Europe? *Where to,* and *how?*"[10] More than a year passed before Abrams managed to obtain visas for them (and for other refugees) to enter Mexico. By late October 1941 Steimer and Fleshin had made their way to Portugal, and in December they sailed for Vera Cruz.

By the time they were reunited with Abrams, Samuel Lipman had become a victim of Stalinism, and another old friend, Hyman Lachowsky, had in all likelihood become—or was about to become—a victim of Hitlerism. In the late 1930s Lipman, then about forty, a professor of economic geography in Moscow, and a member of the Communist Party, was murdered in the Stalinist purges. (His wife, Ethel Bernstein, was sent to a Soviet concentration camp; she would be released after ten years and told that her imprisonment had been a mistake.)[11] Lachowsky had returned to Minsk in 1922. If, as seems probable, he had stayed there, he would have been fifty years old when German troops overran the city in the summer of 1941. Within a year the Nazis had murdered nearly all the Jews who lived in Minsk. On July 31, 1942, a Nazi official boasted that "Jewry has been completely eliminated" in the Minsk region.[12]

Many others who had been involved in the Abrams case had also passed away, although not so violently. Judge Henry DeLamar Clayton of Alabama had died of pernicious anemia in December 1929, just a few days after resigning his federal district judgeship. Oliver Wendell Holmes remained on the Supreme Court until January 1932, when, nearly ninety-one years of age, he retired. He told his friend, Sir Frederick Pollock, "My idleness is pretty busy and I enjoy it greatly and should like it better if it was a little idler."[13] Holmes passed away in 1935, Pollock in 1937. John M. Ryan, the Assistant United States Attorney who had handled the Abrams trial, continued to work for the federal prosecutor's office, although his interests shifted from radicalism to real estate fraud. He died in 1940 at the age of sixty-nine. Louis D. Brandeis remained on the Supreme Court until 1939. In October 1941, at the age of eighty-five, he suffered a fatal heart attack.

In the days following United States entry into the Second World War, it is unlikely that any of those who had a hand in suppressing radicals in the First World War (with the possible exception of J. Edgar Hoover) knew of Abrams' and Steimer's reunion in Mexico City. Thomas J. Tunney, whose Bomb Squad had arrested the anarchists, had moved to Port Washington, Long Island, where he operated a private detective agency.[14] Alfred Bettman and John Lord O'Brian, the special assistants to the Attorney General who had approved the Sedition Act prosecutions, had resumed the practice of law, Bettman in Cincinnati and O'Brian in Washington. Bettman would soon decide that Franklin D. Roosevelt's Department of Justice handled the problems of espionage and enemy aliens "with much greater discretion, self-control and decency than did the Department in World War I," while O'Brian would take a government job, serving as general counsel for the War Production Board.[15] Francis G. Caffey, the United States Attorney who had drawn up the indictments in the Abrams case, was now a federal district judge for the Southern District of New York, a position to which he had been appointed in 1929.[16] John H. Wigmore had retired from Northwestern University Law School, but had not modified his view that freedom of speech in wartime should not be confused with freedom of thuggery.[17]

Those who had sided with the anarchists in the earlier conflict, however, might very well have known of their reunion. Certainly their lawyer, Harry Weinberger, who in 1939 had hoped a way could be found for Steimer and Fleshin to return to the United States, learned they had reached Mexico. Over the years Weinberger had continued to defend unpopular causes, but the attack on Pearl Harbor forced him to reassess his pacifist convictions. In "A Rebel's Interrupted Autobiography," an essay published at the time, Weinberger explained, "I, too, crusader against war as I am and have been, was one of the people in favor of a declaration of war."[18] Kate Richards O'Hare, Mollie Steimer's onetime prison mate in Jefferson City, had become an outspoken crusader for prison reform. She divorced her husband, married Charles C. Cunningham, an engineer, and moved to California. In 1938 she was appointed Assistant Director of the Department of Penology and had an opportunity to introduce some of the reforms she had championed, such as the segregation of youthful offenders from hardened criminals.[19] Zechariah Chafee was still teaching at Harvard Law School. In June 1941 he had completed a revision of his 1920 volume, *Freedom of Speech,* which was published as *Free Speech in the United States.* Reviews of the earlier edition, he wrote, "have led me to reshape the presentation of some passages, particularly in the chapter on the Abrams case." He explained that he had tried to take into account critics who said that he had shown "excessive solicitude for the persons who were prosecuted and deported" and had been "too harsh toward the promoters of suppression."[20]

As for Jacob Abrams, he had remained in Mexico City, where he edited a Yiddish-language newspaper. He dreamed of returning to the United States, but the conditions attached to the commutation of his sentence made that impossible. In 1938 a friend reported that "Jake and Mary are very unhappy in Mexico City and very anxious to get out of there; in addition to being political refugees, they are also *Jews* like all of us and are not welcome even in Mexico."[21] Although Abrams' efforts to obtain a visa failed, they apparently prompted Adolf A. Berle, a State Department official, to ask FBI Director J. Edgar Hoover for information about the case in October 1940. Digging through the old, musty files, Hoover produced a highly misleading reply. Abrams "was admittedly formerly associated with a terrorist group in Russia which delighted to set fire to the homes of manufacturers and capitalists"; he had organized a group which "advised conscripts how to evade military service"; he had been "arrested for printing and distributing seditious literature opposing the draft"; he had been found marching through the streets of East Harlem, on the night of August 23, 1918, "distributing copies of leaflets entitled 'The Hypocrisy of the United States and Her Allies,' and 'Toilers Awake' as well as a pamphlet written in Hebrew entitled 'Workers Wake Up.' " Hoover pointed out, correctly, that Abrams had not taken out citizenship papers, had admitted he was an anarchist, and, on November 23, 1921, had been deported to Russia.[22]

The next effort to obtain a visa had a more tragic motivation. By the early 1950s Abrams had been diagnosed as having throat cancer, and friends and relatives thought his last hope was to obtain treatment at a clinic in Philadelphia. Mary Abrams drafted a letter to Eleanor Roosevelt, imploring her to use her influence to obtain permission for Abrams to return. She said she was writing since Mrs. Roosevelt was the official representative to the United Nations, and was "a great humanitarian and a person who possesses enough intelligence to understand that you don't go on punishing a person for over 30 years just because he had a DIFFERENT OPINION on events than that of the Government in power."[23] But the letter was apparently never sent. In May 1952 U.S. immigration authorities seemed ready to grant Abrams a temporary visa, but the Department of Justice objected. In June a six-week visa was finally granted, and Abrams underwent radiation treatment at Temple University Hospital. He was operated on in November and in December was permitted to return to Philadelphia for further treatment.

Despite these efforts, Steimer reported, "His state is as bad as it can be."[24] Steimer described Abrams' final days. They were "horrible," she said; "he was only one day at home (after his arrival from the States) when he suddenly got a terrible attack, was taken to the clinic from where he never returned." The medical intervention and the blood transfusions "only prolonged the agony." Steimer was at his bedside on June 10, 1953, when, unable to speak, he beckoned for a pencil and paper, and wrote, "take care of Mary."[25] Four hours later he died. Mary Abrams was inconsolably distraught and remained so until her death in January 1978. Earlier a friend had commented that "spiritually she is not longer of this world. She belongs to the past, and to Abrams."[26]

The event responsible for her husband's arrest in 1918—United States intervention in Russia—also belonged to the past. The American troops dispatched by President Woodrow Wilson that fateful summer remained in eastern Siberia for nearly two years, under the command of General William S. Graves. They provided arms and equipment to the counter-revolutionary forces led by Admiral Alexander V. Kolchak. Graves tried to prevent any military clash between his men and the pro-Bolshevik forces, but under the circumstances his efforts could not be entirely successful. On June 25, 1919, Russian partisans attacked a force of seventy-five Americans at Romanovka, killing twenty-four men and wounding twenty-five. Wilson, subjected to scathing criticism for maintaining an army in Russia long after the armistice had been signed, had to fabricate excuses. By late December 1919, however, Secretary of State Robert Lansing informed him that Kolchak's forces were collapsing, the Bolsheviks were approaching eastern Siberia, and "the people seem to prefer them to the officers of the Kolchak regime." Lansing predicted that "if we do not withdraw we shall have to wage war against the Bolsheviki."[27] Wilson bowed to the inevitable. The exodus of 5,000 Americans from Vladivostok then began, and the last soldier departed on April 1, 1920. As one observer wrote, "There was no cheering and little to be said."[28]

Congress, in an action that went almost unnoticed, repealed the Sedition Act. In December 1920 the House took up a seemingly unexceptional Joint Resolution. Since the United States was still technically at war with Germany, the Resolution stated that in applying the provisions of any wartime acts which were to be operative until the "termination of the present war," the date the Resolution took effect "shall be construed and treated" as the date the war ended. The Resolution did not specify which wartime acts were included. When asked if it would repeal the Espionage Act of June 15, 1917, a sponsor explained that it was meant only to repeal "the portion of the espionage law to which there is objection," that is, the Sedition Act of May 18, 1918, which was technically an amendment to section 3 of the Espionage Act. Two Congressmen made brief statements, one opposing repeal and the other favoring it. The House approved the Resolution.[29]

In February 1921 the Senate amended the Resolution to make it more explicit. It now provided that the May 18, 1918 amendment to section 3 of the Espionage Act "is hereby repealed, and that said section 3 of said act approved June 15, 1917 is hereby revived and restored with the same force and effect as originally enacted." Senator Thomas Walsh of Montana, who had been instrumental in the enactment of the 1918 measure, offered an amendment, which was hastily approved, to ensure that no one who had been indicted under that measure, or who was still facing trial, would be affected by the recision. The Senate then adopted the Joint Resolution, which went into effect on March 3, 1921.[30] So the law which had produced *Schenck* remained on the books, but not the law which had produced *Abrams.*

The "clear and present danger" standard which Justice Oliver Wendell Holmes had formulated and then refined in those cases had a longer and more controversial life. To describe the ways in which Supreme Court Justices applied, modified, or rejected that standard would be to write a history of civil liberties in the fifty years after 1919. "Clear and present danger" provided a criterion for deciding First Amendment cases throughout the 1920s, 1930s, and 1940s. Although it became increasingly fashionable to criticize the standard during the 1950s, Justices continued to invoke Holmes's dissent in the Abrams case to support a right to freedom of expression well into the 1960s.[31] But in June 1969 the nine Justices decided that "clear and present danger," even in its most libertarian form, was not sufficiently speech-protective. In *Brandenburg* v. *Ohio,* they adopted instead the direct incitement test.

The case grew out of the conviction of a Ku Klux Klan leader under a state criminal syndicalism act which made it a crime to advocate "the duty, necessity, or propriety" of using violence "as a means of accomplishing industrial or political reform." The Ohio legislature had enacted the measure in 1919, the very year in which the Supreme Court had upheld the conviction of Jacob Abrams and his comrades and they had gone to jail. Now, overturning the Ohio statute, the Court declared in a unanimous opinion that free speech guarantees "do not permit a State to forbid or proscribe advocacy of the use of force or of law violation except where such advocacy is directed to inciting or producing imminent lawless action and is likely to incite or produce such action." Justice William O. Douglas wrote a concurring opinion in which he added, "The line between what is permissible and not subject to control and what may be made impermissible and subject to regulation is the line between ideas and overt acts." To justify that conclusion, Douglas reviewed the Court's decisions in the six World War I Espionage and Sedition Act cases—*Schenck, Frohwerk, Debs, Abrams, Schaefer,* and *Pierce*—and cited Holmes's dissent in *Abrams:* "Congress certainly cannot forbid all effort to change the mind of the country."[32]

The Court had therefore accepted two ideas that Harry Weinberger, Zechariah Chafee, and other civil libertarians had advanced fifty years earlier: the requirement that "intent" and "incitement" be proven. Yet *Brandenburg* did not—and could not—reject at least one aspect of the "clear and present danger" standard. The Court said that speech, even when made with the requisite intent and for the purpose of incitement, still had to be "likely to incite or produce" imminent lawless action in order for the government to restrict it. That seemed to be merely another way of saying that speech also had to create something like a "clear and present danger." And, again, Douglas approvingly quoted Holmes's view, stated in *Abrams,* that "only the present danger of immediate evil or an intent to bring it about" warranted the limiting of speech.

In 1969, when the Supreme Court adopted this construction of the First Amendment, only Mollie Steimer, among the defendants in the Abrams case, was still alive. She and Senya Fleshin had spent the intervening years in Mexico City, working in their photography studio, SEMO, and eventually acquiring Mexican citizenship. They continued to correspond with friends in the United States. But the anarchist movement had long since vanished, a victim of government repression, the deportation of its leaders, factional quarrels, disillusionment with the Russian Revolution, the increasing assimilation of Jews and other immigrants, and the growing disenchantment with ideals that had once seemed compelling. "The English speaking anarchist movement is dead in this country," one supporter wrote in 1924, and she added,

"Even the Jewish movement is backward, and taken up with differences and quarrels."[33] By 1928 Alexander Berkman recognized that "our movement, everywhere, is degenerating into a swamp of petty personal quarrels, accusations and recriminations."[34] Emma Goldman came to a similar conclusion. "Actually there is no Anarchist movement anywhere in the world. What we have got is so insignificant, so piffling it is ridiculous to speak of an Anarchist organized movement."[35] One of the few remaining diehards commented in 1934 that she and other anarchists "have had the acute pain of watching our movement dwindle to nil."[36] As doubts and uncertainties increased, a friend told Steimer that in bygone days "issues seemed so much clearer. The revolution was apparently right around the corner, we were so sure of ourselves and what we should do!"[37]

So the years of exile in Mexico were, for Steimer and Fleshin, years of frustration, heightened by a realization that the movement to which they had devoted their lives had failed. But they offered no apologies for the path they had chosen. When someone suggested to Steimer that she and Fleshin write their autobiographies, she replied, "Both of us feel that whatever we did in our lives was because WE HAD TO DO SO. We fought injustice in our humble way as well as we could; and if the result was prison, hard labour, deportations and lots of suffering, well, this was something that every human being who fights for a better humanity has to expect. . . . I don't feel important enough to write my autobiography. We fought tyranny ever since our early youth wherever we met with it as simple rank and filers and because of an inner conviction that a society of rich and poor, luxury and misery, ignorance and brutality is wrong, and MUST BE CHANGED. But we don't look for any credit for what we did. . . . Consequently we prefer to remain in the shadow."[38] Mollie Steimer died in Cuernavaca on July 23, 1980, at the age of eighty-three. Senya Fleshin died the following year.

Steimer and Abrams, Lipman and Lachowsky, and Jacob Schwartz, too, had paid a heavy price for voicing their inner convictions, a price none of them could have foreseen when they emigrated to America, embraced radicalism, or denounced United States intervention in Soviet Russia. Their efforts did not reduce the inequality, misery, or injustice in the world, much less the brutality. Yet the action these five Russian immigrants took in the summer of 1918 had far-reaching consequences. The Abrams case led Justice Oliver Wendell Holmes to discover more libertarian possibilities in the "clear and present danger" standard. Fifty years later, even as the Supreme Court adopted the direct incitement standard, Holmes's *Abrams* dissent was cited and an aspect of it was incorporated into the more libertarian test. The Abrams case contributed, therefore, to a process of judicial reconsideration which eventually placed freedom of speech on a firmer constitutional basis. As radicals, especially as anarchists, Jacob Abrams and the others hardly had this goal in mind, yet it was surely a goal worth achieving. As Mollie Steimer once commented in another context, "And if we can say about someone that he hasn't lived in vain, it is already a lot, don't you think so?"[39]

# MANUSCRIPT COLLECTIONS, LOCATIONS, AND ABBREVIATIONS

*Library of Congress, Washington D. C:* Newton D. Baker MSS; Albert Burleson MSS; George Creel MSS; William R. Day MSS; Felix Frankfurter MSS; Thomas Gregory MSS; Warren Harding MSS; Samuel Gompers Letterbooks; AFL Records in the Gompers Era; Judson King MSS; Amos Pinchot MSS; Louis Post MSS; Theodore Roosevelt MSS; Thomas Walsh MSS; Charles Warren MSS; William Howard Taft MSS; Joseph Tumulty MSS; Willis Van Devanter MSS; Woodrow Wilson MSS.

*National Archives and Records Centers*

*Washington D. C:* Records of the Bureau of Investigation (BI-MSS); Records of the Department of Justice (DJ-MSS); Records of the Military Intelligence Division (MID-MSS); Records of the Pardon Attorney; Records of the Supreme Court; Records of the U.S. Commission on Industrial Relations.

*Military Ocean Terminal, Bayonne:* Records of the U.S. District Court, Southern District, New York; Records of the U.S. Attorneys and Marshals: World War I Cases.

*Philadelphia:* Records of the U.S. District Court, Eastern District, Pennsylvania.

*Freedom of Information Act* (FOIA): Records of the Bureau of Investigation (BI-MSS [FOIA]); Records of the Bureau of Prisons (BP-MSS [FOIA]); Records of the State Department; Records of the Bureau of Immigration; Records of the Office of Naval Intelligence.

*Tamiment Institute, New York University:* Alexander Berkman MSS; Emma Goldman MSS; New York Bureau of Legal Advice MSS; Rose Pastor Stokes MSS.

*Butler Library, Columbia University:* Robert Minor MSS; Lincoln Steffens MSS.

*New York Public Library:* Emma Goldman MSS; Rose Pesotta MSS.

*YIVO Institute for Jewish Research, New York City:* Michael Cohn MSS.

*Jewish Labor Bund Archives, New York City:* Joseph Cohen MSS.

*Municipal Archives, New York City:* John F. Hylan MSS; John P. Mitchel MSS.

*New York State Archives, Albany:* Records of the Joint (Lusk) Committee to Investigate Seditious Activity.

*Syracuse University Library:* Granville Hicks MSS (Charles Recht Diary).

*SUNY-Buffalo Law Library:* John Lord O'Brian MSS.

*Labor-Management Document Center, Cornell University:* Industrial Workers of the World MSS.

*Hoover Institution, Stanford University:* Benjamin Gitlow MSS; Louise Olivereau MSS; John Lord O'Brian MSS.

*Bancroft Library, University of California–Berkeley:* Hiram Johnson MSS; Tom Mooney MSS.

*University of California at Los Angeles Library:* Theodore Perceval Gerson MSS; Lucy Robins Lang MSS.

*State Historical Society of Wisconsin, Madison:* Elizabeth Gurley Flynn MSS; Raymond Robins MSS; Morris Hillquit MSS.

*Sterling Library, Yale University:* Rose Pastor Stokes MSS; Harry Weinberger MSS.

*Beinecke Library, Yale University:* Mabel Dodge MSS; Hutchins Hapgood MSS; Alfred Steiglitz MSS: Carl Van Vechten MSS.

*Northwestern University Law School Library:* John H. Wigmore MSS.

*Joseph M. Regenstein Library, University of Chicago:* Ernst Freund MSS.

*Walter Reuther Library, Wayne State University:* Industrial Workers of the World MSS; Mary Heaton Vorse MSS.

*Seeley G. Mudd Library, Princeton University:* American Civil Liberties Union MSS (ACLU MSS); Roger Baldwin MSS.

*University of Alabama Library:* Henry DeLamar Clayton MSS.

*State of Alabama, Department of Archives and History, Montgomery:* Francis G. Caffey MSS.

*Duke University Library:* Socialist Party of America MSS.

*University of Florida Library:* Margaret Dreier Robins MSS.

*Case Western Reserve Library:* John H. Clarke MSS.

*University of Louisville Law School Library:* Louis D. Brandeis MSS.

*Labadie Collection, University of Michigan:* Ralph Chaplin MSS; Freie Arbeiter Stimme–Max Nettlau MSS; Emma Goldman MSS; Agnes Inglis MSS; Joseph Labadie MSS.

*Microfilming Corporation of America:* Eugene Debs MSS.

*Schlesinger Library, Radcliffe College:* Emma Goldman MSS.

*Houghton Library, Harvard University:* Joseph Ishill MSS; John Reed MSS; Oswald Garrison Villard MSS.

*Harvard Law School Library:* Louis D. Brandeis MSS; Lawrence G. Brooks MSS; Zechariah Chafee MSS; Learned Hand MSS; Oliver Wendell Holmes MSS.

*International Institute for Social History* (IISG): Alexander Berkman MSS; Emma Goldman MSS; Rudolf Rocker MSS; Steimer–Flechine MSS.

*University Publications of America:* U.S. Military Intelligence Reports: Surveillance of Radicals in the U.S. 1917–1941 (MIR-MSS).

# NOTES

### Prologue—A Farewell Dinner

1. This account is based on reports in the New York *Tribune* and New York *Call*, November 22, 1921; Mollie Steimer to Harry Weinberger, November 19, 1921, Weinberger MSS, Box 2; J. R. Proctor to Assistant Chief of Staff, November 22, 1921, Military Intelligence Division MSS; Edward J. Brennan to Director, December 14, 1921, FBI MSS (FOIA) 61–406.

### 1. Anarchism and War

1. Mollie Steimer to Milly Rocker, March 14, 1948, Rocker MSS.

2. Lucien Wolf, *The Legal Sufferings of the Jews in Russia* (London, 1912), p. 49.

3. Samuel Joseph, *Jewish Immigration to the United States* (New York, 1914), p. 66.

4. A. V. Dicey, "Introduction," in Wolf, *Legal Sufferings,* p. vii.

5. Reports of the Immigration Commission, IV, *Emigration Conditions in Europe* (Washington, 1911), p. 98.

6. Reports of the Immigration Commission, XXXVII, *Steerage Conditions* (Washington, 1911), pp. 13–23.

7. *Ibid.*, pp. 24–29.

8. E. H. Mullan, "Mental Examination of Immigrants: Administration and Line Inspection at Ellis Island," *U.S. Public Health Reports* (May 18, 1917), pp. 3–7.

9. *Ibid.* "Favus" is a skin disease caused by a fungus.

10. T. Clark and J. W. Schereschewsky, "Trachoma: Its Character and Effects," *U.S. Public Health Bulletin,* No. 19 (1907), p. 5.

11. *Ibid.*

12. E. H. Mullan, "Mentality of the Arriving Immigrants," *U.S. Public Health Bulletin* No. 90 (1917), p. 80.

13. Alfred C. Reed, "Going

Through Ellis Island," *Popular Science Monthly*, LXXXII (January 1913), 8–9.

14. Victor Safford, *Immigration Problems: Personal Experiences of an Official* (New York, 1925), p. 244.

15. Williams cited in Thomas M. Pitkin, *Keepers of the Gate: A History of Ellis Island* (New York, 1975), p. 46.

16. Mary Van Kleeck, *Women in the Bookbinding Trade* (New York, 1913), p. 219.

17. *The International Bookbinder*, XX (December 1919), 395.

18. Van Kleeck, *Women in Bookbinding*, p. 146.

19. *The International Bookbinder*, XX (January 1919), 24.

20. *Ibid.*, XX (August 1919), p. 250.

21. *Ibid.*, XX (April 1919), 124.

22. *Ibid.*, XIX (April 1918), 98.

23. *Ibid.*, XIX (June 1918), 164.

24. *Ibid.*, XX (January 1919), 12.

25. See *Ibid.*, XX (September 1919), 339, for a typical example.

26. *The Fur Worker*, October 10, 1916; April 3, 1917.

27. *Ibid.*, March 6, 1917.

28. *Ibid.*, July 1917.

29. *Ibid.*, November 1919.

30. *Ibid.*, January 2, 1917.

31. Louis I. Harris, *A Clinical and Sanitary Study of the Fur and Hatters' Fur Trade* (New York City, Department of Health monograph series, No. 12, December 1915), *passim.*

32. *Ibid.*

33. *The Ladies' Garment Worker*, IX (October 1918), p. 27.

34. Charles H. Winslow, *Conciliation, Arbitration, and Sanitation in the Dress and Waist Industries of New York City* (U.S. Bureau of Labor Statistics, Bulletin No. 145, April 10, 1914), p. 164.

35. Sue Ainsley Clark and Edith Wyatt, *Making Both Ends Meet: The Income and Outlay of New York Working Girls* (New York, 1911), p. 120.

36. Winslow, *Conciliation*, p. 30.

37. J. W. Schereschewsky, *The Health of Garment Workers* (U.S. Public Health Service, Bulletin No. 71, May 1915), p. 99.

38. Mollie Steimer to Milly Rocker, March 14, 1948, Rocker MSS.

39. *Ibid.*

40. Roger Baldwin (ed.), *Kropotkin's Revolutionary Pamphlets* (New York, 1927), p. 109.

41. Peter Kropotkin, *The Conquest of Bread* (London, 1906), p. 195.

42. *Ibid.*, p. 13

43. *Ibid.*, p. 155.

44. *Ibid.*, p. 188.

45. Baldwin, *Kropotkin's Revolutionary Pamphlets*, p. 63.

46. Kropotkin, *Conquest of Bread*, p. 35.

47. *Ibid.*, p. 184.

48. Baldwin, *Kropotkin's Revolutionary Pamphlets*, pp. 97, 100.

49. Michael Bakunin, *God and the State* (New York, 1970 ed.), p. 25.

50. James Joll, *The Anarchists* (Cambridge, 1980), p. x notes that anarchism combined elements of a "religious faith and a rational philosophy."

51. Mollie Steimer to Margaret Marsh, January 15, 1978; Jacob Abrams to Harry Weinberger, March 3, 1920, Weinberger MSS.

52. Kropotkin, *Conquest of Bread*, p. 188.

53. New York *Sun*, July 14, 1914.

54. Joseph Spivak, "Der Lebnsveg fun Jacob Abrams," in Central Cultural Israelita de Mexico, *J. Abramsbuch* (Mexico City, 1956), pp. 9–13; interviews with Hilda Kovner Adel, April

14, 1973; Paul Rose, January 25, 1974; Sonya Deanin, September 18, 1974. These interviews were conducted by Paul Avrich, who generously made his notes available.

55. *Trial* Transcript, p. 160.

56. Kehillah of N. Y. C., *The Jewish Communal Register of New York City 1917–1918* (New York, 1918), pp. 487, 1006. See also Jeffrey Gurock, *When Harlem Was Jewish* (New York, 1979), chs. 2 and 3.

57. *Ibid.*, pp. 865, 1341.

58. Paul Avrich, *The Modern School Movement: Anarchism and Education in the United States* (Princeton, 1980), p. 20.

59. *The Blast*, June 1, 1917.

60. Richard Drinnon, *Rebel in Paradise: A Biography of Emma Goldman* (Boston, 1961), p. 231; Alexander Berkman, "The Surgeon's Duty," *Mother Earth Bulletin*, January 1918.

61. Cited in Drinnon, *Rebel in Paradise*, p. 231.

62. Milly Rocker to Mollie Steimer, August 4, 1946, Rocker MSS.

63. *U.S.* v. *Ves Hall*, Great Falls (Mont.) *Tribune*, January 27, 1918, reprinted in *Congressional Record*, 65th Congress, 2nd Session, p. 4560; Helena (Mont.) *Independent*, January 25, 1918.

64. 40 *Stat.* 219 (1917).

65. *Cong. Rec.*, 65–2, p. 4560.

66. Aaron Gutfeld, "The Ves Hall Case, Judge Bourquin, and the Sedition Act of 1918," *Pacific Historical Review*, XXXVII (May 1968), 171–72.

67. *Cong. Rec.*, 65-2, p. 4561.

68. John Lord O'Brian to Thomas W. Gregory, February 27, 1918, O'Brian MSS, Box 17.

69. Thomas Walsh to Thomas W. Gregory, March 26, 1918; Gregory to Walsh, March 29, 1918, Walsh MSS, Box 269.

70. Alvin H. Hansen, "Alfred Bettman," *Journal of American Institute of Planners*, XI (January 1945), 39.

71. Alfred Bettman, "A Beginning and a Prophecy, Cincinnati: 1916," [May 1917] in Arthur C. Comey, ed., *City and Regional Planning Papers by Alfred Bettman* (Cambridge, 1946), pp. 3–4.

72. Alfred Bettman to Felix Frankfurter, December 26, 1941, Frankfurter MSS, Box 24.

73. Alfred Bettman, "Regulation of Free Speech," April 25, 1919, O'Brian MSS, Box 18.

74. Bettman to O'Brian, September 1, 1918, *ibid.*, Box 17.

75. Bettman, "Regulation of Free Speech," *ibid.*, Box 18.

76. Bettman to O'Brian, July 5, 1918, *ibid.*, Box 17.

77. Bettman to O'Brian, December 9, 1918, *ibid.*, Box 17.

78. O'Brian to Gregory, February 27, 1918, *ibid.*, Box 17.

79. John M. Maguire to Zechariah Chafee, July 31, 1919, Chafee MSS, Box 14.

80. Bettman to Chafee, September 20, 1919, *ibid.*, Box 14.

81. *Cong. Rec.*, 65–2, pp. 3003–4.

82. *Ibid.*, p. 4559.

83. R. Lockey to Walsh, April 17, 1918, Walsh MSS, Box 269.

84. *Cong. Rec.*, 65–2, pp. 4645, 4648.

85. *Ibid.*, p. 4826.

86. Roosevelt to Miles Poindexter, May 22, 1918, Roosevelt MSS, Reel 404; Roosevelt to Frank B. Kellogg, April 12, 1918, *ibid.*, Reel 402; New York *Call*, May 9, 1918.

87. Bettman to O'Brian, April 15, 1918, O'Brian MSS, Box 18.

88. O'Brian to Walsh, April 16, 1918, Walsh MSS, Box 269.

89. *Cong. Rec.*, 65–2, p. 6049.

90. *Ibid.*, pp. 6181–86.

91. 40 *Stat.* 553–4 (1918).

92. Cited in Donald Johnson, *The Challenge to American Freedoms* (Lexington, Ky., 1963), p. 71.

93. Baldwin to House, January 22 and 24, 1918, ACLU MSS, Vol. 26.

94. Baldwin to John Haynes Holmes, May 8, 1918, *ibid.*, Vol. 26.

95. Bettman to O'Brian, May 10, 1918, O'Brian MSS, Box 18.

96. Gregory to Wilson, May 14, 1918, Wilson MSS, Reel 356.

97. Gregory to Wilson, October 18, 1918, *ibid.*, Reel 375.

98. Gregory to Wilson, May 14, 1918, *ibid.*, Reel 356.

99. Mollie Steimer to Emma Goldman, January 5, 1930, Steimer–Flechine MSS.

100. Statement of Mollie Steimer, August 24, 1918, Military Intelligence Division MSS.

101. Cited in Robert J. Maddox, *The Unknown War* (San Rafael, 1977), p. 39.

102. Cited in George F. Kennan, *The Decision to Intervene* (Princeton, 1958), p. 392.

103. Cited in Lloyd C. Gardner, *Safe for Democracy* (New York, 1984), p. 182.

104. Karel Capek, ed., *President Masaryk Tells His Story* (New York, 1935), p. 282.

105. Cited in Edward P. Newman, *Masaryk* (London, 1960), p. 163.

106. Masaryk to Wilson, August 5, 1918, Wilson MSS, Reel 98.

107. Cited in N. Gordon Levin, *Woodrow Wilson and World Politics* (New York, 1968), p. 105.

108. Cited in Kennan, *Decision to Intervene,* p. 391.

109. Cited in *ibid.*, p. 395.

110. Cited in *ibid.*, pp. 396–97.

111. The text is provided in *ibid.*, pp. 482–85.

112. *Ibid.*, p. 413.

113. *Ibid.*, p. 415.

114. Taft to Gus Karger, August 10, 1918, Taft MSS, Reel 552.

115. Joint Conference of National Executive Committee and State Secretaries, August 10–12, 1918, Socialist Party MSS, Reel 7.

116. Leaflet [n.d.] in possession of Paul Avrich; Steimer to Milly Rocker, March 14, 1948, Rocker MSS.

## 2. THE ARRESTS

1. New York *Herald Tribune* and New York *World,* August 23, 1918.

2. Nicholas Biddle to Director, Military Intelligence Branch, August 30, 1918, Military Intelligence Division MSS, Series 105106–1619 (MID MSS).

3. *Ibid.*

4. *Ibid.*

5. *Trial* transcript, p. 16.

6. Statement of Hyman Rosansky, August 23, 1918, MID MSS.

7. *Ibid.*

8. Steimer to Milly Rocker, March 14, 1948, Rocker MSS; Steimer to Emma Goldman, January 5, 1930, Steimer–Flechine MSS.

9. Biddle to Director, August 30, 1918, MID MSS.

10. New York *Call,* August 25, 1918.

11. *Ibid.*

12. *Trial* transcript, p. 99.

13. *Ibid.*, pp. 66, 68.

14. *Ibid.*, pp. 67, 113.

15. New York *Evening World* and New York *Journal,* August 24, 1918.

16. New York *World,* August 25, 1918.

17. *New York Times,* August 25, 1918.

18. *U.S.* v. *Jacob Abrams et al.*, p. 252.

19. *Trial* transcript, pp. 218–19.

20. Biddle to Director, August 30, 1918, MID MSS.

21. Thomas J. Tunney, *Throttled! The Detection of the German and Anarchist Bomb Plotters* (Boston, 1919), p. 2.

22. Arthur Woods, "Reasonable Restrictions upon Freedom of Assemblage," *American Sociological Review,* IX (December 1914), 29–45.

23. Arthur Woods, *Policeman and Public* (New Haven, 1919), pp. 77–78.

24. Roosevelt to Woods, August 17, 1917; Woods to Roosevelt, August 21, 1917, Roosevelt MSS, Reels 394, 243.

25. Tunney, *Throttled!,* pp. 160, 175.

26. *Ibid.*, p. xi.

27. *Ibid.*, pp. 252, 273.

28. *Brewing and Liquor Interests and German Propaganda.* Hearings before a Subcommittee of the Committee on the Judiciary, U.S. Senate, 65th Cong., 2nd–3rd Sessions (Washington, 1919), pp. 2678–79.

29. Tunney, *Throttled!,* pp. 246, 247, 276.

30. *New York Times,* November 10, 1917.

31. New York *Tribune,* December 13, 1917.

32. New York *Herald Tribune,* August 5, 1914.

33. *New York Times,* November 8, 1918.

34. *Ibid.*, August 14, 1919.

35. Statement of Hyman Lachowsky, August 23, 1918, MID MSS.

36. *Trial* transcript, pp. 214–18.

37. *Ibid.*, pp. 716–17.

38. *Ibid.*, pp. 660, 470, 711.

39. *Ibid.*, p. 660.

40. Statement of Samuel Lipman, August 23, 1918, MID MSS.

41. *Ibid.*

42. *Trial* transcript, pp. 661–64.

43. *Ibid.*, pp. 470–74, 610.

44. *Ibid.*, p. 477.

45. *Ibid.*, p. 475.

46. Statement of Jacob Abrams, August 23, 1918, MID MSS.

47. *Trial* transcript, p. 475.

48. Statement of Jacob Schwartz, August 23, 1918, MID MSS.

49. Statement of Gabriel Prober, August 23, 1918, *ibid.*

50. Statement of Mollie Steimer, August 23, 1918, *ibid.*

51. *Trial* transcript, p. 709.

52. *Ibid.*, pp. 745–46, 280.

53. Biddle to Director, Military Intelligence Branch, October 25, 1918, MID MSS.

54. Boris Aurin, "A Narrative of the 'Third Degree' " [n.d.], American Civil Liberties Union MSS, Vol. 91. A shorter version was published in *Freedom* I (January 15, 1919), pp. 3, 5.

55. Michael Fiaschetti, *"You Gotta Be Rough"* (Garden City, 1930), pp. 240–42.

56. Cornelius W. Willemse, *Behind the Green Lights* (Garden City, 1931), p. 543.

57. Zechariah Chafee *et al.*, *The Third Degree* (New York, 1931), p. 90.

58. Biddle to Director, August 30, 1918, MID MSS.

59. Caffey to Potter, September 4, 1918, *ibid.*

60. Francis G. Caffey, "Suffrage Limitations at the South," *Political Science Quarterly*, XX (March 1905), 56, 61.

61. Caffey to M. J. Jusserand, October 16, 1917; Caffey to Samuel W. Catts, November 2, 1917, Francis G. Caffey MSS.

62. *New York Times*, July 15, 1917.

63. Bettman to O'Brian, June 3, 1918; Bettman to Attorney General, June 3, 1918, O'Brian MSS, Box 17.

64. O'Brian to Attorney General, June 4, 1918, *ibid.*

65. Upton Sinclair to Caffey, May 3, 1918; Caffey to Sinclair, May 10, 1918, Wilson MSS, Reel 96.

66. Charles Recht, "Autobiography," Chapter 2, pp. 15–16, in Granville Hicks MSS.

67. New York *Call*, April 26, 1918.

68. Abrams was also indicted for possessing a forged draft classification card, and Lipman for possessing fraudulent classification and registration cards, but they were not prosecuted on these charges.

69. Caffey to Attorney General, November 1, 1918, Department of Justice MSS (DJ MSS).

70. Copies of the indictments can be found in the DJ MSS.

71. Caffey to Attorney General, October 21, 1918, DJ MSS.

72. O'Brian to Caffey, October 25, 1918, *ibid.*

73. Caffey to Attorney General, November 1, 2, 1918, *ibid.*

74. Caffey to Attorney General, November 2, 1918, *ibid.*

75. Bettman to Solicitor General, November 6, 1918, *ibid.*

76. Bettman to Zechariah Chafee, October 27, 1919, Chafee MSS, Box 14.

77. Bettman to O'Brian, July 13, 1918, O'Brian MSS, Box 17.

78. Recht, "Autobiography," ch. 2, p. 14, Hicks MSS.

79. Rose Weiss to Frances Witherspoon, May 20, 1919, New York Bureau of Legal Advice MSS, Box 4.

80. Hale to Tom Mooney, September 23, 1920, Mooney MSS, Box 5.

81. Harry Weinberger, "A Rebel's Interrupted Autobiography," *American Journal of Economics and Sociology*, II (October 1942), 111–22.

82. Cited in Jerold Auerbach, *Unequal Justice* (New York, 1976), p. 100.

83. Weinberger, "Rebel's Interrupted Autobiography," *loc. cit.*, p. 115.

84. *Ibid.*, p. 114.

85. Henry George, *Progress and Poverty* (New York, 1948 ed.), pp. 544–52.

86. *Ibid.*, p. 368.

87. Harry Weinberger to Lyman Abbott, October 17, 1917, cited in Willard Cates, Jr., "Harry Weinberger: A Civil Libertarian and His Times, 1915–1942," (Senior thesis, Yale University, 1964).

88. Speech by Harry Weinberger before the Joint Public Health Committee, March 4, 1915, Weinberger MSS, Box 49.

89. *Ibid.*

90. Harry Weinberger, "Vaccination and the Law," *The Open Door*, VII (November 1917), 5–6.

91. *Jacobson* v. *Massachusetts,* 197 U. S. 11 (1905).

92. Weinberger, "Rebel's Interrupted Autobiography," *loc. cit.*, p. 114.

93. Mark Twain, *The Mysterious Stranger and Other Stories* (New York, 1922 ed.), pp. 119–20.

94. Weinberger to Goldman, January 5, 1915; November 9, 1916, Weinberger MSS, Box 28.

95. Goldman to Agnes Inglis, June 29, 1917, Goldman MSS (Labadie).

96. Fred D. Ragan, "An Unlikely Alliance: Tom Watson, Harry Weinberger, and the World War I Draft," *The Atlanta Historical Journal,* XXV (Fall 1981), 27–29.

97. *New York Times,* December 14, 1917.

98. *Selective Draft Law Cases,* 245 U. S. 366, 390 (1917).

99. Weinberger to Tom Watson, January 9, 1918, cited in Cates, "Harry Weinberger," p. 4.

100. Goldman to Weinberger, January 8, 1918, Weinberger MSS, Box 28.

101. Weinberger to Goldman, January 15, 1918, *ibid.*

102. Weinberger to George Chase, April 24, 1919, ACLU MSS, Vol. 108.

103. Weinberger to George Chase, April 18, 1919, *ibid.*

104. Goldman to Weinberger, September 1, 1918, Weinberger MSS, Box 28.

105. Weinberger to Abrams, September 10, 1918, *ibid.*, Box 1.

106. Weinberger to Abrams, September 11, 1918, *ibid.*

107. Weinberger to Abrams, September 28, 1918, *ibid.*

108. Demurrer, September 25, 1918, Records of the U. S. District Court, Southern District, New York (C-14-458).

## 3. The Trial

1. New York *World,* October 12, 1918; *New York Times,* October 12, 1918; *ibid.*, September 17, 1918.

2. New York *World,* October 15, 1918.

3. *Ibid.*, October 12, 1918.

4. *New York Times,* October 18, 1918.

5. *Ibid.*, October 16, 1918.

6. "Harlem's War Activities Many and Varied," *Harlem Magazine,* VII (October 1918), 9, 14.

7. Steffens to Allen H. Suggett, October 15, 1918, Lincoln Steffens MSS, Series III, Reel 2.

8. New York *Tribune,* October 16, 1918.

9. "Motion Pictures and the War," *Current Opinion,* LXIV (June 1918), 402; *New York Times,* April 5, 1918; *ibid.*, April 29, 1918.

10. Gregory to Wilson, September 9, 1918, Woodrow Wilson MSS, Reel 353. For the slacker raids, see Joan Jensen's history of the American Protective League, *The Price of Vigilance* (Chicago, 1968), pp. 203–18.

11. Charles DeWoody to A. Bruce Bielaski, August 7, 1918, Bureau of Investigation MSS, File 124895.

12. Baldwin to John Lord O'Brian, September 13, 1918, American Civil Liberties Union MSS, Vol. 107.

13. Stokes to Olive Dargan, July 30, 1918, Rose Pastor Stokes MSS (Yale), Box 3.

14. Caroline A. Lowe to Eugene V.

Debs, August 28, 1918, Debs MSS, Reel 2.

15. A-105, "Bolsheviki and Anarchist," October 25, 1918, Military Intelligence Reports MSS, Reel 10.

16. For the influenza epidemic, see Alfred W. Crosby, *Epidemic and Peace, 1918* (Westport, Conn., 1976).

17. J. J. Keegan, "The Prevailing Pandemic of Influenza," *Journal of the American Medical Association*, LXXI (September 28, 1918), 1050.

18. U. S. Treasury Department, *Public Health Reports*, XXXIII (November 8, 1918), 1933.

19. John W. Nuzum *et al.*, "Pandemic Influenza and Pneumonia in a Large Civil Hospital," *Journal of the American Medical Association*, LXXI (November 9, 1918), 1562.

20. Royal S. Copeland, "Fighting Influenza With Transit Systems," *The American City*, XIX (November 1918), 388.

21. Cited in Crosby, *Epidemic and Peace*, p. 47.

22. Keegan, "Prevailing Pandemic of Influenza," 1050.

23. New York *World*, October 18, 1918.

24. Lincoln Steffens to Allen H. Suggett, October 15, 1918, Steffens MSS, Series III, Reel 2.

25. Goldman to Weinberger, October 27, 1918, Weinberger MSS, Box 28.

26. Steimer to Goldman, January 5, 1930, Steimer–Flechine MSS.

27. Emma Goldman, *Living My Life* (New York, 1931), II, 666.

28. Upton Sinclair, *Boston* (New York, 1928), p. 177.

29. New York *Call*, November 13, 1920.

30. Political Prisoners Defense and Relief Committee, *Sentenced to Twenty Years Prison* (New York, 1918), pp. 10–12, 14–15.

31. Boris Aurin, "A Narrative of the 'Third Degree,' " ACLU MSS, Vol. 91.

32. New York *Call*, November 13, 1920.

33. Death Certificate, Jacob Schwartz (New York City Bureau of Records).

34. Weinberger to Zechariah Chafee, February 4, 1920, Chafee MSS, Box 29.

35. Jeremiah A. O'Leary, *My Political Trial and Experiences* (New York, 1919), p. 207.

36. "In Re: Anarchists Held in Tombs, N. Y., Awaiting Trial," October 15, 1918, BI-MSS (FOIA), 61–158.

37. O'Leary, *Political Trial*, pp. 208–11.

38. A-105, "Meeting in Memory of Schwartz," October 26, 1918, MIR-MSS, Reel 10.

39. "Meeting Held in Memoriam of Jacob Schwartz . . . October 25, 1918," Alexander Berkman MSS (Tamiment), Box 1.

40. Report, September 17, 1918, enclosed with "Bolsheviki Movement in America," October 2, 1918, MIR-MSS, Reel 12.

41. "Meeting Held in Memoriam . . .," Berkman MSS, Box 1.

42. A-105, "Meeting in Memory," October 26, 1918, MIR-MSS, Reel 10.

43. *Nolle prosequi*, November 10, 1931, Records of the U.S. District Court, Southern District, New York.

44. Note [November 1918?], John Reed MSS, Box 30.

45. Hand to Caffey, July 9, 1918, Learned Hand MSS, Box 15.

46. Cited in Walter J. Fleming, *Civil War and Reconstruction in Alabama* (Cleveland, 1911), pp. 385–86; Victoria Hunter Clayton, *White and Black Under the Old Regime* (Milwaukee, 1899), p. 178.

47. Clayton, *White and Black*, pp. 61, 129, 131–32, 165, 188.

48. *New York Times*, February 13, 1916.

49. New York *Herald Tribune*, October 14, 1918.

50. Clayton to John Sharp Williams, October 8, 1918, Henry D. Clayton MSS, Box 530.

51. New York *Herald Tribune*, October 14, 1918.

52. See Karl Rodabaugh, "Congressman Henry D. Clayton, Patriarch in Politics: A Southern Congressman During the Progressive Era," *The Alabama Review*, XXXI (April 1978), 110–20.

53. Thomas McAdory Owen, *History of Alabama and Dictionary of Alabama Biography* (Spartanburg, 1978; reprint of 1921 ed.), I, 551–53.

54. Clayton to George Sutherland, December 15, 1916, Hand MSS, Box 17.

55. Clayton to A. Mitchell Palmer, July 21, 1915, Woodrow Wilson MSS, Reel 535.

56. Gompers to Clayton, November 19, 1914, American Federation of Labor—Samuel Gompers MSS, Reel 78.

57. Karl Rodabaugh, "Congressman Henry D. Clayton and the Dothan Post Office Fight: Patronage and Politics in the Progressive Era," *The Alabama Review*, XXXIII (April 1980), 125–49.

58. Clayton to S. H. Dent, January 19, 1916; Secretary to John Sharp Williams, January 21, 1916, Clayton MSS, Box 526.

59. Clayton to Ollie M. James, August 12, 1916, *ibid.*, Box 527.

60. Clayton to Hand, April 21, 1917; Clayton to George Sutherland, December 15, 1916, Hand MSS, Box 17.

61. Clayton to Henry C. Walthour, March 15, 1917, Clayton MSS, Box 527.

62. Clayton to John Sharp Williams, October 8, 1918, *ibid.*, Box 530.

63. *Congressional Record*, 62nd Congress, 3rd Session (February 19, 1913), p. 3418.

64. *New York Times*, January 7, 1916.

65. Bertram Clayton to Henry Clayton, April 5, 1917, Clayton MSS, Box 528.

66. Clayton to Alice K. Davis, June 4, 1918, *ibid.*, Box 529.

67. Clayton to Bettie Clayton, November 21, 1918, *ibid.*, Box 530.

68. Harry Weinberger to Agnes Inglis, February 11, 1920, Weinberger MSS, Box 1.

69. Clayton to Jeff D. Clayton, October 3, 1918, Clayton MSS, Box 530.

70. Clayton to George Stuart, September 5, 1918, *ibid.*, Box 530.

71. Clayton to George Stuart, September 9, 1918, *ibid.*, Box 530.

72. Clayton to "Dear Little Mother [-in-law]," September 9, 1918, *ibid.*, Box 530.

73. Clayton to George S. Graham, September 18, 1918, *ibid.*, Box 530.

74. Clayton to D. C. Allen, October 10, 1918, *ibid.*, Box 530.

75. Caffey to Zechariah Chafee, June 10, 1920, Chafee MSS, Box 29.

76. Weinberger to Agnes Inglis,

February 11, 1920, Weinberger MSS, Box 1.

77. Weinberger to Zechariah Chafee, February 20, 1920, Weinberger MSS, Box 1; Weinberger to Chafee, February 4, 1920, Chafee MSS, Box 29.

78. *Trial* transcript, pp. 839–40.

79. Charles DeWoody to Francis G. Caffey, September 28, 1918, Records of the U.S. Attorneys and Marshals: World War I Cases, Box 94.

80. Weinberger to Chafee, February 4, 1920, Chafee MSS, Box 29.

81. Nicholas Biddle to Director, Military Intelligence, October 25, 1918, MID-MSS.

82. *Trial* transcript, p. 254.

83. Caffey to Attorney General, December 18, 1918, Department of Justice MSS.

84. *Trial* transcript, p. 341.

85. *Ibid.*, p. 138.

86. *Ibid.*, pp. 123–25.

87. *Ibid.*, pp. 224, 219, 260.

88. *Ibid.*, pp. 172–93.

89. *Ibid.*, pp. 302–3.

90. Diary, October 17, 1918, Robins MSS.

91. *Trial* transcript, p. 320.

92. Edgar Sisson, *One Hundred Red Days* (New Haven, 1931), pp. 39–42, 208–9, 262.

93. *Ibid.*, p. 291.

94. Sisson Memorandum, May 31, 1918, Albert S. Burleson MSS, Box 21.

95. "For Creel from Sisson," [n.d.], Wilson MSS, Reel 100.

96. The committee, consisting of J. Franklin Jameson and Samuel N. Harper, inspected the sixty-eight documents for a week. Unsure about the authenticity of fifteen documents, they declared, "we have no hesitation in declaring that we see no reason to doubt the genuineness or authenticity" of the fifty-three others. For devastating critiques of the Jameson-Harper report, see George Blakey, *Historians on the Homefront* (Lexington, Ky., 1970), pp. 98–104, and Carol Gruber, *Mars and Minerva* (Baton Rouge, 1975), pp. 151–57.

97. Mary E. Dreier, *Margaret Dreier Robins: Her Life, Letters, and Work* (New York, 1950), p. 25.

98. William Hard, *Raymond Robins' Own Story* (New York, 1920), pp. 6–7.

99. Sisson, *One Hundred Red Days*, p. 214.

100. Hard, *Robins' Own Story*, pp. 138–39. See also Sister Anne Vincent Meiburger, *Efforts of Raymond Robins Toward the Recognition of Soviet Russia and the Outlawry of War, 1917–1933* (Washington, 1958).

101. Report by Raymond Robins [June 1918], pp. 10, 26, Hiram Johnson MSS, Part III, Carton 12; Robins to Margaret Dreier Robins, September 5, 1918, enclosing copy of *Anaconda Standard* of same date, Margaret Dreier Robins MSS, Reel 55; Hard, *Robins' Own Story*, p. 242.

102. Memo for the Chief of Staff, "Bolsheviki propaganda in the U.S.," July 22, 1918, MIR-MSS, Reel 33.

103. Raymond to Margaret Robins, September 15, 1918, Margaret Dreier Robins MSS, Reel 55.

104. Raymond to Margaret Robins, September 15, 1918; Margaret to Raymond Robins, May 1, 1919, Margaret Dreier Robins MSS, Reel 55.

105. Robins to Theodore Roosevelt, August 24, 1918, Roosevelt MSS, Reel 289.

106. Robins to Alex Gumberg, July 19, 1918, Robins MSS, Reel 4.

107. Raymond to Margaret Robins, September 15, 1918, Margaret Dreier Robins MSS, Reel 55.

108. Reed to Margaret Robins, Robins MSS, Reel 4.

109. Robins to Theodore Roosevelt, October 15, 1918, Roosevelt MSS, Reel 295.

110. Gifford Pinchot to Robins, October 17, 1918, Robins MSS, Reel 4.

111. New York *World*, October 15, 1918.

112. *Trial* transcript, p. 320.

113. *Ibid.*, pp. 321, 323.

114. *Ibid.*, pp. 329–50.

115. Diary, October 18, 1918, Robins MSS.

116. Albert Rhys Williams, *Journey into Revolution* (Chicago, 1969), pp. 315–16.

117. Joshua Kunitz, "Albert Rhys Williams: A Biographical Sketch," in Williams, *Through the Russian Revolution* (New York, 1967 ed.), p. lxvii.

118. *Trial* transcript, pp. 351–68.

119. *Ibid.*, pp. 374–75.

120. George Kennan, *Russia Leaves the War* (Princeton, 1958), pp. 454, 498.

121. *Trial* transcript, pp. 373–74.

## 4. THE CONVICTION

1. *New York Times*, October 22, 1918.

2. "Evidence—Province of the Court," *Yale Law Journal*, XXX (1920), 196.

3. *Trial* transcript, p. 387.

4. *Ibid.*, pp. 380–81.

5. *Ibid.*, p. 453.

6. *Ibid.*, p. 489.

7. *Ibid.*, p. 389.

8. *Ibid.*, p. 398.

9. *Ibid.*, p. 389.

10. *Ibid.*, pp. 426–28.

11. *Ibid.*, p. 433.

12. *Ibid.*, pp. 434–36.

13. *Ibid.*, pp. 443–46.

14. *Ibid.*, pp. 521–22.

15. *Ibid.*, pp. 529–30.

16. *Ibid.*, p. 545.

17. *Ibid.*, p. 483.

18. *Ibid.*, pp. 549–50.

19. *Ibid.*, pp. 559–60.

20. *Ibid.*, p. 592.

21. *Ibid.*, pp. 603–4.

22. *Ibid.*, pp. 640, 638.

23. *Ibid.*, p., 641.

24. *Ibid.*, p. 642.

25. *Ibid.*, p. 718.

26. *Ibid.*, pp. 453–54.

27. Kate Richards O'Hare to Frank O'Hare, May 18, 1920, in O'Hare, *Dear Sweethearts* (St. Louis, 1920); Emma Goldman, *Living My Life* (New York, 1931), II, 701.

28. New York *Call*, October 18, 1918.

29. Kate Richards O'Hare to Frank O'Hare, May 23, 1920, in O'Hare, *Dear Sweethearts;* Goldman, *Living My Life*, II, 701.

30. New York *Call*, November 13, 1920.

31. *Ibid.*

32. Steimer to Goldman, January 5, 1930, Steimer–Flechine MSS.

33. Steimer to Paul Avrich, April 18, 1975. Paul Avrich graciously permitted me to consult his file of correspondence with Mollie Steimer.

34. New York *Call*, October 18, 1918.

35. *New York Times,* October 23, 1918.

36. *Trial* transcript, p. 683.

37. *Ibid.,* pp. 687–88.

38. *Ibid.,* pp. 689–94.

39. *Ibid.,* pp. 695–97.

40. *Ibid.,* pp. 697–99.

41. *Ibid.,* pp. 700–3.

42. *Ibid.,* p. 703.

43. *Ibid.,* p. 828.

44. *Ibid.,* p. 708.

45. *Ibid.,* pp. 708–9.

46. *Ibid.,* p. 713.

47. *Ibid.,* p. 707.

48. New York *Tribune,* October 24, 1918; Emma Goldman to Stella Ballantine, November 3, 1918, Goldman MSS (IISG), XVI–9.

49. *Trial* transcript, p. 755.

50. Political Prisoners Defense and Relief Committee, *Sentenced to Twenty Years Prison* (New York, 1918), pp. 21–29. The leaflet was written by Leonard Abbott.

51. Unidentified newspaper clipping enclosed in Mollie Steimer to Margaret Marsh, April 28, 1978. I am indebted to Margaret Marsh for permission to consult her file of correspondence with Mollie Steimer.

52. New York *Call,* October 24, 1918.

53. *Trial* transcript, pp. 766–67.

54. *Ibid.,* p. 769.

55. *Ibid.,* pp. 770–74.

56. *Ibid.,* pp. 774–78.

57. *Ibid.,* pp. 774–76.

58. *Ibid.,* p. 786.

59. *Ibid.,* pp. 793–95.

60. *Ibid.,* pp. 802–3.

61. *New York Times,* October 22, 1918.

62. New York *Call,* October 24, 1918.

63. Weinberger to H. J. Seligman, November 2, 1918, Weinberger MSS, Box 1.

64. *Trial* transcript, p. 812.

65. *Ibid.,* p. 814.

66. Unidentified newspaper clipping enclosed in Steimer to Marsh, April 28, 1978.

67. New York *Tribune,* October 24, 1918.

68. Joseph and Manya Spivak to Jacob Abrams, October 24, 1918. The telegram is in the possession of Paul Avrich, who kindly made it available to me.

69. Clayton to Charles C. Thach, September 16, 1918, Clayton MSS, Box 530.

70. *Trial* transcript, pp. 822–26.

71. *Ibid.,* pp. 826–28.

72. *Ibid.,* pp. 828–29.

73. *Ibid.,* pp. 829–32.

74. *Ibid.,* p. 837.

75. *Ibid.,* pp. 832–35.

76. *Ibid.,* pp. 844–46.

77. *Ibid.,* pp. 846–48.

78. *Ibid.,* pp. 850–53.

79. *Ibid.,* pp. 853–55.

80. *Ibid.,* pp. 856–63.

81. *Ibid.,* pp. 864–65.

82. *Ibid.,* pp. 865–69.

83. *Ibid.,* pp. 869–71.

84. New York *Call,* October 26, 1918.

85. *New York Times,* October 28, 1918.

86. Hugo H. Ritterbusch to Clayton, October 26, 1918, Clayton MSS, Box 530.

87. "An American Citizen" to Clayton, October 22, 1918, *ibid.*

88. "American Bolsheviks Get Twenty Years," *The Negro Worker,* Steimer–Flechine MSS.

89. Goldman, *Living My Life,* II, 667; Goldman to Harry Weinber-

ger, October 27, 1918, Weinberger MSS.

90. A-105 Report "The anarchist group and the Bolsheviki," October 30, 1918, MIR-MSS, Reel 10.

91. "Our Ferocious Sentences," *The Nation*, November 1918, p. 504.

92. Weinberger, "Answering Memorandum for Plaintiffs-in-Error on Motion to Admit to Bail," November 7, 1918, Weinberger MSS, Box 2. (Most of the legal documents can also be found in the U.S. District Court MSS, and in the Department of Justice MSS.)

93. Clayton, "Order," enclosed as Exhibit A in Weinberger, "Motion to Admit Plaintiffs-in-Error to Bail," October 29, 1918, *ibid.*

94. "Assignments of Error," enclosed as Exhibit B in Weinberger, "Motion to Admit Plaintiffs-in-Error to Bail, *ibid.*

95. Hughes to Bettman, October 31, 1918, DJ-MSS.

96. Caffey to Bettman, November 2, 1918, *ibid.*

97. Todd, "Memorandum for the United States on Motion to Admit Plaintiffs-in-Error to Bail," November 5, 1918, Weinberger MSS, Box 2.

98. Weinberger, "Answering Memorandum," *ibid.*

99. *Ibid.* The case cited was *Hudson* v. *Parker*, 156 U.S. 277.

100. Weinberger to Learned Hand, December 3, 1918, Weinberger MSS, Box 1. (Caffey waived the additional bail already set for Abrams and Lipman, who had also been indicted for violation of the Selective Service Act.)

101. These transactions are recorded on the Criminal Docket, 509-15-23, in the U.S. District Court MSS.

102. Blossom to Weinberger, November 23, 1919, Weinberger MSS, Box 1.

103. Weinberger to Eugene Boissevain, November 13, 1918, *ibid.*

104. Clayton to Weinberger, November 23, 1918, *ibid.*

105. Weinberger to Emma Goldman, April 25, 1919, *ibid.*, Box 28.

106. Weinberger, "Answering Memorandum," *ibid.*, Box 2.

107. Anna L. Fox to Weinberger, February 14, 1919, *ibid.*, Box 1.

108. Weinberger to Goldman, May 8, 1919, *ibid.*, Box 28.

109. Goldman to Weinberger, May 18, 1919, *ibid.*

110. Clayton to Caffey, February 24, 1919, DJ MSS.

111. A-105, "IWW and Bolsheviki Activities," November 19, 1918, MIR-MSS, Reel 33.

## 5. THE SURVEILLANCE STATE

1. J. G. Tucker, "In Re: Samuel Lipman," October 15, 1919, Bureau of Investigation MSS, Reel 302.

2. *Fong Yue Ting* v. *United States*, 149 U.S. 698.

3. *Yamataya* v. *Fisher*, 189 U.S. 86.

4. See Jane Perry Clark, *Deportation of Aliens from the United States to Europe* (New York, 1931), ch. 2; Howard L. Bevis, "The Deportation of Aliens," *University of Pennsylvania Law Review*, LXVIII (January 1920), 97–119.

5. Act of February 5, 1917 (39 Stat. 874).

6. *Lopez* v. *Howe,* 259 Fed. 401.

7. *U.S.* v. *Stuppiello,* 260 Fed. 483.

8. Act of October 16, 1918 (40 Stat. 1012).

9. *Congressional Record,* 65th Congress, 2nd Session, pp. 8109, 8111, 8125.

10. *Ibid.*, pp. 8939–40.

11. *Ibid.*, p. 8117.

12. Caminetti to Caroline A. Lowe, March 21, 1919, American Civil Liberties Union MSS, Vol. 84.

13. *CR,* 65-2, p. 8111.

14. John Dillon and Leonard Arnold to Commanding Officer, December 20, 1918, MIR-MSS, Reel 11.

15. S-500, "In re: Russian Bolsheviki," January 31, 1919, BI-MSS, Reel 96.

16. Lipman to Berkman, March 7, 1919, BI-MSS, Reel 87A.

17. "Weekly Meeting—Ferrer Modern School," May 4, 1919, Lusk Committee MSS, Box 5.

18. O-22 Reports, June 28, August 16, 1919, *ibid,* Box 4.

19. O-22 Report, October 14, 1919, *ibid.*

20. Robert K. Murray, *Red Scare* (Minneapolis, 1955), p. 79. The man killed in the blast was apparently Carlo Valdinocci; see William Young and David E. Kaiser, *Postmortem: New Evidence in the Case of Sacco and Vanzetti* (Amherst, 1985), pp. 20–21.

21. *New York Times,* August 14, 1919.

22. Enright to Hylan, November 15, 1918, John F. Hylan MSS, Box 28.

23. New York *Call,* March 10, 1919.

24. *New York Times,* March 31, 1920.

25. Enright to Hylan, February 3, 1919, Hylan MSS, Box 27.

26. Enright to Hylan, June 25, 1919, *ibid.*, Box 44.

27. *Annual Report of the Police Commissioner, 1919* (New York, 1920), p. 53.

28. Frank Donner, *The Age of Surveillance* (New York, 1980), p. 33.

29. Cited in *ibid.*, p. 34.

30. Cited in Max Lowenthal, *The Federal Bureau of Investigation* (New York, 1950), pp. 83–84. *See also* Richard Gid Powers, *Secrecy and Power: The Life of J. Edgar Hoover* (New York, 1987), pp. 63–74.

31. "Memorandum Upon the Work of the Radical Division," August 1, 1919 to March 15, 1920, BI-MSS, Reel 302.

32. *Ibid.*

33. *Ibid.*

34. Hoover, "Report Upon New York Trip," October 8–9, 1919, *ibid.*

35. *Ibid.*

36. Hoover to Colonel A. B. Cox, August 14, 1920, MIR-MSS, Reel 33.

37. War Department, *Annual Report, 1919* (Washington, 1920), p. 331; *ibid., 1920* (Washington, 1921), p. 222.

38. John B. Trevor to Director, May 2, 1919, MIR-MSS, Reel 12.

39. Nicholas Biddle to Director, November 1, 1918, *ibid.*, Reel 10.

40. Archibald Stevenson to John B. Trevor, January 15, 1919, *ibid.*, Reel 12.

41. Morris Hillquit to Seymour Stedman, January 22, 1920, Morris Hillquit MSS, Reel 2.

42. Stevenson to Nicholas Biddle, November 12, 1918, MIR-MSS, Reel 12.

43. Stevenson to Biddle, November 23, 1918, *ibid.*, Reel 11.

44. Dunn to Biddle, November 29, 1918, *ibid.*

45. *New York Times,* January 28, 1919.

46. On the Lusk Committee, *see* Lawrence H. Chamberlain, *Loyalty and Legislative Action* (Ithaca, 1951), ch. 1; Julian F. Jaffe, *Crusade Against Radicalism* (Port Washington, 1972); and Patricia Wesson Wingo, "Clayton R. Lusk: A Study of Patriotism in New York Politics, 1919–1925," (Ph. D. Diss., Univ. of Georgia, 1966).

47. Clayton R. Lusk, "Hatching Revolution in America," *Current Opinion,* LXXI (September 1921), 294.

48. *Annual Report, 1919,* p. 54.

49. Memorandum on Organization, Lusk Committee MSS, Box 2.

50. *New York Times,* June 7, 1919.

51. BB, "In re: Analysis of Individuals Engaged in Anarchist Activities," March 19, 1920, BI-MSS, Reel 96-B.

52. "Memorandum upon the Work of the Radical Division," *ibid.,* Reel 302.

53. "Convention of the Russian Soviets," [March 24, 1919], Lusk Committee MSS, Box 5.

54. "Re: John Reed *et al.,* Bolshevik Meeting," May 20, 1918, MIR-MSS, Reel 4.

55. "In re: Mass Meeting to Celebrate the Birth of Eugene V. Debs," November 5, 1919, BI-MSS, Reel 61-B.

56. U-25, "In Re: Radical, Industrial Situation in New York City," April 20, 1918, *ibid.,* Reel 97-B.

57. O-99 Report, January 2, 1918, MIR-MSS, Reel 33.

58. M. J. Driscoll to Stevenson, June 7, 1919, Lusk Committee MSS, Box 3.

59. John Purdie Report, April 13, 1919, *ibid.,* Box 5.

60. "May Day Meeting at Forward Hall," May 1, 1919, *ibid.*

61. Margaret M. Scully to R. W. Finch, October 28, 1919, *ibid.,* Box 3.

62. Benjamin Levy Report, August 3, 1919, *ibid.,* Box 4.

63. Levy Report, July 4, 1919, *ibid.*

64. Levy Report, July 25, 1919, *ibid.*

65. Acting Chief to W. M. Offley, January 30, 1919, BI-MSS, Reel 97-B; see also Gary T. Marx, "Thoughts on a Neglected Category of Social Movement Participant: The Agent Provocateur and the Informant," *American Journal of Sociology,* LXXX (September 1974), 418–20.

66. C. L. Converse to W. L. Moffat, Jr., February 17, 1919, MIR-MSS, Reel 12.

67. "Radical Meeting," April 25, 1919, Lusk Committee MSS, Box 5.

68. George F. Lamb to Director, October 4, 1920, BI-MSS, Reel 97-B.

69. Marion Barling (pseudo, Margaret M. Scully) reports, October 30–31, and November 5–6, 1919, are in the Lusk Committee MSS, Boxes 3 and 4.

70. R. W. Finch, "In Re: Confidential Informant B-10," November 20, 1918, BI-MSS, Reel 96-B.

71. C. J. Scully, "In Re: Anarchist Soviet Bulletin," December 5, 1919, *ibid.,* Reel 271.

72. J. P. McDevitt, "Re: . . . Minna Lowensohn," December 29, 1919, *ibid.*

73. Victor Valjaveo, "In re: Anarchists Organization of the World," December 6, 1919, *ibid.,* Reel 96-B.

74. Frank B. Faulhaber, "In re: Anarchist Activities," September 22, 1919, *ibid.,* Reel 271.

75. *The Anarchist Soviet Bulletin* (April 1919).

76. *Ibid.* (June 1919).

77. *Ibid.*

78. *Ibid.* (September 1919).

79. *Ibid.* (August 1919).

80. Steimer to Goldman, January 5, 1930, Steimer–Flechine MSS.

81. "In re: Radical Activities in New York," January 30, 1919, MIR-MSS, Reel 12. See also the "Autobiographical Note" in Marcus Graham (ed.), *MAN! An Anthology* (London, 1974), pp. viii–xxi.

82. Hutchins Hapgood, *A Victorian in the Modern World* (New York, 1939), p. 327.

83. J. P. McDevitt, "Re: Emma Goldman . . .," December 29, 1919, BI-MSS, Reel 271.

84. On Havel, see Paul Avrich, *The Modern School Movement* (Princeton, 1980), pp. 121–24.

85. "Special Memo for Chief," December 30, 1919, BI-MSS, Reel 95-B.

86. J. P. McDevitt, "The Anarchist Soviet Bulletin . . .," January 19, 1920, *ibid.*, Reel 271.

87. Hoover, "Report of Radical Section," October 10, 1919, *ibid.*, Reel 302.

88. Reports on "American Anarchist Federated Commune Soviets," by Frank B. Stone, August 12, 1919, and G. J. Crystal, August 19, 1919, *ibid.*, Reel 271.

89. Copies of the leaflet are in the Weinberger MSS, Box 3.

90. Unidentified clipping in Department of Justice MSS.

91. Emmet T. Drew, "Special Report," May 20, 1920, BI-MSS, Reel 271.

92. Hoover to Anthony Caminetti, October 14, 1919, *ibid.*, Reel 301.

93. Weinberger to Caminetti, March 14 and 17, 1919, Weinberger MSS, Box 2.

94. Hoover, "Report of Radical Section," October 3, 1919, BI-MSS, Reel 302.

95. Newspaper clippings, September 18, 1919, enclosed in Steimer to Margaret Marsh, April 27, 1978.

96. The deposition is in the Weinberger MSS, Box 3.

97. New York *Globe*, September 18, 1919, enclosed in Steimer to Marsh.

98. Frank Faulhaber, "In re: Anarchist Activities, September 30, 1919," and Mortimer J. Davis, "In re: American Anarchist Federated Commune Soviet," September 24, 1919, BI-MSS, Reel 278.

99. Faulhaber, "Anarchist Activities," September 22, 1919, MID-MSS.

100. C. J. Scully, "In re: Mollie Steimer," September 25, 1919, BI-MSS, Reel 278.

101. Davis, "In re: American Anarchist . . .," September 24, 1919, *ibid.*

102. Hoover, "Report of Radical Section," October 3, 1919, *ibid.*, Reel 302.

103. George F. Lamb to Frank Burke, September 30, 1919, *ibid.*, Reel 278.

104. *Ibid.*

105. Davis, "In re: Mollie Steimer," October 11, 1919, *ibid.*

106. Davis, "In re: Gus Alonen and Carl Paivio, October 1919, *ibid.*, Reel 243.

107. *New York Times*, October 11, 1919.

108. A copy of the indictment is in the Weinberger MSS, Box 3. William Winters and Ida Luchofsky were indicted along with Steimer.

109. C. J. Scully, "In re: Mollie

Steimer Anarchist," October 20, 1919, BI-MSS, Reel 278.

110. Davis, "In re: Mollie Steimer," October 28, 1919, *ibid.*

111. *Ibid.*

112. *Ibid.*

113. Emma Goldman, *Living My Life* (New York, 1970 ed.), p. 705.

114. Steimer to Goldman, January 5, 1930, Steimer–Flechine MSS.

115. Frederic C. Howe, *The Confessions of a Reformer* (New York, 1925), pp. 129, 113. *See also* Roy Lubove, "Frederic C. Howe and the Quest for Community in America," *The Historian*, XXXIX (February 1977), 270–91.

116. Howe, *Confessions*, pp. 138–39.

117. *Ibid.*, p. 243.

118. *Ibid.*, pp. 253, 257; Howe to Eugene Lyons, August 8, 1919, Elizabeth Gurley Flynn MSS; Frederic C. Howe, "Turned Back in Time of War," *The Survey*, XXXVI (May 6, 1916), 152.

119. "Investigation of Ellis Island Proposed," *The Survey*, XXXVI (July 29, 1916), 446.

120. Howe to Oswald Garrison Villard, October 1, 1915, Villard MSS (1790).

121. Howe to Lincoln Steffens, September 17, 1918, Steffens MSS, Series II, Reel 1.

122. Howe to Albert de Silver, May 17, 1919, ACLU MSS, Vol. 106.

123. Howe, *Confessions*, p. 267.

124. "A Deportee," "My Experiences in the Deportation Wave," [n.d.], ACLU MSS, Vol. 132.

125. Cited in Thomas Pitkin, *Keepers of the Gate: A History of Ellis Island* (New York, 1975), pp. 123–25.

126. Howe, *Confessions*, pp. 279–82.

127. *Ibid.*, pp. 280–81.

128. *Ibid.*, pp. 282, 327–28.

129. *Conditions at Ellis Island.* Hearings before the House Committee on Immigration and Naturalization, House of Representatives, 66th Congress, 1st Session (Washington, 1920), pp. 59–60, 76–79.

130. Steimer to Weinberger, October 24, 1919, Weinberger MSS, Box 2.

131. Mollie Steimer, "To My Comrades," *Freedom*, I (October–November 1919), 8–9.

132. *New York Times;* New York *Call*, October 29, 1919.

133. Steimer to Weinberger, November 6, 1919, Weinberger MSS, Box 2.

134. Kate Claghorn, *The Immigrant's Day in Court* (New York, 1923), pp. 363–64.

135. New York *Call*, November 8, 1919.

136. *Ibid.*

137. Weinberger to A. Mitchell Palmer, February 13, 1920, DJ-MSS.

138. *The Anarchist Soviet Bulletin* (April 1920).

139. Weinberger to Emma Goldman, November 24, 1919, Weinberger MSS, Box 28.

## 6. THE SUPREME COURT

1. *Schaefer* v. *United States*, 251 U.S. 466.

2. Weinberger to Jerome [Weiss], [n.d.], Weinberger MSS, Box 1.

3. Robert M. Cover, "The Left, the Right, and the First Amendment: 1918–1928," *Maryland Law Review*, XL (1981), 354.

4. Robert B. Highsaw, *Edward Douglass White: Defender of the Conservative Faith* (Baton Rouge, 1981), p. 53.

5. *Ibid.*, p. 35.

6. *Ibid.*, pp. 159–60.

7. *Ibid.*, p. 151.

8. James F. Watts, "Joseph McKenna," in Leon Friedman and Fred L. Israel (eds.), *The Justices of the United States Supreme Court, 1789–1969* (New York, 1969), III, 1726.

9. Matthew McDevitt, *Joseph McKenna: Associate Justice of the United States* (Washington, 1946), p. 105.

10. Watts, "Joseph McKenna," p. 1727.

11. *Schaefer* v. *United States*, 251 U.S. 456.

12. Joseph E. McLean, *William Rufus Day: Supreme Court Justice from Ohio* (Baltimore, 1946), pp. 53–54.

13. For many years Day was president of the National McKinley Memorial Association. See Day to Charles E. Bury, November 7, 1915, Day MSS, Box 4.

14. McLean, *Day*, p. 18.

15. *Ibid.*, p. 161.

16. Van Devanter to Winslow Van Devanter, November 1, 1918, Van Devanter MSS, Box 11.

17. Van Devanter to J. H. Farley, February 12, 1920, *ibid.*, Box 12.

18. Alexander M. Bickel and Benno C. Schmidt, Jr., *The Judiciary and Responsible Government, 1910–1921* (New York, 1984), pp. 331–32.

19. John Kirby, Jr., to William Howard Taft, March 15, 1912, Taft MSS, Reel 435.

20. *Pierce et al.* v. *United States*, 252 U.S. 239.

21. Bickel and Schmidt, *Judiciary and Responsible Government*, p. 353.

22. David Burner, "James C. McReynolds," in Friedman and Israel (eds.), *Justices of the Supreme Court*, III, 2023.

23. *Berger* v. *United States*, 255 U.S. 22.

24. Bickel and Schmidt, *Judiciary and Responsible Government*, p. 345.

25. Burner, "James C. McReynolds," p. 2024.

26. Bickel and Schmidt, *Judiciary and Responsible Government*, p. 354.

27. *Ibid.*, p. 355.

28. *Ibid.*, p. 354.

29. *Ibid.*, p. 357. See also Clarke to William Howard Taft, October 31, 1922, Clarke MSS.

30. Clarke to Baker, October 14, 1918, Baker MSS, Reel 4.

31. Clarke to Wilson, November 18, 1918, Wilson MSS, Reel 102.

32. Hoyt Landon Warner, *The Life of Mr. Justice Clarke* (Cleveland, 1959), pp. 100, 75.

33. Highsaw, *White*, p. 154.

34. Mark DeWolfe Howe, *Justice Oliver Wendell Holmes: The Proving Years, 1870–1882* (Cambridge, 1963), pp. 280–81.

35. Oliver Wendell Holmes, *The Common Law* (Boston, 1881; 1963 ed.), pp. 5, 36–38.

36. *Ibid.*, pp. 88, 118.

37. *Patterson* v. *Colorado*, 205 U.S. 454.

38. *Moyer* v. *Peabody*, 212 U.S. 78.

39. Charles P. LeWarne, *Utopias on Puget Sound, 1885–1915* (Seattle, 1975), pp. 212–20.

40. *Fox* v. *State of Washington*, 236 U.S. 273.

41. Holmes to Learned Hand, June 24, 1918, in Gerald Gunther, "Learned

Hand and the Origins of Modern First Amendment Doctrine: Some Fragments of History," *Stanford Law Review*, XXVII (1975), 757.

42. Holmes to Wigmore, November 17, 1915, John Wigmore MSS.

43. Holmes to Hand, June 24, 1918, in Gunther, "Learned Hand," *loc. cit.*

44. Holmes to Laski, July 7, 1918, in Mark DeWolfe Howe (ed.), *Holmes–Laski Letters*, (New York, 1963 ed., abridged by Alger Hiss), I, 160–61.

45. *Transcript, United States* vs. *Charles T. Schenck, et al.*, Records of the U.S. District Court, Eastern District, Pennsylvania.

46. *Schenck* v. *United States*, 249 U.S. 47.

47. Kane to the Attorney General, August 29, 1917, Records of the U.S. Attorney, Eastern District, Pennsylvania.

48. The leaflets may be found in the *Transcript, U.S.* vs. *Schenck.*

49. *Schenck* v. *United States*, 249 U.S. 47.

50. Kane to the Attorney General, August 29, 1917, Records of the U.S. Attorney.

51. F. L. Garbarino, "Socialist Party," August 31, 1917, *ibid.*

52. *Schenck* v. *United States*, 249 U.S. 47.

53. *Transcript, U.S.* vs. *Schenck*, pp. 241, 245, 249.

54. *Schenck* v. *United States*, 249 U.S. 47.

55. *Frohwerk* v. *United States*, 249 U.S. 204.

56. *Ibid.*

57. *Debs* v. *United States*, 249 U.S. 211.

58. Debs to Bolton Hall, July 6, 1918, Eugene V. Debs MSS.

59. *Debs* v. *United States*, 249 U.S. 211.

60. Howe (ed.), *Holmes–Laski Letters*, I, 139; John Stuart Mill, *On Liberty* (1859; New York, 1974 ed.), p. 119.

61. Fred D. Ragan, "Justice Oliver Wendell Holmes, Jr., Zechariah Chafee, Jr., and the Clear and Present Danger Test for Free Speech: The First Year, 1919," *Journal of American History*, LVIII (June 1971), 36; Gunther, "Learned Hand," *loc. cit.*, p. 720.

62. *Ibid.*, pp. 755–56.

63. *Ibid.*, pp. 758–60, 741.

64. Oscar Kraines, *The World and Ideas of Ernst Freund* (University of Alabama, 1974), p. 148; Grace Abbott to Freund, June 26, 1922, Freund MSS.

65. Ernst Freund, "The Debs Case and Freedom of Speech," *The New Republic*, XIX (May 3, 1919), 13–15.

66. *Ibid.* See also Harry Kalven, Jr., "Professor Ernst Freund and *Debs* v. *United States*," *The University of Chicago Law Review*, XL (Winter 1973), 235–39.

67. Cited in Douglas H. Ginsburg, "Afterword," *ibid.*, 244.

68. Howe (ed.), *Holmes–Laski Letters*, I, 152–53.

69. Mark DeWolfe Howe (ed.), *Holmes–Pollock Letters*, 2 vols., (Cambridge, 1961), II, 7; Holmes to John Wigmore, June 7, 1919, Wigmore MSS.

70. Howe (ed.), *Holmes–Laski Letters*, I, 142–43.

71. Zechariah Chafee, "Freedom of Speech in War Time," *Harvard Law Review*, XXXII (June 1919), 932–73.

72. Cited in Ragan, "Justice Oliver Wendell Holmes," *loc. cit.*, p. 43.

73. Howe (ed.), *Holmes–Laski Let-*

*ters,* I, 144; Howe (ed.), *Holmes–Pollock Letters,* II, 8. Holmes's list of all the books he read in 1919 can be found in the Holmes MSS, Reel 61.

74. James Ford Rhodes, *History of the Civil War* (New York, 1917), p. 68.

75. *Ibid.,* pp. 354–55.

76. Harold J. Laski, *Authority in the Modern State* (New Haven, 1919), pp. 55–56, 78–79.

77. Howe (ed.), *Holmes–Laski Letters,* I, 155.

78. Graham Wallas, *The Life of Francis Place* (London, 1919), p. 255.

79. Howe (ed.), *Holmes–Pollock Letters,* II, 22–24.

80. John Locke, *The Second Treatise of Government,* XIV, §159.

81. Howe (ed.), *Holmes–Laski Letters,* I, 162.

82. *Ibid.,* I, 156.

83. F. S. Marvin, *The Century of Hope* (Oxford, 1921 ed.).

84. Howe (ed.), *Holmes–Laski Letters,* I, 147–48.

85. *Ibid.,* I, 165.

86. Weinberger to Tom Watson, September 20, 1919, Weinberger MSS, Box 2.

87. *Brief* for Plaintiffs-in-Error, pp. 11–17.

88. Weinberger to Abrams, August 22, 1919, Weinberger MSS, Box 1.

89. *Brief* for Plaintiffs-in-Error, pp. 24, 35–40.

90. *Ibid.,* pp. 43–47, 50–51.

91. Bettman to Attorney General, May 3, 1919, John Lord O'Brian MSS, Box 17.

92. Bettman to Solicitor General, March 14, 1919, *ibid.,* Box 17.

93. Weinberger to Palmer, May 28, 1919, DJ-MSS.

94. Weinberger to Palmer, August 9, 1919, *ibid.*

95. Baker to Palmer, September 23, 1919; Palmer to Baker, September 29, 1919, DJ-MSS.

96. Stewart to Palmer, September 27, 1919, *ibid.*

97. Stewart to Secretary of State, September 25, 1919, *ibid.*

98. *Brief* on Behalf of the United States, pp. 8–9, 33.

99. *Ibid.,* pp. 19–21.

100. *Ibid.,* p. 28.

101. *Abrams et al.* v. *United States,* 250 U.S. 616.

102. Dean Acheson, *Morning and Noon* (New York, 1965), p. 119.

103. *Mr. Justice Holmes' Opinions,* October Term, 1919, Oliver Wendell Holmes MSS.

104. Howe (ed.), *Holmes–Pollock Letters,* II, 29.

105. Holmes to Mrs. Nina Gray, December 10, 1919, Holmes MSS, Reel 23.

106. *Mr. Justice Holmes' Opinions,* October Term, 1919, Holmes MSS.

107. *Abrams et al.* v. *United States,* 250 U.S. 616; Cover, "The Left, the Right, and the First Amendment, *loc. cit.,* p. 373; Gunther, "Learned Hand," *loc. cit.,* p. 743. For more critical interpretations of the dissent, see G. Edward White, "Looking at Holmes in the Mirror," *Law and History Review,* IV (Fall 1986), 458–59; Yosil Rogat and James F. O'Fallon, "Mr. Justice Holmes: A Dissenting Opinion—the Speech Cases," *Stanford Law Review,* XXXVI (1984), 1349–1406; David M. Rabban, "The First Amendment in Its Forgotten Years," *Yale Law Journal,* XC (1981), 514–80.

108. Howe (ed.), *Holmes–Pollock Letters,* II, 32.

109. Howe (ed.), *Holmes–Laski Letters,* I, 175.

110. *Ibid.*, I, 220, 231, 585.

111. Pound to Holmes, November 26, 1919, Holmes MSS, Reel 26.

112. Zechariah Chafee, "A Contemporary State Trial," *Harvard Law Review*, XXXIII (April 1920), 769, 771.

113. Gunther, "Learned Hand," *loc. cit.*, p. 760.

114. Hand to Chafee, December 3, 1919, Learned Hand MSS, Box 15.

115. Clayton to Ryan, November 17, 1919, Henry DeLamar Clayton MSS, Box 531.

116. Ryan to Hand, November 20, 1919, Hand MSS, Box 15.

117. Samuel Lipman to Minnie Levin, March 20, 1921, Bureau of Prisons MSS (FOIA).

## 7. The Response

1. E. T. Needham, "In re: Samuel Lipman, J. J. Ballam, and Jacob Abrams, Bolshevists," December 4, 1919, BI-MSS, Reel 302. It appears that Ballam did not meet Abrams and Lipman until November 17. So the third "Russian fugitive" might have been Paul Rose, a friend of Abrams and Lipman, who claimed that he accompanied them "with the intention of smuggling them over to Mexico." Paul Rose interview with Paul Avrich, January 25, 1974.

2. Needham, "In re: Samuel Lipman," December 4, 1919, BI-MSS, Reel 302.

3. New Orleans *Times-Picayune;* Boston *Globe;* New York *World*, all December 3, 1919.

4. Lipman to Minnie Levin, March 20, 1921, BP-MSS (FOIA).

5. Abrams to Weinberger, [n.d.], Weinberger MSS, Box 1.

6. Palmer to Caffey, December 6, 1919, DJ-MSS.

7. Weinberger to Assistant United States Attorney, December 17, 1919, Weinberger MSS, Box 2.

8. Statement of Hyman Lachowsky, *ibid.*, Box 2.

9. Statement of Jacob Abrams, December 26, 1919, *ibid.*, Box 1.

10. Statement of Samuel Lipman, December 26, 1919, *ibid.*, Box 2.

11. Weinberger to Lachowsky, December 17, 1919, *ibid.*, Box 2.

12. "Hyman Lachowsky," October 21, 1919, BI-MSS, Reel 301, citing report of August 21, 1919.

13. Mollie Steimer to Paul Avrich, May 15, 1979.

14. Caffey to Palmer, January 6, 1920, DJ-MSS.

15. Weinberger to Abrams, December 29, 1919, Weinberger MSS, Box 1.

16. Weinberger to Lachowsky, December 12, *ibid.*, Box 2; Weinberger to Abrams, December 24, 1919, *ibid.*, Box 1.

17. C. W. German, "An Unfortunate Dissent," *University of Missouri Bar Bulletin*, XXI (1920), 75–80.

18. Edward S. Corwin, "Freedom of Speech and Press Under the First Amendment: A Resume," *Yale Law Journal*, XXX (1920), 54.

19. Day Kimball, "The Espionage Act and the Limits of Legal Toleration," *Harvard Law Review*, XXXIII (1920), 442–49.

20. Cited in William Roalfe, *John Henry Wigmore: Scholar and Reformer* (Evanston, 1977), p. 84. A superb appraisal of Wigmore's work, particularly

*The Principles of Judicial Proof* (1913), can be found in William Twining, *Theories of Evidence: Bentham and Wigmore* (Stanford, 1985).

21. Holmes to Lady Pollock, October 24, 1902, in Howe (ed.), *Holmes–Pollock Letters,* I, 108.

22. Wigmore to Holmes, April 29, 1894, John H. Wigmore MSS; Roalfe, *Wigmore,* p. 12.

23. Roalfe, *Wigmore,* p. 83.

24. *Ibid.,* p. 94.

25. *Ibid.,* p. 95.

26. *Ibid.,* p. 29.

27. Wigmore to Holmes, February 6, 1916, Wigmore MSS.

28. Holmes to Wigmore, February 12, 1916, *ibid.*

29. Wigmore to Franklin K. Lane, July 20, 1915, *ibid.*

30. Roalfe, *Wigmore,* pp. 123–25.

31. Wigmore memorandum for General Crowder, [n.d.], Wigmore MSS.

32. Wigmore, "Report of the Publicity Plans for Registration Day," August 16, 1918, *ibid.*

33. Wigmore, "Guaranteeing One Hundred Percent Registration," July 29, 1918, *ibid.*

34. Wigmore, "Measures Required for Identifying Registrants," August 1, 1918, *ibid.*

35. Roalfe, *Wigmore,* p. 146.

36. Wigmore to Holmes, December 6, 1920, April 1, 1921, Wigmore MSS.

37. John H. Wigmore, "Abrams v. U.S.: Freedom of Speech and Freedom of Thuggery in War-time and Peacetime," *Illinois Law Review,* XIV (1920), 539–61.

38. Caffey to Stewart, April 8, 1920, DJ-MSS.

39. Stewart to Charles F. Clyne, April 13, 1920, *ibid.*

40. Roalfe, *Wigmore,* p. 150.

41. Harold Helboug to Wigmore, April 9, 1920, Wigmore MSS.

42. Wigmore, "Abrams v. U.S.," *loc. cit.,* p. 559.

43. Edmund Burke, *Reflections on the Revolution in France* (1790; New Rochelle, 1966), p. 263. For a sympathetic account of Wigmore's critique of Holmes, see Lee C. Bollinger, *The Tolerant Society: Freedom of Speech and Extremist Speech in America* (Oxford, 1986), pp. 18–23, 141–42.

44. Howe (ed.), *Holmes–Pollock Letters,* II, 42.

45. John Gorham Palfrey, "Introduction," in *ibid.,* p. xv.

46. *Ibid.,* p. xiii.

47. Sir William Holdsworth memorial in *Law Quarterly Review,* LIII (April 1937), 178–79.

48. Cited in *ibid.,* p. 182.

49. Sir Frederick Pollock, *The Genius of the Common Law* (New York, 1912), pp. 2, 124.

50. Sir Frederick Pollock, *Essays in Jurisprudence and Ethics* (London, 1882), pp. 163–65.

51. *Ibid.,* p. 173; Sir Frederick Pollock, *The Expansion of the Common Law* (London, 1904), pp. 105–6.

52. Howe (ed.), *Holmes–Pollock Letters,* I, 245.

53. *Ibid.,* II, 39.

54. *Ibid.,* II, 165.

55. *Ibid.,* II, 166.

56. John Pollock, *The Bolshevik Adventure* (London, 1919), pp. 30, 196–97.

57. Howe (ed.), *Holmes–Pollock Letters,* II, 5.

58. *Ibid.,* II, 31–32.

59. *Ibid.,* II, 44–45; Pollock to Ernst Freund, March 21, 1921, Freund MSS.

60. Sir Frederick Pollock, "Abrams v. United States," *Law Quarterly Review*, XXXIII (October 1920), 334–38.

61. L. G. C. [Louis G. Caldwell], "Abrams v. United States," *Illinois Law Review*, XIV (March 1920), 601–7; K. N. L. [Karl N. Llewellyn], "Free Speech in Time of Peace, *Yale Law Journal*, XXIX (January 1920), 337–44.

62. Stewart to Weinberger, January 20, 1921, DJ-MSS.

63. (Howe, ed.), *Holmes–Pollock Letters*, II, 65.

64. Pollock to Weinberger, February 5, 1921, Weinberger MSS, Box 2.

65. Holmes to John Wigmore, February 12, 1916, Wigmore MSS.

66. Holmes to Brandeis, [n.d.], Louis D. Brandeis MSS, 5–13 (Harvard Law School); cited in Cover, "The Left, the Right, and the First Amendment," *loc. cit.*, 381.

67. Louis D. Brandeis, *Other People's Money* (New York, 1914; 1932 ed.), pp. 17–19. For a critique of Brandeis's work, see Thomas K. McCraw, *Prophets of Regulation* (Cambridge, 1984), pp. 112–14.

68. Cited in Alexander M. Bickel and Benno C. Schmidt, Jr., *The Judiciary and Responsible Government* (New York, 1984), pp. 384, 378. For the fight over confirmation, see A. L. Todd, *Justice on Trial* (New York, 1964).

69. Cited in Samuel J. Konefsky, *The Legacy of Holmes and Brandeis* (New York, 1956), p. 94.

70. Holmes to Felix Frankfurter, December 3, 1925, cited in Philippa Strum, *Louis D. Brandeis: Justice for the People* (Cambridge, 1984), p. 311.

71. David Riesman cited in *ibid.*, p. 314.

72. Brandeis-Frankfurter Conversations, August 8, 1923, Brandeis MSS (Harvard Law School), 114–18.

73. *Schaefer* v. *U.S.*, 251 U.S., 466–501. Justice John H. Clarke wrote a separate dissent in the case.

74. Brandeis-Frankfurter Conversations, August 8, 1923, Brandeis MSS.

75. *Schaefer* v. *U.S.*, 251 U.S., 495.

76. *Pierce et al.* v. *U.S.*, 252 U.S., 239–73.

77. Robert L. Morlan, *Political Prairie Fire: The Nonpartisan League, 1915–1922* (Minneapolis, 1955), p. 171.

78. *Gilbert* v. *State of Minnesota*, 254 U.S., 325–43. Chief Justice Edward I. White dissented separately.

79. Cover, "The Left, the Right, and the First Amendment," *loc. cit.*, 381.

80. Konefsky, *Legacy of Holmes and Brandeis*, p. 218.

81. Holmes to Brandeis, [n.d.], Brandeis MSS (Harvard Law School), Reel 3; *see also* Holmes to Felix Frankfurter, December 22, 1920, Holmes MSS, Reel 21.

82. Brandeis to Chafee, May 19, 1921, in Melvin I. Urofsky and David W. Levy, *Letters of Louis D. Brandeis*, (Albany, 1975), IV, 558–59.

83. Arthur E. Sutherland, *The Law at Harvard* (Cambridge, 1967), p. 254.

84. Zechariah Chafee, "Freedom of Speech," *New Republic*, XVII (November 16, 1918), 66–69.

85. Zechariah Chafee, "Legislation Against Anarchy," *ibid.*, XVIII (July 23, 1919), 379–85. See also Donald L. Smith, *Zechariah Chafee, Jr.: Defender of Liberty and Law* (Cambridge, 1986), chs. 1–3.

86. Peter H. Irons, " 'Fighting

Fair:' Zechariah Chafee, Jr., The Department of Justice, and the 'Trial at the Harvard Club,' " *Harvard Law Review,* XCIV (April 1981), 1218–22.

87. Cited in *ibid.*, p. 1224.

88. "Recommendation for Amnesty," [ca. March 12, 1920], Harry Weinberger MSS, Box 3.

89. Cited in Irons, " 'Fighting Fair,' " *loc. cit.*, pp. 1222–23.

90. Weinberger to Chafee, February 4, 1920, Zechariah Chafee MSS, Box 29 (11).

91. Zechariah Chafee, "A Contemporary State Trial—The United States *Versus* Jacob Abrams *Et Al.*," *Harvard Law Review,* XXXIII (April 1920), 747–74.

92. Chafee to Stephenson, April 27, 1920, Chafee MSS, Box 29 (19).

93. Chafee to John Maguire, May 22, 1920, *ibid.*, Box 14 (18).

94. Caffey to Chafee, June 10, 1920, *ibid.*, Box 29 (19).

95. Cited in Irons, " 'Fighting Fair,' " *loc. cit.*, p. 1219.

96. Zechariah Chafee, *Freedom of Speech* (New York, 1920), ch. 3; "Minutes of Conversation with Ryan," [n.d.], Chafee MSS, Box 29 (21); Galley proofs, *ibid.*, Box 29 (20).

97. Cited in Irons, " 'Fighting Fair,' " *loc. cit.*, p. 1228.

98. *Charges of Illegal Practices of the Department of Justice,* Hearings before a Subcommittee of the Committee on the Judiciary, 66th Congress, 3rd Session (Washington, 1921), pp. 188, 207.

99. Cited in Irons, " 'Fighting Fair,' " *loc. cit.*, p. 1229.

100. Ryan to Robert P. Stewart, February 23, 1921, Bureau of Investigation MSS, Reel 44.

101. Cited in Irons, " 'Fighting Fair,' " *loc. cit.*, p. 1229

102. Cited in Fred D. Ragan, "The 'Trial' at the Harvard Club Reconsidered," p. 10. I am indebted to Professor Ragan for sending me this paper.

103. Cited in *ibid.*, p. 10.

104. Chafee to Louis D. Brandeis, May 29, 1921, Brandeis MSS, Reel 48.

105. Chafee to Upton Sinclair, September 19, 1922, enclosing "Mr. Lowell and the Harvard Club Meeting about Professor Chafee," Chafee MSS, Box 34 (19).

106. Chafee to Brandeis, May 29, 1921, Brandeis MSS, Reel 48.

107. Sutherland, *The Law at Harvard,* p. 257.

108. Chafee to Hand, June 1, 1920, Learned Hand MSS, Box 15 (26).

109. Chafee to Brandeis, May 29, 1921, Brandeis MSS, Reel 48.

110. Chafee to Holmes, May 1921, Oliver Wendell Holmes MSS, Box 41 (12).

111. Lowell to Chafee, June 27, 1921, Chafee MSS, Box 14 (16).

112. Cited in Ragan, "The 'Trial' at the Harvard Club Reconsidered," p. 12.

113. Chafee to Lowell, September 30, 1921, Chafee MSS, Box 14 (16).

114. Lowell to Chafee, October 1, 1921, *ibid.*

115. "A Contemporary State Trial—The United States *Versus* Jacob Abrams *Et Al.*," *Harvard Law Review,* XXV (November 1921), 9–14.

116. Chafee, "A Contemporary State Trial," *loc. cit.*, p. 774.

117. John, Viscount Morley, *Recollections* (New York, 1917), II, 269–70.

118. Zechariah Chafee, *Freedom of Speech,* p. 290. See also Jerold S. Auerbach, "The Patrician as Libertarian:

Zechariah Chafee, Jr. and Freedom of Speech," *New England Quarterly*, XLII (December 1969), 511–31; and Jonathan Prude, "Portrait of a Civil Libertarian: The Faith and Fear of Zechariah Chafee, Jr., *Journal of American History*, LX (December 1973), 633–56.

119. Judson King to Thomas Walsh, January 10, 1921, Thomas I. Walsh MSS, Box 232.

120. King to Chafee, July 30, 1921, Chafee MSS, Box 29 (3).

121. Chafee to Upton Sinclair, September 19, 1922, Chafee MSS, Box 34 (19).

## 8. PRISON

1. John Koren, "Report of Special Committee on 'The Status of Political Offenders and Their Treatment in Prisons,' " *Proceedings of the Annual Congress of the American Prison Association, 1919* (Indianapolis, 1920), pp. 77–82.

2. "Report of the Warden . . . United States Penitentiary, Atlanta, Ga.," in *Report of the Attorney General for the Fiscal Year, 1921* (Washington, 1921), pp. 600–642.

3. Department of Corrections, City of New York, *Report for the Year 1918* (New York, 1919), p. 49.

4. Bouck White, *Letters from Prison* (Boston, 1915), pp. 114–15.

5. Julian Hawthorne, *The Subterranean Brotherhood* (New York, 1914), p. 241.

6. Cited in Frank Tannenbaum, *Osborne of Sing Sing* (Chapel Hill, 1933), p. 10.

7. Workers' Defense Union, press release, November 24, 1919, ACLU-MSS, Vol. 108.

8. David J. Rothman, *Conscience and Convenience: The Asylum and its Alternatives in Progressive America* (Boston, 1980), p. 141.

9. Hawthorne, *Subterranean Brotherhood*, p. 63.

10. Cited in Tannenbaum, *Osborne*, p. 7.

11. Department of Corrections, City of New York, *Report for the Year 1920* (New York, 1921), p. 39.

12. William Van De Wall, "Music as a Means of Discipline," *Proceedings . . . of the American Prison Association, 1922* (Indianapolis), p. 152.

13. Hawthorne, *Subterranean Brotherhood*, p. 79.

14. Tannenbaum, *Osborne*, p. 31.

15. National Commission on Law Observance and Enforcement (Wickersham Commission), *Report on Penal Institutions, Probation and Parole* (Washington, 1931), p. 44.

16. Cited in Tannenbaum, *Osborne*, pp. 23–24.

17. Joseph Z. Terrell, "Prison Discipline," *Proceedings . . . of the American Prison Association, 1921* (Indianapolis, 1922), pp. 154–58.

18. George W. Kirchwey, "The Human Element in Prison Discipline," *Proceedings . . . of the American Prison Association, 1919* (Indianapolis, 1920), p. 91.

19. Frank Tannenbaum, *Wall Shadows: A Study in American Prisons* (New York, 1922), p. 111.

20. Thomas Mott Osborne, *Society and Prisons* (New Haven, 1916), p. 133.

21. Tannenbaum, *Wall Shadows*, p. 38.

22. City of New York, *Report of the*

*Department of Corrections, 1921* (New York, 1922), p. 107.

23. State of New York, *Twenty-Sixth Annual Report of the State Commission of Prisons* (Ossining, 1921), p. 161.

24. James Malcolm (ed.), *The New York Red Book* (Albany, 1919), pp. 158–59; *The New York Times,* August 2, 1918; May 18, 1919; November 3, 1919; November 4, 1919.

25. *Ibid.,* p. 155.

26. *Ibid.,* p. 156.

27. City of New York, *Report of the Department of Corrections, 1920* (New York, 1921), p. 56.

28. State of New York, *Twenty-Sixth Annual Report,* p. 156.

29. City of New York, *Report of the Department of Corrections, 1920,* p. 60.

30. State of New York, *The Eightieth Annual Report of the Prison Association of New York, 1924* (Albany, 1925), p. 90.

31. Mary M. Lilly Deposition, April 20, 1920, Records of the U.S. District Court; City of New York, *Report of the Department of Corrections, 1919* (New York: 1920), p. 23; *ibid., 1920,* p. 62.

32. Steimer to Emma Goldman, January 5, 1930, Steimer–Flechine MSS.

33. *Ibid.*

34. Max Stirner [Johann Kaspar Schmidt], *The Ego and His Own* (New York, 1918; 1963 ed.), pp. 298, 286–87.

35. Lilly Deposition, April 20, 1920, Records of the U.S. District Court.

36. Steimer to Goldman, January 5, 1930, Steimer–Flechine MSS.

37. James A. Hamilton to Weinberger, November 24, 1919, Harry Weinberger MSS, Box 1.

38. Steimer to Goldman, January 5, 1930, Steimer–Flechine MSS.

39. *Ibid.*

40. *Ibid.*

41. Lilly Deposition, April 20, 1920, Records of the U.S. District Court.

42. Steimer to Goldman, January 5, 1930, Steimer–Flechine MSS.

43. Lilly to Weinberger, December 31, 1919, Weinberger MSS, Box 1.

44. Lilly Deposition, April 20, 1920, Records of the U.S. District Court.

45. Fannie E. Smith Deposition, April 20, 1920, *ibid.*

46. Steimer to Weinberger, January 20, 1920, Weinberger MSS, Box 2.

47. Steimer to Weinberger, February 8, 1920, *ibid.*

48. Steimer to Goldman, January 5, 1930, Steimer–Flechine MSS.

49. Steimer to Weinberger, February 8, 1920, Weinberger MSS, Box 2.

50. Weinberger to James A. Hamilton, March 2, 1920, Weinberger MSS, Box 1.

51. Smith Deposition, April 20, 1920, Records of the U.S. District Court.

52. City of New York, *Report of the Department of Corrections, 1919* (New York, 1920), p. 23.

53. Weinberger to A. Mitchell Palmer, April 7, 1920, DJ-MSS.

54. Caffey to Weinberger, April 3, 1920, Weinberger MSS, Box 2.

55. Assistant Attorney General William L. Frierson to Weinberger, April 10, 1920, DJ-MSS.

56. Lilly Deposition, April 20, 1920, Records of the U.S. District Court.

57. Judge John C. Knox order de-

nying motion in United States vs. Abrams and Mollie Steimer, April 24, 1920, Weinberger MSS, Box 3.

58. *The New York Times,* May 1, 1920.

59. *Globe and Commercial Advertiser,* January 25, 1921.

60. Lilly Deposition, April 20, 1920, Records of the U.S. District Court.

61. Steimer to Goldman, January 5, 1930, Steimer–Flechine MSS.

62. Works Progress Administration, *Atlanta: A City of the Modern South* (New York, 1942), p. 193. The "huge walls of stone" description is in a letter Samuel Lipman wrote to his lawyer, Weinberger MSS, Box 2.

63. Atlanta *Constitution,* January 24, 1902; U.S. Bureau of Prisons, *Handbook of Correctional Institution Design and Construction* (Washington, 1949), p. 42.

64. Atlanta *Constitution,* January 25, 1950.

65. "Report of the Warden," in *Annual Report of the Attorney General of the United States for the Year 1921* (Washington, 1921), p. 601; *ibid., 1920,* pp. 653, 651.

66. *Ibid., 1921,* p. 632.

67. Berkman to M. Eleanor Fitzgerald, March 31, 1918, BI-MSS, Reel 87-A; Berkman, "Persecution of Politicals in U.S.A.," *Freedom* (London), XXXIV (February 1920), 8.

68. F. H. Denhay to Weinberger, March 14, 1919, Weinberger MSS, Box 30.

69. Berkman to M. Eleanor Fitzgerald, March [?], 1918, BI-MSS, Reel 87-A.

70. Debs to Theodore Debs, July 5, 1920, Eugene V. Debs MSS, Reel 3.

71. Nick Salvatore, *Eugene V. Debs: Citizen and Socialist* (Urbana, Ill., 1982), p. 315.

72. [Ammon] Hennacy to "Dear Comrades," March 24, 1918, ACLU-MSS, Vol. 26. See also, "Political Prisoners in Atlanta Federal Prison, 1920," Socialist Party MSS, Reel 9.

73. Lipman to Ethel Bernstein, April 13, 1921, Bureau of Prisons MSS (Freedom of Information Act). I have corrected errors in spelling and punctuation in the prison letters. Under the Freedom of Information Act, I obtained access to typewritten copies made by the Bureau of Prisons, not of course to the originals. But it is apparent that some of the spelling errors were made by the persons who transcribed the letters (because of the sometimes illegible handwriting) not by the authors. For example, in one letter Steimer undoubtedly wrote "Gegan and the bomb squad," but the typewritten copy says: "Cogan and the lamb squad." Moreover, since English was not the prisoners' native language, they often spelled words phonetically. They were not permitted to write in Yiddish, Polish, or Russian, except when Lipman wrote to family members in Poland.

74. T. M. Reddy to Chief, January 21, 1921, BI-MSS (FOIA).

75. Vincent M. Hughes to Chief, February 17, 1921, BI-MSS, Reel 1.

76. Reddy to Hughes, February 25, 1921, BI-MSS (FOIA).

77. Edward B. Chastain to Chief, July 28, 1921, BI-MSS (FOIA).

78. Lipman to Mrs. Fishman, March 14, 1921, BP-MSS (FOIA).

79. Lipman to Weinberger, March 7, 1921, Weinberger MSS, Box 2.

80. Lipman to Jacob Lipovsky, May 9, 1921, BP-MSS (FOIA).

81. Abrams to Mary Abrams, April 4, 1921, BI-MSS, Reel 1.

82. Abrams to Weinberger, January 20, 1920, November 13, 1920, Weinberger MSS, Box 1.

83. Zerbst to Attorney General, May 13, 1920, DJ-MSS.

84. Lipman to Mrs. Fishman, March 14, 1921, *ibid.*

85. Rose Bernstein to Weinberger, June 2, 1920; Weinberger to Zerbst, June 1, 1920; Zerbst to Weinberger June 5, 1920, Weinberger MSS, Box 1.

86. Lachowsky to Mrs. Bluma Lachowsky, March 20, 1921, BP-MSS (FOIA).

87. Lipman to Weinberger, January 21, 1920, Weinberger MSS, Box 2.

88. Abrams to Joseph and Manya Spivak, February 22, 1921, BP-MSS (FOIA).

89. Lipman to Ethel Bernstein, March 9, 1921, BP-MSS (FOIA).

90. Lachowsky to Rose Brownstein, April 17, 1921, BP-MSS (FOIA).

91. Abrams to Mary Abrams, September 19, 1921, BP-MSS (FOIA).

92. *Report of the Attorney General for the Fiscal Year 1921* (Washington, 1921), p. 717.

93. Abrams to Joseph Spivak, February 22, 1921, BP-MSS (FOIA).

94. Lachowsky to Rose Brownstein, June 26, 1921, March 12, 1921, BP-MSS (FOIA).

95. Lachowsky to Rose Gordon, August 14, 1921, BP-MSS (FOIA).

96. Lachowsky to Rose Brownstein, July 10, 1921, BP-MSS (FOIA).

97. Lachowsky to Rose Brownstein, September 25, 1921, BP-MSS (FOIA).

98. Lachowsky to Anna Rand, June 28, 1921, BP-MSS (FOIA).

99. Lachowsky to Anna Linggs, June 23, 1921, BP-MSS (FOIA).

100. Lachowsky to Weinberger, July 18, 1921, Weinberger MSS, Box 2.

101. Lachowsky to Rose Gordon, September 4, 1921, BP-MSS (FOIA).

102. Lachowsky to Rose Brownstein, March 27, 1921, BI-MSS, Reel 1; Lachowsky to Anna Linggs, October 16, 1921, BP-MSS (FOIA).

103. Abrams to Mary Abrams, February 21, 1921, BP-MSS (FOIA).

104. Abrams to Mary Abrams, July 11, 1921, BP-MSS (FOIA).

105. Abrams to Mary Abrams, March 14, 1921, BP-MSS (FOIA).

106. *Ibid.*

107. Mary Abrams to Jacob Abrams, August 11, 1921, BP-MSS (FOIA).

108. Abrams to Mary Abrams, April 18, 1921, BP-MSS (FOIA).

109. *Ibid.*

110. Abrams to Mary Abrams, June 21, 1921, BP-MSS (FOIA).

111. Abrams to Mary Abrams, September 12, 1921, BP-MSS (FOIA).

112. Lipman to Weinberger, October 29, 1921, Weinberger MSS, Box 2.

113. Lipman to Bernstein, May 2, 1919, BI-MSS, Reel 1.

114. Lipman to Weinberger, November 16, 1920, Weinberger MSS, Box 2

115. Bernstein to Lipman, January 24, 1920, Military Intelligence Records MSS, Reel 33.

116. Bernstein to Lipman, December 24, 1920, BP-MSS (FOIA).

117. Bernstein to Lipman, February 11, 1921, BP-MSS (FOIA).

118. Bernstein to Lipman, February 28, 1921, BI-MSS, Reel 1.

119. Lipman to Bernstein, May 2, 1919, BI-MSS, Reel 1.

120. Lipman to Bernstein, August

22, 1921, BP-MSS (FOIA); May 22, 1921, BI-MSS, Reel 1.

121. Lipman to Bernstein, June 8, 1921, BI-MSS, Reel 1.

122. Lipman to Weinberger, November [?], 1921, Weinberger MSS, Box 2.

123. Floyd Calvin Shoemaker, *Missouri and Missourians,* 4 vols. (Chicago, 1943), III, 128–29.

124. Weinberger to O'Hare, April 28, 1920, Weinberger MSS, Box 1.

125. This account relies on Neil K. Basen, "Kate Richards O'Hare; The 'First Lady' of American Socialism, 1901–1917," *Labor History* XXI (Spring 1980), 165–99.

126. Cited in *ibid.,* p. 183.

127. "Drink, Its Cause and Cure," (1913), in Philip S. Foner and Sally M. Miller (eds.), *Kate Richards O'Hare: Selected Writings and Speeches* (Baton Rouge, 1982), p. 85.

128. " 'Nigger' Equality" (1912), in *ibid.,* p. 48.

129. "Shall Women Vote?" (1914), in *ibid.,* p. 97; Basen, "O'Hare," *loc. cit.,* p. 197.

130. Kate Richards O'Hare, *Law and the White Slaver* (St. Louis, 1911), p. 5.

131. P. E. Marrinan, "Re: Kate Richards O'Hare," July 15, 1917, MIR-MSS, Reel 6.

132. "United States vs. Kate Richards O'Hare," Department of Justice, Bulletin No. 49, in Walter Nelles, *Espionage Act Cases* (New York, 1918), pp. 45–47.

133. Martin J. Wade, "Education in Americanism," Speech to the Iowa State Bar Association, June 28, 1917, p. 18.

134. Bernard J. Brommel, "Kate Richards O'Hare: A Midwestern Pacifist's Fight for Free Speech," *North Dakota Quarterly,* XLIV (Winter 1976), 5–19.

135. *O'Hare v. United States* (October 28, 1918), 253 Fed. 540.

136. O'Brian to Attorney General, April 12, 1919, John Lord O'Brian MSS, Box 17.

137. O'Brian to Attorney General, May 27, 1919; O'Brian to Pardon Attorney, May 28, 1919; O'Brian to Attorney General, May 28, 1919, O'Brian MSS, Box 17.

138. Kate Richards O'Hare, *In Prison* (New York, 1923), pp. 181–83.

139. Lynn Frazier to Woodrow Wilson, September 13, 1919, Records of the Pardon Attorney, Box 1.

140. O'Hare, *In Prison,* p. 87, 91–92.

141. O'Hare to Frank P. O'Hare, December 14, 1919, in *Dear Sweethearts: Letters from Kate Richards O'Hare to her Family* (St. Louis, 1920).

142. O'Hare, *In Prison,* pp. 65–66.

143. Goldman to Harry Weinberger, July 27, 1919, Weinberger MSS, Box 28.

144. O'Hare, *In Prison,* pp. 96–97.

145. O'Hare to Frank P. O'Hare, May 25, 1919, in *Dear Sweethearts.*

146. O'Hare, *In Prison,* p. 115.

147. *Ibid.,* pp. 110–11.

148. The Osborne Association, *Handbook of American Prisons and Reformatories* (New York, 1938), p. 199.

149. Goldman to Harry Weinberger, July 27, 1919, Weinberger MSS, Box 28.

150. O'Hare to Frank P. O'Hare, August 14, 1919, September 28, 1919, in *Dear Sweethearts;* see also O'Hare to Otto Branstetter, February 24, 1920, Socialist Party MSS, Reel 9.

151. O'Hare to Frank P. O'Hare, May 23, 1920, in *Dear Sweethearts;* O'Hare, *In Prison,* p. 132.

152. E. T. Drew, "Kate Richards O'-Hare," June 18, 1920, BI-MSS, Reel 76.

153. Steimer to Stella Ballantine, May 9, 1920, Elizabeth Gurley Flynn MSS.

154. Steimer to Fannie Steimer, May 9, 1920, Flynn MSS.

155. Steimer to Stella Ballantine, May 9, 1920, *ibid.*

156. Steimer to Fannie Steimer, May 9, 1920, *ibid.*

157. Steimer to (?) [August] 1921, Weinberger MSS, Box 2.

158. Painter to Weinberger, August 5, 1921, Weinberger MSS, Box 1.

159. Steimer to Margaret Marsh, April 8, 1978. I am indebted to Margaret Marsh for providing me with a copy of this letter.

160. Steimer to Fannie Steimer, August 22, 1920, Flynn MSS.

161. Steimer to Lipman, Abrams, and Lachowsky, March 24, 1921, BP-MSS (FOIA).

162. Steimer to Harry Weinberger, July 3, 1921, Weinberger MSS, Box 2.

## 9. Exile

1. Hapgood to Wilson, November 18, 1918, Thomas H. Gregory MSS, Box 1.

2. Wilson to Gregory, November 20, 1919, *ibid.*

3. Gregory to Wilson, November 29, 1918, *ibid.*

4. Wilson to Hapgood, December 2, 1918, Woodrow Wilson MSS, Reel 157.

5. Gregory to William Redfield, February 20, 1919, cited in Donald Johnson, *Challenge to American Freedoms* (Lexington, Ky., 1963), p. 112.

6. Gregory to Wilson, March 1, 1919, Wilson MSS, Reel 173.

7. Steffens to Allen Suggett, June 28, 1919, Steffens MSS, Series III, Reel 2.

8. Wilson to Tumulty, June 28, 1919, Albert Burleson MSS, Box 24.

9. Palmer to Wilson, June 28, 1919, Wilson MSS, Reel 173.

10. Palmer to Wilson, July 30, 1919, *ibid.*, Reel 376.

11. Wilson to Palmer, August 1, 1919, *ibid.*

12. Palmer to Wilson, August 12, 1919, *ibid.*

13. Weinberger to Palmer, May 28, 1919, November 5, 1919, *ibid.*

14. Weinberger to Norman Thomas, November 26, 1919, Weinberger MSS, Box 2.

15. *Attorney General Palmer on Charges Made by Louis F. Post and Others.* Hearings before the Committee on Rules, House of Representatives, 66th Cong., 2nd Sess., (1920), I, 6. *See also* Dominic Candeloro, "Louis F. Post and the Red Scare of 1920," *Prologue* (Spring 1979), XI, 41–55.

16. Post to Weinberger, August 4, 1920, Weinberger MSS, Box 2.

17. Weinberger to Post, September 29, 1920, *ibid.*

18. Weinberger to Lipman, February 2, 1920, *ibid.*

19. Lachowsky to Weinberger, February 3, 1920, *ibid.*

20. Steimer to Weinberger [January 1920], *ibid.*

21. Weinberger to Steimer, January 23, 1920, *ibid.*

22. Application for Executive Clemency, January 23, 1920, *ibid.*

23. Harry W. L. Dana to Weinberger, April 18, 1920, *ibid.*, Box 1.

24. Weinberger to Stewart, May 27, 1920, DJ-MSS.

25. Special Assistant to the Attorney General [J. E. Hoover] Memo to Mr. Scott, April 18, 1920, BI-MSS, Reel 61-B.

26. Weinberger to Abrams, August 2, 1920, Weinberger MSS, Box 1.

27. Weinberger to Abrams, August 13, 1920, *ibid.*

28. Under Secretary of State Norman H. Davis to A. Mitchell Palmer, August 25, 1920, DJ-MSS.

29. R. T. S[cott] to Stewart, September 7, 1920, *ibid.*

30. Palmer to Secretary of State, September 9, 1920, *ibid.*

31. Minutes of Conference between the Attorney General and Representatives of the American Federation of Labor, September 14, 1920, AFL Records in the Gompers Era MSS, Reel 121.

32. Weinberger to Palmer, September 29, 1920, Weinberger MSS, Box 2.

33. Palmer to Weinberger, October 2, 1920, *ibid.*

34. Palmer to Weinberger, January 22, 1921, *ibid.*

35. Steimer to Weinberger, January 27, 1921, *ibid.*

36. *Report of the Attorney General for 1921* (Washington, 1921), p. 717.

37. Weinberger to Abrams, Lipman, Lachowsky, and Steimer, February 10, 1921, Weinberger MSS, Box 1.

38. Abrams to Weinberger, February 17, 1921, *ibid.*

39. Steimer to Weinberger, February 17, 1921, *ibid.*, Box 2.

40. Weinberger to Wilson, February 10, 1921, *ibid.*

41. Weinberger to Tumulty, March 1, 1921, *ibid.*

42. Creel to Weinberger, February 14, 1921, *ibid.*, Box 1.

43. Baker to Weinberger, March 2 or 3, 1921, *ibid.*

44. Weinberger to Hapgood, February 16, 1921, *ibid.*

45. Hapgood to Weinberger, February 19, 1921, *ibid.*

46. *New York Times,* July 25, 1921.

47. *Ibid.*, October 8, 1921.

48. Statement, July 19, 1922, Warren G. Harding MSS, Reel 187.

49. Cited in James M. Giglio, *H. M. Daugherty and the Politics of Expediency* (Kent State, 1978), p. 125.

50. Cited in *ibid.*, p. 142.

51. Daugherty to Harding, December 17, 1921, Harding MSS, Reel 178.

52. Daughterty to Weinberger, June 29, 1921, Weinberger MSS, Box 2.

53. New York *Call,* July 7, 1921.

54. M. J. Davis, Special Report, July 16, 1921, BI-MSS, Reel 64.

55. Weinberger to Gregory Weinstein, June 30, 1921, Weinberger MSS, Box 2.

56. Weinberger to Bernstein, June 30, 1921, *ibid.*, Box 1.

57. Recht to Weinberger, July 22, 1921, *ibid.*, Box 2.

58. Weinberger to Abrams *et al.*, June 30, 1921, *ibid.*

59. Lachowsky to Weinberger, July 18, 1921, *ibid.*

60. Weinberger to Daughterty, July 19, 1921, *ibid.*

61. Weinberger to Steimer, June 28, 30, 1921, *ibid.*

62. Steimer to Weinberger, July 3, 1921, *ibid.*

63. Steimer to Weinberger, July 6, 1921, *ibid.*

64. Weinberger to Finch, August 19, 1921, *ibid.*

65. Hoover to D. C. Poole, August 9, 1921, BI-MSS (FOIA).

66. Abrams to Weinberger, October 31, 1921, Weinberger MSS, Box 1.

67. Finch to Daugherty, October 6, 1921, Harding MSS, Reel 212.

68. Daugherty to Harding, October 7, 1921, *ibid.*

69. Harding to Daugherty, October 10, 1921, *ibid.*

70. Daugherty to Weinberger, October 12, 1921, Weinberger MSS, Box 2.

71. Daugherty to Harding, October 17, 1921, Harding MSS, Reel 212.

72. Abrams and Lipman to Weinberger, October 21, 1921, Weinberger MSS, Box 1.

73. Lipman to Weinberger, October 28, 1921, *ibid.*, Box 2.

74. New York *Call*, October 28, 1921.

75. Robert E. Todd to Weinberger, November 9, 1921, Weinberger MSS, Box 2.

76. Abrams to Weinberger, November 2, 1921, *ibid.*, Box 1.

77. Weinberger to Morris Berman, November 9, 1921, *ibid.*

78. Steffens to Hays, November 1, 1921, Steffens MSS, Series II, Reel 1.

79. Lipman to Weinberger, November 23, 1921, Weinberger MSS, Box 2.

80. Abrams to Weinberger, November 23, 1921, *ibid.*

81. This account is based on reports in the New York *Call*, *The New York Times*, and The New York *World*, November 24, 1921.

82. New York *Daily News*, November 24, 1921.

83. Weinberger to Todd, November 23, 1921, Weinberger MSS, Box 2.

84. New York *Call*, November 24, 1921.

85. Weinberger to Goldman and Berkman, January 22, 1922, MIR-MSS, Reel 3.

86. *The New York Times*, November 24, 1921.

87. Steimer statement, [n.d.], Weinberger MSS, Box 2.

88. "Mollie Steimer Et Al Anarchists deported on S/S Estonia," November 25, 1921, BI-MSS (FOIA).

89. *Ibid.*

90. "Memorandum for Mr. Hoover," December 2, 1921, *ibid.*

91. Baltic-American Line Brochure, Weinberger MSS, Box 3.

92. Steimer to Weinberger, December 20, 1921, *ibid.*, Box 2.

93. Lipman to Weinberger, December 20, 1921, *ibid.*

94. *The New York Times*, December 14, 1921.

95. Steimer to Weinberger, December 20, 1921, Weinberger MSS, Box 2.

96. "Berkman's Diary," MIR-MSS, Reel 3.

97. Goldman to Stella Ballantine, December 31, 1921, *ibid.*

98. Weinberger to Goldman and Berkman, January 22, 1922, *ibid.*

99. Robert C. Tucker (ed.), *The Lenin Anthology* (New York, 1975), p. 379.

100. *Ibid.*, p. 353.

101. Cited in Paul Avrich, *The Russian Anarchists* ([Princeton, 1967], New York, 1978 ed.), p. 182.

102. *Ibid.*, p. 183.

103. George Leggett, *The Cheka: Lenin's Political Police* (Oxford, 1981), p. 17.

104. Cited in Lennard D. Gerson, *The Secret Police in Lenin's Russia* (Philadelphia, 1976), p. 78.

105. Leggett, *The Cheka*, p. 198.

106. Cited in Gerson, *Secret Police*, p. 34. See also Robert Blobaum, *Feliks Dzierzynski and the SDKPiL: A Study in the Origins of Polish Communism* (New York, 1984).

107. Cited in Avrich, *Russian Anarchists*, p. 189.

108. Cited in *ibid.*, p. 197.

109. Cited in Alexander Berkman, "The Kronstadt Rebellion" (1922), in Berkman, *The Russian Tragedy* (Montreal, 1976), p. 73.

110. Cited in Avrich, *Russian Anarchists*, p. 230. *See also* Paul Avrich, *Kronstadt 1921* (Princeton, 1970).

111. Berkman to M. Eleanor Fitzgerald, March 3, 1921, cited in Harold Joel Goldberg, "The Anarchists View the Bolshevik Regime, 1918–1922," (Ph. D. diss., Univ. of Wisconsin, 1973), p. 168.

112. Cited in Richard Drinnon, *Rebel in Paradise* (Chicago, 1961; Boston, 1970 ed.), p. 237

113. Roger Baldwin (ed.), *Letters from Russian Prisons* (New York, 1925), pp. 253–55. Alexander Berkman was the principal editor of this volume.

114. Goldman to Stella Ballantine, July 23, 1921, Michael Cohn MSS (YIVO).

115. Goldman to Agnes [Inglis?], August 27, 1921, cited in Goldberg, "Anarchists View Bolshevik Regime," p. 170.

116. *Ibid.*, p. 198.

117. Goldman to Stella Ballantine, July 23, 1921, Cohn MSS.

118. Cited in Leggett, *The Cheka*, p. 321.

119. Goldman to Carl [Newlander], March 26, 1921, Goldman MSS (IISG), XVIII-A.

120. Goldman to Weinberger, December 9, 1921, Weinberger MSS, Box 28.

121. Steimer to Weinberger, December 20, 1921, Weinberger MSS, Box 2.

122. Lipman to Weinberger, December 20, 1921, *ibid.*

123. Lachowsky to Rose Brownstein, September 12, 1921, BP-MSS (FOIA).

124. Steimer to Paul Avrich, April 18, 1975. I am indebted to Professor Avrich for providing a copy of this letter.

125. Lipman to Steimer, August 23, 1928, Steimer–Flechine MSS.

126. Gerson, *Secret Police*, p. 249.

127. Baldwin (ed.), *Letters from Russian Prisons*, p. 108.

128. Steimer to Berkman, December 4, 1922, Cohn MSS.

129. Baldwin (ed.), *Letters from Russian Prisons*, pp. 95–99.

130. Steimer to Milly Rocker, March 14, 1948, Rocker MSS.

131. Goldman to Hutchins Hapgood, November 20, 1923, Hapgood MSS.

132. Steimer, "On Leaving Russia," *Freedom*, XXXVIII (January 1924), 2; "The Communists as Jailers," *ibid.* (May 1924), 22–23.

133. Abrams to Steimer, October 13, 1925; [November] 2, 1925, Steimer–Flechine MSS.

134. Berkman to Flechine, November 30, 1925, *ibid.*

135. Lipman to Steimer, November 23, 1925, *ibid.*

136. Lipman to Steimer, May 8, 1924, *ibid.*

137. Lipman to Steimer and Flechine, November 10, 1925, *ibid.*

138. Lipman to Steimer, August 23, 1928, *ibid.* I am indebted to Carol Sheade for a translation of the Russian.

139. Steimer to Paul Avrich, April 18, 1975.

## EPILOGUE: A REUNION IN MEXICO CITY

1. Steimer to Milly and Rudolf Rocker, December 23, 1941, Rocker MSS.

2. Goldman to Alexander Berkman, March 26, 1932, March 6, 1932, Goldman MSS (IISG), XIII-B.

3. Steimer to Milly and Rudolf Rocker, April 8, 1935, Rocker MSS; Steimer to Albert de Jong, September 28, 1934, Steimer–Flechine MSS.

4. Steimer to Anna, Abe, and Selma, May 15, 1940, Rocker MSS.

5. Michael R. Marrus and Robert O. Paxton, *Vichy France and the Jews* (New York, 1981), p. 67.

6. Adele Cantor, *Tears and Joys of a War-Time Deportee* (London, 1946), p. 6. A copy of this mimeographed memoir is in the Yad Vashem Library in Jerusalem.

7. Fleshin to Rose Pesotta, July 8, 1940, Pesotta MSS, Box 12.

8. Steimer to "My dearest ones," August 11, 1940, *ibid;* Steimer to Abe, August 11, 1940, Rocker MSS.

9. Steimer to Dolly, February 23, 1942, Steimer–Flechine MSS.

10. Steimer to Rose Pesotta, August 19, 1940, Rocker MSS.

11. Steimer to Paul Avrich, April 18, 1975. I am indebted to Professor Avrich for providing a copy of this letter.

12. Cited in Martin Gilbert, *The Holocaust* (New York, 1985), p. 403.

13. Howe (ed.), *Holmes–Pollock Letters,* II, 307.

14. Tunney died at the age of seventy-seven. An obituary appeared in *The New York Times,* January 27, 1952.

15. Bettman to Felix Frankfurter, April 17, 1943, Frankfurter MSS, Box 24. Bettman died at the age of seventy-one. For O'Brian's tribute to his friend, see *American Institute of Planners Journal,* XI (Autumn 1945), pp. 1–6. O'-Brian died in 1973 at the age of ninety-nine.

16. Caffey's obituary appeared in *The New York Times,* September 21, 1951.

17. Wigmore died in April 1943, at the age of seventy-nine.

18. Harry Weinberger, "A Rebel's Interrupted Autobiography," *American Journal of Economics and Sociology,* II (October 1942), p. 121. On March 5, 1944, at the age of fifty-eight, Weinberger died suddenly of a heart attack.

19. See Foner and Miller (eds.), *Kate Richards O'Hare,* pp. 30–31.

20. Zechariah Chafee, *Free Speech in the United States* (Cambridge, 1941), pp. xii–xiii. In 1956 the seventy-year-old Chafee retired from Harvard. He died the following year. See Donald L. Smith, *Zechariah Chafee, Jr.: Defender of Liberty and Law* (Cambridge, 1986), pp. 268–71.

21. Rose Pesotta to Steimer, November 22, 1938, Flechine–Steimer MSS.

22. Berle to Hoover, October 4, 1940; Hoover to Berle, October 17, 1940, Department of State MSS (FOIA).

23. Mary Abrams to Eleanor Roosevelt, [n.d.], Steimer–Flechine MSS.

24. Steimer to Rose Pesotta, May 10, 1952, *ibid.*

25. Steimer to Spivak, August 10, 1953, *ibid.*

26. Augustin Souchy to Steimer, August 31, 1960, *ibid.*

27. Cited in Betty Unterberger, *America's Siberian Expedition, 1918–1920* (Durham, N. C., 1956), p. 177.

28. Robert J. Maddox, *The Unknown War with Russia* (San Rafael, 1977), p. 131.

29. *Congressional Record,* December 13, 1920, pp. 293–94.

30. *Ibid.,* February 26, 1921, pp. 3937–39.

31. See Frank B. Strong, "Fifty Years of 'Clear and Present Danger': From Schenck to Brandenburg—And Beyond," in Philip B. Kurland (ed.), *Free Speech and Association* (Chicago, 1975), pp. 302–41.

32. *Brandenburg* v. *Ohio,* 395 U.S. 444, 450–52.

33. Lillian Kisliuk to Steimer, January 30, 1924, Steimer–Flechine MSS.

34. Berkman to Steimer and Fleshin, September 28, 1928, *ibid.*

35. Cited in Stevenson, "Ideology of American Anarchism," p. 330.

36. Bessie Kimmelman to Berkman, May 27, 1934, Alexander Berkman MSS (IISG), 1.

37. Lillian Kisliuk to Steimer, June 25, 1946, Steimer–Flechine MSS.

38. Steimer to Renee, November 3, 1960, *ibid.*

39. Steimer to "My dear ones," July 10, 1943, *ibid.*

# SELECTED BIBLIOGRAPHY

Acheson, Dean. *Morning and Noon.* New York, 1965.

"A Contemporary State Trial—The United States *Versus* Jacob Abrams *Et Al.,*" *Harvard Law Review,* XXV (November 1921).

Auerbach, Jerold S. "The Patrician as Libertarian: Zechariah Chafee, Jr. and Freedom of Speech," *New England Quarterly,* XLII (December 1969).

———. *Unequal Justice.* New York, 1976.

Avrich, Paul. "Anarchist Lives: Mollie Steimer and Simon (Senya) Fleshin," in Abe Bluestein, ed. *Fighters for Anarchism.* New York, 1983.

———. *The Modern School Movement: Anarchism and Education in the United States.* Princeton, 1980.

———. *Kronstadt 1921.* Princeton, 1970.

———. *The Russian Anarchists.* Princeton, 1967.

Bakunin, Michael. *God and the State.* (1882) New York, 1970.

Baldwin, Roger, ed. *Kropotkin's Revolutionary Pamphlets.* New York, 1927.

Baldwin, Roger [and Alexander Berkman], eds. *Letters from Russian Prisons.* New York, 1925.

Baron, Salo W. *The Russian Jew Under Tsars and Soviets.* New York, 1976.

Basen, Neil K. "Kate Richards O'Hare; The 'First Lady' of American Socialism, 1901–1917," *Labor History,* XXI (Spring 1980).

Baxendall, Rosalyn F. "Elizabeth Gurley Flynn: The Early Years," *Radical America,* VIII (1975).

Belknap, Michal. "The Mechanics of Repression: J. Edgar Hoover, The Bureau of Investigation and the Radicals, 1917–1925," *Crime and Social Justice,* VII (Spring/Summer 1977).

Berkman, Alexander. *The Russian Tragedy.* (1922) Montreal, 1976.

Berman, Hyman. "Era of the Protocol: A Chapter in the History of the International Ladies Garment Workers' Union, 1910–1916," (Ph. D. Diss., Columbia University, 1956).

Bevis, Howard L. "The Deportation of Aliens," *University of Pennsylvania Law Review*, LXVIII (January 1920).
Bickel, Alexander M., and Benno C. Schmidt, Jr. *The Judiciary and Responsible Government, 1910–1921.* New York, 1984.
Blakey, George. *Historians on the Homefront.* Lexington, Ky., 1970.
Blobaum, Robert. *Feliks Dzierzynski and the SDKiL: A Study in the Origins of Polish Communism.* New York, 1984.
Bollinger, Lee C. *The Tolerant Society: Freedom of Speech and Extremist Speech in America.* Oxford, 1986.
Brandeis, Louis D. *Other People's Money.* New York, 1914.
Brommel, Bernard J. "Kate Richards O'Hare: A Midwestern Pacifist's Fight for Free Speech," *North Dakota Quarterly*, XLIV (Winter 1976).
Burke, Edmund. *Reflections on the Revolution in France.* (1790) New Rochelle, 1966.
Caffey, Francis G. "Suffrage Limitations at the South," *Political Science Quarterly*, XX (March 1905).
Caldwell, Louis G. "Abrams v. United States," *Illinois Law Review*, XIV (March 1920).
Candeloro, Dominic. "Louis R. Post and the Red Scare of 1920," *Prologue*, XI (Spring 1979).
Cantor, Adele. *Tears and Joys of a War-Time Deportee.* London, 1946.
Cary, Lorin Lee. "The Bureau of Investigation and Radicalism in Toledo, Ohio: 1918–1920," *Labor History*, XXI (Summer 1980).
Cates, Willard, Jr. "Harry Weinberger: A Civil Libertarian and His Times, 1915–1942" (Senior Thesis, Yale Univ., 1964).
Central Cultural Israelita de Mexico. *J. Abramsbuch.* Mexico City, 1965.
Chafee, Zechariah. "A Contemporary State Trial," *Harvard Law Review*, XXXIII (April 1920).
Chafee, Zechariah *et al. The Third Degree.* New York, 1931.
Chafee, Zechariah. *Freedom of Speech.* New York, 1920.
———. "Freedom of Speech in War Time," *Harvard Law Review*, XXXII (June 1919).
———. *Free Speech in the United States.* Cambridge, 1941.
———. "Legislation Against Anarchy," *New Republic*, XVIII (July 23, 1919).
Chamberlain, Lawrence H. *Loyalty and Legislative Action.* Ithaca, 1951.
Claghorn, Kate. *The Immigrant's Day in Court.* New York, 1923.
Clark, Jane Perry. *Deportation of Aliens from the United States to Europe.* New York, 1931.
Clark, Sue Ainsley, and Edith Wyatt. *Making Both Ends Meet: The Income and Outlay of New York Working Girls.* New York, 1911.
Clayton, Victoria Hunter. *White and Black Under the Old Regime.* Milwaukee, 1899.
Coben, Stanley. *A. Mitchell Palmer: Politician.* New York, 1963.
Cohen, Joseph. *The Jewish Anarchist Movement in the United States: A Historical Review and Personal Reminiscences.* Philadelphia, 1945.

Comey, Arthur C., ed. *City and Regional Planning Papers by Alfred Bettman.* Cambridge, 1946.

Corwin, Edward S. "Freedom of Speech and Press Under the First Amendment: A Resume," *Yale Law Journal,* XXX (1920).

Cover, Robert M. "The Left, the Right, and the First Amendment: 1918–1928," *Maryland Law Review,* XL (1981).

Crosby, Alfred W. *Epidemic and Peace, 1918.* Westport, Conn., 1976.

Donner, Frank. *The Age of Surveillance.* New York, 1980.

Dreier, Mary E. *Margaret Dreier Robins: Her Life, Letters, and Work.* New York, 1950.

Drinnon, Richard. *Rebel in Paradise: A Biography of Emma Goldman.* Boston, 1961.

Drinnon, Richard, and Anna Maria Drinnon, eds. *Nowhere at Home: Letters from Exile of Emma Goldman and Alexander Berkman.* New York, 1975.

Dubofsky, Melvin. *We Shall Be All: A History of the Industrial Workers of the World.* Chicago, 1969.

Epstein, Melech. *Jewish Labor in the U.S.A. An Industrial, Political and Cultural History of the Jewish Labor Movement.* 2 vols., New York, 1950–1953.

Falk, Candace. *Love, Anarchy, and Emma Goldman.* New York, 1984.

Filene, Peter. *Americans and the Soviet Experiment 1917–1933.* Cambridge, 1967.

Fleming, Walter J. *Civil War and Reconstruction in Alabama.* Cleveland, 1911.

Fogelson, Robert. *Big-City Police.* Cambridge, Mass, 1977.

Foner, Philip S., and Sally M. Miller, eds. *Kate Richards O'Hare: Selected Writings and Speeches.* Baton Rouge, 1982.

Freund, Ernst. "The Debs Case and Freedom of Speech," *The New Republic,* XIX (May 3, 1919).

Friedman, Leon, and Fred L. Israel, eds. *The Justices of the United States Supreme Court, 1789–1969.* 4 vols., New York, 1969.

Gardner, Lloyd C. *Safe for Democracy.* New York, 1984.

George, Henry. *Progress and Poverty.* (1879) New York, 1948.

Gengarelly, W. Anthony. "The Abrams Case: Social Aspects of a Judicial Controversy," *Boston Bar Journal* (March, April 1981).

German, C. W. "An Unfortunate Dissent," *University of Missouri Bar Bulletin,* XXI (1920).

Gerson, Lennard D. *The Secret Police in Lenin's Russia.* Philadelphia, 1976.

Giglio, James M. *H. M. Daugherty and the Politics of Expediency.* Kent State, 1978.

Gilbert, Martin. *The Holocaust.* New York, 1986.

Goldberg, Harold Joel. "The Anarchists View the Bolshevik Regime, 1918–1922," (Ph. D. Diss., Univ. of Wisconsin, 1973).

Goldman, Emma. *Living My Life.* 2 vols., New York, 1931.

Goren, Arthur. *New York Jews and the Quest for Community: The Kehillah Experiment, 1908–1922.* New York, 1970.

Graham, Marcus, ed. *MAN! An Anthology.* London, 1974.

Gruber, Carol. *Mars and Minerva.* Baton Rouge, 1975.

Gunther, Gerald. "Learned Hand and the Origins of Modern First Amendment Doctrine: Some Fragments of History," *Stanford Law Review*, XXVII (1975).
Gurock, Jeffrey. *When Harlem Was Jewish.* New York, 1939.
Gutfeld, Aaron. "The Ves Hall Case, Judge Bourquin, and the Sedition Act of 1918," *Pacific Historical Review*, XXXVII (May 1968).
Hapgood, Hutchins. *A Victorian in the Modern World.* New York, 1939.
Hard, William. *Raymond Robins' Own Story.* New York, 1920.
Highsaw, Robert B. *Edward Douglass White: Defender of the Conservative Faith.* Baton Rouge, 1981.
Holmes, Oliver Wendell. *The Common Law.* Boston, 1881.
Howe, Frederic C. *The Confessions of a Reformer.* New York, 1925.
Howe, Mark DeWolfe, ed. *Holmes–Laski Letters.* 2 vols., New York, 1953.
———. *Holmes–Pollock Letters.* 2 vols., Cambridge, 1941.
Howe, Mark DeWolfe. *Justice Oliver Wendell Holmes: The Proving Years, 1870–1882.* Cambridge, 1963.
Irons, Peter H. " 'Fighting Fair:' Zechariah Chafee, Jr., The Department of Justice, and the 'Trial at the Harvard Club,' " *Harvard Law Review*, XCIV (April 1981).
Jaffe, Julian F. *Crusade Against Radicalism.* Port Washington, N.Y., 1972.
Jensen, Joan. *The Price of Vigilance.* Chicago, 1968.
Johnson, Donald. *The Challenge to American Freedoms.* Lexington, Ky., 1963.
Joll, James. *The Anarchists.* Cambridge, 1980.
Joseph, Samuel. *Jewish Immigration to the United States.* New York, 1914.
Josephson, Harold. "The Dynamics of Repression: New York During the Red Scare," *Mid-America*, LIX (October 1977).
Kalven, Harry, Jr. "Professor Ernst Freund and *Debs* v. *United States*," *The University of Chicago Law Review*, XL (Winter 1973).
Kendrick, Jack E. "Alabama Congressmen in the Wilson Administration," *The Alabama Review*, XXIV (October 1971).
Kennan, George F. *The Decision to Intervene.* Princeton, 1956.
———. *Russia Leaves the War.* Princeton, 1958.
Kennedy, David. *Over Here. The First World War and American Society.* New York, 1980.
Kessner, Thomas. *The Golden Door: Italian and Jewish Immigrant Mobility in New York City 1880–1915.* New York, 1977.
Kimball, Day. "The Espionage Act and the Limits of Legal Toleration," *Harvard Law Review*, XXXIII (1920).
Konefsky, Samuel J. *The Legacy of Holmes and Brandeis.* New York, 1956.
Kraines, Oscar. *The World and Ideas of Ernst Freund.* University of Alabama, 1974.
Kropotkin, Peter. *The Conquest of Bread.* (1892) New York, 1927.
Kuznets, Simon. "Immigration of Russian Jews to the United States: Background and Structure," *Perspectives in American History*, IX (1975).
Lasch, Christopher. *The American Liberals and the Russian Revolution.* New York, 1962.
Laski, Harold J. *Authority in the Modern State.* New Haven, 1919.

Leggett, George. *The Cheka: Lenin's Political Police.* Oxford, 1981.
Levin, Gordon N. *Woodrow Wilson and World Politics.* New York, 1968.
Levine, Louis. *The Women's Garment Workers.* New York, 1924.
LeWarne, Charles P. *Utopias on Puget Sound, 1885–1915.* Seattle, 1975.
Llewellyn, Karl N. "Free Speech in Time of Peace," *Yale Law Journal,* XXIX (January 20, 1920).
Locke, John. *The Second Treatise of Government.* (1690) New York, 1953.
Lowenthal, Max. *The Federal Bureau of Investigation.* New York, 1950.
Lubove, Roy. "Frederic C. Howe and the Quest for Community in America," *The Historian,* XXXIX (February 1977).
Maddox, Robert J. *The Unknown War with Russia.* San Rafael, 1977.
Marrus, Michael R., and Robert O. Paxton. *Vichy France and the Jews.* New York, 1981.
Marsh, Margaret. *Anarchist Women,* 1890–1920. Philadelphia, 1981.
Marx, Gary T. "Thoughts on a Neglected Category of Social Movement Participant: The Agent Provocateur and the Informant," *American Journal of Sociology,* LXXX (September 1974).
Mason, Alpheus Thomas. *Brandeis: A Free Man's Life.* New York, 1946.
McCraw, Thomas K. *Prophets of Regulation.* Cambridge, 1984.
McDevitt, Matthew. *Joseph McKenna: Associate Justice of the United States.* Washington, 1946.
McLean, Joseph E. *William Rufus Day: Supreme Court Justice from Ohio.* Baltimore, 1946.
Meiburger, Sister Anne Vincent. *Efforts of Raymond Robins Toward the Recognition of Soviet Russia and the Outlawry of War, 1917–1933.* Washington, D.C., 1958.
Mill, John Stuart. *On Liberty.* (1859) Baltimore, 1974.
Miller, Sally M. *Victor Berger and the Promise of Constructive Socialism, 1910–1920.* Westport, Conn., 1973.
Morlan, Robert L. *Political Prairie Fire: The Nonpartisan League, 1915–1922.* Minneapolis, 1955.
Murphy, Paul L. *World War I and the Origins of Civil Liberties in the United States.* New York, 1979.
Murray, Robert K. *Red Scare.* Minneapolis, 1955.
Nadell, Pamela S. "The Journey to America by Steam: The Jews of Eastern Europe in Transition," *American Jewish History,* LXXI (December 1981).
Nelles, Walter. *Espionage Act Cases.* New York, 1918.
Newman, Edward P. *Masaryk.* London, 1960.
O'Hare, Kate Richards. *Dear Sweethearts.* St. Louis, 1920.
———. *In Prison.* New York, 1923.
O'Leary, Jeremiah A. *My Political Trial and Experiences.* New York, 1919.
O'Neill, William. *The Last Romantic: A Life of Max Eastman.* New York, 1978.
The Osborne Association. *Handbook of American Prisons and Reformatories.* New York, 1938.
Osborne, Thomas Mott. *Society and Prisons.* New Haven, 1916.

Owen, Thomas McAdory. *History of Alabama and Dictionary of Alabama Biography.* (1921) Spartanburg, 1978.

Paper, Lewis J. *Brandeis.* Englewood Cliffs, N.J., 1983.

Perlin, Terry. "Anarchist Communism in America 1890–1914," (Ph. D. Diss., Brandeis Univ., 1970).

Pesotta, Rose. *Bread Upon the Waters.* New York, 1944.

———. *Days of Our Lives.* Boston, 1958.

Peterson, H. C., and Gilbert C. Fite. *Opponents of War, 1917–1918.* Seattle, 1957.

Pitkin, Thomas M. *Keepers of the Gate: A History of Ellis Island.* New York, 1975.

Pohlman, H. L. *Justice Oliver Wendell Holmes and Utilitarian Jurisprudence.* Cambridge, 1984.

Polenberg, Richard. "Progressivism and Anarchism: Judge Henry D. Clayton and the Abrams Trial," *Law and History Review,* III (Fall 1985).

Political Prisoners Defense and Relief Committee. [Leonard D. Abbott]. *Sentenced to Twenty Years Prison.* New York, 1918.

Pollock, John. *The Bolshevik Adventure.* London, 1919.

Pollock, Sir Frederick. "Abrams v. United States," *Law Quarterly Review,* XXXIII (October 1920).

———. *Essays in Jurisprudence and Ethics.* London, 1882.

———. *The Expansion of the Common Law.* London, 1904.

———. *The Genius of the Common Law.* New York, 1912.

Powers, Richard Gid. *Secrecy and Power: The Life of J. Edgar Hoover.* New York, 1987.

Preston, William. *Aliens and Dissenters: Federal Suppression of Radicals, 1903–1933.* Cambridge, 1963.

Prude, Jonathan. "Portrait of a Civil Libertarian: The Faith and Fear of Zechariah Chafee, Jr.," *Journal of American History,* LX (December 1973).

Rabban, David M. "The First Amendment in Its Forgotten Years," *Yale Law Journal,* XC (1981).

Ragan, Fred D. "The 'Trial' at the Harvard Club Reconsidered."

———. "An Unlikely Alliance: Tom Watson, Harry Weinberger, and the World War I Draft," *The Atlanta Historical Journal,* XXV (Fall 1981).

———. "Justice Oliver Wendell Holmes, Jr., Zechariah Chafee, Jr., and the Clear and Present Danger Test for Free Speech: The First Year, 1919," *Journal of American History,* LVIII (June 1971).

Roalfe, William. *John Henry Wigmore: Scholar and Reformer.* Evanston, Ill., 1977.

Rodabaugh, Karl. "Congressman Henry D. Clayton and the Dothan Post Office Fight: Patronage and Politics in the Progressive Era," *The Alabama Review,* XXXIII (April 1980).

———. "Congressman Henry D. Clayton, Patriarch in Politics: A Southern Congressman During the Progressive Era," *The Alabama Review,* XXXI (April 1978).

Rogat, Yosil, and James F. O'Fallon. "Mr. Justice Holmes: A Dissenting Opinion—the Speech Cases," *Stanford Law Review,* XXXVI (1984).

Rosenstone, Robert A. *Romantic Revolutionary: A Biography of John Reed.* New York, 1975.

Rothman, David J. *Conscience and Convenience: The Asylum and Its Alternatives in Progressive America.* Boston, 1980.

Safford, Victor. *Immigration Problems: Personal Experiences of an Official.* New York, 1925.

Salvatore, Nick. *Eugene V. Debs: Citizen and Socialist.* Urbana, Ill., 1982.

Sisson, Edgar. *One Hundred Red Days.* New Haven, 1931.

Smith, Donald L. *Zechariah Chafee, Jr.: Defender of Liberty and Law.* Cambridge, 1986.

Steimer, Mollie. "On Leaving Russia," *Freedom,* XXXVIII (January 1924).

———. "The Communists as Jailers," *Freedom,* XXXVIII (May 1924).

Stevenson, Billie Jeanne Hackley. "The Ideology of American Anarchism, 1880–1910," (Ph. D. Diss., Univ. of Iowa, 1972).

Stirner, Max. *The Ego and His Own.* (1843) New York, 1918.

Strong, Frank B. "Fifty Years of 'Clear and Present Danger': From Schenck to Brandenburg—and Beyond," in Philip B. Kurland, ed., *Free Speech and Association.* Chicago, 1975.

Strum, Philipa. *Louis D. Brandeis: Justice for the People.* Cambridge, 1984.

Sutherland, Arthur E. *The Law at Harvard.* Cambridge, 1967.

Szajkowski, Zosa. "Double Jeopardy—The Abrams Case of 1919," *American Jewish Archives,* XXIII (April 1971).

———. *Jews, Wars, and Communism.* 3 vols., New York, 1972–1977.

Tannenbaum, Frank. *Osborne of Sing Sing.* Chapel Hill, 1933.

———. *Wall Shadows: A Study in American Prisons.* New York, 1922.

Todd, A. L. *Justice on Trial.* New York, 1964.

Tucker, Robert C., ed. *The Lenin Anthology.* New York, 1975.

Tunney, Thomas J. *Throttled! The Detection of the German and Anarchist Bomb Plotters.* Boston, 1919.

Twain, Mark. *The Mysterious Stranger and Other Stories.* New York, 1922.

Twining, William. *Theories of Evidence: Bentham and Wigmore.* Stanford, 1985.

Unger, Sanford. *FBI.* New York, 1976.

Unterberger, Betty. *America's Siberian Expedition 1918–1920.* Durham, N.C., 1956.

Urofsky, Melvin I., and David W. Levy. *Letters of Louis D. Brandeis.* 5 vols., Albany, 1971–1978.

Van Kleeck, Mary. *Women in the Bookbinding Trade.* New York, 1913.

Van Vleck, William C. *The Administrative Control of Aliens: A Study in Administrative Law and Procedure.* New York, 1932.

Wallas, Graham. *The Life of Francis Place.* London, 1919.

Warner, Hoyt Landon. *The Life of Mr. Justice Clarke.* Cleveland, 1959.

Weill, Joseph. *L'Histoire des Camps d'Internement.* Paris, 1946.

Weinberger, Harry. "A Rebel's Interrupted Autobiography," *American Journal of Economics and Sociology,* II (October 1942).

Wexler, Alice. *Emma Goldman: An Intimate Life.* New York, 1984.

White, Edward G. "Looking at Holmes in the Mirror," *Law and History Review,* IV (Fall 1986).

Whitfield, Stephen J. *Scott Nearing: Apostle of American Radicalism.* New York, 1974.

Wigmore, John H. "Abrams v. U.S.: Freedom of Speech and Freedom of Thuggery in War-time and Peace-time," *Illinois Law Review,* XIV (1920).

Williams, Albert Rhys. *Journey into Revolution.* Chicago, 1969.

———. *Through the Russian Revolution.* New York, 1921.

Williams, David J. "Without Understanding: The F.B.I. and Political Surveillance, 1908–1941," (Ph. D. Diss., Univ. of New Hampshire, 1981).

Wingo, Patricia Wesson. "Clayton R. Lusk: A Study of Patriotism in New York Politics, 1919–1925" (Ph. D. Diss., Univ. of Georgia, 1966).

Wolf, Lucien. *The Legal Sufferings of the Jews in Russia.* London, 1924.

Woods, Arthur. *Policeman and Public.* New Haven, 1919.

———. "Reasonable Restrictions upon Freedom of Assemblage," *American Sociological Review,* IX (December 1914).

Young, William, and David E. Kaiser. *Postmortem: New Evidence in the Case of Sacco and Vanzetti.* Amherst, Mass., 1985.

# INDEX

## FOR THE BEST IN PAPERBACKS, LOOK FOR THE